Safety and Security in Tourism: Relationships, Management, and Marketing

Safety and Security in Tourism: Relationships, Management, and Marketing has been co-published simultaneously as *Journal of Travel & Tourism Marketing,* Volume 15, Numbers 2/3/4 2003.

The *Journal of Travel & Tourism Marketing*™ Monographic "Separates"

Editor-in-Chief K. S. (Kaye) Chon

Below is a list of "separates," which in serials librarianship means a special issue simultaneously published as a special journal issue or double-issue *and* as a "separate" hardbound monograph. (This is a format which we also call a "DocuSerial.")

"Separates" are published because specialized libraries or professionals may wish to purchase a specific thematic issue by itself in a format which can be separately cataloged and shelved, as opposed to purchasing the journal on an on-going basis. Faculty members may also more easily consider a "separate" for classroom adoption.

"Separates" are carefully classified separately with the major book jobbers so that the journal tie-in can be noted on new book order slips to avoid duplicate purchasing.

You may wish to visit Haworth's website at . . .

http://www.HaworthPress.com

. . . to search our online catalog for complete tables of contents of these separates and related publications.

You may also call 1-800-HAWORTH (outside US/Canada: 607-722-5857), or Fax 1-800-895-0582 (outside US/Canada: 607-771-0012), or e-mail at:

docdelivery@haworthpress.com

Safety and Security in Tourism: Relationships, Management, and Marketing, edited by C. Michael Hall, PhD, Dallen J. Timothy, PhD, and David Timothy Duval, PhD (Vol. 15, No. 2/3/4, 2003). *Examines tourism safety and security issues in light of the September, 2001 terrorist attacks on the United States.*

Wine, Food, and Tourism Marketing, edited by C. Michael Hall, PhD (Vol. 14, No. 3/4, 2003). *"ONE OF THE WORLD'S FOREMOST RESEARCHERS IN CULINARY TOURISM TAKES THE FIELD TO A NEW LEVEL. . . ." (Erik Wolf, MA, Director, International Culinary Tourism Association)*

Tourism Forecasting and Marketing, edited by Kevin K. F. Wong, PhD, and Haiyan Song, PhD, (Vol. 13, No. 1/2, 2002). *"A VALUABLE RESOURCE for policymakers in both the private and public sectors . . . Makes a significant contribution to the field of tourism forecasting by bringing together many different research methodologies with data on tourism flows from around the world." (Pauline J. Sheldon, PhD, Interim Dean and Professor, School of Travel Industry Management, University of Hawaii at Manoa)*

Japanese Tourists: Socio-Economic, Marketing and Psychological Analysis, edited by K. S. (Kaye) Chon, Tustomo Inagaki, and Taji Ohashi (Vol. 9, No. 1/2, 2000). *Presents recent studies on the socioeconomic, marketing, and psychological analysis of Japanese tourists.*

Geography and Tourism Marketing, edited by Martin Oppermann, PhD (Vol. 6, No. 3/4, 1997). *"Casts much light on how insights from geography can be applied to, and gained from, tourism promotion. . . . Well-written, informative, and interesting, and the issues are important." (David Harrison, PhD, Co-ordinator of Tourism Studies, School of Social and Economic Development, University of the South Pacific, Suva, Fiji)*

Marketing Issues in Pacific Area Tourism, edited by John C. Crotts, PhD, and Chris A. Ryan, PhD (Vol. 6, No. 1, 1997). *"A significant volume on the marketing issues that face the region. Nicely complements existing texts and will carve its own distinctive niche as a reference work. . . . Valuable to students of tourism marketing both inside and outside of the Pacific region." (C. Michael Hall, PhD, Professor and Chairperson, Tourism and Services Management, Victoria University of Wellington, New Zealand)*

Recent Advances in Tourism Marketing Research, edited by Daniel R. Fesenmaier, PhD, Joseph T. O'Leary, PhD, and Muzaffer Uysal, PhD (Vol. 5, No. 2/3, 1996). *"This book clearly marks the current advancement in tourism marketing research. . . . Tourism marketing researchers and academics can gain useful insights by reading this text." (Journal of the Academy of Marketing Science)*

Economic Psychology of Travel and Tourism, edited by John C. Crotts, PhD, and W. Fred van Raaij, PhD (Vol. 3, No. 3, 1995). *"A fresh and innovative volume that expands our understanding of consumers in the tourism market. . . . Will be a useful reference for scholars and graduate students working in tourism psychology and marketing." (Dr. Stephen L. J. Smith, Professor, Department of Recreation and Leisure Studies, University of Waterloo, Ontario, Canada)*

Communication and Channel Systems in Tourism Marketing, edited by Muzaffer Uysal, PhD, and Daniel R. Fesenmaier, PhD (Vol. 2, No. 2/3, 1994). *"Loaded with information on a variety of topics that provides readers with a solid background of the topic as well as introduces them to new ideas. . . . A valuable resource." (Robert M. O'Halloran, PhD, Associate Professor, School of Hotel, Restaurant & Tourism, University of Denver)*

Published by

The Haworth Hospitality Press®, 10 Alice Street, Binghamton, NY 13904-1580 USA

The Haworth Hospitality Press® is an imprint of The Haworth Press, Inc., 10 Alice Street, Binghamton, NY 13904-1580 USA.

Safety and Security in Tourism: Relationships, Management, and Marketing has been co-published simultaneously as *Journal of Travel & Tourism Marketing,* Volume 15, Numbers 2/3/4 2003.

The development, preparation, and publication of this work has been undertaken with great care. However, the publisher, employees, editors, and agents of The Haworth Press and all imprints of The Haworth Press, Inc., including The Haworth Medical Press® and The Pharmaceutical Products Press®, are not responsible for any errors contained herein or for consequences that may ensue from use of materials or information contained in this work. Opinions expressed by the author(s) are not necessarily those of The Haworth Press, Inc.

Cover design by Jennifer M. Gaska

Library of Congress Cataloging-in-Publication Data

Safety and security in tourism : relationships, management, and marketing / C. Michael Hall, Dallen J. Timothy, David Timothy Duval, editors.
     p. cm. – (The journal of travel & tourism marketing monographic separates)
"Co-published simultaneously as Journal of Travel & tourism marketing, volume 15, numbers 2/3/4 2003."
Includes bibliographical references and index.
     ISBN 0-7890-1916-7 (hard cover : alk. paper) – ISBN 0-7890-1917-5 (soft cover : alk. paper)
1. Tourism–Social aspects. 2. Travel–Safety measures. 3. Terrorism–Psychological aspects.
I. Hall, Colin Michael, 1961- II. Timothy, Dallen J. III. Duval, David Timothy, 1970- IV. Journal of travel & tourism marketing. V. Series.
G155.A1S25 2003
910'.68'4–dc22

     2003020406

Safety and Security in Tourism: Relationships, Management, and Marketing

C. Michael Hall
Dallen J. Timothy
David Timothy Duval
Editors

Safety and Security in Tourism: Relationships, Management, and Marketing has been co-published simultaneously as *Journal of Travel & Tourism Marketing*, Volume 15, Numbers 2/3/4 2003.

THHP

The Haworth Hospitality Press®
An Imprint of The Haworth Press, Inc.

New York • London • Victoria (AU)
www.HaworthPress.com

Indexing, Abstracting & Website/Internet Coverage

This section provides you with a list of major indexing & abstracting services. That is to say, each service began covering this periodical during the year noted in the right column. Most Websites which are listed below have indicated that they will either post, disseminate, compile, archive, cite or alert their own Website users with research-based content from this work. (This list is as current as the copyright date of this publication.)

Abstracting, Website/Indexing Coverage . . . . Year When Coverage Began

- *Academic Search: data base of 2,000 selected academic serials, updated monthly: EBSCO Publishing* 2003

- *Business Periodicals Index (BPI) <http://www.hwwilson.com>* . . 1999

- *CIRET (Centre International de Recherches et d'Etudes Touristiques) <http://www.ciret-tourism.com>* 2000

- *CNPIEC Reference Guide: Chinese National Directory of Foreign Periodicals* 1995

- *Emerald Management Reviews (formerly known as Anbar Management Intelligence Abstracts) <http://www.emeraldinsight.com/reviews/index.htm>* 1998

- *Hospitality Research-At-a-Glance Index* 1998

- *IBZ International Bibliography of Periodical Literature <http://www.saur.de>* 1995

- *International Hospitality and Tourism Database, The* 1995

- *Leisure, Recreation & Tourism Abstracts, c/o CAB International/CAB ACCESS <http://www.cabi.org>* 1993

- *Lodging, Restaurant & Tourism Index* 1992

- *Management & Marketing Abstracts* 1992

(continued)

- *Restaurant Information Abstracts* 1998
- *Sage Urban Studies Abstracts (SUSA)* 1992
- *Sociological Abstracts (SA)* <http://www.csa.com> .... *
- *SPORTDiscus* <http://www.sportquest.com/> 1994
- *Tourism Insight* <http://www.tourisminsight.com> 2003
- *TOURISM: an international interdisciplinary journal* 1998
- *Travel Research Bookshelf, a current awareness service of the "Journal of Travel Research," published by the Travel & Tourism Association* 1998
- *Wilson Business Abstracts* <http://www.hwwilson.com> 1995
- *Wilson OmmFile Full Text: Mega Edition (only available electronically)* <http://www.hwwilson.com> 1995
- *World-of-Islands* <http://www.world-of-islands.com> 1999
- *Worldwide Hospitality & Tourism Trends Database ("WHATT" Database) International CD-ROM research database for hospitality students, researchers, and planners with 3 international editorial bases, and functions with support of the Hotel & Catering International Management Association (HCIMA)* 1996

*Exact start date to come.

Special Bibliographic Notes related to special journal issues (separates) and indexing/abstracting:

- indexing/abstracting services in this list will also cover material in any "separate" that is co-published simultaneously with Haworth's special thematic journal issue or DocuSerial. Indexing/abstracting usually covers material at the article/chapter level.
- monographic co-editions are intended for either non-subscribers or libraries which intend to purchase a second copy for their circulating collections.
- monographic co-editions are reported to all jobbers/wholesalers/approval plans. The source journal is listed as the "series" to assist the prevention of duplicate purchasing in the same manner utilized for books-in-series.
- to facilitate user/access services all indexing/abstracting services are encouraged to utilize the co-indexing entry note indicated at the bottom of the first page of each article/chapter/contribution.
- this is intended to assist a library user of any reference tool (whether print, electronic, online, or CD-ROM) to locate the monographic version if the library has purchased this version but not a subscription to the source journal.
- individual articles/chapters in any Haworth publication are also available through the Haworth Document Delivery Service (HDDS).

Safety and Security in Tourism: Relationships, Management, and Marketing

CONTENTS

ABOUT THE EDITORS

C. Michael Hall, PhD, is Professor and Head of the Department of Tourism at the University of Otago in New Zealand. He is also Honorary Professor in the Department of Marketing at the University of Stirling in Scotland. He is a co-editor of Current Issues in Tourism and is the author or editor of a number of books, chapters, and journal articles on a range of tourism, gastronomy, geography, and regional development topics. His current research projects focus on issues of temporary mobility, regional development, competition and cooperation, food and wine tourism, and cool climate wines and horticultural production.

Dallen J. Timothy, PhD, is Associate Professor at Arizona State University in Tempe and Visiting Professor of Heritage Tourism at Sunderland University, England. His research interests include the politics of tourism, tourism in developing countries and peripheral regions, heritage tourism, shopping tourism, and tourism planning. He is the author of several books and a wide range of journal articles on these subjects.

David Timothy Duval, PhD, is Lecturer in the Department of Tourism at the University of Otago in New Zealand. His research interests include VFR tourism and return visits, migration, mobility and tourism, aviation and transport policies and alliances, seasonality in rural environments, and spatial analysis. He is also interested in transnational identities and diasporic communities in the context of post-colonial environments.

Security and Tourism:
Towards a New Understanding?

C. Michael Hall
Dallen J. Timothy
David Timothy Duval

SUMMARY. The article provides a review of the expansion of the concept of security and the relationship of security to tourism. It is argued that the concept of security has become transformed from one of collective security and common defence to embrace notions of common and co-operative security. Despite the damage done to the concept of collective security because of the United States led invasion of Iraq, the development of common security structures through collective, multilateral frameworks such as the United Nations remains important for the expansion of security concerns to cover the environment, health and economic threats. The article also notes that tourism and supranational tourism organizations have little influence on peace and security agendas although such agendas are important for tourism. Nevertheless, particularly at the micro-level, appropriate tourism development may serve as a means to

---

C. Michael Hall (E-mail: cmhall@business.otago.ac.nz) and David Timothy Duval (E-mail: dduval@business.otago.ac.nz) are affiliated with the Department of Tourism, University of Otago. Dallen J. Timothy is affiliated with the Department of Recreation Management and Tourism, Arizona State University.

[Haworth co-indexing entry note]: "Security and Tourism: Towards a New Understanding?" Hall, C. Michael, Dallen J. Timothy, and David Timothy Duval. Co-published simultaneously in *Journal of Travel & Tourism Marketing* (The Haworth Hospitality Press, an imprint of The Haworth Press, Inc.) Vol. 15, No. 2/3, 2003, pp. 1-18; and: *Safety and Security in Tourism: Relationships, Management, and Marketing* (ed: C. Michael Hall, Dallen J. Timothy, and David Timothy Duval) The Haworth Hospitality Press, an imprint of The Haworth Press, Inc., 2003, pp. 1-18. Single or multiple copies of this article are available for a fee from The Haworth Document Delivery Service [1-800-HAWORTH, 9:00 a.m. - 5:00 p.m. (EST). E-mail address: docdelivery@haworthpress.com].

10.1300/J073v15n02_01

ward off potential future conflict over resource and environmental secu-
rity. *[Article copies available for a fee from The Haworth Document Delivery
Service: 1-800-HAWORTH. E-mail address: <docdelivery@haworthpress.com>
Website: <http://www.HaworthPress.com> © 2003 by The Haworth Press, Inc.
All rights reserved.]*

KEYWORDS. Collective security, common security, environmental
security, tourism security, invasion of Iraq

Security is a concept that is, at present, central not just to tourism but to the
wider world. This is not just a result of the events of September 11th 2001 and
the terrorist attacks which occurred in the United States but is also the result of
major shifts in American foreign policy, and the consequent American-led invasion of Iraq, ongoing concerns regarding the armed expression of religious
and political fundamentalism, and fears for economic and personal health and
well-being. These security concerns not only affect individual tourism decision-making but also have a broader influence on economic and political confidence, which in turn affects the wider environment within which the tourism
industry operates and in which individual destinations are perceived.

Security fears are not new to the world. The twentieth century witnessed
two world wars, numerous regional conflicts and civil wars, and the threat of
nuclear annihilation during the "Cold War" between the United States-led industrialised West and the state-communist East led by the Soviet Union. It is
therefore perhaps of no great surprise that the notion of security, at least in
terms of global politics, has its grounding in the post-Second World War and
Cold War period. However, as this article argues, the so-called security cer-
tainties of the Cold War, at least in relation to notions of friend and foe, have
given way to conceptions of security that extend beyond ideas of national security and therefore encompass a wide range of issues at scales ranging from
the global to the individual. Under these new concepts of security, threats are
generated not just from military actions but also from such global issues as environmental change, resource scarcity, international crime, health, biosecurity,
and challenges to sustainable development, to name just a few (Butfoy, 1997).

Tourism is irrevocably bound up with the concept of security. Tourist behaviour and, consequently, destinations, are deeply affected by perceptions of
security and the management of safety, security and risk. Moreover, with
events in 2003 related to the war in Iraq, concerns over a new strain of pneumonia and general travel safety demonstrated the tourism industry is highly
vulnerable to changes in the global security environment. In addition, high se-

curity risk concerns have a ripple effect throughout the industry in that security risks at one location may be perceived to influence the wider region or, during major security concerns, the entire tourism system. For example, the new form of pneumonia known as Severe Acute Respiratory Syndrome (SARS) emanating from Guangzhou and Hong Kong was not only spread internationally through modern aviation services but also resulted in a number of countries issuing travel warnings regarding travel to some destinations in East Asia and health security measures at their own borders ("Terrifying for Asia," 7 April 2003). East Asian air stocks were falling, flights were being cut, and all this in a business environment made all the more difficult for tourism because of the invasion of Iraq, concerns over the price of oil, and threats of economic recession. Within this climate it is therefore not surprising that, for the tourism industry at least, security is now seen as more than just the safety of tourists. Nevertheless, at a macro-analytical level tourism has tended to focus on the threats posed by political insecurity and uncertainty (e.g., Richter and Waugh, 1986; Gartner and Shen, 1992; Hall and O'Sullivan, 1996; Hall and Oehlers, 2000).

Although "Tourism as a Force for Peace" has been a popular positive message relayed by the industry, consultants and some academics in recent years, the reality is that tourism has very little influence on peace and security issues, at least at the macro level, and that tourism is far more dependent on peace than peace is on tourism. Indeed, as one of the industries which has been hurt the most by the war in Iraq, some may see it as perhaps surprising how quiet industry voices were with respect to the invasion. For example, while the World Tourism and Travel Council (WTTC) had issued a press release on the economic impacts of the Iraq War (WTTC, 2003), noting that a prolonged war in Iraq would lead to the loss of more than three million jobs in the worldwide travel and tourism industry and eliminate more than US$30,000 million of economic value in 2003, no comment was made regarding the appropriateness of government decision-making with respect to Iraq. Instead, the WTTC President, Jean-Claude Baumgarten, stated, "In the event this worst case scenario takes place, we will look for immediate and decisive action from governments to protect and secure this vital world industry," with the press release going on to note that "Baumgarten called for strong and proactive public-private partnerships to develop emergency contingency plans that would help mitigate the impact of events. Key interventions might range from tax breaks to increased levels of investment by governments in security, tourism promotion and infrastructure" (WTTC, 2003). Similarly, in a letter to member states of the World Tourism Organization (WTO), Francesco Frangialli, Secretary-General of the World Tourism Organization, also commented on the potential impacts of the war on international tourism, noting, "it is not the purpose of this letter to pass judgment on the political dimension of this conflict–it is not the World Tourism Organization's place to do so. It is our mission, however, to underline whenever necessary tourism's contribution to peace, and conversely, its vulnerability to acts or war and terrorism" (WTO, 2003: 1). Nevertheless, he did go on to state, "During this difficult period for the Arab-Muslim world, it is important for it to be able to use tourism, as many of its governments wish to do, as an instrument of openness and as a channel of communication with the rest of the international community" (WTO, 2003: 3). It may, of course, be argued that it is both difficult, because of the range of opinions that may exist within such organisations, and inappropriate, because of the inherently political nature over the issues surrounding the invasion of Iraq, for the WTTC and WTO to comment publicly on political and international security issues. But if tourism is seriously a force for peace, as both organizations have subscribed to, why should it be?

The above question lies at the heart of understanding the nature of security. The same letter by Secretary-General Frangialli to member states regarding the Iraq crisis went on to highlight the importance of:

- "the International Year of Ecotourism declared by the United Nations, and the inclusion of tourism in the Plan of Action adopted by the World Summit on Sustainable Development in Johannesburg."
- the international recognition of tourism "as an important tool in the fight against poverty, and the STEP (Sustainable Tourism for Eliminating Poverty) initiative, undertaken in conjunction with UNCTAD" aimed at enhancing this contribution.
- the growth of the "influence" and "visibility" of the WTO in the international community as it begins its transformation into a specialized agency of the United Nations.
- tourism as a stakeholder in multilateral cooperation within the framework of the United Nations system which "will be felt more strongly and more urgently than ever . . . Beyond the Iraq crisis and upon its conclusion."

Such areas fall under the realm of security. Environmental, social and economic issues, as well as the system of international governance by which such concerns are governed, now clearly lie within contemporary understandings of security (Boulding, 1991). Such a broadening of ideas of security is reflective of the changed notion of politics beyond that found in many dictionaries as "the science and art of government, the science dealing with the form, organisation and administration or a part of one, and with the regulation if its relations with other states" (Tansey 1995: 5). Instead, we are concerned with who gets what, when, how; and the interactions of values and interests in policy and decision-making (Hall, 1994; Hall and Jenkins, 1995). Concerns which, arguably, cover all aspects of human existence.

THE NEW SECURITY AGENDA

Contemporary notions of security have evolved from Cold War-era security concerns (Table 1). During this period (1948-1990), conventional wisdom in the West was that the core goal of security policy should be the enhancement of stability. The alternatives were presented as either nuclear Armageddon or appeasement. In this period, security was based on the notion of deterrence, the logic of which was that if either side pushed the other into using nuclear weapons then it would set off a trail of nuclear escalation in which no one survived, otherwise known as the doctrine of Mutual Assured Destruction (MAD).

Deterrence dominated Western strategic policy and thinking until the late 1970s (Butfoy, 1993). Despite increasing global economic interdependence, deterrence was seen as the most realistic way of keeping Soviet power at bay. However, by the late 1970s increasing protests occurred regarding the deployment of US nuclear forces to Europe, particularly with respect to enhanced radiation warheads ("neutron bombs") and new missile systems. Such deploy-

TABLE 1. Key Concepts Used in the Debate on International Security

Collective Security	Based on the idea that states should join together to enforce international law, primarily relating to prohibiting aggression, sometimes applied to enforcement of the legal dimensions of environmental security.
Collective Defence	Another term to describe traditional alliances, e.g., NATO. Often confused with collective security; the major difference is that collective defence is more exclusionary and is based on notions of national, as opposed to international, interest.
Common Security	Based on notions of interdependence, a focus on the safety of individual people as opposed to states, and a multi-dimensional perspective in which non-defence ideas of security are given significance. Key concept of the Palme Commission (1982).
Cooperative Security	A limited, and relatively conservative, adaptation of common security with the focus on promoting mutual reassurance between states.

After Butfoy, 1997

ments were the subject of protests by a renewed peace movement, fuelled by the belligerent anti-Soviet rhetoric of U.S. President Ronald Reagan and the lack of new initiatives from Moscow, and concerns over the economic costs of such weapons systems (Butfoy, 1997). It was therefore within this setting that a seminal document in the evolution of the concept of security was published. This was the 1982 Report of The Independent Commission on Disarmament and Security Issues, entitled *Common Security: A Blueprint for Survival* (referred to as the Palme Commission Report, after its chairman, Swedish Prime Minister Olof Palme). (The Independent Commission on Disarmament and Security Issues, 1982; hereafter referred to as the Palme Commission.) The report was driven by the idea that the arms race was economically and socially wasteful, harmful to the prospects for development in the Less Developed World, and–more than anything else–dangerous. According to the Palme Commission, there was a "drift towards war" (Palme Commission, 1982: xiii); the world seemed to be "marching towards the brink of a new abyss" (Palme Commission, 1982:1). The Report noted that:

> nations must strive for objectives more ambitious than stability, the goal of the present system in which security is based on armaments. For stability based on armaments cannot be sustained indefinitely. There is always the danger that the fragile stability of an international system based on armaments will suddenly crumble, and that nuclear confrontation will take its place. A more effective way to ensure security is to create positive processes that can lead to peace and disarmament. It is essential to create an irreversible process, with a momentum such that all nations cooperate for their common survival. (Palme Commission, 1982: 7)

When first released, the idea of common security proposed by the Palme Report was seen by many as politically and strategically naïve (Butfoy, 1997). Nevertheless, the idea of common security helped reframe wider debates over security. It did this in four ways. First, it added extra emphasis to the concept of "non-offensive defence," meaning the desirability of developing a defence posture which achieved military security without creating counter-productive threats (Butfoy, 1997). Second, the idea further publicised the usefulness of "confidence building measures" (CBMs) designed to promote mutual reassurance. Third, the focus on common interests led to a reconsideration of the security implications of interdependence. Fourth, the issues of the Less Developed Countries were brought onto the political centre stage with, for instance, poverty being portrayed as a potential security issue (Butfoy, 1997).

Ironically, given the Soviet Union's posture for much of the Cold War period on defence and security issues, it was the accession of Mikhail Gorbachev as the Soviet leader which led to the Soviets embracing some elements of the common security agenda and its wider influence on security discourse as well as practical politics in terms of the collapse of the Iron Curtain. Indeed, Gorbachev's reforms which were informed by the "New Thinking" were one of the political sources for the rapid growth of people-power in Eastern Europe and the collapse of state repression as an acceptable way of providing long-term security (Butfoy, 1997).

Following the collapse of the Cold War divisions, the common security message has been expanded even further to include the economy (Gurr, 1985), human rights, welfare, the environment (Myers, 1989, 1993; Boulding, 1991), food (Maxwell and Frankenberger, 1992; Cohen and Pinstrup-Andersen, 1998), and water (Falkenmark and Lundqvist, 1998; World Water Assessment Programme, 2001) as part of the discourse on security (Brown, 1977; Ullman, 1983; Mathews, 1989; Romm, 1993). These new notions of security are strongly embedded in support for the collective security provided, in theory, by the United Nations system and which underlie the importance of multilaterism in a wide range of international fields (Imber, 1994; Commission on Global Governance, 1995). Nevertheless, such an understanding of security has not been universally adopted, and even though the Clinton-Gore administration had embraced some elements of the common security agenda with respect to the environment, these were lost in the development of the notion of cooperative security which placed emphasis on reassurance, CBMs, arms control, and transparency. Indeed, such a direction also highlights the potential development of a north-south or core-periphery security model in which the security prospects of the "core" rule-based liberal-democratic industrial world are perceived as greatly different from the relatively lawless, undemocratic "periphery" (e.g., "rogue states") in much of the rest of the world.

The notion of environmental security arguably developed as an off-shoot of concerns over defence security in the 1970s and 1980s (Holst, 1989; Myers, 1989; Käkönen, 1994; Stern, 1995). Concerns over the potential impact of a nuclear winter following a nuclear war provided a basis for other international environmental problems, such as the nuclear disaster in Chernobyl, burning oil wells in Kuwait following the liberation of that country in 1991, and global climate change, have all contributed to an appreciation of the security dimensions of ecological inter-dependence (Mische, 1989; Käkönen, 1994; Levy, 1995a, 1995b; Elliott, 1998). At least four sets of relationships between more traditional notions of security and the concept of environmental security may be identified. First, the relationship between environmental security and the potential for resource wars fought over increasingly scarce resources such as oil and water (Gurr, 1985; Käkönen, 1988; Homer-Dixon, 1991, 1994; Molvær, 1991; Homer-Dixon et al., 1993; Dolatyar and Gray, 2000; Haftendorn, 2000;

Maxwell and Reuveny, 2000). Second, direct threats to environmental health because of environmental change and biosecurity threats, some of which may be deliberately induced by human action (Alexander, 2000). Third, the mass migration of ecological refugees who are abandoning resource-poor or damaged areas (Holst, 1989). Refugee flows often generate new resource, political, economic and cultural tensions in those nations which receive them (Jamieson, 1999). Fourth, there is the environmentally destructive capability of the military itself (Kakonen, 1994; Kirchner, 2000). Although linked to the concept of sustainable development, the notion of environmental security is not universally accepted although it does have a number of significant supporters such as former US Vice President Al Gore (1992) and Norman Myers (1989, 1993). For example, Myers' (1993) book, *Ultimate Security*, provided an analysis of a range of case studies (focussing on regional resource wars and global ecological threats), which collectively seek to demonstrate that environmental and resource degradation is inseparable from economic and political insecurities and which perhaps foresaw some of the oil resource access and ownership issues arising out of the 2003 invasion of Iraq.

Issues of environmental security have themselves broadened into notions of food and water security. For example, the UN Food and Agricultural Organization (FAO) has a food security programme which states that "Food security exists when all people, at all times, have physical and economic access to sufficient, safe and nutritious food to meet their dietary needs and food preferences for an active and healthy life" (FAO, *http://www.fao.org/spfs/*). Key features of the programme include attention to such concerns as participation, technology transfer, gender sensitivity, social equity, economic and environmental sustainability, and South-South cooperation. Perhaps not surprisingly therefore such concerns also exist within the area of water security (World Water Assessment Programme, 2001). However, what would also be apparent to many readers is that such concerns are also central issues for tourism and tourism researchers, practitioners and academics also seek to come to terms with the relationship between tourism and sustainable development. For example, in the same way that discussions of sustainable tourism refer to the significance of the broader discussions of sustainable development so the World Water Assessment Programme (2001) in discussing "Achieving Water Security in the Twenty-First Century" highlights the need to keep "a focus on the first principle of the Rio Declaration: Human beings are at the centre of concerns for sustainable development. They are entitled to a healthy and productive life in harmony with nature" (World Water Assessment Programme, 2001: 2).

The relationship between security and sustainable development may clearly pose a new agenda for research on tourism and security, and the development of a broad range of answers to the questions of "security from what and secure to do what?" Nevertheless, to some extent several of these issues are already being anticipated in the wider tourism literature, although they are subject to substantial contestation (Hall and Lew, 1998; Mowforth and Munt, 1998; Butcher, 2003). With few exceptions, however, traditional ideas of state security, which have been applied to a set of conditions that guarantees the ability of a nation to protect its territorially bounded community of citizens and pursue its national interests free from both real and imagined impediments and threats, have been applied in tourism. State security concerns clearly have the capacity to affect the flow of international travellers because of the desire of some states to deter undesirable visitors—whether on the basis of wealth, health, creed, or crime. Indeed, in concluding their book on tourism and migration relations, Hall and Williams (2002) cite Bauman's (1998) discussion of the human consequences of globalisation which juxtaposes the tourist and the vagabond as the two extreme character types of contemporary mobility and a metaphor for the new, emergent, stratification of global society. Entry visas are being progressively phased out in many parts of the world (although new requirements are being introduced in parts of Eastern Europe and the CIS) as part of the deregulation of desired human mobility and the encouragement of future growth in international tourism in particular: "But not passport control. The latter is still needed—perhaps more than ever before—to sort out the confusion which the abolition of visas might have created: to set apart those for whose convenience and whose ease of travel the visas have been abolished, from those who should have stayed put—not meant to travel in the first place" (Bauman, 1998: 87). Tourists travel because they want to. Vagabonds travel because they have no choice. As Bauman (1998: 92-93) notes, "The tourists move because they find the world within their (global) reach irresistibly attractive—the vagabonds move because they find the world within their (local) reach unbearably inhospitable . . . What is acclaimed today as 'globalization' is geared to the tourists' dreams and desires . . . Vagabonds are travellers refused the right to turn into tourists."

One important area of national security–tourism relationships centres on national borders. Borders as limits of national space and sovereignty have been at the center of myriad international conflicts throughout history, and there are few places in the world that have not been affected directly or indirectly by some form of border altercation. Today, many forms of territorial disputes and border conflicts abound where the discord relates to the exact location of a shared border (particularly relevant in places of high natural resource amenity); one country's unilateral and despotic manipulation of the boundary and its functions; the misuse or overexploitation of natural resources like water, forests, fish and oil that overlap national lines; and, clearly, who is allowed to cross such borders (Allcock et al., 1992; Timothy, 2001).

Some border and territorial conflicts are highly problematic in places of significant tourist interest. One example is Taba, a popular tourist resort, which was developed by the Israelis in 1982 near the border with Egypt. After Israel's withdrawal from the Sinai, there was conflict between Egypt and Israel about where the new international boundary should be located. Based on historical boundary documents, Egypt claimed a more eastward location. Despite the absence of a set border, the Israelis began developing beachfront tourist facilities in the 700-metre wide disputed territory. Despite political and legal efforts by Israel, the small tract of land, including the booming tourist facilities, was awarded to Egypt in 1988 by an international arbitration council (Kemp and Ben-Eliezer, 2000; Timothy, 2001). Some other notable examples of territorial and boundary disputes directly affecting tourism including Spain-Gibraltar, India-China, Canada-USA, Russia-China, Cyprus, and Thailand-Cambodia. However, it should also be noted that in some cases tourism may be deliberately exploited as a means to reinforce claims to sovereignty of disputed areas (Hall 1994).

Obviously border and territorial disputes usually hinder the successful and continuous development of tourism in unstable borderlands. However, they also affect tourism development within the national interior of countries, as boundaries become essentially impenetrable in both real and perceived terms, which in turn limits access to the national core by visitors from abroad. Likewise, and similar to other forms of conflict, border and territorial disputes nearly always create uncertainty in the minds of potential travellers who intentionally avoid the countries or regions where such conflicts occur.

National security concerns in the post-September 11th environment have not only influenced travel behaviour but have also affected the direct personal security measures employed to protect the travelling public. By extension, and as Hall (2002) argued, not only is the media significant in terms of the images that surround travel and specific destinations and which influence travel decision-making, but the media also has a substantial impact on the policy measures which governments take with respect to tourist safety and security: "The stringency of application of security measures has previously ebbed and flowed in light of responses to terrorist attacks and hijackings and perceptions of risk and security and subsequent commercial and consumer pressures for convenient and cheaper travel. Even given the undoubted enormity of the events of September 11 it is highly likely that they will ebb and flow again" (Hall, 2002: 462, 465). This is not to minimise the enormous and varied impacts of the terrorist attacks of September 11th both in the United States (Beirman, 2003; Chen and Noriega, this volume; Floyd et al., this volume; Green et al., this volume; Kingsbury and Brunn, this volume) and elsewhere (McKercher and Hui, this volume).

The media is clearly critical in influencing both tourist and political reactions to political and international security issues (Hall and O'Sullivan, 1996; Carter, 1998; Hall, 2002). However, it is also important to recognise that the American experience with terrorist attacks as a means of political expression has been experienced elsewhere around the world (Richter and Waugh, 1986; Enders and Sandler, 1991; Buckley and Klemm, 1993; Aziz, 1995; de Albuquerque and McElroy, 1999; Wahab, 1996; Wall, 1996; Sönmez, 1998; Leslie, 1999; Sönmez et al., 1999; Soemodinoto et al., 2001; Fallon, this volume; Thapa, this volume) with the development of subsequent potential models for understanding the means by which the tourism industry may react to such situations (Anson, 1999; Ioannides and Apostolopoulos, 1999; Mansfield, 1999; Sönmez et al., 1999). At a different scale, though still highly significant for tourists' individual feelings of safety as well as perceptions of destinations, is the extent to which tourists may be victims of crime (Nicholls, 1976; Fujii and Mak, 1980; Walmsley et al., 1983; Chesney-Lind and Lind, 1986; Kelly, 1993; Hall et al., 1995; Pizam and Mansfield, 1996; Prideaux, 1996; Ryan and Kinder, 1996; Pizam et al., 1997; Michalko, this volume). This latter issue has been of longstanding interest to students of tourism, particularly in relation to the social dimensions of tourism, although what is criminal in one context may not be in another (Hall and O'Sullivan, 1996). Nevertheless, terrorism, war and crime has been the more normal security focus of tourism, although, as with the wider notion of national security, ideas of the relationship between tourism and security have also shifted.

Another significant perception and management issue for tourism, not least because of recent concerns over the global movement of SARS, is that of biosecurity. The implications of biosecurity issues for tourism were clearly illustrated in the impacts of the outbreaks of foot and mouth in the UK in 2001, which substantially restricted access to rural areas (Sharpley and Craven, 2001; Coles, this volume; Ritchie et al., this volume) and are paralleled by concerns over the potential for travellers to transmit diseases between human populations (e.g., Berkelman et al., 1994; Wilson, 1995; Cookson et al., 2001), particularly when globalisation processes actually encourage greater human mobility.

Economic security has also become an area of concern for the tourism industry, particularly in light of the impacts of the Asian financial crisis on tourism in the region (Hall and Page, 2000; de Sausmarez, this volume). Significantly, the Asian financial crisis indicated the interconnectedness of security issues, as the economic crisis also became transformed into a social and political crisis as people lost their jobs, and prices on some fundamental goods, including rice, increased in some parts of East Asia. In some cases, tourists were the objects of such unrest (Fallon, this volume), although, significantly, it is notable that throughout Asia tourism was seized upon as one of the industries that could potentially greatly assist in economic and financial recovery and in the provision of employment (Hall and Page, 2000).

The increased recognition of the wide ranging nature of threats which fit under the ambit of security have also given rise to attention to crisis and disaster management strategies (Faulkner, 2001; Faulkner and Vikulov, 2001; Beirman, 2003; Cushnahan, this volume; Prideaux, this volume). Undoubtedly, attention to the tourist decision making process with respect to security issues (Lovelock, this volume; McLaurin, this volume) is important. However, there is also a clear need, as Santana (this volume) has pointed out, to go beyond the rhetoric, and to look at some of the fundamentals of security and the means by which security issues and concerns are interrelated and embedded in the very nature of tourism.

CONCLUSION

Our notions of security have broadened significantly since the end of the Cold War. This was, in large part, due to the impetus provided by the debate on common security. This debate provided for contestation of the legitimacy and appropriateness of a traditional notion of security as something that was primarily concerned with the defence of the nation state. Indeed, this "old thinking" was viewed by many exponents as being a major source of insecurity in itself (Butfoy, 1997). Instead, security ideas now tend to stress more global and people-centred perspectives with greater emphasis on multilateral frameworks of security management (Johnston, 1992). However, security concerns will undoubtedly continue to also focus on deterrence and the containment of threats to international order, particularly from "rogue states." These conceptions of security will continue to influence tourism, although the influence of tourism on security will likely continue to be minimal. Nevertheless, the term security resonates with deep seated longings to be safe and these feelings undoubtedly have importance not only for travellers but also those people who are dependent on the business of tourism. In the search for an ethical basis for tourism it will therefore be interesting to see whether greater stress will be put on moving beyond the rhetoric of tourism as a force for peace to tourism actually providing a firm foundation for human well-being.

This volume was borne out of the impacts of September 11th and is being concluded at a time when American tanks are on the bridges of Baghdad and the fear of SARS is possibly having an even greater impact on the international tourism industry than the Iraq invasion and fears of economic recession. Several airlines are facing bankruptcy and destinations from the Caribbean to Asia are suffering declines in tourism numbers. These are, indeed, times of insecurity. However, out of the current crisis for the tourism industry also comes an awareness that the nature of security has changed, possibly forever. Although crime, terrorism and national security concerns will continue to be important, as this volume testifies, health, social and environmental issues are also becoming a part of the lexicon of tourism security and are also becoming related to ideas of sustainable development. Perhaps just as importantly the new discourse of security recognises just how interdependent and interconnected the world is. This discourse is not appreciated by all governments given the implications that arise from it with respect to the need to respect multilateral and global frameworks on issues as seemingly diverse as global climate change, human rights, peace keeping, the environment and, of course, national security. Nevertheless, it is a discourse that is continuing to grow and in an increasingly globalised world should find substantial resonance in the field of tourism studies. In 1994 Kaplan referred to "the coming anarchy" with respect to the prospect of greater international conflict in relation to resource and environmental security. In the twenty-first century we hope that the burning oil wells of Iraq are not harbingers of just such anarchy but instead trust that the notion of collective security will provide a basis for stability in which tourism will continue to thrive and human well-being enhanced.

REFERENCES

Alexander, G.A. (2000). Ecoterrorism and Nontraditional Military Threats. *Military Medicine*, 165(1): 1-5.

Allcock, J.B., Arnold, G., Day, A.J., Lewis, D.S., Poultney, L. Rance, R., & Sagar, D.J. (1992). *Border and Territorial Disputes*, Third Edition. London: Longman.

Anson, C. (1999). Planning for Peace: The role of tourism in the aftermath of violence. *Journal of Travel Research*, 38(1): 57-61.

Aziz, H. (1995). Understanding Attacks on Tourists in Egypt. *Tourism Management*, 16: 91-95.

Bauman, Z. (1998). *Globalization: The Human Consequences*. London: Polity Press.

Beirman, D. (2003). *Restoring Tourism Destinations in Crisis: A Strategic Marketing Approach*. Sydney: Allen and Unwin.

Berkelman, R.L., Bryan, R.T., Osterholm, M.T., LeDuc, J.W., & Hughes, J.M. (1994). Infectious Disease Surveillance: A Crumbling Foundation. *Science*, 264: 368-70.

Boulding, E. (1991). States, Boundaries and Environmental Security in Global and Regional Conflicts. *Interdisciplinary Peace Research*, 3(2): 78-93.

Brown, L. (1977). Redefining Security. *Worldwatch Paper No. 14*. Washington, DC: Worldwatch Institute.

Buckley, P. and Klemm, M. (1993). The decline of tourism in Northern Ireland: The causes. *Tourism Management*, 14: 184-94.

Butcher, J. (2003). *The Moralisation of Tourism: Sun, Sand . . . and Saving the World*. London: Routledge.

Butfoy, A. (1993). Rationalising The Bomb? Strategic Studies and the US Nuclear Umbrella. *The Australian Journal of Politics and History*, 40(2): 145-61

Butfoy, A. (1997). *Common Security and Strategic Reform: A Critical Analysis*. London: Macmillan, London.

Carter, S. (1998). Tourists and Traveler's Social Construction of Africa and Asia as Risky Locations. *Tourism Management*, 19: 349-58.

Chen, R.J.C., & Noriega, P., The Impacts of Terrorism: Perceptions of Faculty and Students on Safety and Security in Tourism. *Journal of Travel and Tourism Marketing*, 15(2/3): 81-97.

Chesney-Lind, M. and Lind, I.Y. (1986). Visitors as Victims: Crimes Against Tourists in Hawaii. *Annals of Tourism Research*, 13: 167-91.

Cohen, M.J. and Pinstrup-Andersen, P. (1998) Food Security and Conflict. *Social Research*, 66(1): 375-416.

Coles, T. (2003). A Local Reading of a Global Disaster: Some Lessons on Tourism Management from an *Annus Horribilis* in South West England. *Journal of Travel and Tourism Marketing*, 15(2/3): 173-97.

Commission on Global Governance (1995). *The Report of the Commission on Global Governance, Our Global Neighbourhood*. Oxford: Oxford University Press.

Cookson, S.T., Carballo, M., Nolan, C.M., Keystone, J.S., & Jong, E.C. (2001). Migrating Populations–A Closer View of Who, Why, and So What, *Journal of Emerging Infectious Diseases*, 7(3) (Supplement, June): 551.

Cushnahan, G., (2003). Crisis Management in Small-Scale Tourism. *Journal of Travel and Tourism Marketing*, 15(4): 323-38.

deAlbuquerque, K., & McElroy, J. (1999). Tourism and Crime in the Caribbean. *Annals of Tourism Research*, 26(4): 968-84.

de Sausmarez, N. (2003). Malaysia's Response to the Asian Financial Crisis: Implications for Tourism and Sectoral Crisis Management. *Journal of Travel and Tourism Marketing*, 15(4): 217-31.

Dolatyar, M. and Gray, T.S. (2000). The Politics of Water Scarcity in the Middle East. *Environmental Politics*, 9(3): 65-88.

Elliott, L. (1998). *The Global Politics of the Environment*. London: Macmillan.

Enders, W., & Sandler, T. (1991). Causality between transnational terrorism and tourism: The case of Spain. *Terrorism*, 14: 49-58.

Falkenmark, M., & Lundqvist, J. (1998). Towards Water Security: Political Determination and Human Adaptation Crucial. *Natural Resources Forum*, 22(1): 37-50.

Fallon, F. (2003). After the Lombok Riots, Is Sustainable Tourism Achievable? *Journal of Travel and Tourism Marketing*, 15(4): 139-58.

Faulkner, B. (2001). Towards a Framework for Tourism Disaster Management. *Tourism Management*, 22(2): 135-147.

Faulkner, B., & Vikulov, S. (2001). Katherine, Washed Out One Day, Back on Track the Next: A Post Mortem of a Tourism Disaster. *Tourism Management*, 22(4): 331-44.

Floyd, M.F., Gibson, H., Pennington-Gray, L., & Thapa, B. (2003). The Effect of Risk Perceptions on Intentions to Travel in the Aftermath of September 11, 2001. *Journal of Travel and Tourism Marketing*, 15(2/3): 19-38.

Food and Agricultural Organization (FAO) (nd). *Special Programme for Food Security*, http://www.fao.org/spfs/ accessed 1 April 2004.

Fujii, E.T., & Mak, J. (1980). Tourism and Crime: Implication for Regional Development Policy. *Regional Studies*, 14: 27-36.

Gartner, W.C., & Shen, J. (1992). The Impact of Tiananmen Square on China's Tourism Image. *Journal of Travel Research*, 30(4): 47-52.

Gore, A. (1992). *Earth in the Balance: Ecology and the Human Spirit*. New York: Houghton Mifflin.

Green, C.G., Bartholomew, P., & Murrmann, S. (2003). New York Restaurant Industry: Strategic Responses to September 11, 2001. *Journal of Travel and Tourism Marketing*, 15(2/3): 63-79.

Gurr, T.R. (1985). On the Political Consequences of Scarcity and Economic Decline. *International Studies Quarterly*, 29: 51-75.

Haftendorn, H. (2000). Water and International Conflict. *Third World Quarterly*, 21(1): 51-68.

Hall, C.M. (1994). *Tourism and Politics*. Chichester: John Wiley.

Hall, C.M. (2002). Travel Safety, Terrorism and the Media: The Significance of the Issue-Attention Cycle. *Current Issues in Tourism*, 5(5): 458-66.

Hall, C.M., & Jenkins, J. (1995). *Tourism and Public Policy*. London: Routledge.

Hall, C.M., & Lew, A. (Eds.) (1998). *Sustainable Tourism Development: Geographical Perspectives*. Harlow: Addison-Wesley Longman.

Hall, C.M., & Oehlers, A. (2000). Tourism and politics in South and Southeast Asia: political instability and policy. In C.M. Hall and S.J. Page (Eds.), *Tourism in South and South-East Asia: Critical Perspectives* (pp. 77-94), Oxford: Butterworth-Heinemann.

Hall, C.M., & O'Sullivan, V. (1996). Tourism, Political Instability and Social Unrest. In A. Pizam and Y. Mansfield (Eds.), *Tourism, Crime and International Security Issues* (pp. 105-21), Chichester: John Wiley.

Hall, C.M., & Page, S. (Eds.) (2000). *Tourism in South and South-East Asia: Issues and Cases*. Oxford: Butterworth-Heinemann.

Hall, C.M., Selwood, J., & McKewon, E. (1995). Hedonists, Ladies and Larrikins: Crime, Prostitution and the 1987 America's Cup. *Visions in Leisure and Business*, 14(3): 28-51.

Hall, C.M., & Williams, A.M. (2002). Conclusions: Tourism-migration Relationships. In C.M. Hall and A.M. Williams (Eds), *Tourism and Migration: New Relationships Between Production and Consumption* (pp. 277-89). Dordrecht: Kluwer.

Holst, J.J. (1989). Security and the Environment: A Preliminary Explanation. *Bulletin of Peace Proposals*, 20(2): 123-8.

Homer-Dixon, T.F. (1991). On the Threshold: Environmental Changes as Causes of Acute Conflict. *International Security* 16: 76-116.

Homer-Dixon, T.F. (1994). Environmental Scarcities and Violent Conflict: Evidence from Cases. *International Security*, 19: 5-40.

Homer-Dixon, T.F., Boutwell, J.H. & Rathjens, G.W. (1993). Environmental Change and Violent Conflict. *Scientific American*, February: 38-45.

Imber, M. (1994). *Environment, Security and UN Reform*. London: Macmillan.

Ioannides, D., & Apostolopoulos, Y. (1999). Political instability, war and tourism in Cyprus: Effects, management and prospects for recovery. *Journal of Travel Research*, 38(1): 51-6.

Jamieson, J.W. (1999). Migration as an Economic and Political Weapon. *Journal of Social, Political and Economic Studies*, 24(3): 339-48.

Johnston, R.J. (1992). Laws, States and Super-States: International Law and the Environment. *Applied Geography*, 12: 211-28.

Käkönen, J. (1988). *Natural Resources and Conflicts in the Changing International System: Three Studies on Imperialism*. Brookfield: Avebury.

Käkönen, J. (Ed.) (1994). *Green Security or Militarized Environment*. Aldershot: Dartmouth Publishing Company.

Kaplan, R. (1994). The Coming Anarchy. *The Atlantic Monthly*, February: 45-76.

Kelly, I. (1993). Tourist Destination Crime Rates: An Examination of Cairns and the Gold Coast, Australia. *Journal of Tourism Studies*, 4(2): 2-11.

Kemp, A., & Ben-Eliezer, U. (2000). Dramatizing Sovereignty: The Construction of Territorial Dispute in the Israeli-Egyptian Border at Taba. *Political Geography*, 19: 315-44.

Kingsbury, P.D., & Brunn, S.D. (2003). Freud, Tourism, and Terror: Traversing the Fantasies of Post-September 11 Travel Magazines. *Journal of Travel and Tourism Marketing*, 15(2/3): 39-61.

Kirchner, A. (2000). Environmental Protection in Time of Armed Conflict. *European Environmental Law Review*, 9(10): 266-71.

Leslie, D. (1999). Terrorism and Tourism: The Northern Ireland situation–A look behind the veil of certainty. *Journal of Travel Research*, 38(1): 37-40.

Levy, M.A. (1995a). Time for a Third Wave of Environment and Security Scholarship? *The Environmental Change and Security Project Report*, 1: 44-6.

Levy, M.A. (1995b). Is the Environment a National Security Issue? *International Security*, 20(2): 35-62.

Lovelock, B. (2003). New Zealand Travel Agent Practice in the Provision of Advice for Travel to Risky Destinations. *Journal of Travel and Tourism Marketing*, 15(4): 259-79.

Mansfeld, Y. (1999). Cycles of War, Terror, and Peace: Determinants and Management of Crisis and Recovery of the Israeli Tourism Industry. *Journal of Travel Research*, 38(1): 30-6.

Mathews, J.T. (1989). Redefining Security. *Foreign Affairs*, 68(Spring): 162-77.

Maxwell, J.W., & Reuveny, R. (2000) Resource Scarcity and Conflict in Developing Countries. *Journal of Peace Research*, 37(3): 301-22.

Maxwell, S., & T. Frankenberger (1992). *Household Food Security Concepts, Indicators, and Measurements*. New York: UNICEF.

MacLaurin, T.L. (2003). The Importance of Food Safety in Travel Planning and Destination Selection. *Journal of Travel and Tourism Marketing*, 15(4):233-57.

McKercher, B. & Hui, E.L.L. (2003). Terrorism, Economic Uncertainty and Outbound Travel from Hong Kong. *Journal of Travel and Tourism Marketing*, 15(2/3): 99-115.

Michalko, G. (2003). Tourism Eclipsed by Crime: The Vulnerability of Foreign Tourists in Hungary. *Journal of Travel and Tourism Marketing*, 15(2/3): 159-72.

Mische, P. (1989). Ecological Security and the Need to Reconceptualize Sovereignty. *Alternatives*, 14: 389-427.

Molvær, R.K. (1991). Environmentally Induced Conflicts?: A Discussion Based on Studies from the Horn of Africa. *Bulletin of Peace Proposals*, 22: 175-88.

Mowforth, M. and Munt, I. (1998) *Tourism and Sustainability: Development and New Tourism in the Third World*. London: Routledge.

Myers, N. (1989). Environment and Security. *Foreign Policy*, 74(Spring): 23-41.

Myers, N. (1993). *Ultimate Security: The Environmental Basis of Political Stability*. New York: W.W. Norton & Co.

Nichols, L.L. (1976). Tourism and Crime. *Annals of Tourism Research*, 3: 176-81.

Pizam, A. & Mansfield, Y. (Eds.) (1996). *Tourism, Crime and International Security Issues*. Chichester: John Wiley & Sons.

Pizam, A., Tarlow, P., & Bloom, J. (1997). Making Tourists Feel Safe: Whose Responsibility is it? *Journal of Travel Research*, 36(1): 23-8.

Prideaux, B. (1996). The Tourism Crime Cycle: A Beach Destination Case Study. In A. Pizam and Y. Mansfield (Eds.), *Tourism Crime and International Security Issues* (pp. 59-75). Chichester: Wiley.

Prideaux, B. (2003). The Need to Use Disaster Planning Frameworks to Respond to Major Tourism Disasters: Analysis of Australia's Response to Tourism Disasters in 2001. *Journal of Travel and Tourism Marketing*, 15(4): 281-98.

Richter, L.K. & Waugh, W.L., Jr. (1986). Terrorism and tourism as logical companions. *Tourism Management*, 7: 230-38.

Ritchie, B.W., Dorrell, H., Miller, D. & Miller, G.A. (2003). Crisis Communication and Recovery for the Tourism Industry: Lessons from the 2001 Foot and Mouth Disease Outbreak in the United Kingdom. *Journal of Travel and Tourism Marketing*, 15(2/3): 199-216.

Romm, J.J. (1993). *Defining National Security: The Nonmilitary Aspects*. New York: Council on Foreign Relations Press.

Ryan, C., & Kinder, R. (1996). The Deviant Tourist and the Crimogenic Place. In A. Pizam and Y. Mansfield (Eds.), *Tourism Crime and International Security Issues* (pp. 23-36). Chichester: Wiley.

Santana, G. (2003). Crisis Management and Tourism: Beyond the Rhetoric. *Journal of Travel and Tourism Marketing*, 15(4): 299-321.

Sharpley, R., & Craven, B. (2001). The 2001 Foot and Mouth crisis–rural economy and tourism policy implications: A comment. *Current Issues in Tourism*, 4(6): 527-37.

Soemodinoto, A., Wong, P., & Saleh, M. (2001). Effect of prolonged political unrest on tourism. *Annals of Tourism Research*, 28, 1056-60.

Sönmez, S. (1998). Tourism, Terrorism, and Political Instability. *Annals of Tourism Research*, 25(2): 416-56.

Sönmez, S., Apostolopoulos, Y., & Tarlow, P. (1999). Tourism in Crisis: Managing the Effects of Terrorism. *Journal of Travel Research*, 38(1): 13-8.

Stern, E.K. (1995). Bringing the Environment In: The Case for Comprehensive Security. *Cooperation and Conflict*, 30(3): 211-37.

Tansey, S. (1995). *Politics: The Basics*, London: Routledge.

Terrifying for Asia, worrying for the world. *The Economist*, April 7 2003, http://www.economist.com/PrinterFriendly.cfm?Story_ID=1680078 accessed 4 April.

Thapa, B. (2003). Tourism in Nepal: Shangri-La's Troubled Times. *Journal of Travel and Tourism Marketing*, 15(2/3): 117-38.

The Independent Commission on Disarmament and Security Issues (the Palme Commission) (1982) *Common Security: A Blueprint for Survival*. New York: Simon & Schuster.

Timothy, D.J. (2001). *Tourism and Political Boundaries*. London: Routledge.

Ullman, R.H. (1983). Redefining Security. *International Security*, 8: 129-53.

Wahab, S. (1996). Tourism and terrorism: Synthesis of the problem with emphasis on Egypt. In A. Pizam and Y. Mansfeld (Eds.), *Tourism, Crime and International Security Issues* (pp. 175-86). New York: Wiley.

Wall, G. (1996). Terrorism and Tourism: An Overview and an Irish Example. In A. Pizam and Y. Mansfeld (Eds.), *Tourism, Crime and International Security Issues* (pp. 143-58). New York: Wiley.

Walmsley, D.J., Boskovic, R.M., & Pigram, J.J. (1983). Tourism and crime: An Australian perspective. *Journal of Leisure Research* 15: 136-55.

Wilson, M.E. (1995). Travel and the Emergence of Infectious Diseases. *Journal of Emerging Infectious Diseases*, 1(2): 39-46.

World Tourism and Travel Council (WTTC) (2003). *The Potential Impact of an Iraq War on Travel & Tourism*, undated, *http://www.wttc.org/News6.htm*, accessed 1 April 2003

World Water Assessment Programme (2001). *Water Security: A Preliminary Assessment of Policy Process Since Rio*, prepared by the World Water Assessment Programme as a contribution to the International Conference on Freshwater (Bonn, December 2001) and the World Water Development Report, WWAP/WWDR/2001/001. New York: United Nations World Water Assessment Programme (WWAP)

The Effect of Risk Perceptions on Intentions to Travel in the Aftermath of September 11, 2001

Myron F. Floyd
Heather Gibson
Lori Pennington-Gray
Brijesh Thapa

SUMMARY. This study examined the relationship between perceived risk and travel intentions among residents in the New York City area. The timing of the survey (November 2001) provided opportunity to examine the effect of perceived risk on travel intentions during the period of aftershock following September 11, 2001. The study found that intentions to take a pleasure trip in the next 12 months (at the time of the survey) was related to safety concerns, perceived social risk, travel experience and income. Results from the study hold potential for better understanding risk perceptions and their impact on travel behavior and in

---

Myron F. Floyd, Heather Gibson, Lori Pennington-Gray, and Brijesh Thapa are affiliated with the Center for Tourism Research and Development, Department of Recreation, Parks and Tourism, University of Florida, P.O. Box 118209, Gainesville, FL 32611-8209 USA.

Address correspondence to Myron F. Floyd at the above address (E-mail: mfloyd@ hhp.ufl.edu).

[Haworth co-indexing entry note]: "The Effect of Risk Perceptions on Intentions to Travel in the Aftermath of September 11, 2001." Floyd, Myron F. et al. Co-published simultaneously in *Journal of Travel & Tourism Marketing* (The Haworth Hospitality Press, an imprint of The Haworth Press, Inc.) Vol. 15, No. 2/3, 2003, pp. 19-38; and: *Safety and Security in Tourism: Relationships, Management, and Marketing* (ed: C. Michael Hall, Dallen J. Timothy, and David Timothy Duval) The Haworth Hospitality Press, an imprint of The Haworth Press, Inc., 2003, pp. 19-38. Single or multiple copies of this article are available for a fee from The Haworth Document Delivery Service [1-800-HAWORTH, 9:00 a.m. - 5:00 p.m. (EST). E-mail address: docdelivery@haworthpress.com].

10.1300/J073v15n02_02

the marketing of travel services during periods of uncertainty like that following September 11, 2001. *[Article copies available for a fee from The Haworth Document Delivery Service: 1-800-HAWORTH. E-mail address: <docdelivery@haworthpress.com> Website: <http://www.HaworthPress.com> © 2003 by The Haworth Press, Inc. All rights reserved.]*

KEYWORDS. Social risk, travel experience, marketing, travel services, risk perception

INTRODUCTION

Travel and tourism is the world's largest industry and also represents the top three industries in many countries (Goeldner, Ritchie, and McIntosh, 2000). In 2000, the travel and tourism industry accounted for US$ 474 billion with 697 million international arrivals (World Tourism Organization, 2002). In the same year, the United States of America was the top earner of international tourism receipts (US$ 82 billion) that represented about 18% of total world market share. A record number of 50.9 million (7.3% of world market share) international tourists visited the US, whereby Canada (14.6 million), Mexico (10.3 million), Japan (5.1 million), the United Kingdom (4.7 million) and Germany (1.8 million) were the top five countries of visitor origination (American Hotel and Lodging Association, 2001). Besides inbound tourism, the US generated 35.4 million outbound trips by air, which resulted in US$ 65 billion (13.7% of world market share) in tourist spending in 2000 (World Tourism Organization, 2001). In addition, total domestic person-trips (person traveling 50 miles one way or more away from home and/or overnight) was registered at 998 million for 2000, in which 75% was related to leisure travel (pleasure, personal, other), 14% was business and 8% was combined business/pleasure (Travel Industry Association, 2001a).

Two years ago on September 11, 2001 the terrorist attacks on the World Trade Center (New York) and the Pentagon (Washington, D.C.) changed the inbound, outbound and domestic flow of tourists as the industry came to an abrupt halt as air transportation was grounded until September 13th. The effective shut-down resulted in mass cancellation of domestic and international inbound and outbound flights that left hundreds of thousands of travelers stranded. Early estimates by the International Air Transport Association (IATA) noted a direct loss of about US$ 10 billion during the week (World Tourism Organization, 2001). More importantly, consumer confidence in the safety and security of travel decreased significantly. Based on a survey conducted by Simmons Market Research to assess the immediate aftershocks among respondents who had air travel plans during the next 12 months, 39% noted the events of September 11 would have a large to very large effect on their plans and subsequent decision to travel, while 44% noted little to no effect. Among business travelers, 62% indicated that the events of September 11 would have little to no effect on their plans, while 20% indicated a large to very large effect (Simmons Market Research Bureau, 2001). Another survey conducted by Yesawich, Pepperdine and Brown found that 63% of leisure travelers were not likely to change plans; 35% intended to cancel a domestic trip, while 60% planned to take fewer international trips. Conversely, 67% were not likely to change plans; 38% planned to cancel a domestic trip, and 52% intended to take fewer international trips (Visit Florida, 2001a). Similarly, the Travel Industry Association of America reported that 70% of all Americans who had trips planned had not changed their plans, while only 12% reported cancellations, and others postponed or changed their travel plans. In addition, about 60% of Americans expressed intent of taking a leisure trip in the next six months (Travel Industry of America, 2001c).

In the weeks following September 11, about two-thirds of US leisure travelers indicated reluctance to fly, while 55% of business travelers planned to drive when feasible as opposed to fly to their respective destinations. Consequently, Amtrak–the nation's railway–experienced a 60% increase in its ridership ("Reality check on the rails," 2001). The airline industry experienced the brunt of the financial losses with low passenger volume, which led to reduction in routes and staff personnel. Major US carriers such as American Airlines experienced 33.7% decrease in passengers during September 2001; Continental Airlines noted a decrease of 31%, and Northwest Airlines reported a 30.7% decrease compared to the past year (Visit Florida, 2001b). Similarly, international carriers also felt the reverberations as British Airways cut 190 weekly scheduled flights, which included 36 inbound flights to the U.S. ("British Airways to cut 190 flights," 2001). Moreover, Air Canada moved to cut 5,000 employees due to a 30% decrease in reservations, and also decreased its flight schedule by 20% (Michaels and Coleman, 2001). Overall, in October of 2001, there was a 23% decrease in domestic passenger volume while a decrease of 37% was reported for international volume ("Passenger traffic is down 23%," 2001).

The reluctance to fly or travel had adverse impacts on other sectors of the tourism industry as hotel occupancy rates plummeted, business trips and vacations were cancelled, and workers industry-wide were laid off. The lodging industry experienced major setbacks as occupancy rates in major tourist destinations such as central Florida were down to 44.6% in September, but has fared better in the subsequent months (Visit Florida, 2001a). Lodging properties that depend on meeting, conventions and exhibitions (US$ 96 billion industry) did not fare any better, as meeting cancellations accounted for more than $1 billion in lost US business. Corporate and convention travel experienced more than a 40% decrease in attendance in September and modest improvements in October (Hotel and Motel Management, 2001a). Besides low occupancies, layoffs were imminent in the lodging industry especially for the luxury/upscale market segment. For example, the Wyndham Hotel Company laid off 1,600 employees (Hotel and Motel Management, 2001b), and Adam's Mark terminated 20% of its managers at 24 properties (Daniels, 2001). In the subsequent weeks after September 11, it was estimated that among the 260,000 hotel and restaurant employees who belonged to the Hotel Employees and Restaurant Employees International Union, more than one-third reported to have lost their jobs (Visit Florida, 2001b). Other notable sectors such as the rental car companies followed the same fate with layoffs.

Consumer confidence in November 2001 was more encouraging with 62% of Americans planning to take a leisure trip within the next six months, largely capitalizing on travel deals and incentives. Such deals and incentives were attractive as 56% indicated that airline discounts would increase their frequency of travel. Fifty-three percent of Americans indicated hotel offers would increase their frequency of travel; 45% reported special offers within their home state, while 44% noted travel tax credits (Travel Industry Association, 2001d). However, among the 38% that did not plan to take a leisure trip in the next 6 months varying reasons were reported for not traveling. With the growing down turn in the economy, 42% reported economic concerns; 16% noted not enough time; 12% identified health reasons, while 14% noted the overall safety of travel which included airline safety (Travel Industry Association, 2001d).

Overall, post-September 11 had immediate severe aftershocks on the tourism industry especially in the subsequent three months. Income generation, job creation and tax revenue collection was curtailed due to the erosion of consumer confidence. International arrivals in the US during September 2001 decreased by 29% (Visit Florida, 2001c), while the growth rate of arrivals during September-December declined by 20.4% in North America (World Tourism Organization, 2002). What had been "something that happened in foreign countries" and was a concern for those who traveled internationally, terrorism was now a major consideration when traveling domestically within the US. While the US had not been immune to terrorism attacks on their home soil with the 1993 World Trade Center bombing, the bombing of the Oklahoma Federal building in 1995 and the pipe bomb exploding at the 1996 Olympics in Atlanta, the severity of the September 11 attacks was unprecedented in terms of lives lost and physical destruction, not only in the US but compared with previous incidents around the world. While US jetliners had been hijacked many times before especially in the mid-1980s (e.g., TWA 847 hijacked between Athens and Rome in 1985; and a Pan Am flight hijacked in Karachi in 1986), the planes had always landed and while lives were lost, many more were saved. Using a hijacked plane as a missile was something new and inconceivable. The reaction was also instantaneous. While Sönmez (1998) noted that the reaction to terrorism among tourists is frequently delayed by about three months as people have already made their plans and are unwilling to change them, this time the impact on tourism was immediate. The purpose of this paper was to investigate the perceptions of risk and travel intentions of US residents in the months following September 11, 2001.

BACKGROUND LITERATURE

Travel surveys consistently find that safety and security are important concerns among tourists (Poon and Adams, 2000). The literature has focused on four major risk factors pertinent to tourism: (1) war and political instability (Clements and Georgiou, 1998; Gartner and Shen, 1992; Hall and O'Sullivan, 1996; Hollier, 1991; Ioannides and Apostolopoulos, 1999; Mansfeld, 1996; 1999; Richter, 1992; 1999; Pitts, 1996; Seddighi, Nuttall and Theocharous, 2000; Teye, 1986; Wall, 1996); (2) health concerns (Carter, 1998; Cossens and Gin, 1994; Lawton and Page, 1997); (3) crime (Brunt, Mawby and Hambly, 2000; Dimanche and Leptic, 1999; Pizam, 1999; Pizam, Tarlow and Bloom, 1997); and (4) terrorism (Aziz, 1995; Brady and Widdows, 1988; Bar-On, 1996; Enders, Sandler and Parise, 1992; Leslie, 1999; Richter and Waugh, 1986; Sönmez, 1998; Sönmez and Graefe 1998a, 1998b; Sönmez, Apostolopoulos and Tarlow 1999). In recent years the influence of natural disasters on tourism demand has also received attention (Faulkner, 2001; Mazzocchi and Montini, 2001). Of these five factors, risks associated with potential terrorism attacks and political instability have been identified as particularly influential in changing travel intentions, even among experienced travelers (Sömez and Graefe, 1998a). Sönmez (1998) suggests that when faced with the threat of terrorism tourists tend to engage in a number of behaviors including substituting risky destinations with safer alternatives and generalizing potential risks to other countries in the region affected. She also notes that tourists exhibit cultural variations in their reactions, with US tourists most likely to perceive higher levels of risk in foreign destinations.

Sönmez, Apostolopoulos and Tarlow (1999) note that travel statistics from around the world clearly suggest that tourism demand decreases as the perception of risks associated with a destination increases. Richter (1983) explains that when tourists are victimized worldwide media broadcasts exacerbate perceptions of risk associated with a particular destination. Sönmez and Graefe (1998b) found that perceptions of risk or safety concerns are of paramount importance in the decision making process of tourists since they can alter rational decision-making as it pertains to travel modes and choice of a destination. As a result of media coverage, perceived risks associated with a particular destination could actually outweigh actual conditions in the travel decision making process causing whole regions to be perceived as risky (Sönmez, 1998).

In one the earliest studies of travel and risk, Roehl and Fesenmeier (1992) drew on consumer behavior models to identify seven types of risk (e.g., Brooker, 1983; Cheron and Ritchie, 1982) that might be associated with travel decisions. The type of risks included in their study included equipment, financial, physical, psychological, satisfaction, social, and time risks. The authors found that social risk did not seem to be related to the perceptions of risk associated with pleasure travel. More importantly, Roehl and Fesenmeier found that it was possible to identify differences among tourists in their perceptions of risk with some tourists more risk averse than others. Sönmez and Graefe (1998a, 1998b) added health, political instability and terrorism risks to the seven risk factors investigated by Roehl and Fesenmeier. Based on a sample of middle-aged experienced international travelers, they found that tourism was generally not regarded as risky; however, terrorism and political instability were identified as factors of particular concern. Sönmez and Graefe (1998a) found that while individuals with higher education and income levels held more favorable attitudes towards international travel demographic variables alone were not good predictors of risk perception related to travel. Instead, favorable attitudes to international travel and risk seeking, along with higher income levels, best predicted the likelihood that a person would travel when faced with terrorism and political instability. While previous travel experience did not seem to impact the decision making process in this regard, individuals who had previously visited a destination tended to report that they would not avoid that destination in the future. Although, Matzursky (1989) suggests that future travel behavior may be influenced not just by the extent of past travel experience but by the nature of previous travel as well. Indeed, Sönmez and Graefe (1998a) postulate that experiencing or witnessing a terrorist behavior may have more influence on future travel decisions regardless of how experienced the traveler might be. Furthermore, Pizam and Fleischer (2002) found that while the severity of a terrorist attack will depress tourism demand in the short term (six to nine months after), the frequency of terrorist attacks is more important in determining whether tourists will travel to a particular destination in the long term as tourists perceive a destination to be risky and will tend to avoid it (Sönmez and Graefe, 1998b).

Following from this literature, the objective of the present study was to describe the risk perceptions of residents in the New York City area and observe the relationship between risk perceptions and travel intentions. In addition to being the site of the World Trade Center (WTC) attacks, the New York City area is the leading designated market area for television advertising in the US. The timing of the survey (November 2001) provided an opportunity to examine the effects of perceived risk on travel intentions during the period of aftershock following September 11, 2001.

DATA AND METHODS

Data for this study were obtained through a telephone survey of households in the New York City designated market area (DMA). DMAs are delineated by A.C. Nielson/Nielson Media Research, Inc. to determine market share in television viewing and is a basis for advertising placement. "A DMA consists of all counties whose largest viewing share is given to stations of the same market area" (Nielson Media Research, Inc. 2002). The NYC DMA is comprised of northern New Jersey, New York City, southeast Pennsylvania and Connecticut. The survey was administered by a private data collection firm using computer assisted telephone interviewing (CATI). Potential respondents were screened prior to the survey so that the resulting sample only included respondents who were 18 years and older, who were the primary decision-maker in the household and who had taken a pleasure trip in 12 months prior to the survey. The survey queried respondents on past trips and future travel intentions, risk perception, information search and socio-demographic characteristics. A total of 365 out of 1,647 eligible households participated in the study; complete interviews were obtained from 348 households. The response rate was 22%. Concern about the low response rate and nonresponse bias was addressed by a follow-up survey with 57 nonrespondent households. The follow-up survey revealed some differences between respondents and nonrespondents. Respondents were more likely to be women (60%, [$\Pi^2 = 4.19$, p. $= .041$]) and were slightly older than nonrespondents (respondents mean $= 50.61$ vs. nonrespondents $= 47.67$). The age difference was not statistically significant ($t = 1.66$, NS). Nonrespondents reported a greater likelihood of traveling in the next 6 to 12 months (79%) compared to respondents (53%) ($\Pi^2 = 16.78$, p. $= .000$). When asked about information sources used to plan pleasure trips, non-respondents were likely to use the Internet (37% never use); whereas respondents were not as likely to use the Internet ($\Pi^2 = 11.21$, p $= .024$). There were no differences between respondents and nonrespondents in use of travel agencies for travel information and education attainment. The results and conclusions of the study should be received in light of these differences.

Measures

Travel intention, the dependent variable, was measured by asking respondents if they intended to take a pleasure trip in the next 12 months (from the time of the survey). The responses were coded 0 for NO and 1 for YES. Three sets of measures served as independent variables. First, risk perception was measured by a 15-item Likert scale asking respondents to state their agreement or disagreement with statements developed for this study. These items focused on risk associated with pleasure travel *at the time of the study*. A principal components factor analysis was used to derive three subscales for use in subsequent data analysis. The details of this procedure and resulting measures are described below. A second measure of risk perception was adapted from the work of Sönmez and Graefe (1998b), Roehl and Fesenmaier (1992), and Moutinho (1987). Respondents were asked to rate eight types of risk in terms of the level of risk each posed to pleasure travel *at any time*. The types of risks included financial risk, health risk, physical risk, crime risk, terrorism risk, social risk, psychological risk and risk of natural disasters. The response format and codes were as follows: *None (coded 1), Very Low (2), Low (3), Moderate (4), High (5), Very High (6)*. Following previous studies (e.g., Sönmez and Graefe, 1998b), individual risk items were included in subsequent analyses, rather than creating an index. The third set of variables consisted of control variables. In order to observe the effect of risk perception on travel intentions, the potential mediating effects of income, education, age, gender and travel experience were statistically controlled. Income and education were measured by ordinal categories. Age was calculated from birth year and treated as a continuous variable. The number of pleasure trips taken by plane in the past 12 months (from the time of survey) served as an indicator of travel experience.

Logistic regression was used to examine the effects of risk perceptions, risk types and background variables on travel intentions since the dependent variable was dichotomous. The logistic regression model to be estimated can be expressed as:

$$\ln[P / (1 - P) = \beta_0 + \beta_{xi}$$

where P is the probability of taking a trip in the next 12 months, β_0 is the intercept, and βx_i is the set of parameters to be estimated associated with the independent variables. Three coefficients are highlighted in this study: the beta coefficients, odds ratios, and a pseudo-R^2 (Nagelkerke R^2). The beta coefficients represent the effect of a change in an independent variable on the log-odds of an event occurring (e.g., travel in the next 12 months or not traveling). They show the individual contribution of an independent variable in explaining travel intention holding all other variables constant. Thus, the possible confounding effects of variables such as income can be controlled. R^2 is highlighted to provide some measure of how well the set of independent variables explain the likelihood of taking a pleasure trip. Odds ratio is reported in order to compare relative influence of the independent variables on travel intentions. An odds ratio represents the increase in odds of an event occurring when the value of the independent variable increases by one unit. A complete discussion of logistic regression techniques can be found in Hosmer and Lemeshow (1989).

FINDINGS

Risk Perceptions

Principal components factor analysis with varimax rotation was performed on the 15-item risk perception scale. Based on the results of this procedure, three measures of risk perceptions were constructed (Table 1). Five factors with eigen values over 1.0. were extracted. Statements reflecting feelings of comfort and anxiety about travel were labeled *travel risk* and constituted factor 1 ($\forall = .75$). Factor 2 contained statements indicating *destination risk* ($\forall = .66$). Factor 3 appeared to reflect concerns about *safety concerns* as an attribute of travel decision making ($\forall = .53$). A fourth factor consisting of two items seemed to tap risk in international versus domestic travel. A fifth factor consisted of just one item. Following convention, factors with reliabilities (alpha) of less than .50 were not employed in subsequent analyses. Therefore, only the first three factors were used to develop measurement scales of risk beliefs. Each of these factors exhibited adequate internal consistency and reliability. Scales were constructed by summing the scores on individual items and dividing by the number of items in the scale. The factor analysis results of scale items are shown in Table 1.

Risk Types

In order to measure respondents' perceptions of risk associated with travel at any time, they were asked about the level of risk they perceived to be associated with eight types of risk. Across the eight risk types, mean values corre-

TABLE 1. Factor Analysis Results of 13 Items Used to Measure Risk Perception (N = 448)

Items and Factors Labels	Loadings	Means	Standard Deviation	Eigen Value	Alpha	% Variance Explained	Cumulative Variance Explained
Factor 1 (Travel Risk)		3.24	0.87	3.75	.75	24.98	24.98
I feel nervous about traveling right now	.79	3.27					
Traveling is risky now	.78	3.12					
Because of terrorism large theme parks should be avoided	.60	3.67					
I would feel very comfortable traveling right now*	.56	2.93					
Factor 2 (Destination Risk)		2.45	.70	1.58	.66	10.52	35.50
Travel to natural areas such as national parks is not risky	.78	2.38					
Trips to natural area scenic attractions are safe right now	.70	2.51					
Vacation travel is perfectly safe	.60	2.74					
Visiting art galleries/ museums are safe tourist activities	.51	2.15					
Factor 3 (Safety Concerns)		2.23	.87	1.42	.53	9.46	44.96
Safety is the most important attribute a destination can offer	.81	2.32					
Safety is a serious consideration when choosing a travel destination	.67	2.14					
Additional security measures at airports make traveling safe	.56	2.18					
Factor 4 (International vs. Domestic Travel)		2.80	.03	1.18	.47	7.87	52.83
International travel is just as safe as domestic travel	.79	2.77					
Domestic travel is just as risky as international travel	.78	2.83					

Note: Each item consisted of a 5-point Likert scale, ranging from 1 "strongly agree" to 5 "strongly disagree."
*This item was reverse coded.

sponded with the "low" response on the perceived risk measure. The means ranged from a low of 2.86 (SD = 1.40) for *social risk* to a high of 3.22 (SD = 1.29) for *financial risk*. The disapproval of family, friends and associates represented the lowest amount risk associated with the respondents' vacation travel intentions or plans. Losing money due to a cancellation posed the greatest risk in vacation travel. It is noteworthy that risk of being involved in a terrorist act was associated with a low level of risk. The percentage of respondents who rated this type of risk as very low or low was 62.4%. The wording of the instructions and the questionnaire item (i.e., "pleasure travel at any time) obviously can affect responses to this question. However, considering the temporal context in which they survey took place, and level of media saturation concerning terror attacks, this was a surprising finding.

Effect of Risk on Intentions to Travel

To examine how risk perceptions impacted intentions to travel intentions, a logistic regression model in which the dependent variable was intentions to "take a pleasure trip in the next 12 months" was estimated. A general measure of travel intentions (rather than intentions to travel to a specific destination) was used to gain insight into how risk influenced general propensity to travel during the aftershock of the 9-11 events. Eighty-one percent of the respondents (n = 281) reported that they intended to take a pleasure trip in the next 12 months (from the time of the survey). Consistent with other surveys of consumer confidence during November 2001, there was a strong indication of resurgence of pleasure travel in the U.S. following September 11. Table 2 shows the effects of risk perception and other independent variables on the odds of a taking a pleasure in the next 12 months versus not taking a trip. Table 2 shows four statistically significant effects on intentions to travel. Two of the effects were shown to be attributed to risk perceptions. The other effects were associated with travel experience and income. It is important to note that the effects of risk perceptions were observed while controlling for income, education, age, gender, and travel experience.

Safety concerns (Factor 1) exhibited a positive effect on intentions to travel. Higher values on this scale indicate disagreement. That is, respondents who were more likely to disagree that safety was an important consideration in travel decisions were more likely to travel in the next 12 months. A one unit increase on the safety concern scale increases the odds of taking a pleasure trip by 1.70 times. As one might expect, individuals less concerned about safety would show greater propensity to travel than individuals who placed greater weight on safety concerns. These results are consistent with those reported in the literature (Poon and Adams, 2000). For example, Sönmez and Graefe (1998a), based on a sample of U.S. residents, reported that safety was a factor in decision making related to international destinations and rural destinations.

Social risk, the disapproval of vacation choices by family, friends and associates was associated with a lower likelihood of taking a pleasure trip in the next 12 months. While the odds ratio for this variable was less than 1 (Table 3), risking disapproval of family, friends, and associates had a statistically nega-

TABLE 2. Frequencies, Percentages and Means for Risk Types

Response	Risk Types (Frequencies/Percentages)							
	Financial	Health	Physical	Crime	Terrorism	Social	Psychological	Natural Disaster
None	44/12.6	36/10.3	28/8.0	32/9.2	32/9.2	77/22.1	37/10.6	30/8.6
Very Low	49/14.1	62/17.8	56/16.1	52/14.9	104/29.9	61/17.5	64/18.4	84/24.1
Low	111/31.9	123/35.3	125/35.9	136/39.1	113/32.5	108/31.0	141/40.5	141/40.5
Moderate	88/25.3	97/27.9	113/32.5	94/27.0	64/18.4	54/15.5	79/22.7	73/21.0
High	44/12.6	27/7.8	22/6.3	29/8.3	25/7.2	32/9.2	22/22.7	17/4.9
Very High	12/3.4	3/0.9	4/1.1	5/1.4	10/2.9	16/4.6	5/1.4	3/0.9
Mean	3.22	3.07	3.16	3.15	2.93	2.86	3.00	2.92
SD	1.29	1.12	1.08	1.11	1.18	1.40	1.10	1.03

Note: Each risk type was measured on a 6-point scale, ranging from 1 "None (no risk)" to 6 "Very High."

TABLE 3. Logistic Regression Analysis of Risk Perception Factors, Risk Types, and Selected Control Variables on Overall Travel Intentions (N = 348)

Independent Variables	B	p	Odds Ratio
Factor 1 (Travel Risk)	.327	.133	1.386
Factor 2 (Destination Risk)	.145	.585	1.155
Factor 3 (Safety Concerns)	.535	.012	1.708
Financial Risk	−.153	.249	.858
Health Risk	−.092	.600	.912
Physical Risk	.365	.083	1.440
Crime Risk	−.143	.427	.867
Terrorism Risk	−.042	.790	.959
Social Risk	−.405	.002	.667
Psychological Risk	.189	.258	1.209
Natural Disasters Risk	.096	.574	1.101
Experience	.600	.013	1.823
Age	−.012	.242	.988
Gender	−.251	.460	.778
Income	.147	.004	1.158
Education	.117	.288	1.124
Constant	−2.102	.176	

Nagelkerke R^2 = .255; −2 Log likelihood = 297.455; Percent classified correctly = 81.8%.

tive effect on the odds of taking a pleasure trip in the next year. It is interesting to observe that of the eight types of risk in the model, social risk was the lone statistically significant risk type. Roehl and Fesenmaier's (1992) study suggested that social risk was unrelated to pleasure travel. Although, Sönmez and Graefe (1998a) found that social risk was important in considering trips to Europe but not for travel to other world regions.

Consistent with previous research on past travel experience, greater air travel experience was associated with a greater likelihood of taking a pleasure trip. Number of air trips taken in the previous 12 months prior to the survey was the best predictor of travel intentions. An odds ratio of 1.83 showed that the odds of taking a trip in the next 12 months were roughly two times more likely given a one unit increase in travel experience. Among the socio-demographic variables, income was the sole statistically significant predictor of travel intentions. A one unit increase in income resulted in 1.8 times increased odds of taking of pleasure trip in the next 12 months.

· The overall model explained about 26% of the variation in the log of the odds of travel intentions (versus not taking a pleasure trip). To summarize, safety concerns, social risk, air travel experience and income were the best predictors of travel intentions in our sample. Further indication of the significance of these variables can be gained by comparing the fit (log-likelihood) of the model containing the full set of independent variables to a model without these four variables. A reduced model without the four significant independent variables explained 11% of the variation in the log of the odds of taking a pleasure in the next 12 months (versus not taking a trip). A comparison of the full model (-2 Log likelihood = 297.455) with the reduced model (-2 Log likelihood = 306.99) indicated that inclusion of the four variables resulted in a superior model ($\Pi^2 = 24.85$, d.f. = 12, p. $\leq$ 05). The significance of these findings for future research and marketing practice are discussed below.

DISCUSSION AND CONCLUSIONS

The objective of this study was to examine the effect of perceived risk on travel intentions in the aftermath of the September 11 events. The sample, consisting of households from the New York City area, is significant because of its proximity to "Ground Zero" and because of its importance as the leading designated market area in the U.S. The set of events created a unique opportunity to study risk perception and travel behavior for research and marketing aims.

This study identified three factors associated with perceived risk towards travel. These risk perceptions were consistent with previous literature (Roehl and Fesenmaier, 1992). Interestingly, of the three factors observed in this study, travel risk exhibited the strongest level of agreement, whereas safety concerns had the least level of agreement. This is particularly interesting given the time that the survey was conducted.

Examining risk perceptions, risk factors and five mediating variables as predictors of travel intensions revealed that only four items were significant predictors of the intention to travel in the next year. Travel experience emerged as the most significant predictor of travel intentions. This result is consistent with previous research which suggests that past experience might override one's perception of risk. Pinhey and Inverson (1994) posited that previous travel experience might enhance feelings of safety. Sönmez and Graefe's (1998a) study of the risk perceptions associated with international travel supports this hypothesis. While the present study used a different measure of travel experience, it showed that travel experience did not override safety concerns and social risk. This finding should be further explored from both a research and marketing standpoint.

In addition, safety concerns emerged as a significant predictor of travel intentions. This finding is in line with the predictions of protection motivation theory (Rogers, 1975). Protection motivation theory maintains that individuals engage in protective behavior when (1) potential and magnitude for danger is high; (2) probability of occurrence is high; (3) actions to mitigate threat are effective (e.g., choosing alternative destinations or staying home); and (4) relatedly, an individual can control consequences (e.g., money to go elsewhere or time to postpone for safe conditions). It can be argued that these conditions were present following the events of 9-11. The threat level was certainly high, given the lack of specific information initially about the possibility of additional threats and the series of warnings that emanated from U.S. government officials. As described earlier, gross tourism demand fell precipitously following the terror attacks as people chose not to travel until some measure of safety and security was assured. Similarly, while a majority of the sample indicated plans to travel, those with safety concerns were less likely to express intentions to travel in the next 12 months.

Social risks emerged as the only significant predictor among the eight types of perceived risk, including risks associated with physical harm and terrorism. This is similar to Sönmez and Graefe's (1998a, 1998b) findings. Earlier it was noted that question wording could have influenced respondent ratings of the different types of risk. It is also likely that family, friends and associates' fear of terrorism risks and other risks associated with acts of terror is reflected in the social risk measure. Finally, income played a significant role in the intention to travel in the next year. Those with higher incomes were more likely to indicate plans to take a pleasure trip in the next year.

MARKETING IMPLICATIONS

Travelers' concern about safety has been felt in every sector of the industry. Understanding traveler's risk perception and its relationship to travel intention has a number of benefits to marketers in the various sectors. The results of this study suggest that income, past air travel experience, perceived safety concerns and perceived social risks were the best predictors of intentions to travel (in the next 12 months) two months following the 9-11 events. The results suggest that strategies to decrease perceptions of risk might only exist for two of these predictors: safety concerns and social risk. One strategy to mitigate safety concerns and perceived social risk is through persuasive advertising techniques. Persuasive advertising is advertising which increases consumers willingness to travel (von der Fehr and Stevik, 1998).

In response to the disruption of the travel industry following 9-11, the Travel Industry Association of America (TIA) initiated a persuasive advertising campaign. As part of the "Travel Industry Recovery Campaign," President Bush appeared in advertisements encouraging Americans to resume traveling and to see America. Travel was constructed as a patriotic duty of Americans. The ads aired on television in the U.S. and internationally for four consecutive weeks. Research suggested that more than two-thirds of the U.S. population saw the travel recovery ads. When Americans were asked to recall the purpose of the ads, 36% said the ads attempted to convince Americans that they should travel or that it is safe to travel, 28% percent said the ads tried to convince citizens to return to their normal lives, 24% percent said the ads were meant to alleviate fears about safety in the country and 21% said the ads encouraged consumers to spend money to boost the economy. TIA judged the campaign as a success.

The significance of social risk in this study brings to light a less emphasized component of recovery advertising. The results indicated that intentions to travel in the 12 months following 9-11 were related to the risk of family, friends and associates disapproving of vacation choices. In the TIA ads little attention was given to the perception of social risk. Following the events of 9-11, many individuals commented that relationships were first and foremost in the "mind" of the public. Jack Burke (2002) observed that, "The value placed on family and friends increased exponentially with the realization that life is tenuous." In recent years the U.S. has become a more geographically mobile society and since 1990 the percentage of Americans moving greater distances (e.g., different states) has increased. In 2000, 19% percent of all moves in the U.S. were to another county in a different state (Schacter, 2001). Given that a large percentage of U.S. population does not have family or friends who live in the same city or region, a strategic move could have been to capitalize on the importance and need to be with family and friends by dedicating a greater portion of advertising effort to this theme. Perhaps ads dedicated to encouraging people to "travel to see family and friends who you haven't seen" might have helped reduce the social risk associated with travel in the weeks and months immediately after September 11 as well as stimulated more travel (e.g., visiting family and friends).

The finding related to travel experience suggests that altering the product or improving advertising would not alter perceptions of risk. Marketing effort for individuals and market segments with greater traveling experience, particularly greater experience with air travel, would require less attention to safety and risk issues. Given Pearce's (1983; 1996) work on the "Travel Career Ladder," this may make sense. Pearce found that more experienced travelers tend to focus on higher order needs such as self actualization and education rather than lower level needs like food and safety. Therefore, more experienced travelers may be less focused on safety than less experienced travelers. In conclusion, in the post-September 11 era it has become important for destination and other marketers to help travelers cope with past events and the potential acts of terror. While experienced travelers appeared to be less affected by safety and security issues, marketers within the industry are faced with the challenge of assuring other travelers and their families that travel and destinations meet a high standard of safety and security. As stated earlier, in 2000 the U.S. generated 35 million outbound trips by air resulting in $65 billion in tourist spending (World Tourism Organization, 2001). Spending associated with domestic travel is also substantial. Information about the effects of perceived risk and its effect on travel intentions has the potential to contribute to marketing strategies to counter losses associated with perceptions of risk.

LIMITATIONS AND FUTURE RESEARCH

As previously mentioned there may be limitations related to high nonresponse. Nonrespondents tended to be younger males who expressed a greater likelihood of traveling in the next 12 months. Given this finding, it is interesting that the expressed risks were not higher than they were. In general, the respondents indicated fairly low levels of risk. However, given this difference between the sample and the population caution is warranted regarding the generalizability of the findings.

In addition, given the nature of the question regarding intention to travel, care should be taken when interpreting the findings. For example, intention to travel was not specific to a destination or type of trip. Therefore, responses could have varied based on the interpretation of the question. Traveling to see grandchildren in the next county one weekend would have a very different interpretation than taking an international two-week trip.

Nonetheless, the results do provide some insight into significant influences on travel intentions during the aftershocks of a traumatic U.S. domestic terrorism event. This is noteworthy since a majority of previous studies have focused on political instability and terrorism and its effect on tourism in regions outside the U.S. Future research on travel decision-making should assess whether risks are perceived and processed differently in domestic and international travel contexts. The findings related to social risk suggest that cognitive approaches underlying previous studies (e.g., Anderson, 1981, 1982; Kahneman and Tversky, 1979) can be complemented by addressing the social normative pressures associated with family and friends. As suggested earlier, social risk as a predictor of travel intentions has not been a significant component of tourism marketing in general and recovery advertising in particular.

REFERENCES

Anderson, N. (1981). *Foundations of information integration theory.* New York: Academic Press.

Anderson, N. (1982). *Methods of information integration theory.* New York: Academic Press.

Aziz, H. (1995). Understanding attacks on tourists in Egypt. *Tourism Management,* 16: 91-95.

Bar-On, R. R. (1996). Measuring the effects on tourism of violence and of promotion following violent acts. In A. Pizam and Y. Mansfeld (Eds.), *Tourism, crime and international security issues* (pp. 159-174). New York: Wiley.

Brady, J., and Widdows, R. (1988). The impact of world events on travel to Europe during the summer of 1986. *Journal of Travel Research,* 4: 8-10.

British Airways to cut 190 flights. (September 28, 2001). *The Wall Street Journal,* p. A12.

Brooker, G. (1983). An assessment of an expanded measure of perceived risk. In T. Kinnear (Eds.), *Advances in consumer research,* 11 (pp. 439-441). Provo, UT: Association for Consumer Research.

Brunt, P., Mawby, R. and Hambly, Z. (2000). Tourist victimization and the fear of crime on holiday. *Tourism Management,* 21: 417-424.

Burke, J. (2002). Crisis intervention: The relationship factor. http://www.callcenternews.com/newsletters/sample/ccnv6n1_news2.shtml (November 27, 2002).

Carter, S. (1998). Tourists and traveler's social construction of Africa and Asia as risky locations. *Tourism Management,* 19: 349-358.

Cheron, E., and Ritchie, J. R. B. (1982). Leisure activities and perceived risk. *Journal of Leisure Research,* 14: 139-154.

Clements, M.A. and Georgiou, A. (1998). The impact of political instability on a fragile tourism product. *Tourism Management,* 19: 283-288.

Cossens, J. and Gin, S. (1994). Tourism and AIDS: The perceived risk of HIV infection and destination choice. *Journal of Travel and Tourism Marketing,* 3: 1-20.

Daniels, E. (2001). *Adam's Mark trims its top staff.* http://www.jacksonville.com/tu-online/stories/100501/bus_7469128.html (September 25, 2001).

Dimanche, F. and Leptic, A. (1999). New Orleans tourism and crime: A case study. *Journal of Travel Research,* 38: 19-23.

Enders, W., Sandler, T. and Parise, G. F. (1992). An econometric analysis of the impact of terrorism on tourism. *Kyklos,* 45: 531-554.

Faulkner, B. (2001). Towards a framework for tourism disaster management. *Tourism Management,* 22: 135-147.

Gartner, W. C., and Shen, J. (1992). The impact of Tiananmen Square on China's tourism image. *Journal of Travel Research,* 30: 47-52.

Goeldner, C., Ritchie, B., and McIntosh. R. (2000). *Tourism: Principles, practices, and philosophies* (8th edition). New York: Wiley.

Hall, C. M. and O'Sullivan, V. (1996). Tourism, political stability and violence. In A. Pizam and Y. Mansfeld (Eds), *Tourism, crime and international security issues* (pp. 105-121). New York: Wiley.

Hollier, R. (1991). Conflict in the Gulf. *Tourism Management,* 12: 2-4.

Hosmer, D. W. and Lemeshow, S. (1989). *Applied logistic regression.* New York: Wiley.

Hotel and Motel Management. (2001a). *Hospitality industry goes extra mile to revive business.* http://www.hmmonline.com/ho...nds/headlinesdetail.jhtml?headlineID=1105 (November 10, 2001).

Hotel and Motel Management. (2001b). *Kleisner says Wyndham remains financially sound.* http://www.hotelmotel.com/hotelmotel/article/articleDetail.jsp?id=10497 (November 10, 2001).

Ioannides, D., and Apostolopoulos, Y. (1999). Political instability, war and tourism in Cyprus: Effects, management and prospects for recovery. *Journal of Travel Research,* 38: 51-56.

Kahneman, D., and Tversky, A. (1979). Prospect theory: An analysis of decision under risk. *Econometrica,* 47: 263-291.

Lawton, G., and Page, S. (1997) Evaluating travel agents' provision of health advice to travelers. *Tourism Management,* 18: 89-104.

Leslie, D. (1999). Terrorism and tourism: The Northern Ireland situation–A look behind the veil of certainty. *Journal of Travel Research,* 38(1): 37-40.

Mansfeld, Y. (1996). Wars, tourism and the "Middle East" factor. In A. Pizam and Y. Mansfeld (Eds.), *Tourism, crime and international security issues* (pp. 265-278). New York: Wiley.

Mansfeld, Y. (1999). Cycles of war, terror and peace: Determinants and management of crisis and recovery of the Israeli tourism industry. *Journal of Travel Research,* 38: 30-36.

Mazursky, D. (1989). Past experience and future tourism decisions. *Annals of Tourism Research,* 16: 333-344.

Mazzocchi, M., and Montini, A. (2001). Earthquake effects on tourism in central Italy. *Annals of Tourism Research,* 28: 1031-1046.

Michaels, D. and Coleman, Z. (October 1, 2001). Airlines with closest ties to U.S. face a painful future. *The Wall Street Journal*, p. A17.

Moutinho, L. (1987). Consumer behavior in tourism. *European Journal of Marketing*, 21: 1-44.

Nielson Media Research, Inc. (2002). FAQs–*About DMA's and direct broadcast satellite (DBS) providers.* www.nielsonmedia.com/FAQ/index.html (July 24, 2002).

Passenger Traffic Is Down 23%. http://www.orlandosentinel.com/business (November 9, 2001).

Pearce, D. (1983). Travelers' career ladders and travellers' experiences. *Journal of Travel Research*, 22: 16-20.

Pearce, D. (1996). Recent research in tourist behavior. Asia-Pacific *Journal of Tourism Research*, 1: 7-17.

Pinhey, T. K. and Inverson, T. J. (1994). Safety concerns of Japanese visitors to Guam. *Journal of Travel and Tourism Marketing*, 3: 87-94.

Pitts, W. J. (1996). Uprising in Chiapas, Mexico: Zapata Lives, Tourism Falters. In A. Pizam and Y. Mansfeld (Eds), *Tourism, crime and international security issues* (pp. 215-227). New York: Wiley.

Pizam, A. (1999). A comprehensive approach to classifying acts of crime and violence at tourism destinations. *Journal of Travel Research*, 38: 5-12.

Pizam, A., Tarlow, P. E. and Bloom, J. (1997). Making tourists feel safe: Whose responsibility is it? *Journal of Travel Research*, 3: 23-28.

Pizam, A., and Fleischer, A. (2002). Severity versus frequency of acts of terrorism: Which has a larger impact on tourism demand? *Journal of Travel Research*, 40: 337-339.

Plog, S. (1974). Why destination areas rise and fall in popularity. *The Cornell Hotel and Restaurant Administration Quarterly*, 14: 55-58.

Poon, A. and Adams, E. (2000). How the British will travel 2005. *Tourism Intelligence*, Germany: International Bielefeld.

Reality check on the rails. (September 26, 2001). *The Wall Street Journal*, p. B4.

Richter, L. (1983). Tourism politics and political science: A case of not so benign neglect. *Annals of Tourism Research*, 10: 313-315.

Richter, L. (1992). Political instability and tourism in the Third World. In D. Harrison (Ed.), *Tourism and the Less Developed Countries* (pp. 35-46). New York: Wiley.

Richter, L. (1999). After political turmoil: The lessons of rebuilding tourism in three Asian countries. *Journal of Travel Research*, 38: 41-45.

Richter, L. and Waugh, W. L. (1986). Terrorism and tourism as logical companions. *Tourism Management*, 7: 230-238.

Roehl, W. S. and Fesenmaier, D. R. (1992). Risk perceptions and pleasure travel: An exploratory analysis. *Journal of Travel Research*, 2: 17-26.

Rogers, R. W. (1975). A protection motivation theory of fear appeals and attitude change. *The Journal of Psychology*, 91: 93-114.

Schacter, J. (2001). Geographic mobility: Population characteristics, March 1999 to March 2000. *Current Population Reports*. Washington, DC: U.S. Census Bureau.

Seddighi, H. R., Nuttall, M. W. and Theocharous, A. L. (2001). Does cultural background of tourists influence the destination choice? An empirical study with special reference to political instability. *Tourism Management*, 22: 181-191.

Simmons Market Research Bureau. (2001). *Americans divided on air travel says nationwide poll.* http://www.smrb.com (October 10, 2001).

Sönmez , S. (1998). Tourism, terrorism, and political instability. *Annals of Tourism Research*, 25: 416-456.

Sönmez, S., Apostolopoulos, Y. and Tarlow, P. (1999) Tourism in crisis: Managing the effects of terrorism. *Journal of Travel Research*, 38: 13-18.

Sönmez, S. and Graefe, A. R. (1998a). Influence of terrorism risk on foreign tourism decisions. *Annals of Tourism Research*, 25: 112-144.

Sönmez, S. and Graefe, A. R. (1998b). Determining future travel behavior from past travel experience and perceptions of risk and safety. *Journal of Travel Research*, 37: 171-177.

Teye, V. (1986). Liberation wars and tourism development in Africa: The case of Zambia. *Annals of Tourism Research*, 13: 589-608.

Travel Industry Association (2001a). *Domestic research: Travel volume and trends.* http://www.tia.org/Travel/tvt.asp (November 9, 2001).

Travel Industry Association (2001b). *Domestic research: Trip characteristics.* http://www.tia.org/Travel/tripChar.asp (November 9, 2001).

Travel Industry Association (2001c). *Plan to rebuild travel in USA developed by travel industry.* http://www.tia.org/Press/pressrec.asp?Item=144 (November 9, 2001).

Travel Industry Association (2001d). *Third TIA travel confidence survey shows slight increase in American travel intention.* http://www.tia.org/Press/pressrec.asp?Item=157 (November 9, 2001).

Visit Florida (2001a). *How's business–special edition: Market intelligence report for partners.* Unpublished document. October 1, 2001.

Visit Florida (2001b). *How's business–special edition: Market intelligence report for partners.* Unpublished document. October 15, 2001.

Visit Florida (2001c). *How's business–special edition: Market intelligence report for partners.* Unpublished document. January 10, 2002.

von der Fehr, N. M. and Stevik, K. (1998). Persuasive advertising and product differentiation. *Southern Economic Journal*, 65: 113-126.

Wall, G. (1996) Terrorism and tourism: An overview and an Irish example. In A. Pizam and Y. Mansfeld (Eds.), *Tourism, crime and international security issues* (pp. 143-158). New York: Wiley.

World Tourism Organization (2001). *The impact of the attacks in the United States on International Tourism:* http://www.world-tourism.org/marketresearch/recovery/home (September 28, 2001).

World Tourism Organization (2002). *Tourism proves as a resilient and sable economic sector.* www.world-tourism.org/newsroom/Releases/more_releases/june2002/data.htm (June 28, 2002).

Freud, Tourism, and Terror: Traversing the Fantasies of Post-September 11 Travel Magazines

Paul T. Kingsbury

Stanley D. Brunn

SUMMARY. Travel and tourist magazines are major sources of information about destinations, events, accommodations, and transportation. The majority of this information is conveyed visually through colorful, stimulating, and seductive photographs of familiar landscapes and destinations. We examine a dozen popular U.S. travel magazines in the five months following the events of September 11, 2001 to discern the extent to which issues of risk, security, and anxiety are addressed or disavowed in editorials, articles, advertisements, and photographs. There is little mention of the tragic events on the magazine covers, in photographs, and articles; however, editors and regular staff writers often discussed security and risk and their impacts on destinations. In evaluating the magazines' responses, this paper draws on the work of Sigmund Freud and Jacques Lacan to offer the most rigorous utilization of psychoanalytic

Paul T. Kingsbury (E-mail: ptking0@uky.edu) is Visiting Assistant Professor, Department of Geography, Miami University, 216 Shideler Hall, Oxford OH 45056. Stanley D. Brunn (E-mail: Brunn@uky.edu) is Professor, Department of Geography, University of Kentucky, Lexington, KY 40506-0027.

The authors thank Richard Gilbreath, Director of the Cartography Laboratory, Department of Geography, University of Kentucky for preparing Table 1.

[Haworth co-indexing entry note]: "Freud, Tourism, and Terror: Traversing the Fantasies of Post-September 11 Travel Magazines." Kingsbury, Paul T., and Stanley D. Brunn. Co-published simultaneously in *Journal of Travel & Tourism Marketing* (The Haworth Hospitality Press, an imprint of The Haworth Press, Inc.) Vol. 15, No. 2/3, 2003, pp. 39-61; and: *Safety and Security in Tourism: Relationships, Management, and Marketing* (ed: C. Michael Hall, Dallen J. Timothy, and David Timothy Duval) The Haworth Hospitality Press, an imprint of The Haworth Press, Inc., 2003, pp. 39-61. Single or multiple copies of this article are available for a fee from The Haworth Document Delivery Service [1-800-HAWORTH, 9:00 a.m. - 5:00 p.m. (EST). E-mail address: docdelivery@haworthpress.com].

10.1300/J073v15n02_03

theory in tourism studies to date. In so doing, we seek to initiate a belated dialogue between critical tourism research and psychoanalytic approaches deployed in the disciplines of geography and social theory. Psychoanalytic concepts such as "symptom," "ego," "defense," and "fantasy" enable us to critically understand the uncanny disjunctures between the exotic, vulnerable, terrorized, and sunny tourist worlds that traversed the pages of post-September 11 travel magazines. *[Article copies available for a fee from The Haworth Document Delivery Service: 1-800- HAWORTH. E-mail address: <docdelivery@haworthpress.com> Website: <http:// www.HaworthPress.com> © 2003 by The Haworth Press, Inc. All rights reserved.]*

KEYWORDS. Tourism promotion, fantasy, risk, security, psychoanalysis, Freud, travel magazines, September 11

Remember a time not long ago when you could feel that if you took enough precautions before setting off into the unknown, and kept your head after things went seriously awry, you could think your way out of any emergency. When you are a firefighter heading up the stairs of a collapsing World Trade Center tower, well . . . we're in different times now. In saying that, I don't mean to trivialize the subjects we cover. When you are willing to live adventurously, take some risks, you can discover amazing things about yourself; if you're brave enough, maybe you can help to save the world. (John Rasmus, Editor in Chief, *National Geographic Adventure*, December 2001)

INTRODUCTION

The business of security and excitement has always been the *sine qua non* of the travel and tourism industries. Threats to the management of their location, intensity, and relationship are likely to pose problems and even result in disaster for the individuals, corporations, and organizations associated with travel and tourism economies. The immediate repercussions of the events following September 11, 2001 were experienced by those in local and international contexts who not only worked in these sectors, but also used them. Suddenly, words including "terror," "war," and "fear" resounded in private conversations and public commentaries around the world, particularly among those providing transportation to places of leisure, recreation, and entertainment.

This tragic day in North America radically ushered in a new set of challenges to the important and then thriving tourism economies of cities and rural areas in states dependent on traveling individuals and groups. Restaurants, gift shops, hotels, entertainment establishments, airlines and other carriers experienced immediately dramatic decreases in sales and reservations, while many scheduled late-year conventions, sporting events, and excursions were cancelled. According to the *USA Today* newspaper, between September 11, 2001 and December 31, 2002 estimated losses in tourism revenue for U.S. cities and metropolitan areas totaled $12.5 billion.[1] How to understand and respond to these new challenges posed major problems for not only companies and individuals directly related to tourism, but also to those whose business was to promote places, events, and activities under the aegis of travel, leisure, and relaxation. Using psychoanalytic understandings of "symptom," "ego," "defense," and "fantasy," our purpose is to critically examine how prominent U.S. travel magazines, composed of articles, photographs, advertisements, editorials, and other textual features, responded content-wise to the September 11 events which redefined for many tourists the very status of security and excitement as well as transport, destinations, and tourist activities.

THEORETICAL BACKGROUND

Stephen Britton (1991) was one of the first geographers to identify the theoretical shortcomings of traditional studies of tourism locations, visitor flows, and impacts. He called for a more critically engaged and theoretical approach to tourism, one that has been answered during the past decade by Aitchison et al. (2000), Crouch (2000), Hall and Page (1999), Mowforth and Munt (1998), and Ringer (1998). A central focus of these studies has been to conceptualize and document how international tourism often results in severe forms of political-economic exploitation, cultural destruction, increased crime rates, and environmental degradation, especially in Third World development contexts (Albuquerque and McElroy, 1999; Harrison, 1992; Pizam and Mansfield, 1996; Ryan 1993; Smith and Eadington, 1992; Weaver, 1998). Others claim that international tourism actually strengthens indigenous customs, reduces ethnic prejudice, safeguards the resources of women, and even promote world peace (D'Amore, 1988; Fairbairn-Dunlop, 1994; Reisinger, 1994; Var et al., 1994). Less studied topics by tourist geographers and other researchers, but themes related to this paper, include political unrest, violence, risk, and security. Notable examples include Teye's (1986) examination of the impacts of liberation wars on tourism in Zambia; Mathieson and Wall (1986) and Wall (1996) who address religious wars between Israelis and Arabs and in Northern

Ireland as affecting tourist arrivals and economic earnings; Lea (1988) on ethnic conflict and tourism impacts; and Aziz (1995) who examines the impacts
of attacks on tourists within Egypt. We agree with Guangrui's (2002:32) assessment of the economic impacts of tourism in China and declaration that
tourism "can be a risky business." Adams (2001), drawing on Smith's (1996,
1998) concept of "war tourism," introduces a new concept, viz., "danger zone
tourism," in which the state (Indonesia serves as her example) ostensibly offers adventure, high risk, and danger for certain tourists (see also Mihalic,
1996; Smith, 1998). Terrorism as a subject is also infrequently addressed; examples include Richter and Waugh (1966), Sönmez (1998), Pizam and Smith
(2000), and Hall (2001). Hall discusses how states attempt to promote tourism
in spite of internal violence, terrorism, and a questionable human rights record.
Safety and security issues, as they are related to tourism, have neither been topics of major inquiry, nor listed as promising research topics (but see Pearce and
Butler, 1999; Teo et al., 2001; Wall, 2001). Dann (1999) does argue that psychology and psychiatry, as well as geography, history, and political science,
have much to offer in studying relations between tourist development, war, belonging, alienation, and placelessness. He acknowledges, "[a]t the moment we
do not have studies which explore these perennial realities theoretically from a
combination of disciplines and paradigms" (Dann 1999: 21).

It is important to examine tourism from social and behavioral perspectives,
whether related to risk, security, danger, or violence. Two of the most cited
models in tourism studies use psychological approaches. George Doxey's
(1975) "causation theory of visitor-resident irritants" uses a four-stage continuum or "irridex" to theorize tourism development that ranges from "euphoria"
to "antagonism." Stephen Plog's (1974) study looks into "why destination areas rise and fall in popularity by psychographically categorizing tourists into
groups of 'psychocentrics,' who prefer driving to familiar, relaxed 'sun 'n'
fun' destinations, and 'allocentric' people who prefer flying and the freedom
to discover 'strange cultures' in 'non-touristy areas' " (1974: 57). The tour-
ism/psychology interfaces to date, however, have predominantly concentrated
on themes such as pleasure, motivation, consumer behavior, image-percep-
tion, decision-making, and identity creation (see for example, Doxey, 1975;
Goossens, 2000; Morgan and Pritchard, 1999; Plog, 1974; Woodside et al.,
2000). In tourism research there are few explicitly psychological methodological and/or theoretical approaches to violent and terroristic dimensions of travel
and tourism. Furthermore, few psychologically inflected tourism studies adopt
or respond to critical social theoretical frameworks. Critical theorizations and
observations of the unstable, yet seemingly ineluctable nexuses of violence,
enjoyment, anxiety, and pleasure, are central to the concerns of psychoanalysis. Unfortunately, terse criticisms of psychoanalysis in psychologically based

tourism research have resulted in the neglect and misconception of psychoanalytic theory. Plog (1987) declares that:

> [u]nfortunately, the concepts of the id, ego, and superego, and the dynamic psychosexual stages of development do not lend themselves to measurement through personality tests, let alone by means of questionnaires . . . it is our experience that the psychoanalytic-based theories of Freud and most of his disciples have proved to be of very little value in data-based research. Not only are the concepts loose and hard to pin down for research purposes, but the dimensions cannot be tied directly into advertising or promotional programs. (Plog, 1987: 206-09)

When tourism scholars have found it conducive to use psychoanalytic ideas, they do so only in passing (see, for example, MacCannell, 1998: 355). And yet, the psychoanalytic methodologies and theories pioneered by Sigmund Freud, and constantly modified before and since his death (notably by the French psychoanalyst Jacques Lacan), played a crucial role in the development of European critical theory throughout much of the twentieth century (see for example, Baudrillard, 1981; Benjamin, 1968; Deleuze and Guattari, 1983; Marcuse, 1974). Furthermore, in our discipline of geography there is a well-established and burgeoning Anglo-American literature that incorporates a variety of psychoanalytic approaches (Freudian, Lacanian, feminist, Kleinian, Winnicottian, and object-relations theory) to critically examine the psycho-spatialities of power, gender, violence, age, sexuality, racism, embodiment, and landscapes (for example, Aitken, 2001; Nast, 2000; Pile, 1996; Sibley, 1995).

This paper represents the most rigorous utilization of psychoanalytic theory (specifically Freudian and Lacanian) in tourism studies to date and seeks to initiate a belated dialogue between critical tourism research and psychoanalytic approaches in social theory (cf. Bracher, 1989; Davis, 2001). While a thorough inquiry into the reasons for the absence of and challenges that such a dialogue pose are beyond our purview, we pursue this line of inquiry for the following reasons: Psychoanalysis provides a highly spatial, rigorous, and critical theoretical framework that dialectically investigates (inter)subjective, material, symbolic, sexual, and politico-ethical civilities of desire, love, and pleasure *alongside* the discontentment of inhibition, anxiety, and subjugation (see for example, Freud, 1961; Lacan, 1977). Such forces are intensified, relied upon, and pervasive in promoting tourism phenomena like travel magazines. Second, as an alternative to the uncritical psychological tourism studies or, perhaps more accurately, *psyche*-analyses of tourists' interior minds that privilege understandings of "the tourist" as a wholly conscious "Self," endowed with and motivated by individual consumer choices, psychoanalysis asserts the ineluctable and dynamic (un)conscious "work" of desirous, vulnerable, discursive, and sexed *subjects* whose subjectivities are necessarily decentered, partial, and externally "embodied, materialized, in the effective functioning of the social field" (Žižek, 1989: 36). Third, given its theorization of the gaze, luring imaginary relations, linguistic signification, and visual identification, psychoanalysis is extremely adept at understanding magazine representations of phenomena such as September 11. Finally, psychoanalytic approaches provide a way to re-think how power vis-à-vis subjectivity, ideology, and labor regimes are operationalized across various scales in different concrete tourist contexts across the globe. While many critical tourism researchers, including those cited above, acknowledge that tourism is never simply about having innocent fun, a critical study should not neglect the task of theorizing what we call a "politics of enjoyment" in tourism. Such a study would inquire into precisely how anxieties *and* enjoyment maybe constitutive of key topics in critical tourism studies, viz., exploitation, domination, and discrimination (see Kingsbury, forthcoming). Our major thesis is that by theorizing the dialectic or relational modalities of anxiety and enjoyment we can critically help explain the tourism and travel industry's complex *mise en scène* of the lethal and heroic events that took place in New York City, Washington, D.C., and Pennsylvania. Below we list the magazines, describe their contents, and discuss significant features in regards to selected major psychoanalytic concepts.

METHODOLOGY

We examined the contents of eleven popular travel and leisure magazines published in late 2001 and early 2002. These were sold in book and magazine stores and in major shopping centers, downtown areas, and airports. The selection ranged from large circulation ones, such as *National Geographic Traveler* and *Travel + Leisure*, to others for adventure and wilderness travelers, and one specifically relating to Florida's tourist economy. The magazines were: *Condé Nast* November 2001, December 2001, and January 2002; *Backpacker: the Magazine of Wilderness Travel* February 2002; *Florida Travel* November/December 2001; *National Geographic Adventure* December 2001; *National Geographic Traveler* November/December 2001; *National Parks* November/December 2001; *Travel Holiday* December/January 2002; *National Parks* November/December 2001; *Travel + Leisure* December 2001; and *Attaché* US Airways Magazine December 2001. We believe this list provides a valid cross-section of North American travel magazines from which we could discern the post-September 11 tourist worlds both of publishers and travel industries. But we also acknowledge that the contents (covers, illustrations, feature articles, letters to editors, and advertisements) for many monthly magazines are set and also printed four to six weeks (or more) before the date appearing on the cover. In the magazines we examined the themes and phrases used in editorials, concerns expressed in letters to the editors, the messages in advertisements and articles as they relate to events of September 11, and the images and words on the covers.

Magazine Covers

If the contents of a magazine issue can be discerned from the cover, one would conclude that security, safety, risk, anxiety and fear were not important. The titles of articles or sections conveyed messages of escapism coupled with exotic travel, locations, and getaways. *Travel Holiday* for December/January 2002 highlighted its section on "The 25 Best American Escapes Right Now" while *Florida Travel* November/December 2001 included a major section on "7 Sensational Florida Beaches: Plan the Ultimate Golf Getaway. . . ." *National Geographic Traveler* for November/December 2001 described these contents: "11 Yosemite Experiences," "Naples: A Taste of True Italy," and "In Search of the Perfect Soak." *Condé Naste* for December 2001 listed these articles on the cover: "More Sun for Less Money: 25 Great Escapes from Mali to Palm Springs," "Readers Poll: 50 Best Ski Resorts" and "Brazil's Happy Hideaway." The cover of *Travel Holiday* for December/January 2002 had across the center cover "The 25 Best American Escapes Right Now!" Only *Travel + Leisure* December 2001 called attention to any concerns travelers might have, with a section (mentioned at the top of the cover) entitled "Special: Airport Security. Travel Insurance. Assessing Risk" (see Figure 1). This wording was offset by larger words and a snowy rural landscape that described a major part of the issue devoted to "10 Great Places To Spend Christmas." Even *National Parks* made no reference to the concerns travelers might experience; the cover listed articles on "USS Arizona Memorial" and "Species in the Balance." The major feature of *Backpacker* for February 2002 was "Quietest Spots in the U.S." Other articles advertised on the cover were "High Adventure Made Easy" and "Where Animals Go in Winter."

Titles and Editorials

In contrast to the magazine covers, which reflected almost a disregard for the events of September 11, the majority of editorials, even in November/December, articulated concerns that travelers and tourists might have expressed. Security issues were a major focus of the editorial "The All-Seeing Eye" in

FIGURE 1. Cover of Travel + Leisure December 2001

Condé Nast for January 2002. "Travel Under Siege" was the title of the editorial in *National Geographic Traveler* for November/December 2001 and "Freedom to Travel" in *Condé Nast* for November 2001. A very thoughtful essay, "Reshaping Our Future: As Our Nation Faces Uncertain Times, We Must Ask Ourselves a Set of Questions," by the Chairman of the Board, US

Airways appeared in *Attaché* in December 2001. The editor of *Travel + Leisure* entitled her December 2001 editorial "What Is the Role of a Travel Magazine at a Time When Travel Decisions Have Become Complicated by Frightening and Fast Changing World Events?" A sign that changes were evident was apparent in "Family Matters: The Kids Are Ready to Go. Are You Sure You Are?" in *Travel Holiday* December/January 2002. Optimism was expressed in "The Sun Still Shines in Florida" by the president and publisher of *Florida Travel* in the November/December 2001 issue. National healing can come from national treasures and parks; these ideas were conveyed in "Symbols of America" by the president of the National Parks Commission in the November/December 2001 issue of *National Parks*. The editorials expressed a variety of views, from uncertainty and uneasiness about what travel means to Americans to airline and airport security and the impacts of September 11 on the national consciousness.

MAJOR ARTICLES

The magazines also carried a mix of articles and special reports related to September 11 and about specific tourist destinations and opportunities. This juxtaposition of articles on airline security and delays checking into airports, biometric scanning, travel anxiety, or even terrorist threats, *appearing alongside* articles with colorful photographs of beaches, exotic hotels, and smiling people having fun may appear incongruous at the outset. The economic woes facing owners of travel agencies, cruises lines and airlines, and those in traditionally strong tourist destinations were multiple. The 100 most badly impacted cities or proposed state and congressional bailout economic packages were not discussed.

We believe that these worlds of fun, escape, and luxury travel alongside worlds of anxieties and fears related to travel are precisely those issues that tour operators, state travel agencies, and advertisers grappled with after September 11. While not appearing to ignore the events of September 11, our reading of the magazine contents demonstrates much more attention devoted to bargain or exotic places of travel than to fears and anxieties. Arguably, there is a denial of what happened on September 11 and this is evident in the cover photography, advertising, and shorter articles. There is little material provided about what the events meant or might mean to those who are still reluctant to travel; also there were only passing textual references to patriotism, support for firefighters, and victims.

This disjuncture was further evident in words than visual images. Concerns about the travel experience were much more likely to be conveyed in editorials (noted above), letters to editors, and columns by regularly featured writers. The visual contents were much more likely to show exotic and adventure places, promote "escape tourism" and use colorful and seductive photography to lure tourists to familiar destinations. Articles on terrorism and tourism failed to appear; the closest ones being those on airline security and travel advisories, but these subjects were not treated in all magazines.

Advertisements

Of the hundreds of magazine advertisements, less than a handful related specifically to the events of September 11. Perhaps the number reflects the difficulties and anxieties marketing firms had in preparing appropriate advertisements or their conscious decision not to express in words, phrases or images concerns about security, loss of freedom to travel, fear, and risk. Perhaps the publishers themselves decided not to confront the perceived taboos of fantasy and exotic worlds of travel, fun, and entertainment. The few that appeared provide some subtle yet strong messages: "There's never been a better time to celebrate the beauty of our own backyard" is the title of a full-page colorful ad in an eight-page Special Advertising Section in *Condé Nast* in December 2001. The words "American Beauty" were across the top, followed by a horizontal photo of a south Florida beachfront skyline and a text in the middle of the page that listed favorite scenic places, including New Orleans, Miami, and Alaska. The bottom third of the page had a colorful photograph of a western mountain and lake.

USTOA (U.S. Tour Operators Association) placed a full-page ad with the names of 145 sponsors in *National Geographic Adventure* in December 2001. Across the top is a quote from St. Augustine: "The world is a book and those who do not travel read only one page," followed by: "Don't close the book on your right to travel freely. A world of experience, adventure, education, and fun awaits, and the members of the United States Tour Operators Association are ready to help you explore it. Visit www.ustoa.com for more information about our members, their tours and packages, and the USTOA $1 Million Consumer Protection Plan." The sponsors include a wide range of U.S. and non-U.S. travel and tour companies, including airlines, exotic tour companies, tourist destinations, adventure travel, and transport modes. Among the sponsors were Christian Discoveries, Spanish Heritage Vacations, Eco-Challenge Adventure Travel, Collette Discovery Vacations, and American Council for International Studies. In subtle colors beneath the names of sponsors were atlas pages showing northern and northwest Europe and the American flag.

"Paint the Town Red, White and Blue" appeared in *Travel Holiday* January 2002. This full-page ad had a paint roller with a freshly painted American Flag.

Beneath the roller were these words: "New York City's Way of Saying Thanks" followed by attractions to entice the visitor to visit the city's restaurants, Broadway shows, stores, and other attractions at bargain prices. Icons of sponsors, including Coca-Cola, I Love New York, American Express, Delta Airlines, Metropolitan Transportation Authority, Citysearch.com, Paint the Town Red, Inc., and NYC & Company were at the bottom of the page. "Heroes Wanted" appeared in large bold letters in a full-page ad in *Backpacker* February 2002. The subtitle was "You can make an instant contribution to the relief effort with a credit card donation to any of these donations." They included the American Red Cross, Families of NYC Firefighters, and Families of NYC Police. Web addresses were provided for these and two other charities. The employees of Team One and Saatchi & Saatchi Advertising sponsored this ad. The book *From the Ashes: A Spiritual Response to the Attack on America* was advertised in the same issue. The book cover shows someone holding a lighted candle with an American flag in the background.

Views of Travel Operators and Executives

A snapshot of the concerns of 44 travel operators and executives appeared in a five-page section "Trends in Travel" in the December/January 2002 issue of *Travel Holiday*. They included directors of major airlines, regional tourist organizations, state tourist offices, cruise lines, car rentals, resorts, and national tourist divisions, including New Zealand, Jamaica, Switzerland, and Germany. They stated succinctly how the events of September 11 impacted their own business, city, or region. Safety, security, comfort, the importance of travel, and economic optimism were major themes (see Table 1). Close to home destinations, bargain prices and deals, and local/regional attractions were frequently mentioned. Few statements mentioned the importance of patience and reflection or issues of risk and anxiety.

The content analysis yields three important observations. First, while a significant proportion of the magazines (covers, ads, and articles) did not mention September 11 or issues of security and risk, there were poignant sections (editorials, letters by travelers, correspondent articles) that expressed the anxieties borne out of September 11. Second, the predominant message was that while there are drastic changes forthcoming in the travel world, there is also a celebration of how travel and tourist destinations still remain the same. Third, many magazines and advertisers rallied around the notion that tourism and travel were not only ways to overcome the pain of September 11, but also to affirm American freedom and individual heroism and the right (not a privilege) to travel.

TABLE 1A. Content Analysis of "Trends in Travel"

	Cruise Lines — Cruise Lines International	Cunard Line	Holland America	Norwegian Cruise Lines	Orient Lines	Princess Cruises	Radisson Seven Seas Cruises	Royal Caribbean Cruises	U.S. States — Arizona Office of Tourism	Colorado Tourism Office	Kentucky Department of Tourism	Mississippi Division of Tourism	Travel Montana	North Carolina Tourism	Utah Tourism	West Virginia Tourism & Commerce
A Safety and security	■	■					■				■	■				
B Comfort	■	■									■	■				
C Optimistic about recovery	■						■									■
D Uncertainty										■	■					
E Close to home destinations preferred			■	■			■			■	■	■				
F Family and friends important											■					
G Regional and urban destinations preferred																
H Natural surroundings important											■	■				
I What states/countries have to offer														■		
J Americans' bonds with the country																
K Importance of travel in life		■			■						■					
L Freedom to travel								■								
M Joy of travel	■															
N Right to travel		■				■										■
O 9-11 mentioned																
P Fear and anxiety																
Q Bargain prices, good values	■					■										
R Public-private cooperation										■						
S Listen to customers															■	
T Opportunities and challenges		■														
U Americans resolve and resilience										■						
V Patience, reflection, & re-prioritizing life															■	
W Need for flexibility										■						
X "Fantasy"		■														

Key words and phrases in the statements by 44 tourist executives regarding how September 11 affected their sector. The statements are organized by five key psychoanalytic concepts. For example, safety, security, and conflict were key themes by those from cruise lines and tourist offices, whereas introjection, or themes bonding with Americans and boosterism were associated with national government tourist offices.

Source: Compiled from the promotion section in "Trends in Travel," Travel Holiday, December/January 2002.

In examining the magazine covers, titles and editorials, major articles, advertisements, and the views of travel operators and executives, we have illustrated how various textual components contributed to the responses to the events of September 11. In the following section we wish to critically evaluate and interpret the above observations. Specifically, we address and assume that

TABLE 1B

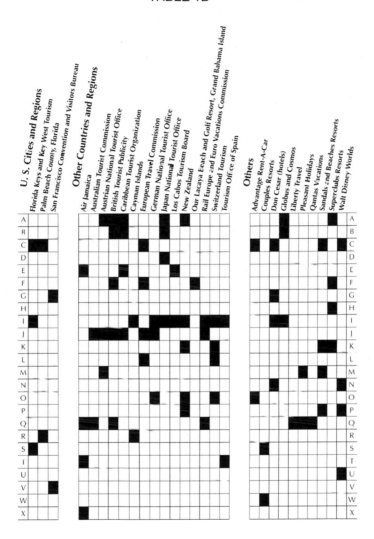

the resistances, omissions, syntheses, contradictions and a host of other choreographed textual meanings, concepts, and processes in the magazines are never "objective" or "impartial," but the mediated outcome of a panoply of (un)conscious subjective decisions immanent to writers' desires, editors' anxieties, and the audience's reading pleasure (cf. Kingsbury, 2002). What follows is an attempt to use psychoanalytic theory to critically evaluate why, how, and to what effect the magazines' discourses capillarize the tremulous social power of the tourism industry in attempts to fix textual meanings that are both constructive of enjoyment and terror in the wake of September 11.

DISCUSSION

Terrorism as Symptom

From a psychoanalytic perspective, September 11 functions for readers as primarily a *symptom* that reverberates throughout the travel magazines (see Žižek, 1989). A symptom is a "foreign body" organized into a "knot" of coded messages and meanings "created so as to avoid a *danger-situation* whose presence has been signaled by the generation of anxiety" (Freud, 1959: 57). Symptoms are permeated with unconscious desire and enjoyment because the subject's ego "proceeds to behave as though it recognized that the symptom had come to stay and that the only thing to do was to accept the situation in good part and draw as much advantage from it as possible" (Freud, 1959: 19). From this perspective, travel magazines attempt to make comfortable and meaningful the "foreign body" that is September 11 through the enjoyment of reading about tourism and travel worlds. For the sake of an anxious tourism industry and its participants, editors, photographers, writers, organizations, and corporations all seek to take advantage of, in one way or another, the unprecedented danger inaugurated by September 11. Our assertion that September 11 can be understood as a symptom that embodies textual desire and enjoyment relies not so much on discovering hidden (latent) desires in the visible (manifest) components of the magazines, as it does on taking into account the intended effects of reading the magazines. As Žižek writes:

> In so far as an ideological text has to be read as a ciphered formation of the unconscious, the reduction of its manifest content to its latent thought, while it is adequate, does not account for its impact, for the fascination it exerts on generations of readers–a third element must intervene, which, of course, is in the underlying economy of *jouissance* [enjoyment]. (Žižek, 1997: 52-3)

We conceive the magazines' strategy and their underlying economy of enjoyment as primarily a defensive one that mobilizes fantasies, that is, where the contents of travel magazines are analogous to the operations of the ego. Our analysis therefore aims to "question our own innocence, to render thematic our own (fantasmatic libidinal) and engagement in" (Žižek, 2001: 57) the magazines, depictions of September 11, and the tourism and travel industries more generally.

Defending Ego-Tourism

How is it possible, then, to equate travel magazines with the mechanisms of the ego? For Freud, the ego is an extremely complex concept that underwent many theoretical modifications. He primarily conceptualizes the ego as a psychical agency charged with the task of synthesizing the moralistic demands of the "superego" and the unconscious desires of the "id." From a Lacanian perspective, the ego is a useful analogy to a travel magazine, because both are objects that mediate with "outside" reality, resist change, and are constructed out of a succession of visual identifications with imaginary and luring images (see Lacan, 1988). For Freud,

> the ego is an organization . . . based on the maintenance of free intercourse and of the possibility of reciprocal influence between all its parts. . . . It is therefore only natural that the ego should try to prevent symptoms from remaining isolated and alien by using every possible method to bind them to itself in one way or another, and to incorporate them into its organization by means of those bonds. (Freud, 1959: 19)

Is not the travel industry's success dependent on and buttressed by representations of its ability to "bind together and unify" (Freud, 1959: 19) and maintain the free intercourse of its terminal hubs, travel agencies, hotel reservations, and information? Successfully writing and publishing a popular post-September 11 travel magazine requires that its contents must bind together and cohere as a pleasing "*imaginary* screen of satisfactions, myths, and so on, which enable the subjects to maintain a distance towards (and thus to 'neutralize') the horrors" (Žižek, 1997: 55) of terrorism. In appeasing its readers, the magazines deliver lines of flight from traumatic and excessive acts aligned with terrorism. Given the need for reassurances of safety in order to enjoy many forms of travel and tourism, an important component that regulates and secures the well being of egos and travel magazines is comparable to what Freud calls the *pleasure principle*: a psychical safeguard that avoids unpleasure by keeping excitation to a constant minimum (see Table 1). Editor Nancy Novgorod (*Travel + Leisure*, December 2001) reassures us that it is "good to provide information so that travels are pleasurable, comfortable, and safe." Sustaining the "peaceable disposition" (Freud, 1959: 21) of the ego and travel worlds represented by the magazines requires a careful incorporation of September 11 by preventing terrorist events from remaining too isolated and alien. Our readings and observations conclude that this incorporation is achieved not by any reference to the historical explanations of the geopolitical and economic conditions that may have led to September 11, but rather, by transforming the events themselves into an affirmation of the resilience of the (U.S.) tourism industry. The magazines demonstrate that the pleasures of travel writing and reading are predicated on not only covering distances, but also keeping distances from the threats posed by and associated with September 11.

Such distancing relies on strategic textual maneuvers or defense mechanisms of the ego that take place in what Lacan calls the "Symbolic" (language, law, and communication), "Imaginary" (meaning and specular imagery), and "Real" (anxiety, trauma, and impossibility) psychical registers. According to Freud, defenses are the "general designation for all the techniques the ego makes use of in conflicts which may lead to neurosis" (Freud, 1959: 98). For example, *repression* (associated with neurosis) is the withdrawal from consciousness of an unwanted thought or signifier by expelling it into the unconscious. This distancing is evident in the frequent withdrawal of signifiers of "terror," "war," or "September 11" from the magazine covers and advertisements. Similarly, *disavowal* defends the ego by refusing to accept the reality of a traumatic scenario. For example, John Rasmus, the Editor in Chief of *National Geographic Adventure* disavows the dangers of travel by narrating with fantasmatic ease the collapse of the WTC and a heroic odyssey to "save the world" evacuated from the restrictions and antagonisms of terrorism (see epigraph). Equally, the Chair and CEO, Royal Caribbean Cruises Ltd. claims that "[w]e are recovering from economic damage by pursuing the everyday activities that were briefly put aside" (*Travel + Leisure*, December 2001). The concerns of travel operators and executives expressed in "Trends in Travel" often mobilized defenses that included *introjection*–the identification or internalization of the characteristics (e.g., resolve and resilience) in order to feel unity with a loved object (e.g., American travelers) and *anticipation*–a more measured defense of planning and guarding against of future problems for the travel industry (see Table 1).

Many defenses of tourism against terrorism are grounded in an attempt to eschew the dismemberment, inconsistencies, and liabilities of a post-September 11 world ridden with threats of hijacking, increased passport controls, and military no-fly zones. In the name of "tourism against terror" the magazines install defenses that elide, elude, and "fill in" the alien and potentially dangerous non-tourist spaces of the world. From a Lacanian perspective such defenses are comparable to fantasies, moreover, "ideological fantasies" (Žižek, 1997) because they stabilize totalizing scenes that guard against a renunciation of enjoyment and the lack in the world of travel or "Other," in short, these fantasies guard against the terror of castration.

Fantasy and the Castration of Tourism

"Fantasy" is a term frequently used by tourism researchers, magazine writers, and tourists alike to conjure up images of exotic, desirable, and elusive activities or locations (see, for example, Dann, 1976). In psychoanalysis, however, fantasy is an extremely complex and important concept that has nothing to do with the "imagination" or "indulgence in the hallucinatory realization of desires prohibited by the Law" (Žižek, 1997: 14). Lacan compares fantasy to a fixed or frozen scene (produced by the jamming of a reel of film in a projector) just before a traumatic event occurs. The purpose of fantasy is to act as an imaginary protective screen to defend ourselves from the threat of castration (see Table 1). In Lacanian theory, castration does not refer to anatomical genital mutilation, but rather to a perceived lack in "the Other" whereby the child perceives that the (m)Other is not complete or self-sufficient and desires something (what Lacan designates the imaginary phallus) beyond the child. Castration involves the child's renunciation of his *or her* attempts to be the imaginary phallus and the subsequent sacrifice of enjoyment required to enter the symbolic order–the world of signifiers that always remains incomplete and beyond our conscious control. According to psychoanalysis, every form of psychopathology involves a refusal to accept castration.

Table 1 illustrates the varying degrees to which writers and corporations accepted or assumed castration vis-à-vis the incompleteness of and renunciation of enjoyment in a post-September 11 world of travel. On the one hand, there were many admissions that "[t]he way we travel has changed" (Thomas J. Wallace, Editor in Chief, *Condé Nast Traveler*, November 2001), "New York is a changed place now" (letter by a New Yorker, *Backpacker*, February 2002), and even that "the travel industry has changed . . . perhaps forever" (letter by Keith Bellows in *Condé Nast Traveler*, January 2002). Many writers and readers' letters, however, stubbornly refused to sacrifice enjoyment obtained prior to September 11 by typically arguing that travel was a "part of way of life, most basic right, freedom worth fighting for." While a significant proportion of magazine editors articulated the loss and sorrow in entering a faltering post-September 11 world, they would quickly attempt to wrestle back some enjoyment. John Rasmus, for example, wrote: "We try to honor them, and everyone who died that day, by continuing to do what we do," whereby what "we do" is "imagining some better times and better places, and learn some more about our world" (*National Geographic Adventure*, December 2001). These affirmations are fantasies because they seek to restore or freeze a world of tourism bereft of the castrating forces of danger and terror in a world, where, according to Governor Jeb Bush (*Travel Holiday*, December/January 2002) although "no one knows what the future will bring" the "sun shines in Florida" where "in spite of everything . . . destinations remain unchanged."

CONCLUSIONS AND FUTURE RESEARCH

Our inquiries into the tourist worlds of post-September 11 critically examined popular U.S. travel magazines by codifying their contents and examining both the anxieties and enjoyment of the subjects (authors, travel agencies, tourists, etc.) in the tourism industry through the use of psychoanalytic concepts. In echoing St. Augustine's quote above, the enjoyment immanent to the texts and images that traverse the magazines' pages (and indeed the act of reading) is no less important, concrete, or political than the enjoyment involved in traveling across the world. Given the reluctance of travel magazines to analyze why September 11 could have happened or how it may be averted in the future, we wonder whether international tourism (with its immense pressures for profit and reliance on enticing people to travel internationally) can ever be popularly represented or exist without resorting to and relying so heavily on defensive ideological fantasies. To what extent, then, can travel magazines afford to "traverse their fantasies," that is, cross the crucial stage in Lacanian psychoanalytic treatment where the subject redefines her/his fundamental relations to the lack in the Other and modifies appropriate modes of defenses and enjoyment (Lacan, 1977: 273). Also, to what extent can travel magazines acknowledge that "America's 'holiday from history' was a fake: America's peace was bought by the catastrophes going on elsewhere?" (Žižek, 2001: 51). To be sure, over recent decades forms of "alternative" or "special interest" tourism have emerged that embody a range of strategies that purport to offer culturally authentic, ecologically sustainable, and politically emancipatory alternatives to the problems associated with mass tourism. But given the deep-seated links between international tourism and the growth of capitalism, the harsh fact that all forms of tourism can reinforce hierarchical relations and skew egalitarian development efforts (Mowforth and Munt 1998), and aggressive post-September 11 calls for "tourism against terrorism," "who can foresee with what success and with what result?" (Freud, 1961: 112). Perhaps tourism, then, is an exceptionalist phenomena, *par excellence*, that is, unique to the historical and contemporary events that have promoted it as a constantly changing economy with new sub-sectors, creative lifestyles, and ingrained capital and psyche institutions (Hollywood, travel media, etc.) and for the most powerful, wealthy, and secular.

We agree with Dann (1999) and consider the interfaces of psychoanalysis, tourism promotion, risk and security ripe for future investigation by geographers and others with varying theoretical and methodological backgrounds, regional expertise, and skills in reading the visual. These inquiries might be using materials published in late 2001 and early 2002 or later. We suggest five themes. *First*, in regards to the print tourism literatures, we think it would be valuable to compare U.S. magazines with those published in Asia, Europe, Australasia, and other major tourist regions. Also, how would major and small city magazines depict travel and tourism destinations and activities, for example, New York, Los Angeles, Miami, Nashville and Portland? What kinds of printed materials (magazines, leaflets, etc.) did the various carriers (airlines, railroads, cruise lines) provide consumers about terrorism, security, and international destinations? *Second*, one could investigate major tourist organizations concerned with tourism and international travel, for example, compare the World Tourism Organization (which acknowledged the terrorist attacks and sought to address salient issues) with the European Union? *Third*, were there any shifts (dramatic or subtle) in the marketing strategies by advertising agencies, whether in photographs, images, coded words, and colors? And were there differences in the international marketing of major destinations among the German, Japanese, Dutch, and Swiss agencies and advertising media? *Fourth*, it would be valuable to examine changes among those directly affected by changes in government policy, terrorism alerts, airport, bus and train security, and tourism promotion. Using quantitative and qualitative research methods, including focus groups, would help tease out differences in regards to nationality, immigration status, age, occupation, gender, and lifestyle. *Fifth*, the immediate and long-term responses of governments are making to the new and different worlds of travel and tourist mobility cannot be ignored. Whether these state responses are unique or coordinated, viz., that tourists are affected by the rights of states, including their own, suggests that the politics and psychologies of tourism are integral components of understanding what is transpiring, where it is and why.

NOTE

1. *USA Today*, 5A, Thursday, October 17, 2002. Source: U.S. Conference of Mayors.

REFERENCES

Adams, K.M. (2001). Danger-zone tourism: Prospects and problems for tourism in tumultuous times. In P. Teo, T.C. Chang, K.C. Ho (Eds), *Interconnected Worlds: Tourism in Southeast Asia* (pp. 265-281). Amsterdam: Pergamon.

Aitchison, C., MacLeod, N.E. and Shaw, S.J. (2000). *Leisure and Tourism Landscapes: Social and Cultural Geographies.* New York: Routledge.

Aitken, S. (2001). *Geographies of Young People: The Morally Constructed Spaces of Identity.* London: Routledge.

Albuquerque, K. de, and McElroy, J.L. (1999). Tourism and crime in the Caribbean. *Annals of Tourism Research,* 26(4): 968-984.

Aziz, H. (1995). Understanding terrorist attacks on tourists in Egypt. *Tourism Management,* 16(2): 91-95.

Baudrillard, J. (1981). *For a Critique of the Political Economy of the Sign.* St. Louis: Telos Press, trans. C. Levin.

Benjamin, W. (1968). *Illuminations.* New York: Harcourt, Brace, and World, trans. H. Arendt.

Bracher, M. (1989). Lacanian theory and the future of cultural criticism. *Newsletter of the Freudian Field,* 3(1 & 2): 102-109.

Britton, S. (1991). Tourism, capital, and place: Towards a critical geography of tourism. *Environment and Planning D: Society and Space,* 9: 451-478.

Crouch, D. (2000). *Leisure and Tourism Geographies: Practices and Geographical Knowledges.* New York: Routledge.

D'Amore, L.J. (1988). Tourism: A vital force for peace. *The Futurist,* 22(3): 23-28.

Dann, G. (1976). The holiday was simply fantastic. *Revue de Tourisme,* 3: 19-23.

Dann, G. (1999). Theoretical issues for tourism's future development. In D.G. Pearce and R.W. Butler (Eds), *Contemporary Issues in Tourism Development* (pp. 13- 30). London: Routledge.

Davis, J.B. (2001). Commentary: Tourism research and social theory–Expanding the focus. *Tourism Geographies,* 3(2): 125-134.

Deleuze, G., and Guattari, F. (1983). *Anti-Oedipus: Capitalism and Schizophrenia.* Minneapolis: University of Minnesota Press, trans. R. Hurley and M. Seem (Eds.).

Doxey, G.V. (1975). A causation of visitor-resident irritants: Methodology and research inferences. In Proceedings of the Travel Research Association 6th Annual Conference, San Diego.

Fairbairn-Dunlop, P. (1994). Gender, culture and tourism development in Western Samoa. In V. Kinnaird and D. Hall (Eds), *Tourism: A Gender Perspective* (pp. 121-141). Chichester: Wiley.

Freud, S. (1959). *Inhibitions, Symptoms and Anxiety.* New York: Norton, trans. A. Strachey.

Freud, S. (1961). *Civilization and Its Discontents.* New York: Norton, trans. J. Strachey.

Goossens, C. (2000). Tourism information and pleasure motivation. *Annals of Tourism Research,* 27(2): 301-321.

Guangrui, Z. (2002). China's tourism since 1978: Policies, experiences, and lessons learned. In A.A. Lew and J. Ap (Eds), *Tourism in China*. New York: The Haworth Hospitality Press.

Hall, C.M. (2001). Tourism and political relationships in Southeast Asia. In P. Teo and T.C. Chang (Eds.), *Interconnected Worlds: Tourism in Southeast Asia* (pp. 13-26). Amsterdam: Pergamon.

Hall, C.M. and Page, S.J. (1999). *The Geography of Tourism and Recreation: Environment, Place and Space*. New York: Routledge.

Harrison, D. (1992). *Tourism and Less Developed Countries*. London: Belhaven.

Kingsbury, P.T. (2002). Science fiction and cinema: The hysterical materialism of pataphysical space. In R. Kitchin and J. Kneale (Eds.), *Lost in Space: Geographies of Science Fiction* (pp. 123-135). New York: Continuum.

Kingsbury, P.T. (Forthcoming). Sun, sand, and psychoanalysis: Jamaican tourism and the politics of enjoyment. *Geoforum*.

Lacan, J. (1977). *The Seminar. Book XI. The Four Fundamentals of Psycho-Analysis*. New York: Norton, trans. A. Sheridan.

Lacan, J. (1988). *The Seminar. Book II. The Ego in Freud's Theory and in the Technique of Psychoanalysis*, 1954-55. New York: Norton, trans. S. Tomaselli.

Lea, J.P. (1988). *Tourism and Development in the Third World*. London: Longman, Harlow.

MacCannell, D. (1998). Making minor places: Dilemmas in modern tourism. In J.M. Fladmark (Ed) *In Search of Heritage: As Pilgrim or Tourist* (pp. 351-362). Dorset: Donhead.

Marcuse, H. (1974). *Eros and Civilization: A Philosophical Inquiry into Freud*. Boston: Beacon.

Mathieson, A. and Wall, G. (1986). *Tourism: Economic, Physical and Social Impacts*. London: Longman.

Mihalic, T. (1996). Tourism and wartime–The case of Slovenia. In A. Pizam and Y. Mansfield (eds.) *Tourism, Crime, and International Security Issues* (pp. 143-158). Chichester: Wiley.

Morgan, N. and Pritchard, A. (1999). *Tourism Promotion and Power: Creating Images, Creating Identities*. New York: Wiley.

Mowforth, M. and Munt, I. (1998). *Tourism and Sustainability: New Tourism in the Third World*. London: Routledge.

Nast, H. (2000). Mapping the "unconscious": Racism and the Oedipal family. *Annals of the Association of American Geographers*, 90(2): 215-255.

Pearce, D.G. (1999). Introduction: issues and approaches. In D.G. Pearce and R.W. Butler (Eds), *Contemporary Issues in Tourism Development* (pp. 1-12). London: Routledge.

Pearce, D.G. and Butler R.W. (Eds), (1999). *Contemporary Issues in Tourism Development*. London: Routledge.

Pile, S. (1996). *The Body and the City: Psychoanalysis, Space and Subjectivity*. New York: Routledge.

Pizam, A. and Mansfield, Y. (1996). *Tourism, Crime and International Security Issues*. Chichester and New York: Wiley.

Pizam, A. and Smith, G. (2000). Tourism and terrorism: A quantitative analysis of major terrorist acts and their impact on tourism destinations. *Tourism Economics*, 6(2): 123-138.

Plog, S.C. (1974). Why destination areas rise and fall in popularity? *The Cornell Hotel and Restaurant Administration Quarterly*, 14(4): 55-58.

Plog, S.C. (1987). Understanding psychographics in tourism research. In J.R.B. Ritchie and C.R. Goeldner (Eds.), *Travel, Tourism, and Hospitality Research* (pp. 203-213). New York: Wiley.

Reisinger, Y. (1994). Tourist-host contact as a part of cultural tourism. *World Leisure and Recreation*, 36: 24-28.

Richter, L.K. and Waugh, W.L., Jr. (1986). Terrorism and tourism as logical companions. *Tourism Management*, 7: 230-238.

Richter, L.K. (1992). Political instability and tourism in the Third World. In D. Harrison (Ed.), *Tourism and Less Developed Countries* (pp. 35-46). London: Belhaven Press.

Ringer, G. (1998). *Destinations: Cultural Landscapes of Tourism*. New York: Routledge.

Ryan, C. (1993). Crime, violence, terrorism and tourism: An accidental or intrinsic relation? *Tourism Management*, 14: 173-183.

Sibley, D. (1995). *Geographies of Exclusion*. New York: Routledge.

Smith, V.L. (1996). War and its tourist attractions. In A. Pizam and Y. Mansfield (Eds.), *Tourism, Crime, and International Security Issues* (pp. 247-264). Chichester: Wiley.

Smith, V.L. (1998). War and tourism: An American ethnography. *Annals of Tourism Research*, 25(1): 202-227.

Smith, Valene L., and Eadington, W.R. (1992). *Tourism Alternatives: Potentials and Problems in the Development of Tourism*. Philadelphia: University of Pennsylvania Press.

Sönmez, S.F. (1998). Tourism, terrorism, and political instability. *Annals of Tourism Research*, 25(2): 416-456.

Teo, P., Chang, T.C. and Ho, K.C. (2001). *Interconnected Worlds: Tourism in Southeast Asia*. New York: Pergamon.

Teye, V.B. (1986). Liberation wars and tourism development in Africa: the case of Zambia. *Annals of Tourism Research*, 13(4): 589-608.

Var, T., Ap, J., and Van Doren, C.S. (1994). Tourism and world peace. In W.F. Theobald (Ed.), *Global Tourism: The Next Decade* (pp. 44-57). Oxford: Butterworth Heinemann.

Wall, G. (1996). Terrorism and tourism: an overview and an Irish example. In A. Pizam and Y. Mansfield (Eds), *Tourism, Crime, and International Security Issues* (pp. 143-158). Chichester: Wiley.

Wall, G. (2001). Conclusion: Southeast Asia, tourism connections–Status, challenges, and opportunities. In P. Teo and T.C. Chang (Eds.), *Interconnected Worlds: Tourism in Southeast Asia* (pp. 312-324). New York: Pergamon.

Weaver, D.B. (1998). *Ecotourism in the Less Developed World*. Wallingford: CAB International.

Woodside, A.G., Crouch, G.I., Mazanec, J.A., Oppermann, M. and Sakai, M.Y. (2000). *Consumer Psychology of Tourism, Hospitality, and Leisure.* New York: CABI Publications.

Žižek, S. (1989). *The Sublime Object of Ideology.* New York: Verso.

Žižek, S. (1997). *The Plague of Fantasies.* New York: Verso.

Žižek, S. (2001). *Welcome to the Desert of the Real.* New York: Wooster Press.

New York Restaurant Industry: Strategic Responses to September 11, 2001

Claudia G. Green
Pat Bartholomew
Suzanne Murrmann

SUMMARY. This research profiles the New York City restaurant industry response to a dramatic drop in business volume following the September 11th terrorist attack. Limited accessibility to the neighborhoods around the site of the World Trade Center challenged restaurants and other businesses to respond and survive the crisis. Through in-depth personal interviews with 14 restaurateurs, we compare the New York City response to the responses of other international tourism destinations

Claudia G. Green is Director of Hotel Management and Associate Professor, Pace University, Lubin School of Business, 1 Pace Plaza, W 446, New York City, NY 10038 (E-mail: cg4500@aol.com). Pat Bartholomew is Professor, City University of New York, New York City College of Technology, 300 Jay Street, Brooklyn, NY 11201 (E-mail: pbartholomew@citytech.cuny.edu). Suzanne Murrmann is Professor, Virginia Tech, Department of Hospitality and Tourism Management, Blacksburg, VA 24060 (E-mail: smurrm@vt.edu).

A special thanks to the selected restaurateurs who agreed to participate in this project by sharing their frank and meaningful experiences with regard to the terrorist attack and subsequent changes in the business environment in Lower Manhattan. With respect for these people, the authors have maintained confidentiality.

[Haworth co-indexing entry note]: "New York Restaurant Industry: Strategic Responses to September 11, 2001." Green, Claudia G., Pat Bartholomew, and Suzanne Murrmann. Co-published simultaneously in *Journal of Travel & Tourism Marketing* (The Haworth Hospitality Press, an imprint of The Haworth Press, Inc.) Vol. 15, No. 2/3, 2003, pp. 63-79; and: *Safety and Security in Tourism: Relationships, Management, and Marketing* (ed: C. Michael Hall, Dallen J. Timothy, and David Timothy Duval) The Haworth Hospitality Press, an imprint of The Haworth Press, Inc., 2003, pp. 63-79. Single or multiple copies of this article are available for a fee from The Haworth Document Delivery Service [1-800-HAWORTH, 9:00 a.m. - 5:00 p.m. (EST). E-mail address: docdelivery@haworthpress.com].

in times of great personal and property losses. We examine the restaurateurs' first response following the terrorist attack followed by their responses to employees, customers, and changes in business volume and
management. *[Article copies available for a fee from The Haworth Document
Delivery Service: 1-800-HAWORTH. E-mail address: <docdelivery@haworthpress.
com> Website: <http://www.HaworthPress.com> © 2003 by The Haworth Press,
Inc. All rights reserved.]*

KEYWORDS. Restaurants, response, crisis, New York City

That day everything just stopped at 9 am in the morning . . . a woman
who works upstairs . . . . said a plane hit the World Trade Center. We
thought it was a little plane. Our manager came in and said there was an
attack: then, I stepped outside and lines of people started forming at the
pay phones. We just left the door open and gave people water, a place to
sit, letting people use the phones because their cells were not working.

One man found out his wife was in the second tower to fall. Then another
guy found out that the building he had just gotten out of collapsed and he
just threw up.

In a way it was like everything I love about the restaurant business,
which is taking care of people. We did not have to charge them for anything. It was kind of like a dream situation where you do not care about
cost, you just make people feel good. In a strange way, I always thought
this was what this business was like at its core. I saw people all around
this area handing out water, helping people, giving them sandwiches and
we just wanted to make people feel good.

INTRODUCTION

In 2000, a record 37.4 million tourists visited New York City. This number
reflects a 28% increase in number of visitors since 1996. In July 2001, Mayor
Rudolph Giuliani reported "tourism continues to be one of the engines power-
ing New York City's economy with a total economic impact of $24.9 billion in
2000" (New York City Government Office, 2001). The desirability of New
York City as a tourist destination was not always so bright. As a matter of fact,
during the post-World War II era, New York City, like other big cities, experienced increased crime and homelessness. It had a reputation as one of the most
dangerous cities with a high crime rate. Concerted public and private efforts
and a strong economy based on a booming stock market in the 1980s contrib-

uted to the changed image of the city, and tourism began to thrive. However, on the morning of September 11, 2001, the terrorist attack on the World Trade Center challenged New York City as a municipality to respond and continues to challenge the viability of the city as tourist destination.

Following the September terrorist attack, New York City tourism suffered an immediate decline. This slowdown was felt across the city, as transportation to and from New York was limited while the city reeled from the impact of the most dramatic and fatal terrorist attack in America. The area most affected by the attack was Lower Manhattan owing to its proximity to the towers of the World Trade Center. The lower portion of the borough of Manhattan was cordoned off as part of the crime scene (Figure 1). For a period of two months,

FIGURE 1. Map

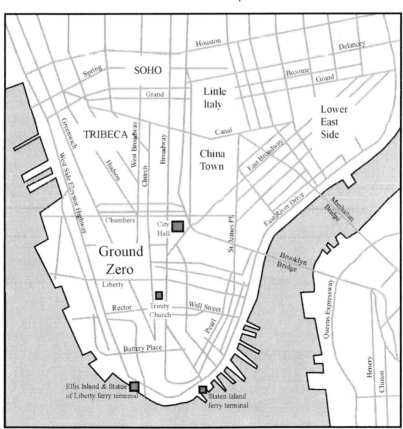

traffic to the immediate area was limited to emergency vehicles only. Eventually, delivery trucks, taxis, and buses were permitted to travel in the area. Finally, in late November, the streets and Holland Tunnel were re-opened. The lack of accessibility to Lower Manhattan was a financial hardship to a variety of businesses including hotels and restaurants. In addition to lack of physical accessibility, many people, residents and tourists included, avoided Lower Manhattan because of reports of poor air quality. Gradually, however, business began to return to the area, but not at the pre 9-11 levels.

The purpose of this research is to explore the recovery strategies employed by lower Manhattan restaurants (below Houston and bounded by the Hudson and East Rivers) after the attacks on September 11, 2001 in terms of immediate response, response to employees, and response to customers.

NATURE OF THE TOURISM INDUSTRY

The World Travel and Tourism Council (WTTC) projected domestic and international business and leisure travel to be a $7.2 trillion business by 2005 and to employ 338 million people. Regardless of its economic stature in the global and domestic economies, tourism is highly susceptible to natural and man-made disasters. According to Richter (1999), tourism planners and entrepreneurs in general have had few plans in place to defend against the instability that would be the result of an act of terrorism. When tourists perceive travel to be less pleasurable due to actual or perceived risks, they exercise their freedom to select other destinations (Sönmez, Apostolopoulos, and Tarlow, 1999). A review of the impact of terrorism in other international destinations has shown that a downturn in travel prevails until public memory of the incident fades (Pizam, 1999).

Following a disaster, it is necessary not only to manage the businesses through the period, but also deal with the needs of customers (Sönmez et al., 1999). Mismanagement during and following a crisis can further destroy the image and delay or prevent recovery (Sönmez et al., 1999). In his study of 300 tourism crises over a ten-year period, Pizam (1999) found a strong positive relationship between the severity of the terrorist attack and the intensity and duration of the effect on the tourism destination viability. Crises that involve mass destruction including loss of life and property (e.g., attack on the World Trade Center) have the strongest impact (Pizam, 1999).

A tourism crisis can occur after a disaster and can be further complicated as media coverage ruins the image of the destination with the resulting decline in visitors and subsequent income to the area (Pizam, 1999). Tourists are able to avoid destinations where risk for safety and security is high. It is, however, recommended that destinations where the risk is high should include a crisis management plan as part of their sustainable development and marketing/management. Using this plan, they have been found more likely to be able to rebuild their image, to reassure visitors, and to support recovery (Sönmez et al., 1999). In a study of crime and violence in tourism, Pizam (1999) developed a typology to describe the dimensions of tourism crises. The dimensions to describe these events are: motives, victims, location, severity, frequency, magnitude, expanse, and duration. In addition, Pizam considered the methods of prevention; parties responsible for prevention; methods used in the recovery; and parties responsible for recovery. In his qualitative analysis of previous tourism destination crises, Pizam (1999) identified the recovery methods as information dissemination, publicity, public relations and marketing. Information dissemination in this context related to providing honest, current and accurate reports of what is and has transpired in the affected area. Publicity and public relations campaigns are begun to let people know that business is back to usual and there is no better place to visit. Increased marketing is needed to promote recovery from the negative consequences and may take the form of price reductions, sales promotions, packaging of products and services, and repositioning the product. Financial support in the form of long-term, low/no-interest government loans help speed up the recovery process.

A 2001 National Restaurant Association industry study revealed that restaurants are the core of the 17.5 million jobs in the U.S. travel and tourism industry (National Restaurant Association, 2001a). The survey found that managers of more than two-thirds of the table service restaurants say that tourists are critical to their business. Further, restaurants with higher guest checks (averaging $25 or more) claimed that 50 percent of their revenue comes from tourists (National Restaurant Association, 2001b). The restaurant industry represents one of the primary segments of tourism with a forecasted contribution to the United States economy of $408 billion in 2002 and $566 billion in 2010 (National Restaurant Association, 2001a). The issues of safety and security and their subsequent impact on the downturn of business have been a topic of concern for a number of years yet few businesses actually have crisis management plans in place.

METHODS

In this study in-depth interviews were used to collect data. An interview protocol was developed and administered to 14 restaurant owners/managers chosen from the *Zagat Survey 2001 Downtown New York City Restaurants*, which was published in an effort to encourage customers to patronize restaurants most impacted by the terrorist attack and subsequent slow down in business.

This study incorporated restaurants from the Lower Manhattan neighborhoods of Soho, Tribeca, Chinatown and the Lower East Side (Figure 1). The Soho District is a fashionable area located halfway between Midtown and the Financial District. The name comes from the fact that it is located SOuth of HOuston Street. The Soho neighborhood features elegant fine dining restaurants and casual street-side cafés, as well as designer boutiques and trendy shops. Art galleries, theaters, showrooms, music venues, nightclubs and lounges can also be found throughout this area.

Tribeca is the district located closest to the site of the former World Trade Center and is bounded by Canal Street, Church Street, Park Place, and the Hudson River. It is part of one of the oldest sections of New York City and rich in historical associations. Its name, however, which stands for TRIangle BElow CAnal Street, is new. The development and growth of Tribeca has a direct relationship to New York City's becoming the business center of America. Some of the old buildings were cleared to erect the World Trade Center, but more during the past few decades the conversions have been from warehouses to living lofts. The accessibility of large, convertible, and originally reasonably priced spaces brought many artists and art organizations into the neighborhood.

New York City's Chinatown is the largest Chinatown in the United States with the largest concentration of Chinese in the western hemisphere and is located below Canal Street on the eastern side of Lower Manhattan. With a population of between 70,000 and 150,000, Chinatown is the favored destination for Chinese immigrants. Both a tourist attraction and home to many Chinese, the area offers hundreds of restaurants, produce and fish markets, and giftshops on crowded streets.

The Lower East Side (LES) is where it all began for generations of immigrants from around the world. In search of opportunity, turn of the century newcomers hit the streets selling their wares. The same entrepreneurial ideals can be seen on the LES today. The neighborhood is sought out for its amazing bargains and has in the last decade become a top destination for fashion, dining, theater and nightlife. The LES is bounded by Houston Street, the Bowery, the Franklin D. Roosevelt (FDR) Drive and Henry Street.

To gather qualitative data using in-depth interviews, owners/managers of 14 restaurants with varying levels of service, different styles of menus, wide-ranging years of operation, and various locations that included Soho, Tribeca, Chinatown, and the Lower East Side were selected. By menu type the restaurants included: American bistros, classic French, 4-star Asian and French, healthy fast food, classic delicatessen, Chinese dim sum, and Middle Eastern. The interview protocol examined how these restaurant businesses faced the dramatic changes initiated by the events of 9/11/01. Interviews included open-ended questions regarding information on employees, hours of operation, levels and type of service, advertising, promotion, public relations, menu discounting, menu items and participation in NYC organized efforts like Restaurant Week. The comments of the restaurateur were recorded and transcribed. Transcripts were reviewed and reported on the consistency and variations in the use of specific strategic responses and the outcome of those responses.

The interviews provided rich data on how restaurants in Lower Manhattan were responding to the changes wrought by the events of 9/11. The restaurant industry's response to the terrorist attack on the World Trade Center are reported in the following format:

- the restaurant's first responses on the day of the attack followed by;
- the restaurant responses to employees;
- the restaurant responses to customers;
- the restaurant responses to changes in business volume and management following the attack.

RESULTS AND DISCUSSION

The First Response

In their interviews, each of the restaurateurs recounted that their first responses on the day of the attack were basically to provide shelter and security for persons in need. Simply opening their doors to people fleeing the World Trade Center area, providing refuge, shelter, restrooms, water and solace. As the realization of the magnitude and the severity of the attack became clear, many restaurants offered people access to their business e-mail and telephones so they could contact loved ones. All of these responses related to the immediacy and uncertainty of the situation. As the reality of the disaster set in, restaurateurs realized that their role must be to provide food to the police officers, fire fighters, and volunteers who were responding to the crisis. The outpouring of sense of community and the desire to help others was extraordinary in the restaurants involved in this study. Virtually every restaurant in this study prepared food for the police, fire fighters, and volunteers at Ground Zero. For instance:

> I had plenty of food in the house. So the day after, the chef and a few assistants came in to work. I told the chef, whatever is going bad, cook it. We cooked for 30 and 100 people came. The police, Con Edison, firemen, they all came in to eat. We fed whoever came through the door, all the volunteers, some of the neighborhood people, but no money changed hands. Then neighborhood people came and donated food, money and we were cooking for 250 a day. This went on for a week, ten days; the restaurant had become a refuge.

> There was this chaos outside. Lines had started forming to use the pay phone. We just left the door open and gave people water, a place to sit, letting people use the phones because their cells weren't working. The next day we started donating stuff to the guys at Ground Zero. Our bread guy gave us bread, our chicken purveyor gave us chickens and a friend bought food at Costco and we just kept making sandwiches. It was important for us and for our employees because there were no customers that first week or two, it gave us a reason to come to work, a way to feel we were helping.

In many instances, restaurants were not paid for the food or the service. Once the restaurant's food supplies were depleted, they obtained more foodstuffs by purchasing them, receiving donations from large food supply vendors, and many cash donations from people in the community.

The Response to Employees

The primary response of owner/managers to employees was to assure their employees of the security of their income and job, and psychologically to let them know they had a safe place to work:

> We were watching outside when the second tower fell and this huge tsunami type tidal wave of blackness started coming at us. We ran back inside and it stopped about three blocks south of us, so we were never engulfed. But my staff were very traumatized by the people, the survivors walking, running uptown on Hudson Street covered in gray ash, some bleeding, hurt or stunned.

The restaurateurs interviewed in this study took reduction in profit and their own salaries to keep their existing employees on payroll. Some did not draw a salary for months. In some instances, employees were working, helping in the effort to prepare food for the emergency workers and support personnel at Ground Zero. In other instances, these employees were paid even though it was not possible to serve out of, or open, the restaurants:

> The whole group would get together at one of our five restaurants in Tribeca, which is only a few blocks from Ground Zero. You have to remember there were 35,000 to 50,000 uniformed services people in this area early on, when the business was still assumed to be rescue, not recovery. We helped to feed them, all those people. They needed our support and the support we could give was to feed them, breakfast, lunch and dinner.

When employees quit owing to problems related to a transportation issue or normal attrition, many restaurateurs did not replace them. In one instance, the restaurateur said he used creative scheduling, even though business was slow, to keep all the staff and so that each staff member would have a place to go and some sense of stability during the times of turmoil and confusion.

The Response to Customers

The customer profile for all businesses in Lower Manhattan changed following 9-11. Prior to this date the customer base consisted of local business people, many employed by the booming financial services industries, international and domestic tourists, shoppers, and local neighbors. Following the attack, which destroyed or damaged approximately 25 million square feet of prime commercial real estate in Lower Manhattan, it was reported that approximately 1,300 businesses were directly harmed. An additional 20,000 businesses were indirectly affected and more than 110,000 jobs were lost from Lower Manhattan (Gargano, 2002). Some of the businesses moved their offices out of Manhattan while still others were individuals who lost their jobs as a result of the attack and subsequently left Manhattan. The restaurateurs responded to customers by making changes in menu format and prices; giving more attention to ambiance; realizing responsibility to the community; and assessing marketing needs (Figure 2).

Menu Format

There were a number of changes in menus which included offering less expensive items, providing cheaper wines, changing portion sizes, opening for

FIGURE 2. Photo

breakfast, and closing for late night as fewer people wanted to stay downtown after midnight or 1 a.m.:

> It wasn't like we were bringing in any new customers, we were catering to our regulars. So what I did was take most of our high-end items off the menu and kept a lot of our signature moderately priced dishes. But no foie gras, no lobster, no expensive steaks. We didn't downscale though, no meatloaf with mac and cheese. Our regulars are looking for our food, so I didn't do any major overhauls but I was very, very sensitive to pricing. We did implement a more casual bar menu with burgers, great pizza, but it didn't replace anything.

In the few days and weeks following the attack, some chefs added items such as burgers, more Italian dishes, and other comfort foods because most of their customers were actually neighbors as opposed to tourists or business people. In addition, one restaurant provided a reduced price *prix fixe* meal that was only available to people who lived in the local community:

We changed the menu for a while. The neighborhood couldn't really get around or out because of barricades and transportation restrictions, so what we did was to accommodate our neighbors and offer a very inexpensive prix fixe menu for $25. Then we went to $45 after Thanksgiving until the New Year when we finally went back to our normal prix fixe of $85/94. There are many ways on a menu to offer a 4-star experience at a reduced price, just no foie gras and lots of chicken. And even when we offered the reduced priced menus customers could always order off the regular menu not putting us out of business.

In another instance, the owner repositioned his Middle Eastern celebration theme restaurant to a Mediterranean theme.

The semi-annual New York Restaurant Week in June and January is a period of time when well known, more upscale restaurants offer a three-course *prix fixe* lunch for $20.01. For the first time in January 2002 dinner was also offered for $30.01. A majority of the restaurateurs interviewed were positive about participating in these semi-annual events even if their participation was minimal. The cost of participating in the collaborative New York Restaurant Week is $2000 per restaurant. Because of the cost, a number of the restaurants with less expensive menu pricing opt to participate in the one-day "Taste of" events which are less costly. In October 2001 there were special promotions by NYC & Company (the New York City Chamber of Commerce equivalent), which included Taste of Tribeca, and Taste of Chinatown, and the restaurants in this study participated in those events as well.

Menu Pricing

The theories on pricing were as varied as the restaurants themselves. While one prominent restaurateur recommended that restaurants should not discount because this alienates the customers, many of the restaurateurs interviewed for this study employed some type of discounting of either menus or beverages or both:

We have always had a very wide selection of different priced wines. We have a wonderful sommelier, who is really committed to getting a bottle of wine that you would feel proud of at $20 or $700. So we always have a wide variety of price ranges in wines we offer, this won't change.

Others said that they felt this was necessary so that customers would feel they were getting a good value for their money. Although many made price changes, most reported that prices were back to normal levels around January 2002:

Discounting is not what we are about. But we did notice that people began to drink more; more glasses of wine than bottles, which was interesting because we are known as a wine destination. People after 9-11 seemed to want to avoid the idea/appearance of indulging in a bottle of wine. Ironically they drank more wine by the glass and we thought they'd order cheap wine by the glass; but they ordered one glass of expensive wine rather than two glasses of cheap wine. People wanted to chill, hang out and what's missing is that sense of frenzy that characterized Soho before 9-11.

Several commented on the price of wines and how the customers were looking for less expensive alternatives in the beverage area. In the area of catered events, a few restaurants reported becoming more competitive, knowing they had to close the business deal during the first call. A well-established deli made no changes in its pricing. The restaurant associated with a large culinary school did not decrease prices either as the managers felt that their prices were already competitive.

Ambiance

Restaurateurs were in tune with a variety of intrinsic factors associated with customer interactions and comfort including ambiance. One particular eatery took steps to support its restaurant as a calming place through the use of music while another reprinted its wine menu and placed it in a soft leather cover to demonstrate tactile comfort and stability. Still others said they did not want to make changes because they wanted to assure the customer of the solidity of their establishment. They stated that consistency and predictability were highly valued by post 9-11 customers. Several others reported that the customers themselves changed the ambiance of the restaurant in that they were more conversant with other customers and with the wait staff. There was a need for social interaction that is not common in New York City restaurants. In the few weeks immediately following the attack of September 11th, many shared their stories with regard to where they were when the attacks occurred or the loss of a friend, loved one or colleague.

Marketing

For the purposes of this research project, we defined marketing as advertising, promotions, and public relations. Most of the restaurateurs interviewed stated that they did not advertise and relied heavily on word of mouth, free publicity via media ratings and reviews, and participation in New York City & Company sponsored Restaurant Weeks. One responded:

I took my budget completely away from print advertising which I feel is so hard to measure. I am doing a lot of direct marketing. I have a web site which brings me tons of business and I do cross promotions that help bring in special events. These things I can gauge, I know they sell out, I see how many people come in with a gift certificate. Advertising is the one area I believe is not giving me the biggest bang for my buck. I don't know what it does for me. I need to see direct results to my bottom line. Like I know how many parties get booked through my website, everything is trackable. But advertising, I don't know.

People know about us through word of mouth, literally and figuratively. We are fortunate because we are such a NYC institution people just come here. We've been here since 1888. And I am talking broadcasting, radio, TV, they all come here to get our opinion or to just use the front of the place as a backdrop to say NYC.

Although most restaurants supported New York Restaurant Week, one restaurateur explained that it cost $2,000 to participate fully. A customer could easily eat at his restaurant for under $20 for lunch and under $30 for dinner. Considering this, there was no need to participate in Restaurant Week. Following 9-11, one of the restaurateurs was particularly creative and aggressive in designing promotions. She began communicating with her existing customers through a mailing where she partnered with local businesses to provide discounts for shopping and eating in Soho during the 2001 holiday season. In January she partnered with a Soho spa offering discounted services to her database and enjoyed a 2-3 percent return rate. In addition, some restaurants have been stepping up their promotions, which include private group food demonstrations by their chefs and partnering with organized walking tours featuring the various ethnic culinary markets and shops in Lower Manhattan.

One event in the spring of 2002 was cited by the restaurants in Tribeca as a rousing success: the Tribeca Film Festival (May 9-12, 2002). Actor Robert DeNiro and his partner, Jane Rosenthal, created a major film festival in just four months. The Tribeca Film Festival, sponsored by several million dollars in seed money from American Express, brought thousands back to the area during a glorious spring weekend and helped fill the restaurants and hotels that had been struggling since 9-11:

> There were organized weekends for Tribeca and Downtown which were quite successful. But I think the real essence of Tribeca, really being ourselves again happened after the Tribeca Film Festival. There was something intangible in the air that came back that day. They expected 3,000 people and 15,000 came. Since then there has been this very uplifting feel, a real going forward feel. It almost seemed like the festival closed a chapter. To me the Tribeca Film Festival was a moment when the lights got turned back on again.

There was disagreement among these entrepreneurs as to the value of a public relations person. Many like to design and track the impact of various promotional strategies they use such as direct mailings to customers and partnering promotions. Others felt that a public relations person was an unnecessary cost. They feel that a positive rating in magazines such as *Time Out* and *New York Magazine*, as well as a good rating in *Zagat Survey New York City Restaurants*, contributes as much to their visibility. But the 3-star+ restaurants in the study all had and kept their full time public relations people on retainer.

The Restaurant Response to Business Volume and Management

The issue of business volume varied among this sample partly as a result of the different styles of service from fast food take out, to deli, to full service. Prior to September 11th, one well-known deli was used to delivering large orders to the World Trade Center areas and providing food for parties and other events. When this business ceased, it made a large difference in sales, which the deli tried to recover by encouraging bus tours to stop for lunches and dinners. Most reported that business even lagged during the holidays since few people were in a mood to celebrate the holidays. If people did celebrate, it was with small, more intimate sized groups:

> People put their parties off, some cancelled, but a lot of them just postponed. After Thanksgiving people began to plan again. We did have some December parties, but the number was much smaller than previous years. There was no feeling of celebration.

> We got through the holidays, which were disappointing. December is usually our best month from both Christmas shoppers eating out and holiday parties but all the Christmas parties were canceling. But we picked up many intimate, smaller groups for the holidays. Ten or 15 people wanted to come out, not to celebrate, because that was considered in poor taste, but they needed to gather and end the year. People were solemn and conscious of not appearing to go overboard.

In addition, the nature of the loss of business was primarily from financial services businesses, tourists, and visitors who lived locally but came to the city for the weekend. Following 9-11, they were prevented from doing so due to tunnel and bridge closures and the reduced accessibility to selected areas of Lower Manhattan. The deli on the Lower East Side and the dim sum parlor in Chinatown also reported huge revenue losses in December because they normally catered parties for businesses in the World Trade Center that month:

Another huge part of our business was lost–the wholesale catering business and the catering business. We sold our products to Windows on the World and to the hotels near the World Trade Center. That business is simply gone. No one did Christmas or holiday parties and Chinatown is never a big destination during those holidays.

A problem we ran into was we did a lot of business downtown, business lunches delivered to the Stock Exchange, Wall Street firms, to the World Trade Centers. We used to deliver huge Christmas orders to the Trade Centers. But that was all gone and it was almost impossible to make deliveries into the other areas down there.

With regard to issues of business management, these owners also looked for other ways to gain control. One owner took the opportunity to re-negotiate her 15-year lease on her restaurant space, which was due to be up in 5 years. She felt that with the business downturn and uncertainty, she might be able to obtain a better deal. Additionally, some business people have started looking closer at the importance of business interruption coverage on their insurance policies. In addition, many applied for and received funding in the form of grants and loans from the local, state, and federal governments and the Small Business Administration (SBA). One of the applicants for the SBA loan changed her mind when she found that it would be necessary to offer her home as collateral on the loan. With the uncertainty around her, she did not feel that was a good decision and withdrew the application. One characteristic revealed in all of the interviews was the lack of ability to predict business. With so many factors having an impact on the downturn of the economy and the potential for future terrorism, business owners proceeded with care.

CONCLUSION

The act of terrorism on U.S. soil has changed life as Americans have known it. Americans' experience with the terrorism so common in other countries far away from U.S. shores has changed them forever. The responses of these restaurateurs follow a pattern identified by several researchers who have explored the impact of terrorism in other international tourism destinations. The most important first response following a tourism crisis or disaster was to deal with the situation and care for the people involved (Sönmez et al., 1999). In New York, on September 11th in Lower Manhattan this was demonstrated as the initial response among the restaurateurs in this study was to provide a safe space and amenities such as access to telephones and e-mail. Furthermore, Pizam (1999) identified the recovery methods as: information dissemination, publicity, public relations and marketing. These responses followed the initial reaction and were implemented to accommodate the changing needs of the customers and to let customers know that Lower Manhattan was open for business and eager to serve. This was seen in the restaurateur responses to employees, customers, and the downturn in business volume. Pizam also suggested that the impact of disasters is greatest when there is loss of life and property. There are no response models developed to forecast how long the impact of the World Trade Center attack will be felt, but the ramifications have been dramatic and ongoing.

Regardless of the downturn in business in Lower Manhattan, there has not been a wholesale collapse of the restaurants in that area since September 11th. This study found that many restaurant managers used similar strategies to deal with the aftermath of the attacks:

- Lower price points on menus via special offers, *prix fixe* meals, and discounts with gift certificates.
- Lower price points for beverage services, wines in particular. This meant offering wines at a lower price point, when necessary.
- Reliance on grants and loans to help bridge the gap; virtually all had availed themselves of some grant or loan at the city, state and/or federal level.
- A reliance on New York City-based efforts to promote the various areas:
  - the Dine Around Downtown Tuesday, May 21 sponsored by Downtown Alliance and Delta Air Lines.
  - the Tribeca Film Festival sponsored in part by American Express.
  - the various Restaurant Weeks in cooperation with NYC & Company.
- A reliance on the goodwill of local residents and tourists to spend whatever dollars they had in downtown businesses.

One consistent characteristic among all of these owners/managers, however, is the feeling of uncertainty about where business will be going in the coming years. In a city notorious for indifference, a new spirit–one of hope, unity and survival was born. Restaurateurs have tried to exemplify and live that spirit as they struggle with the aftermath of a disaster heretofore unseen in the United States:

> There is this feeling in the air of unsureness, I mean you never know if what is happening will be consistent or not. I think it has to do with the war, what's happening at Ground Zero, whether people are staying or leaving NYC. It just doesn't feel like you can know what to expect the way we used to be able to forecast and plan.
>
> Soho is so egotistical, still. People say oh everything is fine. How can it be fine when every time I walk by your store you're empty! We speak the

truth, I tell people that my business is off, this is what I am trying to do to get it back. I am not hesitant to talk about where we are at and we need to go to get back. But so many people feel it is like a curse if you talk about how bad it is. I think you can't go around saying everything is fine when it ain't fine. It solves nothing. But surviving is like keeping 50 balls up in the air at one time, exhausting.

Slowly, slowly regular customers have been coming back. But people have to let go of their fear of travelling/flying. And Chinatown has to solve its parking problems. The real problem is evenings and the tourists aren't back.

People have been trying really hard to get NYC back in people's minds as a place to visit. We have to keep doing that, reminding people why the city is such a unique place to visit.

When we look at the amount of disaster around us, we are doing very well. We are still here. We are paying the bills and we have most everybody working. We really can't complain. It does take a lot more work to get to the same point for the owners and in the kitchen to get to the same point. But we are still off, we are not the same as last year. We are off maybe 20 per cent; but it is a new beginning, like a new normal. We can't look back on what it was, we just have to move forward. In view of the disaster that happened, we are doing very well.

REFERENCES

Gargano, C. (2002). Speech made at the Empire State Development Corporation at the Association for Better New York meeting, Ritz Carlton, 7 May, 2002.

National Restaurant Association (2001a). Restaurants Are a Cornerstone of the Economy. Retrieved July 1, 2001 from the World Wide Web. *http://www.restaurant.org/cornerstone/economy.cfm*

National Restaurant Association (2001b). Travel and Tourism Facts. Retrieved July 1, 2001 from the World Wide Web. *http://www.restaurant.org/tourism/facts2.cfm*

New York City Government Office (2001). Press Release, July 30, 2001.

Pizam, A. (1999). A Comprehensive Approach to Classifying Acts of Crime and Violence at Tourism Destinations. *Journal of Travel Research*, 38(1): 5-12.

Richter, L.K. (1999). After Political Turmoil: The Lesson of Building Tourism in Three Asian Countries. *Journal of Travel Research*, 38(1): 41-45.

Sönmez, S. F., Apostolopoulos, Y. and Tarlow, P. (1999). Tourism in crisis: Managing the effects of terrorism. *Journal of Travel Research*, 38(1): 13-18.

The Impacts of Terrorism:
Perceptions of Faculty and Students
on Safety and Security in Tourism

Rachel J. C. Chen
Pender Noriega

SUMMARY. After the downturn spiral in travel resulting from the Gulf War, marketing professionals had to become extremely creative in trying to attract travelers back to the recreation and tourism markets of the world. However, the events of September 11 inflicted far greater damage to the domestic travel market in the United States than did the Gulf War. The purposes of the study were to examine the perceptions and attitudes of people toward (1) the awareness and acceptance of security measures in travel and tourism, (2) the effects of the September 11 attacks on the tourism industry and industry responses, and (3) the changes of people's travel and recreation behaviors such as destination and activity choices.

Rachel J. C. Chen is Assistant Professor of Tourism Management, Department of Consumer Services Management, University of Tennessee. Pender Noriega is Chair of the Family, Consumer and Health Sciences Division, San Joaquin Delta College.

Address correspondence to: Rachel J. C. Chen, Assistant Professor of Tourism Management, Department of Consumer Services Management, the University of Tennessee, 247 Jessie Harris Building, Knoxville, TN 37996-1911 (E-mail: rchen@utk.edu).

[Haworth co-indexing entry note]: "The Impacts of Terrorism: Perceptions of Faculty and Students on Safety and Security in Tourism." Chen, Rachel J. C., and Pender Noriega. Co-published simultaneously in *Journal of Travel & Tourism Marketing* (The Haworth Hospitality Press, an imprint of The Haworth Press, Inc.) Vol. 15, No. 2/3, 2003, pp. 81-97; and: *Safety and Security in Tourism: Relationships, Management, and Marketing* (ed: C. Michael Hall, Dallen J. Timothy, and David Timothy Duval) The Haworth Hospitality Press, an imprint of The Haworth Press, Inc., 2003, pp. 81-97. Single or multiple copies of this article are available for a fee from The Haworth Document Delivery Service [1-800-HAWORTH, 9:00 a.m. - 5:00 p.m. (EST). E-mail address: docdelivery@haworthpress.com].

The individuals surveyed were asked questions concerning their perceptions regarding the effects of the September 11 attacks on the tourism industry and government/business responses, the relative importance of
safety in destination/activity choice, security measures at airports, and
the changes of their spending patterns, travel decisions, and leisure pursuits. The results of the study indicated that faculty members were more
likely to experience the changes of their life, travel decision, and activity
choices than students. *[Article copies available for a fee from The Haworth
Document Delivery Service: 1-800-HAWORTH. E-mail address: <docdelivery@
haworthpress.com> Website: <http://www.HaworthPress.com> © 2003 by The
Haworth Press, Inc. All rights reserved.]*

KEYWORDS. Terrorists, tourism, travel, security, recreation, students,
faculty

INTRODUCTION

The most recent terrorist attack on U.S. soil, September 11, 2001, has
proven to be the largest human-made disaster in the United States since the
Civil War (Vlahov, Galea, Resnick, Ahern, Boscarino, Bucuvalas, Gold, &
Kilpatrick, 2002). Fatalities in this attack are estimated at 5,000-6,000 people
("Toll from attack at Trade Center is down sharply," 2001). This event has left
a lasting impression on the United States and resulted in a major influence on
the economy, tourism industry, policy adjustments, and the lives/lifestyles of
American citizens. For the travel and tourism industry, especially the domestic
market, to regroup from this travesty will entail a vast amount of creativity on
the part of marketing agencies and professionals. The results of this project
provide useful information to marketing professionals in planning and preparing for marketing future recreation, tourism, and leisure activities.

Terrorism is defined as any act of violence that countries may exchange,
and such acts can be traced back to as early as the mid-1930s. Our previous
major links to terrorism before September 11 included the bombing of Pearl
Harbor by Japan in 1941, which began American involvement in World War II
(Kapila, 2002) and the 1993 attempted attack on the World Trade Center in
New York City, wherein six men collaborated to place a bomb on the basement
level killing six people (Williams, 1998). The individuals convicted of this
previous attack on the Trade Center were issued to serve a 249-year prison
term and faced a $10 million fine (Kuttab, 2001). These previous terrorists at-
tacks did not take the lives of such a large number of civilians nor was public
transportation used to initiate these attacks.

Not since the Gulf War has there been such a downturn in the travel and tourism market as has been caused by the terrorist attack on September 11. The International Tourism Report (1991) revealed the Gulf War might have prevented the United States from reaching its projected surplus forecast of $6 billion in 1991, which was minimal compared to the financial effects of September 11. The United Kingdom Economist Intelligence Unit also indicated that the Gulf War might have caused a decline in the average amount of tourism. The UK Economist Intelligence Unit reported that 1992 was a difficult year for the international travel and tourism industry, as the Gulf War may have depressed travel in 1991 as compared to 1990. Treited and Fockler (1991) stated that while the US represents one of the world's largest travel markets, the US market is mainly domestic. They asserted that 93% of US travel takes place in the United States and not in overseas areas.

Therefore, while the Gulf War had a negative influence on travel in general the United States domestic market would not have witnessed such a major negative impact. However, an article in *The Economist* (1992) did state that Florida and Georgia had witness a reduction in tourism but even this would not have compared to the aftermath of September 11. Since September 11, states such as Florida, California, and Nevada continue to lose revenue. Florida, for instance, employs 7 percent of their total job market to the tourism industry and brings 1.22 million tourists in statewide each year. As a result of the events of September 11, with nearly 20 percent of these employees being laid off, over 240,000 jobs were lost (Dobbs, 2002). Because of the devastating effects of September 11, marketing professionals will be forced to find numerous options and become far more creative to lure travelers back to such a competitive market.

LITERATURE REVIEW

Economy

Some of the economic effects of September 11 are monumental. Miller (2002) noted that unemployment and layoffs result from the hidden recession that was fueled by September 11. According to the Madison School of Business (2001), with a shortage in revenue, corporations were forced to layoff their employees because they could not afford to compensate them for their work. Once laid off, consumer spending decreases because of uncertainty about their prospective job findings, and thus the cycle continues. As Santomero (2002) mentioned, this is the present state of the American economy, a downturn spiral of consumer spending and job termination. The economy shows that this cycle has continued. Dobbs (2002) reported that an economy in a recession would lead to a domino effect in other economic industries. The domino effect was even more apparent in those businesses closely related to the tragedy such as air travel.

The economic downturn has left Americans with social instability and uncertainty and the Gross Domestic Product (GDP) is currently under revision due to negative GDP growth in 2002 (Cohen, 2001). According to Weidenbaum (2001), the GDP of 2001 was about one percent lower than it should have been. In economic terms, it was an approximate reduction of $100 billion and was estimated that the American economy will decrease by 1.8 percent of the total GDP, resulting in a loss of 1.1 million United States jobs. Since travel and tourism is closely linked to the economy, marketing personnel must now develop strategies that will not only meet the financial concerns of the public but of big business in general.

Effects on Travel and Tourism Industry

The Tourism Industry Association (TIA), a nonprofit organization representing all components of the $584 billion travel industry, reported that because of September 11 "453,000 jobs will be lost, which is a 5.6 decrease from previous years" ("Many once thriving cities are suddenly hurting," 2001). For example, the airline industry suffered a great loss and was forced to layoff 20,000 pilots because of travelers' reluctance to transport by air post-September 11 (Santomero, 2002). *The Miami Herald* reported that the airline industry lost "$1 to $2 billion during the first week of the terrorist attacks" (Cohen, 2001). As of March 2002, approximately six months after September 11, the airline industry has reported losses of about $8 million and 95,000 airline jobs have been cut because of September 11. Delta airlines have increased their security measures by an estimation of $50 million. According to Delta representatives, plans are being made to exceed the requirements of the airline industry through technology advancements (Olsen, 2002). These initiatives may be publicized by marketing departments to ensure the public that action is being taken to increase safety and security.

The airlines industry is really stepping up security to try and bring confidence back to its travel market. Added security measures have also been implemented into common tourism destinations to prevent future attacks. A CNN news report stated that through the implementation of surveillance cameras and electronic background checks on employees, terrorism might be less likely to occur (Miller, 2002). These added security measures have also been implemented in some theme parks, hotels, and popular museums. Nonetheless, despite these precautionary measures, the tourism industry reports a steady decline in sales revenue. This decline in sales has a lot to do with the changing lifestyles of Americans as a result of the tragedy. Efforts must be taken by marketing agencies to help counteract this decline.

The travel and tourism industry strives off of family and business travelers. When planning the utilization of marketing dollars, advertisers must be aware that post September 11, studies show that Americans have become more reluctant to travel to certain foreign lands such as Afghanistan, Albania, Algeria, Angola, Burundi, Bosnia, Central African Republic, Columbia, Democratic Republic Columbia, Federal Republic of Yugoslavia, Guinea-Bissau, Indonesia, Iran, Iraq, Israel, Lebanon, Liberia, Libya, Macedonia, Nigeria, Pakistan, Sierra Leone, Solomon Islands, and Somalia (Goodrich, 2002).

Effects on Policies

The government is attempting to implement several new policies to reduce the possibilities of a terrorist attack. The publicizing of the increased concern to reduce terrorism is a method in which the government is not only trying to prevent terrorism but is trying to ensure the public that it is safe to travel, especially within the continental United States. According to policy makers, September 11 could have been prevented with a more detailed and cautious work environment. Several of these new policies of post-September 11 are in regards to privacy issues. Specifically, four policies address privacy issues at the workplace. These four polices include electronic communications, the Internet, the telephone, and video surveillance (Kenen, 2002). While these types of policies may appear not to be related to the travel, recreation, and tourism markets, if they provide a sense of intervention and involvement by the government, they may reduce the perception of the endangerment of travel. Assisting in the publication of these policies may aid in marketing the concerns for safety.

Polices pertaining to student travel has also become a major concern since there are so many foreign students and foreign exchange programs for students. *The Chronicle of Higher Education* reported that a new federal policy would bar Canadians and Mexicans from attending part time colleges in the United States. After a request made by New York, the United States Immigration and Naturalization Service sought clarification on former policies regarding Canadians crossing the border. As a result, the stipulation of this policy (excluding Canadians and Mexicans from enrolling in part-time college classes) is an added security measure to prevent future attacks. To ensure that this policy is adequately followed, the United States Justice Department reports a new database called the Student and Exchange Virtual Information System (SEVIS). This database is a tracking system of all foreign students to reinforce the policy that excludes certain students from enrolling in college classes (Schulz, 2002).

Overview of Previous Surveys Related to the Events of September 11, 2001

In their marketing ventures, marketing professionals must also be aware of some of the post disaster disorders that travelers may bear. Vlahov et al. (2002) stated that post-disaster increases psychological disorders. A telephone survey was conducted among residents of the New York area. Results showed that 24 percent of total respondents have observed their level of alcohol consumption increased, 3.2 percent experienced an increase in marijuana use, and 9.7 percent revealed an increase in the smoking of cigarettes. The remaining 62.5 percent responded that their normal behaviors are unchanged. Based on recent research studies, travelers believe that another terrorist attack is likely in the foreseeable future. A survey conducted by traveler associates that included 800 respondents, 400 that traveled for pleasure and 400 that fit the profile for business travelers, showed that 79 percent of travelers feel another terrorist attack is likely. Regardless of those which want tourism activities to "go back to normal," 58 percent have traveled less as a result of September 11 (Vlahav et al., 2002). Understanding the stress that travelers may bear may assist travel agencies in suggesting destinations and travel times.

The United States economy is unlikely to fall back into a recession this year, according to forecasters of the National Association for Business Economics. Approximately 334 business forecasters were polled and asked a series of questions concerning the future of the American economy. Based on the survey results it appears that 76 percent of those polled are certain that the odds for a double dip in the economy is less than 50-50. In addition, forecasters were asked about monetary policy, 66 percent believe interest rates will increase about 25 to 50 basis points, where 33 percent feel rates will remain unchanged. The Association also believes that economic recovery is underway. They also added a pleasant surprise to the strong numbers they perceive for the economy in the area of consumer spending, economic growth, and stability (Anonymous, 2002).

Security

According to Gorman (2002) the hijackers of September 11 entered the United States with stolen passports. A radio frequency identification tag has been proposed and if approved will be embedded into passports and loaded with information that would confirm the identity of the holder. In security terms, this suggests that these tags could be coupled with biometric technology that for eligibility the passport would only be available for use if the cardholder's fingerprint matched the information in the passport. If this occurred border agencies would be able to track the listings of people through daily emails. However, concerns of the radio frequency identification include questions such as "what other documents this information would be used for the invasion of American's civil liberties?"

Congress has suggested the possibilities of a national identification card. Currently, other countries employ such a card; therefore, they could give the United States some indication of the options and operation of such a card. The national identification card centers around four issues which include: its effectiveness in apprehending terrorists, the extent it would infringe on privacy rights, its abuse by law enforcement officials, and the financial cost of implementing a card. In the security measures sought for the future, the national identification card is well into consideration (Rights and Liberties, 2002).

Driver's license securities are also being reviewed. Several states, including Colorado, Delaware, Georgia, Minnesota, New York, and others are considering restricting licenses of non-United States citizens. If carried out, this restriction would tie one's license to the expiration of their immigration papers. A bill passed in this matter would give the Department of Motor Vehicles (DMV) the authority to contact federal authorities if there is reasonable cause to believe an applicant is an illegal alien (Evans, 2002).

September 11 has spurred on various security measures and new polices in hopes that a similar event or attack will not occur. As a result, one can question how civil liberties and human rights will be affected due to these added precautions. Heymann (2002) analyzed this issue and defined the steps that must occur in order to prevent terrorist attacks. The three ways mentioned include: prevention, consequence management, and punishment. Heymann (2002) detailed that prevention entails four steps that include: (1) learning of a terrorist group's plans in advance by monitoring its efforts, (2) denying all those who do not pass some test of loyalty access to likely targets or to the resources needed to attack those targets, (3) combining the first two steps by discovering who to track through targets and dangerous resources, and (4) detaining without criminal conviction those who are more likely to support an act of terrorism. America must remember to avoid discrimination in the implementation of prevention of terrorism (Heymann, 2002).

STUDY PURPOSE

The research study was designed at the University of Tennessee, USA and was an attempt to more accurately assess the impacts of the terrorist attacks on a local level. The survey instrument was developed by a faculty member in the areas of recreation and tourism management with students assisting in the input and data collection from both graduate and undergraduate (senior) level classes. The purposes of the study were to exam the perceptions and attitudes of people toward (1) the awareness and acceptance of security measures in travel and tourism, (2) the effects of the September 11 attacks on the tourism industry and industry responses, and (3) the changes of individual's travel and recreation behaviors such as destination and activity choices.

METHODS

This study combined on-site interviews and mail surveys to gather data from the faculty, staff, and students at the University of Tennessee. A self-administered questionnaire was delivered to students at the beginning of a class and sent to faculty/staff via campus mails. During the spring (February to April) of 2002, a total of one thousand and one hundred questionnaires were distributed. Of these questionnaires, 908 completed and usable questionnaires were returned, giving a response rate of 83 percent. Returned surveys were coded and entered into a computer. Mean values for a variety of question responses of faculty/staff and student groups were compared using the Statistical Analysis System (SAS) package. After determining normality in data by running a histogram and using the Komogorov-Simirnov statistic with a Lillefors significance level, a non-parametric test (the Mann Whitney test) was used in the study. Mann Whitney test and Chi-Square test were used to test the null hypothesis that no differences existed between two kinds of university populations. The Mann Whitney test was used with interval data and Chi-Square was used with nominal variables. The null hypotheses were rejected if the probability value was less than 0.05. Statistically significant group differences are highlighted and discussed in text.

The people surveyed were asked questions concerning their perceptions regarding the effects of the September 11 attacks on the tourism industry and government/business responses, the relative importance of safety in destination/activity choice, security measures at airports, and the changes of their spending patterns, travel decisions, and leisure pursuits (e.g., shopping, attending populated events, and visiting theme parks, etc.). The results of this project would provide useful information for marketing professionals to assist them in planning, advertising, promotions, and other marketing ventures.

RESULTS

Of 908 useful responses, 714 were students and 192 were faculty and staff. The following is a summary of the key findings related to the travel decisions, behaviors, destination/activity choices, safety, and security measures.

Fly experiences and travel decisions. As illustrated in Table 1, 86% of faculty/staff and students indicated that they were not afraid to fly before September 11, 2001. When asked if they were afraid to fly after September 11, 39% of faculty/staff and 31% of student respondents said "yes" respectively (P < 0.025). Although 49% of faculty/staff and 39% of student respondents have flown in an airplane since September 11, 2001 (P < 0.023), 30% of faculty/staff and 15% of students respondents indicated that the September 11 tragedy changed their traveling decisions (P < 0.0001), and 14% of faculty/staff and 6% of students respondents said that their spending patterns on recreation and travel have changed (P < 0.0001).

Changes of recreation activities. When participants were asked to rate the change of their leisure pursuits after the September 11 attacks (on a 1 to 7 scale, where 1 = no change, 4 = neutral, and 7 = major change), the changes according to faculty/staff were "visiting government buildings" (2.4), "visiting city attractions" (2), and "attending spectator sporting events" (2). To students, the major changes were similar to faculty members' perceptions ["visiting

TABLE 1. Fly Experiences and Travel Decisions

Characteristic	Faculty/Staff	Student	Signif.
Fly Experiences	N = 191	N = 714	
Afraid to fly before 9/11	Yes = 14.14% No = 85.86%	Yes = 13.73% No = 86.27%	0.88[C]
Afraid to fly after 9/11	Yes = 39.15% No = 60.85%	Yes = 30.58% No = 69.42%	0.025**[C]
Travel Behaviors	N = 190	N = 713	
Have flown in an airplane after 9/11	Yes = 49% No = 51%	Yes = 39% No = 61%	0.023**[C]
Traveling decision changed	Yes = 30% No = 70%	Yes = 14.87% No = 85.13%	0.0001**[C]
Spending on recreation and travel changed	Yes = 13.3% No = 86.7%	Yes = 5.61% No = 94.39%	0.0001**[C]

Note: *** = Significant at the 0.01 level. ** = Significant at the 0.05 level. * = Significant at the 0.1 level. Signif. = Significant level. C = Chi-square test.

government buildings" (2.6), "visiting city attractions" (2.1), and "attending spectator sporting events" (2)]. As illustrated in Table 2, the results indicated that the changes of leisure pursuits after the events of September 11 for faculty/staff and students could not be considered statistically different at the 0.05 level.

Destination choices. Differences in the destination choice of faculty/staff and student participants were statistically significant ($p < 0.02$). When asked if they would like to visit New York City, 20% of faculty/staff and 13% of student respondents said "no" respectively. When asked if they would not like to visit New York City, where they would go instead, the most frequent mentioned states and places were: California (e.g., San Diego), Florida, Las Vegas, Hawaii, Bahamas, and Myrtle Beach.

Attitudes toward security measures at the airport. Table 3 shows that when participants were asked about how comfortable the security measures make them feel about flying (on a 1 to 7 scale, where 1 = not at all comfortable, 4 = neutral, and 7 = the most comfortable), the most comfortable levels regarding security measure issues according to faculty/staff were "security officers on the plane" (5.9), "each person's bags being looked through before entering the gates" (5.7), "extra security officers at the airport" (5.6), and "only flight passengers being allowed to go beyond the check-in point" (5.5). For students, the

TABLE 2. Changes of Recreation Activities

Characteristic	Faculty/Staff	Student	Signif. (MW)
Changes of Their Leisure Pursuits	N = 191	N = 711	
Spectator sporting events	1.99	2.02	0.94
Local sporting events	1.78	1.82	0.84
National or state parks	1.8	1.76	0.78
Concerts/theater	1.78	1.81	0.86
Theme parks	1.94	1.95	0.84
Government buildings	2.42	2.6	0.12
City attractions	1.95	2.11	0.15
Historical sites	1.91	2.01	0.29
Museums or art galleries	1.71	1.79	0.44
Shopping malls	1.81	1.83	0.98
Dining	1.63	1.6	0.87

Note: 1 = no change, 7 = major change (reported with average grade). *** = Significant at the 0.01 level. ** = Significant at the 0.05 level. * = Significant at the 0.1 level. Signif. = Significant level. MW = Mann Whitney test.

TABLE 3. Attitudes Toward Security Measures at the Airport

Characteristic	Faculty/Staff	Student	Signif. (MW)
Attitudes Toward Security Measures at the Airport	(N) Average	(N) Average	
Security officers inspecting your car	(N = 185) 5.18	(N = 707) 4.48	0.0001***
Only flight passengers being allowed to go beyond the check-in point	(N = 185) 5.49	(N = 707) 5.06	0.001**
Extra security officers at the airport	(N = 185) 5.64	(N = 707) 5.64	0.99
Each person's bags being looked through before entering the gates	(N = 185) 5.73	(N = 707) 5.35	0.007**
Security officers on the plane	(N = 185) 5.89	(N = 707) 5.84	0.52

Note: 1 = not at all comfortable, 7 = the most comfortable (reported with average grado). *** = Significant at the 0.01 level. ** = Significant at the 0.05 level. * = Significant at the 0.1 level. MW = Mann Whitney test.

most comfortable security measures at the airport were "security officers on the plane" (5.8) and "extra security officers at the airport" (5.6). The least comfortable feelings to students were "security officers inspecting your car before you park at the airport" (4.5). Differences in the "each persons bags being looked through before entering the gates," "only flight passengers being allowed to go beyond the check-in point," and "security officers inspecting your car before you park at the airport" categories for faculty/staff and students were statistically significant at the 0.01 level.

Perceptions of the increased security measures. It is evident from the responses in Table 4, that while going through the increased security measures that have been added to parks, sporting events, airports, and others, above 90% of total respondents felt that they have been treated with respect. Of 185 faculty/staff respondents, 70% indicated that they felt "there have been adequate security measures taken"; 73% indicated that they felt "the events of September 11 have made airports safer from terrorism"; 34% indicated that "their feelings toward foreigners changed since September 11"; 19% indicated that "they felt frustrated when having to go through additional security measures"; and 20% of respondents indicated that they did not feel safe when they attended largely populated events. Of 704 students, 75% indicated that they felt "there have been adequate security measures taken"; 71% indicated that they felt "the events of September 11 have made airports safer from terrorism"; 32% indicated that "their feelings toward foreigners changed since September

TABLE 4. Perceptions of the Increased Security Measures

Characteristic	Faculty/Staff	Student	Signif.
Perceptions of the Increased Security Measures	N = 185%	N = 704%	
Treated with respect	Yes = 95.58% No = 4.42%	Yes = 90.01% No = 9.99%	0.019*C
Adequate security measures taken	Yes = 69.61% No = 30.39%	Yes = 74.64% No = 25.36%	0.17C
Feel frustrated	Yes = 18.68% No = 81.32%	Yes = 23.58% No = 76.42%	0.16C
Feelings toward foreigners changed	Yes = 34.05% No = 65.95%	Yes = 32.39% No = 67.71%	0.67C
Feel safe while attending largely populated events	Yes = 79.78% No = 20.22%	Yes = 87.27% No = 12.73%	0.011*C
9/11 has made airports safer from terrorism	Yes = 72.68% No = 27.32%	Yes = 71.12% No = 28.88%	0.68C

Note: *** = Significant at the 0.01 level. ** = Significant at the 0.05 level. * = Significant at the 0.1 level. Signif. = Significant level. C = Chi-square test.

11"; 24% indicated that "they felt frustrated when having to go through additional security measures"; and (13% of respondents indicated that they did not feel safe when they attended largely populated events.) The results indicated that the two types of university individuals attending largely populated events might be considered as different (statistically different at the 0.05 level).

Government reactions. Shown in Table 5 is the result of responses when participants were asked to evaluate the level of government reaction relative to the events of September 11. The results given were based on a 7-point scale where 1 = very poor, 4 = neutral, and 7 = excellent. "The government's overall reaction to the September 11 terrorist attacks" (5.42), "the government's actions dealing with homeland security" (5.17), and "President George W. Bush is handling the situation" (5.38) were rated by all participants. The faculty/staff ranked "the government's overall reaction" (5.41), "the government's actions dealing with homeland security" (4.99), and "President George W. Bush is handling the situation" (5.12). The students rated "the government's overall reaction" (5.46), "the government's actions dealing with homeland security" (5.22), and "President George W. Bush is handling the situation" (5.46). Differences in the "the government's actions dealing with homeland security" (p < 0.04) and "President George W. Bush is handling the situation" (p < 0.04) categories for faculty/staff and students were statistically significant.

TABLE 5. Government Reactions and the Responses of Businesses

Characteristic	Faculty/Staff	Student	Signif.
Government Reactions[a]	(N) Average	(N) Average	
The government's overall reaction to 9/11	(N = 185) 5.41	(N = 707) 5.46	0.68
The government's actions dealing with homeland security	(N = 185) 4.99	(N = 707) 5.22	0.04**
President George W. Bush is handling the situation	(N = 189) 5.12	(N = 700) 5.46	0.04**
The Responses of Businesses[b]			
American businesses overreacted	(N = 186) 3.48	(N = 696) 4.06	0.0002***
Fear the occurrences of terrorist attacks will happen again	(N = 186) 5.49	(N = 696) 5.03	0.0001***

Note: a: 1 = very poor, 7 = excellent (reported with average grade). b: 1 = not at all, 7 = very much (reported with average grade). *** = Significant at the 0.01 level. ** = Significant at the 0.05 level. * = Significant at the 0.1 level. MW = Mann Whitney test.

The responses of businesses. Participants were asked to rate the level of industry and business reactions relative to the events of September 11. The results given were based on a 7-point scale where 1 = not at all, 4 = neutral, and 7 = very much. "American businesses overreacted" [faculty/staff (3.48), students (4.06)] and "fear the occurrences of terrorist attacks will happen again" [faculty/staff (5.49), students (5.03)] were rated. Differences in the above two categories for faculty/staff and students were statistically significant at the 0.05 level (Table 5).

Tourism industry reactions. The information in Table 6 is of particular importance to future projections by marketing personnel. Participants were also asked to rank how long they think it will take, starting on January 1, 2002, for tourism related industries to recover from the effects of September 11, 2001. Fifty-eight percent of faculty/staff and 48% of students indicated that it will take more than one year for the "Airline Industry" (P < 0.01) to recover from the effects of terrorist attacks; 43% of faculty/staff and 23% of students indicated that it will take more than one year for the "Tourism Industry" (P < 0.0001) to recover from the effects of terrorist attacks; 42% of faculty/staff and 28% of students indicated that it will take more than one year for the "Country's Morale" (P < 0.0001) to recover from the effects of terrorist attacks; and 63% of faculty/staff and 40% of students indicated that it will take more than one year for the "Overseas Travel" (P < 0.0001) to recover from the effects of terrorist attacks.

TABLE 6. Tourism Industry Reactions

Characteristic	Faculty/Staff	Student	Signif.
Tourism Industry Reactions	(N) %	(N) %	
Airline Industry	(N = 189)	(N = 710)	
1-3 months	2.65%	7.18%	
4-6 months	13.76%	15.77%	
7-9 months	8.99%	15.21%	
10-12 months	16.4%	13.38%	
More than one year	58.2%	48.45%	0.01**[C]
Tourism Industry	(N = 189)	(N = 707)	
1-3 months	5.29%	16.27%	
4-6 months	19.58%	25.74%	
7-9 months	16.4%	19.24%	
10-12 months	15.34%	15.28%	
More than one year	43.39%	23.48%	0.0001***[C]
Overseas Travel	(N = 187)	(N = 705)	
1-3 months	2.69%	6.67%	
4-6 months	4.3%	14.61%	
7-9 months	11.29%	20%	
10-12 months	18.28%	18.87%	
More than one year	63.44%	39.86%	0.0001***[C]
Country's Morale	(N = 187)	(N = 702)	
1-3 months	16.58%	26.5%	
4-6 months	13.9%	20.09%	
7-9 months	13.37%	15.1%	
10-12 months	13.9%	10.4%	
More than one year	42.25%	27.92%	0.0001***[C]

(ote: *** = Significant at the 0.01 level. ** = Significant at the 0.05 level. * = Significant at the 0.1 level. C = Chi-square test.

Changes of life. Twenty-four percent of faculty/staff and 14% of student respondents indicated "the terrorists attacks effected them financially." Twenty-six percent of faculty/staff and 15% of student respondents indicated "they have changed their way of life as a result of the terrorist attacks." Differences in the above two categories for faculty/staff and students were statistically significant at the 0.05 level.

Before and after the events of September 11. Table 7 shows the response of the perception of past and future issues. When participants were asked to rate how important different activities and issues were to them before and after the September 11 attacks (on a 1 to 7 scale, where 1 = not at all important, 4 = neutral, and 7 = very important), the changes according to faculty/staff were "recreational activities" [before September 11 (5.28), after September 11 (5.15)], "travel" [before September 11 (4.85), after September 11 (4.69)], and "airport security" [before September 11 (4.77), after September 11 (6.53)]. According to students, the changes were "recreational activities" [before September 11 (5.38), after September 11 (5.3)], "travel" [before September 11 (4.94), after September 11 (4.9)], and "airport security" [before September 11 (4.59), after September 11 (6.23)]. The results indicated that the changes of the importance of travel ($P < 0.09$) and airport security ($P < 0.002$) to faculty/staff and students after the events of September 11 were statistically different.

After the events of September 11. On a scale of 1 to 7 where 1 = not at all, 4 = neutral, and 7 = very, both faculty/staff and student respondents felt the events of September 11 have affected classroom discussions [faculty/staff (4.19), students (4.81); $P < 0.0003$], their travel within the state [faculty/staff (2.21), students

TABLE 7. Before and After the Events of September 11

Characteristic	Faculty/Staff	Student	Signif. (MW)
The Importance	Average	Average	
Recreation activities	Before (N = 190) = 5.28 After (N = 185) = 5.15	Before (N − 709) = 5.38 After (N = 658) = 5.3	0.15 0.17
Travel and tourism	Before (N = 190) = 4.85 After (N = 185) = 4.69	Before (N = 709) = 4.94 After (N = 658) = 4.9	0.22 0.09*
Airport security	Before (N = 190) = 4.77 After (N = 185) = 6.53	Before (N = 709) = 4.59 After (N = 658) = 6.23	0.14 0.002**
Changes After 9/11	Average	Average	
Classroom discussion	(N = 176) 4.19	(N = 707) 4.81	0.000***
Traveling within the state	(N = 190) 2.21	(N = 712) 1.96	0.36
Traveling out of state	(N = 188) .65	(N = 712) 2.38	0.26
Traveling abroad	(N = 185) 3.86	(N = 707) 3.48	0.06*

Note: 1 = not at all, 7 = very much (reported with average grade). *** = Significant at the 0.01 level. ** = Significant at the 0.05 level. * = Significant at the 0.1 level. MW = Mann Whitney test.

(1.96); P < 0.36], their travel out of state [faculty/staff (2.65), students (2.38); P < 0.26], and their travel abroad [faculty/staff (3.86), students (3.48); P < 0.06].

DISCUSSION AND CONCLUSION

Faculty/staff were more likely to experience the changes of their life, travel decisions, and activity choices than students. Students were more likely to feel less comfortable than faculty/staff when they go through the increased security measures at airports. Faculty/staff predict that it will take longer for the tourism related industries to recover from the effects of September 11 than students. More faculty/staff fear the occurrences of terrorist attacks will happen again than students. As a result of September 11, more students think American business overreacted than faculty/staff.

The Gulf War had a negative effect on travel and tourism in the international market and not as much for the domestic market of the United States. The tragedy of September 11 had a devastating effect on the domestic market of the United States. In view of the enormous size of the tragedy that occurred on September 11, it is understandable that there will be a vast amount of apprehension on the part of travelers and tourists to venture any distances that may require air travel. Additionally, an extended period of time will probably have to pass before the travel and tourism industry will come close to regaining their previous level of business. To more effectively provide current information to marketing professionals it is recommended that the same questionnaire be given to the same type of population a year from now to evaluate as to whether there has been a significant change in perceptions.

REFERENCES

Anonymous (2002). Economic forecast: Outlook. *Tax Management Financial Planning Journal*, 18(4): 102-103.

Cohen, R. (2001, October). Post 9/11 considerations and agendas for funders and fundraisers. [Online.] Available: http://www.ncrp.org/mockup/September%2011%20impacts.htm

Dobbs, L. (2002). A post September 11 checkup. *Money*, 33(4): 55-56.

Evans, W. (2002, June 3). Foreign? Suspicious! *The Nation*, 274(21): 22.

Fockler, S. (1991). USA International Tourism Reports (1991), No. 2: 26-47.

Goodrich, J. N. (June, 2002). September 11, 2001 attack on America: A record of the immediate impacts and reactions, in the USA travel and tourism industry. *Tourism Management*, 23(6): 573-580.

Gorman, S. (2002, May 11). A passport that couldn't be lost. *National Journal*, 34(19): 1385.

Heymann, P. B. (2002). Civil liberties and human rights in the aftermath of September 11. *Harvard Journal of Law and Public Policy*, 25(2): 444-458.

Kapila, S. (2002). United States post September 11, 2001 policy impacts on South Asia: An analysis. *South Asia Analysis Group*. [Online.] Available: http://www.saag.org/papers5/paper454.html

Kenen, J. (2002). Democratic campaign chiefs are grandmas. *Politics*. [Online.] Available: http://story.news.yahoo.com/news?tmpl=sotry&u=nm/20020528/pl_nm/politics_democrats

Kuttab, J. (2001). The turning point of 9/11. *Cornerstone Issues*, 23: 1-4.

Madison School of Business (2001). In the hot seat: Tough economy affects recruiting. [Online.] Available: http://www.bus.wisc.edu/update/fall01/0006.htm

Many once thriving cities are suddenly hurting (2001) *New York Times*, 41(1): 34-36.

Miller, K. L. (2002, February 4). The shock of recovery: As national leaders and CEOs gather for the world economic forum in New York, their mission is to start talking the planet out of recession. Irrational exuberance is out–but tempered optimism is taking hold. *Newsweek*, p. 38

Olsen, J. (2002). Delta representatives: Airlines have lost $8 billion since September 11. *The Enterprise*, 31(43): 1.

Rights and Liberties (2002). *Idea Central: The Virtual Magazine of the Electronic Policy Network*. [Online.] Available: http://www.epn.org/whatsnew/subjects/ rights-2.html

Santomero, P. (2002, April 25). The reluctant recession: Why was the recession so mild? *New York: Levy Institute Conference*. [Online.] Available: http://www.phil.frb.org/publicaffairs/speeches/santomero22.html

Schluz, J. (2002). Events of September 11. *Office of International Programs*. [Online.] Available: http://www.international.umn.edu/sept11.html

The Economist (1992). The South: Damn Giving. *The Economist*, 322(7445): 25-26.

The United Kingdom, Economist Intelligence Unit (1993). Prospects for tourism in 1993. *Travel and Tourism Analyst*, 6: 94-110.

Toll from attack at Trade Center is down sharply (2001, November 21) *New York Times*, p. A.1.

Treited, R. & Fockler, S. (1991). The US domestic travel market. *Travel and Tourism Analyst*, 6: 63-76.

Vlahov, D., Galea, S., Resnick, H., Ahern, J., Boscarino, J. A., Bucuvalas, M., Gold, J., & Kilpatrick, D. (2002). Increased use of cigarettes, alcohol, and marijuana among Manhattan, New York, residents after the September 11th terrorist attacks. *American Journal of Epidemiology*, 155(11): 988-996.

Weidenbaum, M. (2001). Economic response to terrorist: Developing new ways of conducting economic activities. *Vital Speeches of the Day*, 68(2): 34-38.

Williams, D. (1998). The Bombing of the World Trade Center in New York City. *International Criminal Police Review*. [Online.] Available: http://www.interpol.int/Public/Publications/ICPR/ICPR469_3.asp

Terrorism, Economic Uncertainty and Outbound Travel from Hong Kong

Bob McKercher
Edith L. L. Hui

SUMMARY. This paper reports on the findings of three consumer surveys conducted in Hong Kong examining and outbound travel frequency and future travel intentions. The surveys were conducted in December, 2000, October, 2001, some three weeks after the September 11th terrorist attacks, and in April/May 2002, thus enabling the researchers to track the immediate and medium term impacts of the 9-11 incident on outbound tourism. The study revealed that a dramatic softening in intentions to travel was reported, yet no apparent differences were noted in overall travel participation rates before and six months after the event. However, consumers have modified their travel activities, taking shorter trips and expressing greater concerns about the safety of travel. The study further reveals that consumer confidence in the safety of outbound travel is returning, but more enduring economic concerns are beginning to affect travel intentions. *[Article copies available for a fee from The Haworth Document Delivery Service: 1-800-HAWORTH. E-mail address: <docdelivery@haworthpress. com> Website: <http://www.HaworthPress.com> © 2003 by The Haworth Press, Inc. All rights reserved.]*

Bob McKercher and Edith L. L. Hui are affiliated with The School of Hotel and Tourism Management, The Hong Kong Polytechnic University, Hung Hom, Kowloon, Hong Kong.

Address correspondence to: Bob McKercher (E-mail: hmbob@polyu.edu.hk).

[Haworth co-indexing entry note]: "Terrorism, Economic Uncertainty and Outbound Travel from Hong Kong." McKercher, Bob, and Edith L. L. Hui. Co-published simultaneously in *Journal of Travel & Tourism Marketing* (The Haworth Hospitality Press, an imprint of The Haworth Press, Inc.) Vol. 15, No. 2/3, 2003, pp. 99-115; and: *Safety and Security in Tourism: Relationships, Management, and Marketing* (ed: C. Michael Hall, Dallen J. Timothy, and David Timothy Duval) The Haworth Hospitality Press, an imprint of The Haworth Press, Inc., 2003, pp. 99-115. Single or multiple copies of this article are available for a fee from The Haworth Document Delivery Service [1-800-HAWORTH, 9:00 a.m. - 5:00 p.m. (EST). E-mail address: docdelivery@haworthpress.com].

http://www.haworthpress.com/store/product.asp?sku=J073
© 2003 by The Haworth Press, Inc. All rights reserved.
10.1300/J073v15n02_06

KEYWORDS. Hong Kong, terrorism, outbound travel

INTRODUCTION

Tourism flows are vulnerable to external and internal shocks, including natural disasters, war, economic recessions, financial crises and, of course, terrorist activities (Sönmez, Apostolopoulos and Tarlow, 1999). The September 11th terrorist attacks on New York and Washington had a profound and immediate impact on global travel. It does not need to be recounted here. It is fair to say, however, that international tourism and air-based domestic tourism effectively ceased in the immediate aftermath of the event ("Travel Industry Faces Different Kind of Aftershock," 2001; WTO, 2001). It is also felt in many quarters that the more important impact was to accelerate the plunge into a global recession, a recession that has been exacerbated by financial scandals and stock market collapses.

Many analysts, therefore, feared that the 9-11 incident had the potential to simultaneously activate a variety of endogenous and exogenous triggers that would invoke a deep and ongoing recession in the global tourism industry (A.A., 2001; anon, 2002; Corcoran, 2002). Yet, at the time of this writing, nearly one year after the incident, it is evident that the impacts have been variable and, globally, not as deep as predicted. Inbound tourism to North America remains weak, as does travel to destinations that are reliant on the American market. US business travel is suffering (YSB, 2002) and traditional US holiday destinations like the Caribbean are struggling (anon, 2001). However, US domestic tourism seems to have been a beneficiary of the tragedy, with media reports suggesting the impacts on predominantly domestic destinations were less than expected (Craver, 2002) as Americans substituted rubber tire traffic for air travel ("More American Families Opt for Road-Trip Vacations," 2002).

Globally, travel declined by 9.2% between September and December 2001 (WTO, 2002), but appears to have recovered quickly since then, especially in the Asia-Pacific region. In spite of immediate post-9-11 predictions of a 10% decline in annual occupancy, Thailand recorded a small net increase in visitors over the year. This was due, in part, to the belief that many tourists from Australia, the UK and US switched their destinations from Indonesia and Malaysia to Thailand because it had no involvement in the war on terrorism ("Thailand Hotel Industry Finishes 2001 at 70.1% Occupancy," 2002). Hong Kong registered strong 12.8% growth in tourist arrivals for the first six months of 2002, fuelled largely by the Mainland Chinese market (HKTB, 2002). Even formerly strife-torn Sri Lanka is poised to make a major return to international tourism since signing a peace agreement with Tamil rebels in early 2002 ("Sri Lankan Tourism Revival Poses New Challenge," 2002).

What has been the longer term impact of the 9-11 terrorist attacks on Asian outbound tourism? This paper discusses the results of three consumer surveys of outbound travel activities and intentions among Hong Kong residents conducted by the School of Hotel and Tourism Management (HTM) at the Hong Kong Polytechnic University. The first survey was conducted in December, 2000 as part of an initiative to develop an in-house longitudinal data set on travel patterns by Hong Kong residents. The second survey was conducted in early October, 2001, some three weeks after the attack on the World Trade Center. A third survey was conducted in late April and early May, 2002, seven months after the incident. The results of the three surveys, therefore, provide time series data examining the travel activity and intentions covering a period from well before the terrorist attack, through its immediate aftermath, to a period some time after the incident, where no further terrorism activity has occurred and after a seemingly successful (though unfinished) military campaign against the perpetrators.

CONTEXT

Disasters are episodic events that disrupt the tourism industry on a regular basis (Sönmez et al., 1999; Faulkner, 2000). Indeed, Barton (1994) says that crises are inevitable in the hospitality industry. Proponents of chaos and complexity theory argue that disasters are an essential aspect of tourism for they push tourism systems to the edge of criticality and induce phase shift that, ultimately, produces a more viable tourism sector (Faulkner and Russell, 1997, 1998; McKercher, 1999). Disasters can take many forms and can include natural events, such as floods, typhoons and earthquakes, or human-induced events, such as war and terrorism. Terrorism, however, is felt to be the most insidious form of disaster. Terrorist attacks on tourists, or terrorist events that affect tourism are surprisingly common. Baron (2001) and Sönmez and Graefe (1998) indicate that terrorist attacks targeting tourists occurred virtually every year since the 1970s. Sönmez and Graefe (1998) further document 29 terrorist incidents involving tourists that occurred between 1993 and 1996. Perhaps even more surprisingly, this issue has been the subject of relatively little academic or industry investigation. Much of what is written in the trade journals relates to disaster planning and disaster mitigation (see, for example Barton, 1994).

By their nature, terrorist acts are designed to exert great psychological impacts, spreading fear and intimidation amongst innocent people. They are violent, random events that put everyone potentially at risk. The stakes for tourism are even higher, for many terrorist attacks are targeted specifically at tourists. As pleasure travelers, most tourists are risk adverse and will seek destinations that provide the maximum personal benefits at the lowest personal risk. The introduction of a significant element of terrorism-induced risk has the potential to affect the travel decision making process (Sönmez and Graefe, 1998), causing people to alter their travel plans, substitute destinations and, in extreme cases, postpone travel plans (Sönmez et al., 1999).

Fortunately, most tourists have relatively short memories and will resume traveling when they feel the immediate threat has passed. As a result, history suggests that disasters tend to have no lasting impact on tourist flows. However, a number of intervening factors influence the duration of the impact. One-off events tend to induce short term impacts, while a persistent history of terrorist attacks can induce more long standing effects on tourist flows (Leslie, 1999). Likewise, the closer the psychological proximity the potential tourist is to a destination, the greater the impact (Clements and Georgiou, 1998). Terrorist events that occur in distant places that few mass tourists visit have much less of an effect than the events that occur in well-known mass destinations. This issue is exacerbated if the destination is generally felt to be a safe destination. Of course, media coverage influences psychological proximity. Events that receive main stream mass media coverage, especially if video footage is presented, have more impact.

The events of September 11th were unprecedented, and from a tourism perspective, it is difficult to perceive how they could have had a stronger impact. New York City, the most famous city in the world, was targeted. It is known to virtually everybody as a financial center, home of the United Nations and its landmarks are known through countless portrayals in film and television. The event was covered globally on live television with hundreds of millions, or possibly billions, of viewers watching the disaster unfold in real time. Moreover, the brazen nature of the attack, its scale and the apparently simple method used, drove home the fact that no one is safe from terrorism. In addition, the use of civil aviation aircraft as tools of mass destruction emphasized how vulnerable airline passengers could be. (Note–it is interesting to observe from the perspective of Hong Kong, more than one year later, the bombing of the Pentagon has become almost a footnote of the day's events. For the most part, 9-11 is remembered as the day the World Trade Center was destroyed.)

In addition, the timing of the event, more than anything else, has proven to have had the most enduring effect. With the American economy teetering on the edge of recession, the direct impact of a cessation in business and pleasure travel, coupled with the indirect shock waves sent through financial markets, accelerated the decline into recession. This event, coupled with emerging financial scandals, high profile bankruptcies and a collapse of the share market has convinced many analysts that a global recession is inevitable.

As stated in the outset of this paper, international tourism flows are subject to exogenous and endogenous factors. While the terrorist event was no doubt a profound exogenous factor, the effect of a global recession, rising unemployment, reduced savings through stock market declines, etc., may also have an effect on travel behavior. This is especially true for a place like Hong Kong that is enduring its greatest recession in more than 50 years. Hong Kong has traditionally been regarded as an economic miracle, enjoying unprecedented growth since the Second World war. However, the late 1990s and early 2000s have been a stressful period, as Hong Kong is suffering from a double dip recession, caused first by the Asian financial crisis and, more recently, by global economic problems. The Territory is struggling with eight percent unemployment, when historical unemployment levels were less than two percent for many decades. In addition, Hong Kong has suffered from deflation for 48 straight months at time of this writing, is enduring a stock market collapse, a collapse in the housing market (prices have fallen by 50% from their 1997 highs) and is struggling with a structural problem in its tax base. In short, once confident Hong Kong has entered into what many analysts fear will be a period of prolonged economic uncertainty.

Pleasure travel has historically been considered a discretionary item that can only be afforded after other more essential items are taken care of. As Gee, Makens and Choy (1989: 48) wrote in the late 1980s "basic necessities, such as food, clothing, and shelter are purchased before pleasure travel becomes an alternative." Indeed, pleasure travel as a discretionary activity has long been preached as a core tourism doctrine (Bull, 1991). Thus, the travel decision is placed within the context of other discretionary activities, such as the purchase of a mink coat (Mill and Morrison, 1985), where the purchase decision for one, by necessity, means forsaking the purchase decision for the other item.

This may have been true once and may still apply in some parts of the developing countries and among low income earners in the developed world. However, many would now argue that tourism is an integral activity for most people, and that a trip, or trips, represent an important component of modern life. Gee et al. (1989: 48) suggest that "in the developed countries of Europe, North America and some countries in Asia and the Pacific, the purchase of travel for vacation and leisure is not considered exceptional for many families." Ryan (1991: 7) further illustrates that "tourism demand would appear to be income inelastic, that is, if there is a reduction in income . . . the demand for tourism does not slacken. Equally, it can be claimed that tourism continues to grow, even if prices increase."

Interestingly, consumers may still feel that travel represents a discretionary activity by expressing a lower intention to travel, but may still exhibit the same propensity to travel. Instead of treating travel as a discretionary activity, it is more likely that tourists exert significant discretion over the type of travel undertaken. Less expensive destinations, modes of transport or accommodation can be substituted for more costly items in times of economic downturns. Also, people may take shorter duration trips or may take fewer trips over the course of a year. In extreme cases, travel may be postponed for a short period of time. In a similar manner, tourists may decide to substitute safer, known or less risky destinations during periods of tension (A.A., 2001).

METHOD

This paper discusses the results of three consumer surveys conducted between December 2000 and May 2002 that were commissioned by the School of Hotel and Tourism Management (IITM) at the Hong Kong Polytechnic University. The first survey was conducted in December 2000 with a sample of 952 respondents. The second survey was conducted in October, 2001 and had a sample of 1,000 respondents. The third survey was conducted in late April and early May, 2002 and also involved 1,000 respondents. This survey was completed some two months after Lunar New Year, the peak outbound tourism period for Hong Kong.

The mode of data collection was by telephone and most interviews were conducted in Cantonese. A modified random digit dialing (mRDD) strategy was employed to generate the sample list of residential telephone numbers. The study population for the survey was individuals who could be accessed by residential phone lines. In addition, potential respondents had to satisfy two qualifying questions: being Hong Kong residents aged 18 or above, and were one of the principal family income earners in the household. Potential respondents were selected by a three-stage randomized process to ensure all residents of Hong Kong had an equal non-zero chance of being selected. Necessary steps, including "making appointments for the not-at-home sampled persons" and re-dialing of the "no-answer" calls, etc., were performed in order to minimize the total survey error.

The questionnaire was based on the original questionnaire developed in 2000 as part of an innovative program developed by HTM to generate time series data on outbound travel patterns from Hong Kong. The first part of the questionnaire described the travel profile of respondents over the previous 12 months. Respondents were asked first if they had participated in an international (i.e., outside of Hong Kong, Macau and the immediate Mainland Chinese hinterland of Guangdong Province) pleasure trip during the previous 12 months, and if so to provide details of their activities. They were then asked if they had taken an overnight pleasure trip to the hinterland of Hong Kong.

The second part of the questionnaire sought information on intended travel over the next 12 months, including the likelihood of traveling internationally, and likely destinations. The effect of the September 11th attacks on future travel plans were also examined in this part of the questionnaire. In addition, questions about the safety of travel and perceptions of safe and unsafe destinations were sought. The final part of the questionnaire provided standard demographic information about respondents.

The questionnaires were modified somewhat across the three survey periods. The initial questionnaire does not include any information on the safety of air travel and the impact of terrorism on tourism. The survey completed in October, 2001, some three weeks after the September 11th attack, gathered detailed information on the immediate effect of 9-11 on future travel plans. Space limitations involved in conducting telephone interviews precluded the inclusion of some of these questions in the 2002 survey. The 2002 study further included questions relating to travel in the intervening period following September 11th.

A sample of 1,000 respondents was targeted in each survey. The demographic profile of the three cohorts of respondents was compared to determine if the three sample populations were comparable. Statistically significant differences were noted, suggesting differences in each of the sample groups. The 2000 sample was generally older and reported lower education and income levels than the other groups. The October 2001 sample tended to have the highest educational standards and also reported, marginally, the highest mean incomes. The April/May 2002 sample tended to be younger. The reader must be aware, therefore, that some of the differences identified may be the result of the sample.

DISCUSSION OF RESULTS

Intentions, Travel Activity and Frequency

A substantial dichotomy between tourist intentions and resultant behavior is evident in the three survey periods. Study participants were asked to indicate their likelihood of taking an international trip in the upcoming 12 months using a seven point Likert scale. In addition, they were asked if they had traveled in the previous 12 months, and in the case of the April/May 2002 survey were also asked if they had traveled after September 11th. As Table 1 indicates, significantly different patterns in intentions to travel are evident between the survey

TABLE 1. Travel Intentions, Activities, Frequency and Duration (Percent)

	Dec 2000	Oct 2001	Apr/May 2002	Test scores
Pleasure travel intentions in 12 months following the survey				
Likelihood of taking an international trip in the next 12 months				
Definitely will travel	29.3	12.1	11.4	Chi Sq = 261.4
Likely to Very Likely	18.6	31.0	31.7	df = 12
Unsure	10.1	18.3	16.4	p = .001
Unlikely to Very Unlikely	11.3	21.4	20.2	
Definitely Not	30.7	17.2	20.2	
Pleasure travel activity in previous 12 months (since Sept 11 for Apr/May survey)				
Did they take an international trip?				
Yes	33.2	38.8	36.9	Chi sq = 6.82
No	66.8	61.2	63.1	df = 2
				p = .033
Pleasure travel frequency over past 12 months				
Average number of trips taken in previous 12 months (among travel active people)	1.77	2.06	1.76 (1.37 trips post Sept 11 –7 months)	F = 2.699 p = .068
Trip duration				
Average length of stay for the trips taken in previous 12 months (nights)	9.15	7.93	6.65	F = 4.36 p = 0.013

conducted prior to the September 11th incident and the two subsequent surveys.

Study participants were much more certain about their intentions in the first, pre-attack baseline survey. More than 60% of respondents stated unequivocally that they either were definitely going to travel or definitely not going to travel. The post-September 11 surveys, on the other hand, revealed a stronger level of uncertainty about international travel among Hong Kong residents. Whereas in the earlier survey fewer than one-third of respondents answered in the range of "unlikely/unsure/likely," more than half of respondents in the latter two surveys responded in this manner. By contrast, only a small proportion of respondents stated that they would definitely travel.

Yet, in spite of this uncertainty, no significant decline in outbound travel was noted in the April/May 2002 survey. Outbound travel in the previous 12 months grew between the December 2000 and October 2001 surveys and has stabilized at around 37% of the population, in spite of the apparent weakening of intentions. No statistically significant differences are noted in gross participation rates in international travel between the October and April surveys (Chi sq = .767, df = 1, p = .203). Moreover, no differences were noted in the mean number of trips taken over the three survey periods. Evidence from the Hong Kong Travel Industry Council (pers. com.) indicates that outbound travel was adversely affected in the immediate aftermath of the terrorist event, but by early 2002 outbound tourism activity had returned to its traditional levels.

Length of Stay

If no long term impact in travel frequency has been noted, have other changes occurred as a result of 9-11? Though travel activity remained rather stable over time, some significant differences in total trip duration were noted among respondents of different surveys (*F* test: 4.36, p = .013), with people adopting shorter holidays over time. The average length of stay was 9.15 nights in 2000, compared to 7.93 nights in 2001 and 6.65 nights in the period following September 11. It is uncertain, however, if the shorter trip duration is a function of 9-11 or of the worsening economic climate. Total trip duration had contracted significantly before the terrorist attacks as the Hong Kong the economy slowed. September 11th seems to have further accelerated the trend to short break holidays. Travel industry professionals also report that people are choosing less expensive holiday options (pers. com.).

Main Destinations and Likely Destinations

Study participants were asked to name the main destinations visited during the previous 12 months and likely future destinations, if they intended to travel in the next 12 months. Somewhat surprisingly, no significant differences were noted in main destination choice (Chi Sq = 5.723, df = 8, p. = .678) and likely future destinations (Chi Sq = 13.614, df = 8, p. = .092) across the three surveys (Table 2). Residents of Hong Kong prefer short break holidays within Asia, followed by longer holidays in the Western Europe, North America, Australia and New Zealand. This pattern has not changed over time, suggesting that in the absence of future terrorist attacks consumer confidence has returned to most destinations.

Likewise, no significant difference was evidenced in the choices of likely destinations between the respondents in their responses in the three surveys. The most popular destination was still Asia, followed by North America and/or West Europe and then Australia/New Zealand. Interestingly, Hong Kong residents express a consistent desire to travel further afield than Asia, but when decisions are ultimately made, they tend to choose short haul destinations.

Change of Travel Plans

The October 2001 and April/May 2002 surveys incorporated questions examining the direct influence of 9-11 and ongoing economic uncertainty on future travel plans. Almost 40 percent of respondents immediately after the September attack stated that they had changed their travel plans (Table 3). Most preferred to change their destinations, while a smaller percentage postponed or canceled travel plans. People have their own ways to reduce psychological threats imposed by the 9-11 incident. Delaying travel plans is a quick fix alternative to changing selected destinations or canceling travel outright. If a choice was available, people would rather delay travel than cancel it.

Lingering concerns about travel are still evident some seven months later, as 24% of respondents continue to feel the combination of the World Trade Center attack and economic problems are causing them to rethink future travel plans. However, it is also encouraging to note that consumer confidence seems to be returning rather quickly as, in the intervening period between October 2001 and April/May 2002, 40% fewer people indicate that they will change travel plans. Further, economic concerns are beginning to take precedence over safety concerns. While safety remains a key issue, a substantially higher proportion of respondents in the 2002 survey identified economic uncertainty as the reason for reconsidering. Likewise, among the majority of respondents who have not changed their travel plans, almost half of the 2002 cohort indicated that they were not planning to travel, compared to less than 40% of the 2001 sample.

TABLE 2. Actual Destinations and Intended Destinations (Percent)

		Dec 2000	Oct 2001	Apr/May 2002	Test score
Main destinations	Where was your main destination in the past 12 months? (%)				
	Australia and New Zealand	5.4	3.9	5.7	Chi Sq = 5.723
	Asia	78.4	80.9	79.8	df = 8
	North America	7.9	5.2	5.1	p = .678
	West Europe	6.0	8.3	7.6	
	Others	2.2	1.7	1.8	
Likely destinations	Which country is most likely to be your main destination in the coming 12 months? (%)				
	Australia and New Zealand	5.6	8.5	5.9	Chi Sq = 13.614
	Asia	70.1	69.0	70.2	df = 8
	North America	14.2	8.9	10.2	p = .092
	West Europe	7.9	10.9	11.5	
	Others	2.3	2.7	2.2	

Note: The percentage is computed by counting responses rather than respondents.

TABLE 3. Change of Travel Plan (Percent)

		Oct 2001	Apr/May 2002	Test score
Change of travel plans	Has WTC attack and economic turmoil caused you to reconsider future travel plans?			
	Yes	38.8	23.9	Chi Sq = 51.578
	No	61.2	76.1	df = 1
				p = .000
	If plans have not changed, why not?			
	Not planning to travel anyway	38.1	49.1	Chi Sq = 16.865
	Decided not to change plans	61.9	50.9	df = 1
				p = .000
Reasons for changing travel plans (among those who indicated they would change their plans)	Safety of travel	49.4	46.8	Chi Sq = 1.759
	Economic impacts on job stability	29.2	36.7	df = 3
	Both travel safety and job stability	18.0	12.8	p = .627
	Others	3.4	3.7	
Types of changes noted among those who changed plans (multiple responses possible)	Postpone your future travel plans?	19.2	28.9	
	Change destinations	22.3	36.0	
	Other (incl. cancel travel plans and not specified)	65.5	51.0	

Safety Concerns

For the most part, consumer confidence is returning in the perceived safety of pleasure travel, with significant differences noted between the Oct 2001 and April/May 2002 cohorts concerning travel safety (Chi Sq = 37.134, df = 1, p = .000) (see Table 4). In total, three-quarters of respondents now feel international pleasure travel is as safe as or more safe than before the attack, compared to only 50% in the immediate aftermath of the incident. Indeed, almost one quarter of respondents in the most recent survey felt that air travel is now safer than in the past.

Similarly, a significant dichotomy was noted among the respondents of the two surveys regarding their perception of the safety of destinations. In October 2001, around 60% respondents felt that some destinations were less safe than before September 11th. This figure drops to 41% by May 2002. When queried further, 14% of the April/May 2002 respondents feel that certain destinations are actually more safe now than they were before September 11th, with the United States and Mainland China being identified as the two countries that are now safer to visit. However, a widespread perception persists that the United States and the Middle East are still unsafe.

DISCUSSION AND CONCLUSION

The study reveals a disparity between intentions and actual travel behavior among Hong Kong residents. The September 11th event, coupled with ongoing economic problems, has manifested itself a higher level of uncertainty about participation in international travel. Yet, some seven months after the event, there has been little or no effect on absolute participation rates. The 9-11 event had an immediate and dramatic effect on outbound travel, effectively stopping discretionary travel for a number of weeks after the event and also changing travel patterns. Demand for travel from Hong Kong to the United States, the Middle East and Western Europe suffered dramatically, while short-haul Asian destinations, in general, and China, in particular, were affected less severely.

However, in the absence of further terrorist attacks, outbound travel participation rates have returned to normal relatively quickly, and by April/May 2002 were at pre-attack levels. This study, therefore, confirms previous studies indicating the short term impact on tourism from terrorism-related events. The study further suggests that events or lack of follow-up terrorist activity after the initial attacks has a greater effect on the return to tourism activity than the scale of the initial event. The prompt reaction by the American Government

TABLE 4. Perception on Safety of Travel (Percent)

	Oct 2001	Apr/May 2002	Test score
Perception on safety of international travel			
Generally do you feel international pleasure travel is:			
More safe than before the attack	11.9	24.4	Chi Sq = 95.351
As safe as before the attack	38.5	51.3	df = 2
Less safe than before the attack	49.6	24.2	p = .000
Perception on safety of destinations			
Are there some destinations that you feel are less safe than before Sept 11?			
Yes	57.3	40.9	Chi Sq = 37.134
No	42.7	59.1	df = 1
			p = .000
Unsafe destinations			
What countries do you feel are less safe to visit?			
Asia	9.9	9.7	Chi Sq = 7.256
North America	54.8	61.7	df = 3
West Europe	12.5	6.9	p = .064
Middle East	22.8	21.7	

Note: The percentage is computed by counting responses rather than respondents.

coupled with a global aviation response to increase safety standards have reduced the risk of travel to acceptable levels.

This study suggests further that travel is seen as a core activity amongst Hong Kong residents and not as a discretionary purchase. While pleasure travel plans were altered immediately after the terrorist attack and ongoing safety and economic concerns have raised questions about future travel activity, Hong Kongers still continue to travel as much as before. The propensity to (participation rate) and frequency (number of trips per person in a 12-month period) of travel have not changed in the periods preceding and following 9-11. However, some changes have been noted in travel behavior as study participants are taking increasingly shorter trips.

Interestingly, while pleasure travel activity has rebounded strongly, consumer confidence is recovering much more slowly. A significant number of Hong Kong residents continue to feel that travel remains less safe and that a number of destinations remain risky. In particular, respondents feel that travel to America still entails a significant amount of risk. These findings suggest that there is a lingering effect of the 9-11 incident on the traveling public's psyche. As such, the apparent recovery in outbound travel may be fragile and could cease if further terrorist attacks occur.

Finally, the study suggests that the concerns about the state of the global economy have the potential to exert a more long-lasting impact than the specific event that triggered economic uncertainty. Consumers are beginning to appreciate that the 9-11 attack was an episodic, though catastrophic event. The deepening recession in Hong Kong, on the other hand, represents an ongoing threat that shows no sign of immediate recovery. It will be interesting to replicate this study in one year's time to see if the trends noted between the October 2001 and April/May 2002 surveys continue.

The September 11th attack on America had a profound impact on global tourism. The duration and extent of the impacts, however, have been variable, with some destinations suffering more than others and source markets taking longer to regain their confidence in international travel than others. The relative geographic and political isolation of Hong Kong from the events, coupled with the concomitant relative geographic and political isolation of its key destinations, have meant that outbound travel here has recovered relatively quickly. What is uncertain is the strength of the recovery. A renewal of terrorism attacks or ongoing doubts about the robusticity of the global economy could put a stop to future outbound travel. Terrorism, therefore, has an immediate but short duration impact on travel flows, while the economy tends to exert a much greater and longer lasting effect on tourism.

REFERENCES

A.A. (2001). *What Impact Will September 11 Have on the Global Hotel Industry?* Arthur Andersen http://hotel-online.com/News/PR2001_4th/Oct01_ImpactAndersen.html (retrieved August 15, 2002).

anon (2001). Dearth of Tourists Strikes Caribbean Like a Hurricane. *The Orlando Sentinel* http://hotel-online.com/News/PR2001_4th/Dec01_CaribbeanDearth.html (retrieved August 15, 2002).

anon (2002). The Hotel Industry–*A Tough 2002 Lies Ahead; Ernst & Young.* Ernst & Young Hospitality Services Group http://hotel-online.com/News/PR2002_1st/Feb02_ HotelStorm.html (retrieved August 15, 2002).

Baron, R.R. (2001). The Effects of Terrorism on Travel and Tourism (unpublished document).

Barton, L. (1994). Crisis Management: Preparing for and Managing Disasters. *Cornell HRA Quarterly*, 35(2): 59-65.

Bull, A. (1991). *The Economics of Travel and Tourism.* Melbourne: Longman Cheshire.

Clements, M.A. and Georgiou, A. (1998). The Impact of Political Instability on a Fragile Tourism Product. *Tourism Management*, 19(3): 283-288.

Corcoran, T.J. Jr. (2002). *What's Ahead for the Industry: Why 2002 is not 1992.* FelCor Lodging Trust http://hotel-online.com/News/PR2002_1st/Jan02_TCorcoran.html (retrieved August 2002).

Craver, R. (2002). Impact of Terrorist Attacks on North Carolina Tourism Was Softer Than Expected. *High Point Enterprise, N.C* http://hotel-online.com/News/2002_ Jul_08/k.HPT.1026227531.html (retrieved August 15, 2002).

Faulkner, B. (2000). Towards a Framework for Disaster Management. *Tourism Management*, 22: 135-147.

Faulkner, B. and Russell, R. (1997). Chaos and Complexity in Tourism: In Search of a New Perspective. *Pacific Tourism Review*, 1(2): 93-102.

Faulkner, B. and Russell, R. (1998). *Movers and Shakers: The chaos makers on the Gold Coast.* Paper presented at the 1998 Australian National Tourism and Hospitality Research Conference, Gold Coast, February 1998.

Gee, C.Y., Makens J.C., and Choy D.J.L. (1989). *The Travel Industry (2nd Ed.).* New York: Van Nostrand Reinhold.

Hall, C.M. (1995). *Introduction to Tourism in Australia (2nd Ed.).* Sydney: Longman Australia.

HKTB (2002). *Hong Kong Tourism Board: June Arrivals Grow 6% to Keep Forecasts Well On Track At Six-month Stage.* Hong Kong Tourist Board http://hotel-online. com/News/2002_Jul_31/b.102.1028215911.html (retrieved August 15, 2002).

Leslie, D. (1999). Terrorism and Tourism: The Northern Ireland Situation–A look behind the veil of certainty. *Journal of Travel Research*, 38: 37-40.

McKercher, B. (1999). A Chaos Approach to Tourism. *Tourism Management*, 20(4): 425-434.

Mill, R.C., and Morrison A.M. (1985) *The Tourism System: An Introductory Text.* Sydney: Prentice-Hall International.

"More American Families Opt for Road-Trip Vacations" (2002). *Chicago Tribune* http://hotel-online.com/News/2002_Jul_19/k.TBT.1027084549.html (retrieved August 15, 2002).

Ryan, C. (1991). *Recreational Tourism: A Social Sciences Perspective.* London: Routledge.

Sönmez, S. and Graefe, A.R. (1998). Influence of Terrorism Risk on Foreign Tourism Decisions. *Annals of Tourism Research*, 25(1): 112-144.

Sönmez, S., Apostolopoulos, Y., Tarlow, P. (1999) Tourism in Crisis: Managing the Effects of Terrorism. *Journal of Travel Research*, 38: 13-18.

"Sri Lankan Tourism Revival Poses New Challenge to Thailand" (2002) *Bangkok Post* http://hotel-online.com/News/2002_Apr_23/k.THT.1019592692.html (retrieved August 15, 2002).

"Thailand Hotel Industry Finishes 2001 at 70.1% Occupancy, Slight Increase from 69.9% in 2000" (2002). *Bangkok Post,* Thailand http://hotel online.com/News/PR2002_1st/Jan02_ThaiHotels.html (retrieved August 15, 2002).

"Travel Industry Faces Different Kind of Aftershock" (2001). The Record, Hackensack, N.J. http://hotel-online.com/News/PR2001_3rd/Sept01_TravelAftershock.html (retrieved August 15, 2002).

WTO (2001). *Crisis Committee of the World Tourism Organization Reports on Response Around the Globe to Restore Travel Confidence.* World Tourism Organization http://hotel-online.com/News/PR2001_4th/Nov01_WTOAction.html (retrieved August 15, 2002).

WTO (2002). *Tourism Proves as a Resilient and Stable Economic Sector.* World Tourism Organization http://hotel-online.com/News/PR2002_2nd/Jun02_WTOTourism.html (retrieved August 2002).

Yesawich, Pepperdine & Brown (2002). *Business Travel Intentions Remain in Doldrums: YP&B Study.* http://hotel-online.com/News/PR2002_1st/YPBStudyJan.html (retrieved August 15, 2002).

Tourism in Nepal:
Shangri-La's Troubled Times

Brijesh Thapa

SUMMARY. The sporadic domestic political instability during the last decade, compounded with the ongoing international war on terrorism in Afghanistan and beyond, has created a substantial decline in tourist visits to Nepal. Safety and security are important aspects of travel destination choice and the perceived risk within Nepal and the South Asian region has mired the pace of international tourist arrivals. The objectives of this paper were to examine the state of tourism in Nepal and the negative repercussions of the political instability and international conflict that has thwarted the potential for growth. *[Article copies available for a fee from The Haworth Document Delivery Service: 1-800-HAWORTH. E-mail address: <docdelivery@haworthpress.com> Website: <http://www.HaworthPress.com> © 2003 by The Haworth Press, Inc. All rights reserved.]*

KEYWORDS. Nepal international arrivals, political instability, terrorism, growth

INTRODUCTION

Tourism in the small Himalayan kingdom of Nepal is a relatively new phenomenon as the country was opened to the Western world in the early 1960s.

Brijesh Thapa is affiliated with the Center for Tourism Research and Development, Department of Recreation, Parks and Tourism, 306 Florida Gym, University of Florida, Gainesville, FL 32611-8209 (E-mail: bthapa@hhp.ufl.edu).

[Haworth co-indexing entry note]: "Tourism in Nepal: Shangri-La's Troubled Times." Thapa, Brijesh. Co-published simultaneously in *Journal of Travel & Tourism Marketing* (The Haworth Hospitality Press, an imprint of The Haworth Press, Inc.) Vol. 15, No. 2/3, 2003, pp. 117-138; and: *Safety and Security in Tourism: Relationships, Management, and Marketing* (ed: C. Michael Hall, Dallen J. Timothy, and David Timothy Duval) The Haworth Hospitality Press, an imprint of The Haworth Press, Inc., 2003, pp. 117-138. Single or multiple copies of this article are available for a fee from The Haworth Document Delivery Service [1-800-HAWORTH, 9:00 a.m. - 5:00 p.m. (EST). E-mail address: docdelivery@haworthpress.com].

http://www.haworthpress.com/store/product.asp?sku=J073
© 2003 by The Haworth Press, Inc. All rights reserved.
10.1300/J073v15n02_07

The country is nestled among the world's highest mountains, the Himalayas, and the world's highest summit, Mt. Everest. The people, the diverse cultures, the majestic grandeur of the sacred Himalayas and the "Shangri-la" mysticism have lured visitors from all corners of the globe. A majority of the international tourists come to Nepal for holiday/pleasure, trekking and mountaineering, predominantly during the tourist season ranging from October to May. Tourist travel occurs within the Kathmandu valley (the international air entry point and the capital city), but the greater part takes place outside the capital at certain destinations, especially at select few protected areas. During the past thirty years, Nepal has experienced an unprecedented growth in tourist arrivals from approximately 6,000 in 1962 to almost 500,000 arrivals, and contributes to 20% of the total foreign exchange (Ministry of Culture, Tourism and Civil Aviation, 2001). However, this influx is steadily decreasing due to the recent heightened political instability and the war on terrorism within the country, the region and beyond.

Tourism is very important to Nepal and is a key industry; so much so that to some extent it represents the third most prominent religion in Nepal after Hinduism and Buddhism. Given the increase in international visitors, the potential to expand this sector to generate more income, employment and other benefits is enormous, considering the low level of tourism development in the country. Due to the economic significance of badly needed foreign exchange, the government's tourism philosophy is to increase tourist arrivals, and subsequently hopes to generate more income, employment, and tax revenues. However, tourism growth is dependent on a number of factors such as development and improvement of infrastructure, information, facilities, access, transportation options, safety and security (Goeldner, Ritchie, and McIntosh, 2000), which are all needed in the case of Nepal. Additionally, tourist demand is subject to change from unpredictable internal and external influences, notably political instability and international conflict (Hall and O'Sullivan, 1996; Richter, 1992), which has consequently hindered the pace of arrivals in the country.

In light of the current state of the world with respect to the U.S.-led war on terrorism, the Indian sub-continent region and the surrounding areas have borne the brunt of a negative publicity campaign among potential tourists from the west. Vivid imagery of the insurgency in the war-affected section of Afghanistan as well as military buildups among the neighboring "nuclear power" countries (India and Pakistan) has had an adverse impact on tourism in the surrounding region. Nepal, a small land locked kingdom between India and China has felt the negative effect as demonstrated by the rapid decline in tourism. Visitor arrivals have decreased at an average of about -40% during the peak season, which has had a major ripple effect on the total economy (Nepal Tourism Board, 2002a).

Besides the international and regional war on terrorism, Nepal has experienced its own struggle due to mounting domestic turmoil. The internal pressure comes from a radical movement (Peoples War Group–PWG) that originated from the mountain communities in the west, now better known as the Maoist. The Maoists began their "People's War" in February 13, 1996 to defeat the current political establishment and create a Peoples' Democratic Republic. This movement has taken over 7,000 lives in the past six years, and with the renewed escalation of violence and attacks on police, army, civilians and infrastructure, the government has had to declare the "Maoist" as terrorists and also imposed a *state of emergency* to curtail the violence (*"Government decides to declare state of emergency,"* 2001; *"Emergency to be prolonged for three months,"* 2002; *"7,073 Nepalis killed during insurgency,"* 2002). The declaration of the emergency by the King upon recommendation from the Prime Minister and the cabinet is based on article 115 of the constitution and notes the following:

> If a grave emergency arises in regard to the sovereignty, national integrity of the Kingdom of Nepal or security of any part thereof, whether by war, external aggression, armed rebellion or extreme economic disarray, His Majesty may, by proclamation, declare or order a state of emergency in respect of whole of the Kingdom of Nepal or any specified part thereof. (*"Government decides to declare state of emergency,"* 2001)

The state of emergency was in effect for six months since November 26, 2001 and was later extended for three months in late May 2002 (*"Emergency to be prolonged for three months,"* 2002). With such an emergency in place, foreign countries have advised or warned their citizens from visiting Nepal. The United States is one of those countries; however, with the significant visit (January 18, 2002) of Secretary of State Colin Powell to Nepal, the U.S. government lifted the travel advisory. Such internal political instability compounded with tensions in the immediate region does not look promising to the once safe haven known as Shangri-la. The international, regional and local war on terrorism has created a *trifecta effect* that Nepal needs to overcome, beginning with the domestic insurgency. Given these circumstances, the purpose of this paper is to examine the challenges to tourism in Nepal and its current struggle to sustain and grow international visitation.

TOURISM IN NEPAL

The first successful ascent of the world's highest mountain, Mt. Everest (8848 m), on May 29, 1953, by Edmund Hillary and Tenzing Norgay Sherpa, raised curiosity about the isolated kingdom as the cauldron of vibrant cultures and the splendor of the Himalayan mountain chain mystified a magnetic charm among potential tourists. Since the early 1960s, visitors have frequented the country with influx from all corners of the globe. During 1966-1970, a growth rate of 266% was experienced which was followed by 95% growth between 1970-1974. Throughout the period between 1962-2001, there has been a positive growth rate in arrivals except in 1984 (-2%), 1989 (-10%), 1993 (-12%), 2000 (-6%) and 2001 (-22%), which were largely the results of political instability in the country (see Table 1).

The distribution of tourists in Nepal has been skewed towards Indians (India) who represent almost 33% of the arrivals, followed by Western European, North American and Japanese markets (Ministry of Culture, Tourism and Civil Aviation, 2001). The Southeast Asian market has been rapidly increasing in percentage terms as tourists in these markets have increased their disposable income, and also there has been more interest in leisure and outdoor recreation. Additionally, tourists from Southeast Asia are attracted to Nepal due to Buddhism, as the city of Lumbini is the birth site of Lord Buddha. Since tourism is seasonal, the Indian market plays an important role as Indian tourists primarily visit during May and June, which compensates for the seasonal decline from other countries. Nepal is a long-haul destination from the major tourist generating regions and it is not surprising to note that the average length of stay has been 11.5 nights with 86% of all visitors coming via air and 14% by land (Ministry of Culture, Tourism and Civil Aviation, 2001).

Besides the famed mountaineering, trekking in the Himalayas still ranks as the major reason to visit as indicated by 43% of all visitors (Nepal Tourism Board, 2001a). Almost all trekking occurs in four popular protected areas: Royal Chitwan National Park (home of the one-horned rhinoceroses as well as the first National Park, established in 1973); Sagarmatha National Park (home of Mt. Everest and the indigenous Sherpa people); Langtang National Park; and Annapurna Conservation Project Area which includes the Upper Mustang Conservation Area. Although visits to protected areas (18% of Nepal is under protected status) have been increasing at an annual rate of 15%, other types of attractions have also gained widespread popularity, namely white-water rafting and wildlife viewing (Ministry of Culture, Tourism and Civil Aviation, 2001; Nepal Tourism Board, 2001a). Additionally, seven sites within the Kathmandu valley, the birth site of Lord Buddha in Lumbini and two natural areas (Royal Chitwan and Sagarmatha National Parks) have been designated as World Heritage Sites (Nepal Tourism Board, 2001a), which has an added appeal for tourists and the specialized Cultural and Heritage tourists' market segments.

The increase in tourist arrivals and consequent increase in foreign exchange earnings has created a tourism dependent economy. International tourism re-

TABLE 1. Tourist Arrivals, Growth Rate and Length of Stay (1962-2001)

Year	Total Number	Growth Rate (%)	By Air[1]	By Land[2]	Length of Stay
1962	6,179	....	....	....	.....
1966	12,567	103	11,206	1,361	.....
1970	45,970	266	36,508	9,462	.....
1974	89,838	95	74,170	15,668	13
1978	156,123	74	130,034	26,089	12
1982	175,448	12	153,509	21,939	13
1983	179,405	2	152,470	26,935	12
1984	176,634	-2	149,920	26,714	11
1985	180,989	3	151,870	29,119	11
1986	223,331	23	182,745	40,586	11
1987	248,080	11	205,611	42,469	12
1988	265,943	7	234,945	30,998	12
1989	239,945	-10	207,907	32,038	12
1990	254,885	6	226,421	28,464	12
1991	292,995	15	267,932	25,063	09
1992	334,353	14	300,496	33,857	10
1993	293,567	-12	254,140	39,427	12
1994	326,531	11	289,381	37,150	10
1995	363,395	11	325,035	38,360	11
1996	393,613	8	343,246	50,367	14
1997	421,857	7	371,145	50,712	10
1998	463,684	10	398,008	65,676	11
1999	491,504	6	421,243	70,261	12
2000	463,646	-6	376,914	86,732	12
2001	362,544	-22	295,681	66,863	11

[1]One International Airport in the Country.
[2]Points of entry (Bhairahawa, Birgung, Dhangadhi, Kakarbhitta, Kodari, Mahendranagar, Nepalgunj).
Source: Compiled from Ministry of Culture, Tourism and Civil Aviation (2001).

ceipts have escalated from US$ 35.2 million in 1979 to US$ 168.1 million in 1999. As of 2001, the reported figure was US$ 136.5 million, a substantial decrease of -18.2% from the previous year (see Table 2). Besides income generation, tourism accounts for 4% of the GDP, and creates more than 250,000 direct and indirect jobs (Nepal Tourism Board, 2001a).

Given the economic importance and dependency, the government made a commitment to promote and develop tourism. A review of the Tourism Master Plan of 1985-1990 indicated a strategy to increase foreign exchange earnings via attracting high budget travelers and subsequent increases in the length of

TABLE 2. Gross Foreign Exchange Earnings (in US$) and Growth Rate

Year	US$ (in millions)	Growth Rate (%)
1979	35.227	-----
1980	51.632	46.6
1981	44.935	−13.0
1982	33.441	−25.6
1983	35.667	6.7
1984	41.273	15.7
1985	39.185	−5.1
1986	50.841	29.7
1987	60.229	18.5
1988	63.502	5.4
1989	68.343	7.6
1990	63.701	−6.8
1991	58.589	−8.0
1992	61.090	4.3
1993	66.337	8.6
1994	88.195	32.9
1995	116.784	32.4
1996	116.644	−0.1
1997	115.904	−0.6
1998	152.500	31.6
1999	168.100	10.2
2000	166.847	−0.8
2001	136.514	−18.2

Source: Compiled from Ministry of Culture, Tourism and Civil Aviation (2001).

stay. Also, a second priority was to create new opportunities for employment through stimulation of the tourism industry. Another objective was to disperse tourists to different regions and promote domestic goods rather than imported products (Banskota and Sharma, 1993). These basic principles mandated in the early Master Plan clearly denote the government's pledge to the tourism sector. Recently, the government has shown a renewed commitment towards tourism as a viable priority largely due to the sustained prospect of foreign exchange earnings. The commitment came as an act of parliament in establishing Nepal Tourism Board (NTB) in 1998; a public and private sector partnership with responsibilities such as destination marketing, diversifying and improving the quality and service of tourism products (Nepal Tourism Board, 2001a).

The NTB replaced the now defunct Department of Tourism and is funded by a 2% Tourism Services fee collected by the Ministry of Finance. During the fiscal year of 2000-2001, the Board was allocated a budget of US$ 1.6 million, of which a generous amount (62%) was earmarked for international promotion and destination marketing (Nepal Tourism Board, 2001a). The NTB has been aggressive with respect to creating thematic campaigns such as "Destination Nepal" to create awareness and interest in various types of tourist products available in Nepal. More importantly, there has been a realization that the image of Nepal is intertwined with trekking and mountaineering themes. To complement and supplement the existing image, marketing campaigns with slogans such as "Mount Everest and More . . . Experience it in Nepal" has provided some measure of success.

Political Instability and Tourism

The trying times of internal instability in Nepal have contributed to the decrease in international arrivals. Nepal has had a positive image as being an exotic, cultural, tranquil, safe and peaceful destination. Over time, the images of South Asia stricken with natural catastrophes and enduring political rhetoric and military exchanges between India and Pakistan have proved to be an encumbrance for tourism growth in Nepal (Richter, 1992). In addition, domestic sporadic events in the last 12 years have demonstrated to be extremely wearisome to the tourism industry, as tourists began to avoid Nepal. Some of the pertinent events and associated highlights are briefly documented in the succeeding paragraphs.

India and landlocked Nepal share an open porous border where Nepalese and Indian nationals do not require a visa or a work permit to work and/or travel in either country. Nepal is considered by India as a "special status" country with preferential economic treatment where trade and transit treaties are generally renewed. However, in late March 1989, the Indian government declined to renew the treaties of trade and transit that resulted in an economic blockade whereby India allowed access for trade and transit at 2 points only. Before the closure of access, there were 15 transit and 21 trading access points (Chand, 2000). Although the rationale behind the crisis (lack of renewal) in the treaties of trade and transit was assumed to be economic, however, speculation was largely associated with India's dissatisfaction of Nepal in the acquisition of weaponry from China. Due to the heavy reliance on India for trade, the Nepalese economy was devastated, as 90% of all imported consumer items had previously come from India. Moreover, goods and products en route to Nepal were stranded resulting in major losses. The prolonged stalemate between the two countries proved destructive to the daily lives of Nepalese citizens as various consumer items were rationed and basic commodities were scarce and not available (Chand, 2000). The effect also transferred to the tourism industry, notably the lodging community. Tourist arrivals decreased by −10%, while −40% decline in Indian arrivals was experienced in 1989 (Ministry of Tourism and Civil Aviation, 2001). Indian tourists may have stayed away from Nepal due to perceived safety and security threats owing to the rising anti-Indian sentiments as a result of the blockade. The gridlock was eventually released in April 1990 due to intensifying international pressure largely from the United States (Chand, 2000).

Following the crisis, a nationalistic pro-democracy movement in Nepal against the three-decade-old Panchayat (partyless) system gained momentum and ultimately became a revolution as the populist demanded a multiparty system. On April 25, 1990, the liberal King Birendra Bir Birkram Shah Dev granted the wishes of the people and chose to remain as a constitutional monarch. During the revolution, mass gatherings, demonstrations and protests were ubiquitous; tourists, notably independent travelers, were caught in the struggle as some ventured to the streets to photograph and witness the civil unrest. Among these travelers, three people were shot and one death was reported in Kathmandu in April 1990 (Schwartz, 1991). Remarkably, the revolution was short-lived and the transition to democracy did not seem to impact the number of tourist arrivals. Overall, tourist arrivals were up 6% in 1990 and 15% in 1991 largely due to the Indian market, which increased 38% in 1990 and 55% in 1991. However, the third country (non-Indian) market experienced about a −1% decrease in 1990, and an increase of approximately 3% in 1991 (Ministry of Culture, Tourism and Civil Aviation, 2001).

With the advent of democracy, numerous political entities were established and with newfound freedom, political parties and various organizations took the liberty of taking their issues to the streets in the form of peaceful protests and demonstrations. Besides street demonstrations, political parties and organizations with various agendas issued calls for "bandhs" which initiated a total shutdown of the country, including commerce and transportation (Chand, 2000). During such closures, riots and violence were usually the norm. Such regularity of closures affected civilian life as well as tourism promotion. Moreover, in the event of violence, travel advisories were issued by western governments, which effectively discouraged travel or resulted in an exodus from Nepal. The intermittent closures, violence and disruption to daily life yielded negative consequences. Although there were increases in total arrivals for 1991 and 1992 following the revolution, an overall decrease of −12% was experienced in 1993. The Indian market noted a −22% drop off, while the third country (non-Indian) market experienced a decline of about −8% (Chand, 2000; Ministry of Culture, Tourism and Civil Aviation, 2001).

Nevertheless, the current tumultuous insecurity created by the "Maoists" is above and beyond what the country has had to face so far. The movement originated in 1996 from the then political party known as the United People's Front spearheaded by Baburam Bhattarai, who envisioned that the recent democracy and associated parliamentary governance was not beneficial to the rural impoverished communities, and a Peoples' Democratic Republic was needed (Mikesell, 2001). The movement established its stronghold in an extremely rural and remote region of western Nepal and eventually spread its tentacles to the neighboring regions via terror tactics on locals, destruction of government offices/properties, and bank robberies. The movement had a slow beginning but has grown and intensified its guerilla offensives against the government in the last few years. In the region of origination and surrounding regions, the Maoist have taken over governance and have claimed to have set up their own institutional framework, which includes tax collection and the creation of a "People's Court." Besides the attack on the establishment, the Maoist rebels have resorted to indiscriminant killing of civilians, civil servants and members of the ruling and major political parties. Infrastructure such as bridges, telecommunication stations, schools and hydroelectric power plants have all been targeted (Chand, 2000; Mikesell, 2001).

The government originally employed the use of the police force to counter the insurgency but failed to curb the violence and atrocities. Subsequently, a special unit within the police force known as the armed paramilitary forces was especially created and deployed with better training and equipment. However, due to the nature of the guerilla warfare among the rebels, success had been fairly limited. The Royal Nepal Army was not mobilized until the rebels launched an audacious offensive at an army barracks that resulted in major casualties in November 2001. Since the imposition of the state of emergency (November 26, 2001) and the declaration of the rebels as "terrorists," the army has had better success in combating the insurgency although difficult challenges still continue.

As of October 31, 2002, the combined casualties based on the Royal Nepal Army's summary since 1996 include 5,111 terrorists, 773 civilians, and 1,189 security personnel (873 civilian police, 97 armed police force and 219 army personnel), while 400 terrorists and 308 army personnel have been documented to be injured. There were 4,366 casualties reported since November 2001, in which 4,050 were terrorists that were killed after the imposition of the state of emergency ("*7,073 Nepalis killed during insurgency*," 2002). These reported casualty numbers have significantly increased in the month of November 2002 with fresh ongoing ambushes and offensives between the terrorists and the security forces. For example, the gruesome concurrent attacks (November 15, 2002) on two mountain district towns in the Jumla and Gorkha region resulted in 60 security personnel casualties, while the government claimed significantly higher numbers for the terrorists (*"60 security men perish in fierce Maoist attacks,"* 2002). In all likelihood, the true number of terrorists killed and or injured could be much higher as many of their dead are hauled off the battle sites, and also the heads of fallen leaders are decapitated to conceal their true identities. This recent fresh wave of attacks was an aftereffect to the three-day mandatory "bandh" (shutdown) imposed upon the nation by the terrorists during November 11-13, 2002. The dates for the symbolic shutdown of traffic and commerce were originally planned to disrupt the November 13 general election as called by the Prime Minister, Sher Bahadur Deuba, who had earlier dissolved the House of Representatives on May 22, 2002. However, the election never came to fruition due to the dramatic change of events, which is explained in the latter sections.

Although the most affected region is the Midwest, erratic tensions and encounters have diffused throughout the country including the capital city, Kathmandu, which has been victimized by sporadic bomb blasts and various associated threats. However, the escalation of violence has especially been evident in numerous mountain regions. As a result, the most popular activity among tourists, i.e., trekking, has been severely impacted. Tourists have also been victims although casualties have yet to be reported. The Maoists leadership has advised tourists against visiting due to the lack of guarantee of their safety. Concomitantly, western governmental entities such as the U.S. State Department has issued travel advisories notifying its citizens to restrict their visits within the confines of the capital city, Kathmandu. An excerpt of the travel advisory issued in May 17, 2002 noted the following:

> Recent reports of threats against and robberies of American trekkers, property destruction suffered by two businesses with an American affiliation, and increased anti-American rhetoric by the Maoist leadership indicate an increased risk to Americans in Nepal. (*"U.S. warns of Maoists attacks upon its citizens,"* 2002)

However, with the two separate killings of locally hired U.S. Embassy security guard employees on December 15, 2001 and November 9, 2002, and the overall deteriorating state of safety and security in Nepal, the U.S. State Department recently issued another major warning on November 22, 2002 until effect until May 20, 2003 which stated the following:

> U.S. citizens should consider deferring non-essential travel to Nepal until the implications of the Maoist-issued press statement for the security of Americans in Nepal can be fully ascertained. Americans currently living in or visiting Nepal should heighten their security precautions and

awareness at this time. While the Maoist press release states that Maoist actions are not targeted at foreign tourists, its repeated threatening references to the "American Mission" implies a heightened risk for both official and private Americans in Nepal. U.S. citizens should vary routes and times of travel, maintain increased vigilance at all times, keep alert for possible surveillance, and report suspicious activities to the U.S. Embassy's Security Officer. (U.S. Department of State, 2002)

As expected, since the declaration of the state of emergency in late November 2001, tourist arrivals have been in the red for all market sectors with ongoing conflicts with subsequent travel warnings and advisories discouraging potential and repeat visitors (Nepal Tourism Board, 2002a).

Besides the escalation of Maoists' destructive and violent activities in the last few years, there were two significant incidents that brought Nepal into the international media limelight, negatively influencing its image. The first notable incident involved the hijacking of an Indian Airlines flight (IC-814) from Kathmandu, Nepal-New Delhi, India on December 23, 1999. This was the first international hijacking conducted through Tribhuvan International Airport. Following the hijacking, all flights to Nepal from India (Indian Airlines) were suspended and eventually resumed after six long months. The suspension of flights to Nepal struck as a major blow to the tourism industry as Indian Airlines was the leading inbound carrier. The Indian market experienced a significant decline throughout the ensuing months in 2000. The immediate reaction in January was a decrease of −54% followed by −44% in February. The overall average decline in arrivals from the Indian market in 2000 was −32%, which was daunting due to the dependency on Indian tourists (Ministry of Culture, Tourism and Civil Aviation, 2001; Nepal Tourism Board, 2001a). However, since the other 12 international carriers had continued their regular operations, as it was the peak tourist season, third country (non-Indians) arrivals showed a positive gain in the aftermath of the hijacking and ended with an overall increase of 5% for 2000 (Ministry of Culture, Tourism and Civil Aviation, 2001).

The second incident was of major historical significance as the Royal family including the King and Queen were massacred on June 1, 2001, *allegedly* by the Crown Prince. The darkest hour in Nepal's history stunned the country and the world. Although the monarchy was relegated to a constitutional head, the symbolic manifestation of the King as a godlike entity brought severe aftershocks to the country as conspiracy theories proliferated from implicating the Maoists to even the current sitting King. The sudden transition to a new monarch (the late King's only surviving younger brother) was initially met with resentment; however, the people have become more sympathetic and shown acceptance of the King. Due to the ongoing political instability and the lack of promised change as bestowed by the political leaders during the 1990 pro-democracy movement, a majority of the public has showed disdain for the government and viewed the monarch as the only entity that could instill positive synergy and change in the country. With the deteriorating state of the country as well as the inability of the Prime Minister to hold general elections on November 13, 2002, and who proposed to postpone it by another year citing political insecurity, the King dramatically took over governance and assumed all executive powers. The King made his surprise announcement via a National Television broadcast on October 4, 2002, when he pronounced that the Prime Minister was relieved from his duties, the Council of Ministers was dissolved, and the elections were to be postponed to a latter date. Also, the Prime Minister had already earlier dissolved the elected House of Representatives. The constitutionality of the King's move has been a subject of debate but he has expressed his commitment to democracy and promised the delivery of governance to the people at an appropriate time, which is currently on an unscheduled timeline (Kantipuronline, 2002). On October 11, 2002, a new Prime Minister, Lokendra Bahadur Chand (a former Prime Minister) was chosen by the King along with several Cabinet Ministers. However, the King asked all political parties to submit names of eligible candidates to form the Council of Ministers, but only a few parties have supported the formation of the new government. The Council of Ministers has since been expanded and now includes politicians and technocrats (Kantipuronline, 2002).

Collectively, the domestic political instability during the past 12 years, combined with the ongoing international war on terrorism in Afghanistan and beyond, has created a major negative impact to tourism for Nepal. Recent statistics communicate the impact, as there has been a total decrease of arrivals at -21% during the 2000-2001 season with -33% decline in the Indian market, and a -17% decline in the third country market (Nepal Tourism Board, 2002a). Prior to the ghastly and largest terrorist attack (World Trade Center, New York and the Pentagon, Washington, D.C., USA) conducted on September 11, 2001, tourist arrivals had shown few improvements; however, the number of arrivals plummeted following those incidents. The impact and repercussions in negative tourist flow was experienced globally.

Overall, the rate of growth (international arrivals) for September-December in 2001 when compared to the previous year during the same period declined by 22.6% for North America; 14.5% for the Caribbean; and 7.7% for Western Europe. There was a change of -8.6% for worldwide arrivals; however, the Middle East witnessed -11.4% decline, while South Asia (Afghanistan, Bangladesh, Bhutan, India, Iran, Maldives, Nepal, Pakistan and Sri Lanka) experienced the most significant decrease at 24.4% (World Tourism Organization,

2002). The South Asian region witnessed an overall decrease of −6.3% for 2000-2001, representing 5.7 million arrivals; however, the growth rate for January-August (before the attacks) in 2001 when compared to the previous year during the same period had actually increased by 1.4% for South Asia (World Tourism Organization, 2002). Therefore, it can be logically deduced that the current war on terrorism in Afghanistan initiated during October 2001 and still ongoing was responsible for the sharp decrease in international visitors to the South Asian region (see Table 3).

In Nepal, the effect of the war in Afghanistan devastated the total arrival numbers as it had decreased to −54% in December 2001. The 2002 season has also shown lackluster arrival numbers. Between January 2002-June 2002, overall tourist arrivals declined by −40%; the Indian market by −19%, while the third country market represented −47% (see Table 4).

The visitor arrivals for select important markets for Nepal are illustrated in Tables 5 and 6. Some of the highlights indicate that the number of arrivals post-September 11 declined for all markets as of June 2002, except for Australia, France, Japan and India who started showing a positive change of growth in June. American arrivals had plunged with an average decline of −50% from September 2001-June 2002. Similarly, U.K. arrivals during the same time period declined by −35%. The summer months are the peak travel season for Indian tourists, and although arrivals to Nepal declined by −41% during

TABLE 3. Visitor Arrivals, Growth Rate, Receipts and Market Share (2000-2001)

	Arrivals (million)			Market Share[d]			Receipts (US$ billion)			Market Share[d]
	2000	2001	%[a]	2001	%[b]	%[c]	2000	2001	%[a]	2001
WORLD	696.7	692.7	−0.6	100	2.9	−8.6	474.4	462.2	−2.6	100
Africa	27.2	28.2	3.8	4.1	6.1	−1.4	10.9	11.7	8.1	2.5
Americas	128.4	120.8	−5.9	17.4	0.3	−20.4	132.8	122.4	−7.8	26.5
East Asia/Pacific	109.1	115.1	5.5	16.6	9.6	−4.2	81.4	82.0	0.8	17.7
Europe	402.7	400.3	−0.6	57.8	1.8	−6.2	233.0	230.1	−1.2	49.8
Middle East	23.2	22.5	−3.1	3.3	0.4	−11.4	11.5	11.2	−2.5	2.4
South Asia[1]	6.1	5.7	−6.3	0.8	1.4	−24.4	4.9	4.7	−5.1	1.0

[a]Growth Rate (2000-2001).
[b]Growth Rate (Comparison of Arrivals from January through August 2000-2001).
[c]Growth Rate (Comparison of Arrivals from September through December 2000-2001).
[d]Market Share in Percent.
[1]South Asia represents: Afghanistan, Bangladesh, Bhutan, India, Iran, Maldives, Nepal, Pakistan and Sri Lanka.
Source: Compiled from World Tourism Organization (2002).

TABLE 4. Visitor Arrivals (by Air) and Growth Rate for January Through December (2000-2001-2002)

Month	Third County Tourists[1]					Indian Tourists					Total Tourists				
	2000	2001	2002	%[a]	%[b]	2000	2001	2002	%[a]	%[b]	2000	2001	2002	%[a]	%[b]
January	15,455	20,611	9,559	35	-54	4,215	5,294	4,017	26	-24	19,670	25,905	13,576	33	-48
February	22,980	24,897	13,256	09	-47	5,020	5,917	3,487	18	-41	28,000	30,814	16,743	11	-46
March	29,723	32,808	17,999	12	-45	5,985	6,023	3,713	01	-38	35,708	38,831	21,712	10	-44
April	30,182	28,454	13,747	-06	-52	7,205	6,871	4,331	-05	-37	37,387	35,325	18,078	-06	-49
May	14,375	14,601	8,819	01	-40	9,705	10,935	7,847	13	-28	24,080	25,536	16,666	06	-35
June	8,940	6,137	5,361	-30	-13	14,897	4,101	8,480	-72	107	23,837	10,238	13,841	-57	-35
July	13,622	10,733		-32		7,638	4,443		-42		21,260	15,176		-29	
August	17,499	14,733		-16		7,465	3,650		-51		24,964	18,383		-26	
September	26,902	20,343		-24		8,880	5,017		-44		35,782	25,360		-29	
October	41,704	29,036		-31		8,095	4,001		-51		49,799	33,037		-34	
November	34,921	20,072		-43		7,675	4,443		-42		42,596	24,515		-43	
December	24,696	11,831		-52		9,135	3,505		-62		33,831	15,336		-54	
Total	280,999	234,256	68,741	-17	-47[c]	95,915	64,200	31,875	-33	-19[c]	376,914	298,456	100,616	-21	-40[c]

[a]Growth Rate (2000-2001).
[b]Growth Rate (2001-2002).
[c]Growth Rate (Comparison of Arrivals from January through June 2001-2002).
[1]Tourists from Other Countries Excluding India.
Source: Compiled from Ministry of Culture, Tourism and Civil Aviation (2001); Nepal Tourism Board (2002a).

September 2001-May 2002, an increase of 107% was identified for June 2002. Likewise, Australia experienced an increase of 150%, and Japan also recorded an increase of 68% when compared to the previous year. However, this particular increase should be recognized within the context of June 2001 when the Royal massacre took place and so base visitor numbers were drastically down (see Tables 5 and 6).

DISCUSSION AND CONCLUSION

Safety and security are important aspects of travel destination choice, as risk perception can influence tourist decision-making and destinations can be severely affected, with substantial negative economic consequences as tourists substitute their vacation destinations or regions (Pizam, Tarlow, & Bloom, 1997; Richter & Waugh, 1986). Risk perception can largely be shaped by the mass media where certain images of a destination are formulated and accordingly attract or detract potential visitors (Hall & O'Sullivan, 1996). For example, based on in-depth interviews with international travelers and travel advice from popular guidebooks, Carter (1998) identified Europe and North America to be perceived as safe, the African continent to be dangerous and avoided, and Asia posed risk but worth the challenge due to its exoticness.

Based on a comparative analysis of arrival numbers in Nepal it is evident that domestic political instability did generate for negative publicity, which resulted in decreased tourist arrivals. In addition, the generalization of perceived risk within the South Asian region due to the war in Afghanistan, and the strained tensions between India and Pakistan can largely be credited with negative tourist flows to Nepal. Such regional effects are evident throughout the world especially among developing countries as western media coverage is scant unless an uprising or a natural calamity exists (Richter, 1992). Such selective media coverage and regional generalization does constrain individual countries' ability to attract visitors.

However, given that the primary source of tourist information is the media, destinations should disclose and be able to provide factual information about political strife in affected regions to avoid confusion and misinformation among the traveling public (Wahab, 1995). The information should be provided early and on a continuing basis especially among the major tourist generating markets to distill negative image formulation (Mansfeld, 1999). Information could be relayed as press releases and supplemented by periodic updates in other communication mediums, notably the Internet, as it seems to offer broader reach. In the case of Nepal, such strategies were implemented the day following the im-

TABLE 5. Visitor Arrivals for Select Markets (by Air) and Growth Rate During July Through December (2000-2001)

Country	July			August			September			October			November			December		
	2000	2001	%[a]	2000	2001	%[a]	2000	2001	%[a]	2000	2001	%[a]	2000	2001	%[a]	2000	2001	%[a]
Australia	204	207	2	246	204	−17	940	825	−12	1,669	1,433	−14	1,444	897	−38	1,061	593	−44
France	997	1,027	3	1,475	1,199	−19	1,531	1,299	−15	4,151	3,529	−15	2,799	1,772	−37	1,028	660	−36
Germany	1,005	639	−36	1,238	919	−26	2,669	2,007	−25	4,486	2,709	−40	2,490	1,878	−25	1,267	707	−44
India	7,637	4,443	−42	7,457	3,650	−51	8,895	5,017	−44	8,086	4,001	−51	7,667	4,443	−42	9,130	3,505	−62
Italy	605	385	−36	1,953	1,659	−15	862	550	−36	1,314	830	−37	983	320	−67	956	313	−67
Japan	1,265	660	−48	2,212	1,568	−29	2,506	1,358	−46	2,771	1,775	−36	5,301	1,992	−62	4,934	2,149	−56
Netherlands	414	362	−13	384	361	−6	1,267	1,065	−16	2,530	2,300	−9	1,465	1,009	−31	1,145	597	−48
Spain	698	597	−15	1,491	1,673	12	1,262	629	−50	1,281	418	−67	616	149	−76	302	96	−68
U.S.A.	1,572	1,320	−16	1,728	1,428	−17	2,973	1,909	−36	5,612	3,066	−45	4,302	2,242	−48	2,667	1,028	−62
U.K.	1,423	1,123	−21	1,410	1,375	−3	2,777	2,307	−17	4,931	4,277	−13	4,545	3,223	−29	2,655	1,511	−43

[a]Growth Rate (2000-2001).
Source: Compiled from Ministry of Culture, Tourism and Civil Aviation (2001); Nepal Tourism Board (2002a).

TABLE 6. Visitor Arrivals for Select Markets (by Air) and Growth Rate During January Through June (2001-2002)

Country	January			February			March			April			May			June		
	2001	2002	%[a]	2001	2002	%[a]	2001	2002	%[a]	2001	2002	%[a]	2001	2002	%[a]	2001	2002	%[a]
Australia	604	366	−39	785	451	−43	1,211	927	−24	1,247	557	−55	477	378	−21	135	338	150
France	893	455	−49	2,023	831	−59	2,332	1,163	−50	2,796	1,331	−52	794	563	−29	201	210	4
Germany	946	653	−31	1,937	1,069	−45	3,389	2,287	−33	2,250	995	−56	883	634	−28	365	257	−30
India	5,294	4,017	−24	5,917	3,487	−41	6,023	3,713	−38	6,871	4,331	−37	10,935	7,847	−28	4,101	8,480	107
Italy	607	178	−71	593	269	−55	884	342	−61	851	476	−44	344	248	−28	167	115	−31
Japan	2,815	1,046	−63	3,700	1,501	−59	3,852	2,263	−41	2,271	1,491	−34	1,010	703	−30	392	658	68
Netherlands	730	397	−46	968	493	−49	1,151	724	−37	905	603	−33	486	197	−59	169	120	−29
Spain	182	63	−65	350	115	−67	335	275	−18	374	196	−48	312	178	−43	107	49	−54
U.S.A.	2,768	1,101	−60	3,105	1,436	−54	4,242	1,695	−60	3,537	1,479	−58	2,463	1,255	−49	1,286	957	−26
U.K.	2,130	1,163	−45	2,784	1,734	−38	4,238	2,639	−38	3,852	1,519	−61	1,773	866	−51	546	491	−10

[a]Growth Rate (2001-2002).
Source: Compiled from Ministry of Culture, Tourism and Civil Aviation (2001); Nepal Tourism Board (2002a).

133

position of the initial state of emergency. An excerpt of the press release noted the following:

> In the aftermath of violence in certain parts of the Kingdom like Dang, Syangja, Solukhumbu, a state of emergency has been declared in Nepal as of 26th November 2001. It is expected that security will be further beefed up and better situation of law and order will prevail in Nepal. Despite the common perception that the word "Emergency" conveys to the casual observer, visitors to Nepal can experience near normalcy in most of the prominent tourist destinations within the country. Emergency in the present context refers to a temporary suspension of political activities by various parties, and more of a preventive measure. (Nepal Tourism Board, 2001b)

In addition, The Nepal Tourism Board officially launched "Destination Nepal Campaign 2002-2003" in January 2002, with two basic objectives: (1) to generate considerable tourism awareness domestically, and (2) to embark on effective international tourism promotion and market repositioning strategy to instill an image of Nepal as a reliable, safe and attractive destination (Nepal Tourism Board, 2002c). The campaign was promoted to coincide with the United Nations' international declarations, such as International Year of the Mountains 2002 and International Year of Ecotourism 2002. Mountain regions, tourism and ecotourism opportunities are in abundance in Nepal and thus made for a logical strategic choice and effort to promote the country.

Due to the economic importance and significance of tourism, the Tourism Board along with the government has been proactive with respect to re-creating and repositioning a favorable image of Nepal as a vacation destination, despite the undulations of political instability within the country, the region and beyond. However, notwithstanding the various promotional activities spearheaded by the Tourism Board, there appears to be a cloud of pessimism among the tourism supply sectors with respect to any potential success. Since the creation of the Nepal Tourism Board, the various segments of the tourism industry have yet to fully embrace the organization and its initiatives. There appears to be disengagement between the Board and the industry that it represents which essentially has led to a lack of a cooperative effort. The Board and the tourism industry should come to a unified effort to promote the country as Nepal as synonymous with trekking and mountaineering in the Himalayas, and an unique and invaluable product as known to potential and repeat visitors. For example, based on a survey among international travelers (about 1,600) that had collectively visited 180 countries, Nepal was voted as the second best country to visit behind New Zealand in the *Wanderlust* (UK based travel magazine) Travel Awards 2001 (Nepal Tourism Board, 2002b). Similarly, in May

2002, Nepal was again voted closely behind New Zealand as the favorite long-haul country among subscribers of two popular U.K. newspapers (*The Observer* and *The Guardian*). Besides Mt. Everest, there are other featured attractions that has received rave reviews, such as the Annapurna Trail, which was recently voted as one of the best 12 walks in the world by *Modern Maturity*, a U.S. based magazine (Nepal Tourism Board, 2002b). Additionally, Nepal has been featured in a documentary as one of the 50 must see destinations before death by British Broadcasting Corporation (BBC TV) aired in late 2002 (*Kathmandu Post*, 2002d). Such accolades are in need to be capitalized upon.

The situational effect in Nepal is not isolated as over the last thirty years; there are numerous examples where political instability, war and terrorism have affected tourism in a country. In Tibet, the nationalist movement of the late eighties led to the declaration of martial law in the capital, Lhasa, which effectively curbed and derailed the growth of tourism (Schwartz, 1991). In 1994, the unsuccessful indigenous uprising led by the Zapatistas of Chiapas against the Mexican government led to substantial decreases in arrivals following the insurgency (Pitts, 1996). Similarly, due to political, economic, ethnic and religious conflicts, Indonesia has had difficulties in attracting visitors including independent travelers since mid-1998 (Adams, 2001; Soemodinoto, Wong, & Saleh, 2001). The situation has been drastically exacerbated since the bombing of a nightclub district in Bali on October 12, 2002, where more than 180 casualties were reported, mostly Australians. Notable examples are also evident in other countries but not limited to these, Croatia (Hall & O'Sullivan, 1996), Cyprus (Clements & Georgiou, 1998; Ioannides & Apostolopoulos, 1999; Mansfeld & Kliot, 1996), Gambia (Sharpely & Sharpley, 1995), Israel (Mansfeld, 1999), Northern Ireland (Anson, 1999; Buckley & Klemm, 1993; Leslie, 1999; Wall, 1996), Peru (Wahab, 1996), Philippines, Pakistan, Sri Lanka (Richter, 1999), Rwanda (Human Rights Watch, 1999; Power, 2001), Turkey (Hall & O'Sullivan, 1996), and Zimbabwe/Zambia (Teye, 1986). However, the management and recovery efforts from political instability, war and terrorism in various regions of the globe have also been evident and should be an optimistic sign for Nepal.

Currently, Nepal is axiomatically in a political conundrum as the international, regional and local war on terrorism has been extremely problematic for tourism growth, especially in the last two years. Concomitantly, the burgeoning efforts to break the impasse via various marketing bonanzas is encouraging and needs total governmental support in the form of political stability. A political solution or quelling of the domestic insurgency is imperative and critical, in order to restore the overall positive tourism growth achieved during the course of last few decades. There is a strong negative correlation between political instability and tourist arrivals, as tourists will simply substitute Nepal products due to perceived risks to safety and security.

REFERENCES

Adams, K. (2001). Danger-zone tourism: Prospects and problems for tourism in tumultuous times. In P. Teo, T. Chang, and K. Ho (Eds.), *Interconnected Worlds: Tourism in Southeast Asia* (pp. 265-281). London: Pergamon.

Anson, C. (1999). Planning for peace: The role of tourism in the aftermath of violence. *Journal of Travel Research*, 38(1): 57-61.

Aziz, H. (1995). Understanding attacks on tourists in Egypt. *Tourism Management*, 16: 91-95.

Banskota, K., and Sharma, B. (1993). *Performance of the tourism sector*. Kathmandu: ICIMOD.

Buckley, P., and Klemm, M. (1993). The decline of tourism in Northern Ireland: The causes. *Tourism Management*, 14: 184-194.

Carter, S. (1998). Tourists and traveler's social construction of Africa and Asia as risky locations. *Tourism Management*, 19: 349-358.

Chand, D. (2000). *Nepal Tourism: Uncensored Facts*. Kathmandu: Pilgrims.

Clements, M., and Georgiou, A. (1998). The impact of political instability on a fragile tourism product. *Tourism Management*, 19: 283-288.

Emergency to be prolonged for three months. (2002). Retrieved on May 24, 2002 from the World Wide Web: www.nepalnews.com

Enders, W., and Sandler, T. (1991). Causality between transnational terrorism and tourism: The case of Spain. *Terrorism*, 14: 49-58.

Gartner, W., and Shen, J. (1992). The impact of Tiananmen Square on China's tourism image. *Journal of Travel Research*, 30(4): 47-52.

Goeldner, C., Ritchie, B., and McIntosh. R. (2000). *Tourism: principles, practices and philosophies* (8th edition). New York: John Wiley and Sons.

Government decides to declare state of emergency. (2001). Retrieved on November 26, 2001 from the World Wide Web: www.nepalnews.com

Hall, C., and O'Sullivan V. (1996). Tourism, political stability and violence. In A. Pizam and Y. Mansfeld (Eds.), *Tourism, Crime and International Security Issues* (pp. 105-121). New York: Wiley.

Ioannides, D., and Apostolopoulos, Y. (1999). Political instability, war and tourism in Cyprus: Effects, management and prospects for recovery. *Journal of Travel Research*, 38(1): 51-56.

Kantipuronline. (2002). *King Gyanendra assumes executive powers*. Retrieved on October 4, 2002 from the World Wide Web: www.kantipuronline.com

Lea, J. (1996). Tourism, *realpolitik* and development in the South Pacific. In A. Pizam and Y. Mansfeld (Eds.), *Tourism, Crime and International Security Issues* (pp. 123-142). New York: Wiley.

Leslie, D. (1999). Terrorism and tourism: The Northern Ireland situation–A look behind the veil of certainty. *Journal of Travel Research*, 38(1): 37-40.

Mansfeld, Y. (1999). Cycles of war, terror, and peace: Determinants and management of crisis and recovery of the Israeli tourism industry. *Journal of Travel Research*, 38(1): 30-36.

Mansfeld, Y. (1996). Wars, tourism and the "Middle East" factor. In A. Pizam and Y. Mansfeld (Eds.), *Tourism, Crime and International Security Issues* (pp. 265-278). New York: Wiley.

Mansfeld, Y., and Kliot, N. (1996). The tourism industry in the partitioned island of Cyprus. In A. Pizam and Y. Mansfeld (Eds.), *Tourism, Crime and International Security Issues* (pp. 187-202). New York.

Mihalic, T. (1996). Tourism and warfare: The case of Slovenia. In A. Pizam and Y. Mansfeld (Eds.), *Tourism, Crime and International Security Issues* (pp. 231-246). New York: Wiley.

Mikesell, S. (2001). The Maoist movement and the threat to democracy in Nepal. *Himalayan Research Bulletin*, 21(1): 17-21.

Ministry of Culture, Tourism and Civil Aviation. (2001). *Summary of Tourism Statistics for 2001*. Kathmandu: His Majesty's Government of Nepal, Ministry of Tourism and Civil Aviation.

Nepal a must see destination. (2002). Retrieved on August 3, 2002 from the World Wide Web: www.nepalnews.com

Nepal Tourism Board. (2001a). *National ecotourism strategy and marketing programme of Nepal*. Kathmandu: NTB.

Nepal Tourism Board. (2001b). *Press-Release on Emergency Declaration*. Retrieved on November 27, 2001 from the World Wide Web: www.welcomenepal.com

Nepal Tourism Board. (2002a). *Monthly Newsletter*. Unpublished Document. Kathmandu: NTB.

Nepal Tourism Board. (2002b). *Nepal wins Observer Travel Award 2002*. Retrieved on, May 29, 2002 from the World Wide Web: www.welcomenepal.com

Nepal Tourism Board. (2002c). *Destination Nepal Campaign 2002-2003*. Retrieved on, January 29, 2002 from the World Wide Web: www.welcomenepal.com

Pitts, W. (1996). Uprising in Chiapas, Mexico: Zapata lives–Tourism falters. In A. Pizam and Y. Mansfeld (Eds.), *Tourism, Crime and International Security Issues* (pp. 215-227). New York: Wiley.

Pizam, A., Tarlow, P., and Bloom, J. (1997). Making tourists feel safe: Whose responsibility is it? *Journal of Travel Research*, 36(3): 23-28.

Power, S. (2001). *Bystanders to genocide. Why the U.S. let the Rwandan tragedy happen*. Retrieved on July 30, 2002 from the World Wide Web: www.TheAtlantic. com/issues/2001/09/power.htm

Richter, L. (1999). After political turmoil: The lessons of rebuilding tourism in three Asian countries. *Journal of Travel Research*, 38(1): 41-45.

Richter, L. (1992). Political instability and tourism in the third world. In D. Harrison (Ed.), *Tourism and the Less Developed Countries* (pp. 35-46). New York: Wiley.

Richter, L., and Waugh, W. (1986). Terrorism and tourism as logical companions. *Tourism Management*, 7: 230-238.

Schwartz, D. (1991). Travelers under fire: Tourists in the Tibetan uprising. *Annals of Tourism Research*, 18(4): 588-604.

Sharpley, R., and Sharpley, J. (1995). Travel Advice: Security or Politics? In *Proceedings of the First Global Research and Travel Trade Conference on Security and Risks in Travel and Tourism* (pp. 168-182). Held at Mid Sweden University, Ostersund, Sweden (June 1995).

Soemodinoto, A., Wong, P., and Saleh, M. (2001). Effect of prolonged political unrest on tourism. *Annals of Tourism Research*, 28, 1056-1060.

Sönmez, S., Apostolopoulos, Y., and Tarlow, P. (1999). Tourism in crisis: Managing the effects of terrorism. *Journal of Travel Research*, 38(1): 13-18.

Sönmez, S. (1998). Tourism, terrorism, and political instability. *Annals of Tourism Research*, 25(2): 416-456.

Teye, V. (1986). Liberation wars and tourism development in Africa: The case of Zambia. *Annals of Tourism Research*, 13(4): 589-608.

U.S. Department of State. (2002). *Nepal Public Announcement*. Retrieved on November 22, 2002 from the World Wide Web: http://www.travel.state.gov/nepal_announce.html

U.S. warns of Maoists attacks upon its citizens. (2002). Retrieved on May 17, 2002 from the World Wide Web: www.nepalnews.com

Wahab, S. (1996). Tourism and terrorism: Synthesis of the problem with emphasis on Egypt. In A. Pizam and Y. Mansfeld (Eds.), *Tourism, Crime and International Security Issues* (pp. 175-186). New York: Wiley.

Wahab, S. (1995). Tourism: A challenge to tourism. In *Proceedings of the First Global Research and Travel Trade Conference on Security and Risks in Travel and Tourism* (pp. 84-108). Held at Mid Sweden University, Ostersund, Sweden (June 1995).

Wall, G. (1996). Terrorism and Tourism: An Overview and an Irish Example. In A. Pizam and Y. Mansfeld (Eds.), *Tourism, Crime and International Security Issues* (pp. 143-158). New York: Wiley.

World Tourism Organization (2002). *Tourism proves as a resilient and stable economic sector*. Retrieved on June 28, 2002 from the World Wide Web: www.world-tourism.org/newsroom/Releases/more_releases/june2002/data.htm

60 security men perish in fierce Maoist attacks. (2002). Retrieved on November 15, 2002 from the World Wide Web: www.nepalnews.com

7,073 Nepalis killed during insurgency. (2002). Retrieved on October 31, 2002 from the World Wide Web: www.nepalnews.com

After the Lombok Riots,
Is Sustainable Tourism Achievable?

Fleur Fallon

SUMMARY. This paper commences with a discussion about aspects of security and safety in relation to tourism. It then looks specifically at the tourism situation for the island of Lombok, Indonesia, after three days of rioting and the subsequent media reporting combined to decimate tourism numbers. Incidents like this severely undermine any idea of sustainability in tourism development. Such incidents also bring into sharp focus the direct and indirect links between tourism and a wide range of social, political and economic issues at the local, national and global levels. It highlights the need for tourism to be integrated into broader social and economic activities. If there is greater involvement by the local community in tourism development, then the risk of violence in

Fleur Fallon is affiliated with the College of Science and Technology, Ningbo University, FAO, P.O. Box 20, Ningbo 315211, Zhejiang, People's Republic of China (E-mail: fleure@asia.com).

The data for this article was gathered as part of the author's PhD study during the period 1998-2001. The author also wishes to acknowledge the invaluable assistance of Dr. Alfons van der Kraan, Dr. Barbara Rugendyke, Dr. Elizabeth Morrell and members of the community on Lombok.

This study was made possible by an Australian Postgraduate Award scholarship and a Keith and Dorothy McKay Travelling scholarship.

[Haworth co-indexing entry note]: "After the Lombok Riots, Is Sustainable Tourism Achievable?" Fallon, Fleur. Co-published simultaneously in *Journal of Travel & Tourism Marketing* (The Haworth Hospitality Press, an imprint of The Haworth Press, Inc.) Vol. 15, No. 2/3, 2003, pp. 139-158; and: *Safety and Security in Tourism: Relationships, Management, and Marketing* (ed: C. Michael Hall, Dallen J. Timothy, and David Timothy Duval) The Haworth Hospitality Press, an imprint of The Haworth Press, Inc., 2003, pp. 139-158. Single or multiple copies of this article are available for a fee from The Haworth Document Delivery Service [1-800-HAWORTH, 9:00 a.m. - 5:00 p.m. (EST). E-mail address: docdelivery@haworthpress.com].

10.1300/J073v15n02_08

relation to tourism is reduced and the likelihood of sustainable development outcomes is enhanced. *[Article copies available for a fee from The Haworth Document Delivery Service: 1-800-HAWORTH. E-mail address: <docdelivery@haworthpress.com> Website: <http://www.HaworthPress.com> © 2003 by The Haworth Press, Inc. All rights reserved.]*

KEYWORDS. Lombok, Indonesia, sustainable tourism development, security

INTRODUCTION

Factors of personal security, or safety, are important criteria by which potential tourists judge the attractiveness of a particular destination (Hall and O'Sullivan, 1996). These factors may relate to the high physical risk in adventure tourism; the risk of becoming a victim of criminal activity such as assault or theft and the risk of being caught in a politically motivated attack by terrorists, or being trapped in a war zone. Hall and O'Sullivan (1996) indicate that there are varying levels of security and political stability. Political instability can range from strikes, protests, riots, acts of terrorism through to coups, civil wars and international wars (Hall, 1994; Hall and O'Sullivan, 1996: 109).

Even under conditions of political stability, a government may not always be benign. A stable government may be authoritarian and repressive, ruthlessly suppressing all opposition. Tourism may flourish under such circumstances and development may be fast-tracked through bureaucratic institutions, as has been the case in the past in Indonesia. The construction of luxury resort enclaves to attract "up-market tourists" in Indonesia, and indeed across Asia, has "resulted in a highly competitive situation, even over-supply, directed at a specific market segment" (Wall, 1998: 237). In Indonesia, tourism grew significantly under Soeharto's authoritarian rule and a national strategy for development was known as the "Trilogy of Development," based on the "three pillars of stability, growth and equal distribution of benefits" (Sunario, 2001; see also Hall, 2000). The highly centralised power system that allowed Soeharto's family and friends to gain economic monopolies in many industry sectors, as well as a hugely unequal distribution of benefits, led to increasing frustration with, and hostility to, Soeharto and to his subsequent downfall in May 1998 (see Aditjondro, 2000). Although emphasis on sustainable development principles has increased internationally parallel with the rapid growth of global tourism, sustainability was not a feature of tourism development in Indonesia during the Soeharto era. For detailed discussions on sustainability in tourism development, see Butler (1998, 1999a); Fallon (2002); Hall and Lew (1998); Harrison (1996); Milne (1998); Mowforth and Munt (1998); Wahab and Pigram (1997); and Weaver and Lawton (1999). Suffice it to say that in this context, tourism, according to sustainable development principles, must integrate economic, community and environmental concerns in a balanced way for long-term equitable distribution of benefits. If local community members are involved in the development of tourism, then the risk of violent opposition is reduced and the likelihood of sustainable development outcomes is increased.

As the situation in Indonesia became more volatile, with economic and political tensions spreading across the archipelago, tourist numbers declined due to the "unstable safety conditions" (Sunario, 2000). The media play a significant role in reporting security related issues about a country and, in so doing, they influence potential tourists in their choice of destination. Hall and Oehlers (2000) demonstrate that media coverage of political and social unrest can have long-term negative impacts on tourist numbers to a given destination, as has been the case in the past, for example, in Cambodia, Sri Lanka, Kashmir and China. Highly publicised reports of criminal incidents that suggest that crime against tourists may be rampant also coincide with declines in international visitors, for example, in Brazil, Papua New Guinea, Republic of South Africa and so on (Pizam, Tarlow and Bloom, 1997: 23). Such types of incidents have also been reported on the world-wide-web for Lombok ("Robbed on Lombok," 1999), but this paper will focus on the impact of three days of rioting in mid-January 2000 on the island's fledgling tourism industry. The scale of devastation and loss of life may appear insignificant in comparison with the catastrophic events of September 11, 2001, in New York and Washington, USA. Yet for a struggling island economy, largely dependent on tourism and with other limited economic opportunities, unlike the USA, the unexpected situation impacted heavily on the local community and gave rise to fears of how the situation would affect national tourism throughout Indonesia.

METHODOLOGY

An integrated process of "open inquiry" was used to gain both qualitative and quantitative data in order to present as broad and as complete a picture of tourism on Lombok as possible. This approach also provided a means of "triangulation" to support the validity of data collected (Watson, Burke and Harste, 1989; see also Berno, 1996; Cukier, 1996; Sandiford and Ap, 1998). The author interviewed key stake-holders in the tourism industry and members of the host community, as well as conducted surveys of fifteen hotels in Mataram and Kute on the south coast of Lombok. These findings are supported by media reports, first-hand observations and the results of tourism market surveys conducted for the provincial tourism department from 1997 to 2001. The author visited Lombok for three months in 1989-1999 and again in June 2000 and June 2001.

BEYOND BALI

Lombok and Sumbawa comprise the province of West Nusa Tenggara (*Nusa Tenggara Barat*, or hereafter, NTB) in Indonesia. Lombok is the smaller of the two islands, just 4,600 square kilometres, situated east of Bali, Indonesia's premier tourist destination. NTB was promoted as a "Beyond Bali" destination, and over a period of ten years had witnessed steady tourism growth. In 1988 there were 44,846 international visitors; in 1997, the number of international visitors peaked at 245,049 (NTB Tourism Office, 2000), more than five times the number predicted in tourism plans. This growth then declined by 22.6 percent to 189,689 in 1999 due to the Indonesian-wide political and economic crisis (*krismon*). The number of international visitors plummeted a further 43.4 percent to just 107,286 international visitors in 2000 following three days of rioting in January 2000. Mataram, the provincial capital, situated in the west of Lombok, became a flash-point, sparking fears of further violence across Indonesia and the disintegration of the Republic ("Islands of discontent," 2000; "Island rent by forces for hire," 2000; "General disorder," 2000; "Indonesian time-bomb," 2000). Christian and Chinese churches, businesses and homes were systematically targeted for looting and destruction. A total of 6,000 people, residents and foreign tourists left the island with over 2,500 people evacuated by air, mostly to Bali ("Calm returns," 2000; see Table 1). Some reporters classified them as refugees ("Mataram refugees," 2000; "Refugees keep flowing," 2000). In less than one week, Lombok achieved international notoriety as a "resort island" ("Christians flee," 2000; see Table 2), but it was the kind of publicity it did not need.

It is estimated that 90 percent of Lombok's 2.8 million population (KMNK, 1999) is Muslim (BPS NTB and BAPPEDA, 2000). Australian newspapers played up religious differences, the alleged military-instigated violence and national unrest with clear warnings for tourists ("Shadowplay," 2000; "Wiranto linked to violence," 2000; "Rioters ignore threat," 2000; "Island rent by forces for hire," 2000; "Outsiders blamed for violence," 2000). In the Indonesian media, religious and political leaders called for calm ("Religious leaders," 2000). In contrast, the safety of the main Indonesian resort island of Bali (Lombok's main competitor for the tourist dollar) was emphasised.[1] Although the media may report a riot, their use of language may exaggerate the event in

TABLE 1. *Jakarta Post* Headlines 18-30 January 2000

Headline	Source	Date
Mob burns 10 churches in Mataram	National News	18 January
One killed in Lombok as violence enters second day	National News	19 January
Lombok remains tense	National News	20 January
Calm returns to Lombok as death toll hits five	National News	21 January
Refugees keep flowing out of Lombok island	National News	22 January
Mataram refugees put heavy strain on Bali	National News	23 January
Religious leaders join forces in preventing riots	National News	23 January
Racial conflicts may hamper tourism recovery	Business News	25 January
Alleged instigators of Lombok riots arrested	National News	29 January
Lombok island post-riots devoid of tourism	Features	30 January

Sources: As listed.

TABLE 2. Newspaper Headlines in Australia 19-22 January 2000

Headline	Source	Date
Christians flee flame of Muslim fury on resort island	*Australian*	19 January
Wiranto linked to violence	*Sydney Morning Herald*	19 January
Police shoot rioters as Lombok burns	*Australian*	20 January
Australian tourists flee riot-torn Lombok	*Sydney Morning Herald*	20 January
Wahid asks: crisis, what crisis?	*Australian*	20 January
Violence traps Australian tourists	*Australian*	20 January
Indonesian time-bomb	*Sydney Morning Herald*	21 January
Rioters ignore threat to shoot on sight as Christian homes looted	*Sydney Morning Herald*	21 January
Outsiders blamed for violence	*Sydney Morning Herald*	22 January
General disorder	*Sydney Morning Herald*	22 January
Island rent by forces for hire	*Australian*	22 January
Islands of discontent	*Australian*	22 January
Shadowplay	*Australian*	22 January

Sources: As listed.

the minds of potential tourists and cause them to choose another destination. In May 2001, the author was asked how tourism on Lombok had been affected by "the war." The questioner was not referring to the conflicts in East Timor, Maluku or Aceh. Her question was qualified by reference to the religious war on Lombok. She meant the riot of January 2000.

Tourism Crisis on Lombok

Notwithstanding its growing tourism industry, prior to 17 January 2000, Lombok was little known in the world at large. On this day, over 5,000 people had gathered for a mass rally in front of military headquarters in the centre of Mataram ("Mob burns," 2000). They were protesting about the central government's inability to stop the violence between Christian and Muslim groups in Maluku where at least 1,700 people had been killed in one year ("Raging inferno," 2000). The crowd became excited by the words of an uninvited speaker, an "agent provocateur," allegedly from outside NTB ("Alleged instigators," 2000; "Lombok remains tense," 2000; "Mob burns," 2000; "Outsiders blamed for violence," 2000).

By early afternoon, a systematic attack began on 77 Christian and Chinese homes and businesses and on 9 churches. Riot instigators paid local Mataram youths to point out the targets. Ironically, on the same day, the Indonesian government revoked the 33-year-old Presidential Instruction that restricted the public observance of Chinese religious practices and traditions ("Government ends bar," 2000). In the mayhem, two nightclubs in central Senggigi, the main tourist area, were destroyed by fire. Immediate neighbours, angered by suspected prostitution ("Return to Lombok," 2000), drugs and constant nightly disturbances from the nightclubs, took the opportunity of the riot to destroy the source of their annoyance (hotel manager, personal communication, June 2000). At other locations, hotel staff and local villagers fiercely protected the tourism establishments. The Mangsit community, north of Senggigi, for instance, erected large signs in Arabic–*Allah-u Akbar* ("God is Great")–and remained on close watch at the Holiday Inn and at the homes of expatriate staff during the crisis ("After the riots," 2000).

In subsequent days, over 1,500 police, naval and military personnel from Java arrived to quell the violence. Orders to shoot rioters and looters were given ("Calm returns," 2000; "One killed," 2000; "Police shoot," 2000; "Rioters ignore threat," 2000). Five people were killed and by Thursday, January 20, a total of 203 alleged rioters and provocateurs were detained, including at least two University of Mataram graduates charged with distributing pamphlets at the rally ("Calm returns," 2000). National Police Chief Lt. Gen. Rusdihardjo claimed that "a certain group of people outside the province" was responsible for the unrest ("Lombok remains tense," 2000; tourism spokesperson, personal communication, July 7, 2001). The Communion of Churches of Indonesia also suspected that the acts of violence were "premeditated, systematic and a threat to the nation's unity" ("Calm returns," 2000). This group expressed disappointment about the slowness of security forces in responding to the unrest on Lombok and enforcing the law.

Tourists have also been slow to return to Lombok and the total number of international and Indonesian visitors for the year 2000 dropped by 30 percent to 233,650 (see Table 3). Room occupancy rates for Lombok hotels plummeted from an average of 42 percent to less than an average of 10 percent in February 2000. After the riot, hotels on Lombok were operating in "survival" mode. Five months later, occupancy rates rose to almost 40 percent (NTB Tourism Office, personal communication, June 2000), but it was acknowledged that consistent occupancy rates of 60 percent are required to achieve reasonable profits. At June 2000, most permanent staff in the hotels surveyed by the author (1999; 2000) had retained their jobs. With more time on their hands, employees took annual leave, renovated rooms, cleaned up hotel grounds and learnt new skills. In this interim period, hotels did not replace permanent staff who resigned. There was little or no work for casual staff, whose numbers declined from 6.4 percent to 2.7 percent of all staff in the fifteen hotels surveyed by the author (1999; 2000). Work experience was stopped for trainees from the local tourism training schools.

Provincial Police Chief, Colonel Sukandri, said damage in Mataram was estimated at more than Rp60 billion. Economic damage in income foregone due to the lack of tourists would be much higher ("Refugees keep flowing," 2000). With at least 30,000 to 40,000 people on Lombok directly or indirectly dependent on tourism ("After the riots," 2000; "Lombok waits for tourists to re-

TABLE 3. Change in Numbers of International Visitors 1996-2000

Country	1996	1997	% change 97-99	1999	% change 99-2000	2000
Australia	44,961	40,245	−14.13	34,558	−54.85	15,601
Germany	31,168	29,586	−18.57	24,093	−47.14	12,736
USA	Na	23,393	−8.66	21,368	−42.7	12,236
Netherlands	25,897	22,131	−19.47	17,821	−55.3	7,962
England	19,199	22,024	−19.04	17,830	−59.19	7,276
Italy	Na	Na		9,852	−45.80	5,340
Japan	Na	Na		8,812	−44.60	4,881
Belgium	Na	Na		7,948	−71.36	2,276
France	Na	Na		7,345	−33.38	4,893
Canada	Na	Na		6,708	−69.56	2,042
Others				33,324	−3.84	32,043
Total	227,453	245,049	−22.60	189,659	−43.43	107,286

Source: Compiled from Rachmad, 1998; NTB Tourism Office, 1997, 2000, 2001.

turn," 2000), the economic impact of the riot will continue to be experienced by the wider Lombok community for a long time. Without tourists, the guides, drivers, beach-vendors and others working on the margins of formal tourism employment need to look for other employment opportunities, even though these opportunities are scarce.

On a positive note, hotel management and other tourism businesses on Lombok made attempts to strengthen community links after the riot. The Starwood Hotel group, of which Senggigi Sheraton is a part, collected Rp42 million from its employees world-wide. This money was used to help staff re-build houses that were burnt down and to supply basic food items such as sugar, cooking oil and rice. Suppliers to the hotels outside Lombok also provided some free services for up to three months after the riot ("After the riots," 2000). The big hotels and smaller tourism operators formed the Senggigi Business Association (SBA) to combine efforts and resources for the benefit of Lombok. The first successful meeting attracted over 100 members and, later, over 400 people worked together to clean up the streets of Senggigi. There was a sense of belonging, synergy and commitment to improving the area and working to encourage a quick return of tourists. The new SBA committee also stressed the importance of education and training for local people to assist them in getting jobs when the economy picks up again ("After the riots," 2000). Some operators within the tourism industry indicated that there were some leadership issues within the SBA about how the organisation should operate. These conflicts need to be resolved for more effective management of environmental and promotional strategies (tourism spokespersons, personal communication, June 2000; July 2001). On another level, business and government officials involved in tourism have not fully integrated their promotional activities. Immediately after the riots, some attempts at integration were made. The provincial government was quick to appeal for calm and for countries to continue sending tourists.

The Governor, Harun Al-Rasyid, put his job on the line regarding security issues. He guaranteed the personal safety of tourists. On 26 January 2000, he wrote to the Japanese and Australian ambassadors, who were advising deferral of non-urgent travel to Lombok and to Indonesia in general. In particular, the widespread media coverage in Australian newspapers, television and travel warnings on the Australian embassy Internet web pages contributed to the more than 50 percent downturn in the number of Australian tourists travelling to Lombok (see Table 3).

Harun Al-Rasyid met with the religious community leaders of NTB to encourage religious and ethnic co-operation and respect. Christian and Muslim people worked together to repair houses and churches. In some instances, Christian homes had been protected by Muslim neighbours, who created superficial damage to the front of these homes, so that rioters would by-pass them (community spokesperson, personal communication June 2000). In an attempt to reverse the downward trend of international visitors, the Governor attended international tourism marts. He also met with nearly 80 travel professionals, Bali-based diplomats and journalists, who travelled to Lombok to assess the current state of security, at the initiative of Lombok-Sumbawa Promotions and the PATA Bali Chapter in March 2000. The group could find no one prepared to defend the actions of January 2000. "Universally, the residents of the island distance themselves in every way possible . . . blaming the events on outside political provocateurs" (*Bali Update*, 2000).

Table 3 shows the sharp decline in the number of international visitors following the January 2000 riots. Europe as a whole is the largest sending area, with 84,889 tourists going to NTB in 1999. This dropped by 42.43 percent to 48,868 tourists in 2000.

Australia retained its rank as the largest single sending country, although it suffered one of the largest decreases in numbers by 54.85 percent to 15,601 tourists in 2000. USA and Canada combined suffered a loss of 49 percent from 28,076 to 14,278 visitors. Japan is the only Asian country to send tourists in significant numbers to NTB. This dropped 44.6 percent from 8,812 visitors in 1999 to 4,881 visitors in 2000. Clearly, the overall decline was largely a result of the specific incident in January 2000 and subsequent media reporting and embassy travel warnings. This was a continuation of the downward trend since 1997. Statistics, media reports, government and tourism business operators each provide only a partial picture of the devastating consequences of the Lombok riots.

Why Did Lombok "Spark" So Easily?

Although no detailed analysis of the causes of the Mataram riot is attempted here, it is necessary to make a few comments, because the political background may have long-term effects on tourism. It is widely believed that the military and the former political élite favoured under Soeharto's rule attempted to destabilise President Wahid by creating unrest across the Indonesian archipelago, sparking tensions and "horizontal conflicts" between religious, ethnic and economic groups (Aditjondro, 2000; "Alleged instigators," 2000; "Calm returns," 2000; "Raging inferno," 2000; "Scene of the crime," 2000; "Refugees keep flowing," 2000; Sirait, 2000). Many Indonesian military and police were relocated to Lombok from East Timor in 1999, and it is believed that some of these men became involved with local militia groups ("Lombok unrest," 2000).

As a response to the lack of trust in the police and the military to fight crime, well-organised local vigilante militia groups, known as *pamswakarsa*, have been set up across Lombok since the early 1990s ("Lombok unrest," 2000; USAID, 2000; journalist, personal communication, June 2001). There are over fifty *pamswakarsa* crime-control groups on Lombok. The two largest are called *Bujak (Pemburu Jejak*–tracker), in Central Lombok, and *Amfibi* ("amphibious," to protect the people on land or sea), in East Lombok with more than 150,000 members ("Lombok unrest," 2000; "Mataram refugees," 2000; "Refugees keep flowing," 2000). Since the economic crisis and the failed harvests of 1997, there has been a significant increase in crime, especially in Central and East Lombok, and increasing frustration about perceived wealth in West Lombok. Tensions existing a century ago (Cederroth, 1996; Van der Kraan, 1976, 1980a, 1980b) between East and West Sasaks still exist, despite a surface appearance of harmony. Most tourism development has occurred in West Lombok, financed by mainly West Lombok, Balinese and Javanese investors, and has served to deepen the divisions between East and West Lombok. The problem is made more complex by the fact that the significant planned tourism development for Central Lombok stalled due to the land disputes and the economic and political crisis (Fallon, 2002). The very limited planned tourism development for East Lombok centres on two islands, Gili Indah to the south, and Gili Sulat to the north, and some overflow from West Lombok in the Gunung Rinjani National Park area. The situation in Maluku, with cries for a *jihad* (holy war) from the extremist Muslim group, *Lashkar Jihad Sunnah Wal Jamaah* (UN, 2000), ignited the anger of impoverished Muslims in East and West Lombok and led to the co-ordinated destruction of Christian and Chinese property in Mataram ("Lombok unrest," 2000).

Eighteen months after the riots, discussions with travel agents and guest-house owners indicated that there are signs that perhaps the influence of the *pamswakarsa* leaders is declining. For instance, according to one travel agent in Mataram:

> The people of Lombok realised that the riot of January 2000 was a big mistake. They realised finally the huge multiplier effect of tourism on the economy. It affected even the *bakso* sellers who wheel their food carts along the streets. While tourists don't generally tend to buy this very cheap food, people who work in the tourism and related industry do. Those who suffered a loss of income due to lack of employment or a reduced share from the service tax paid by tourists, spend less on convenience foods. People are beginning to realise that maybe the *pamswakarsa* does not need to be out on the streets showing a strong presence. Its activities have slowed down considerably. (travel agent, personal communication, July 12, 2001)

And, according to a Kute guest-house owner:

> The *pamswakarsa* tried to persuade me to join the association "for protection." I refused. Another guest-house owner did join *pamswakarsa*, but when a robbery was committed there recently, *pamswakarsa* did not help. Some *pamswakarsa* members are known to have been involved in crime. If you join their association, they want you to give preference to employing their members. I want to know about the background of my staff. My employees are all family related and we would take care of any intruders. We don't have any trouble. People are starting to leave *pamswakarsa*, as the value of joining is diminished. There is a joining fee of Rp120,000, for which members receive a coloured shirt, but little else. (guest-house owner, personal communication, July 14, 2001)

Some of the motivation to be involved in a *pamswakarsa* group may have diminished as people everywhere on Lombok realised the devastating and sudden economic consequences of loss of income due to a non-existent multiplier effect when the tourists fled Lombok in January 2000. The USAID's Office of Transition Initiatives also turned its focus from governance issues to focus on " . . . the potential for conflict, particularly with regard to the role of the *pamswakarsa*" (USAID, 2000: 4). In addition to the need to resolve local community conflicts to strengthen security, strong and consistent integrated marketing efforts need to be made to reassure potential tourists that Lombok is a safe, secure destination, a perception that deteriorated following the 2000 riot.

RESPONSE OF TOURISTS TO SECURITY ISSUES

In tourism market surveys conducted for the NTB Tourism Office since 1997, tourists were asked, among other questions, to rate the quality of safety and privacy and the hospitality of the local people during their stay on Lombok. For each survey, 1,000 tourists completed surveys at hotels, travel agencies and tourism information offices. Responses were slightly more negative for the 2000 survey than for 1997 survey (NTB Tourism Office 1997, 2000, 2001; Rachmad, 1998; see also Table 4).

Indonesian tourists increased their level of dissatisfaction about safety and privacy issues in NTB by more than 8 percent from 1997 to 2000. International tourists demonstrated higher levels of dissatisfaction for this factor and this also increased by 6 percent to 24.7 percent of those surveyed in 2000. Interestingly, international tourists recorded a 10 percent increase in the "good" rating of safety and privacy in 1999, more than 16 percent higher than the rating by Indonesian tourists. Although tourism numbers had decreased due to the na-

TABLE 4. Tourists' Perceptions of Safety and Privacy, Hospitality and Friendliness 1997, 1999, 2000

Factor	2000 % Foreigners	2000 % Indonesian tourists	1999 % Foreigners	1999 % Indonesian tourists	1997 % Foreigners	1997 % Indonesian tourists
Safety and privacy:						
Good	21.7	23.5	39.6	22.8	27.8	24.2
Satisfactory	53.6	60.3	45.2	59.2	53.6	68.0
Not satisfied	24.7	16.2	15.2	18.0	18.6	7.8
Total percentage	100.0	100.0	100.0	100.0	100.0	100.0
Hospitality, friendliness of local people:						
Good	58.2	33.6	74.9	40.7	78.8	40.7
Satisfactory	33.5	58.7	22.3	53.1	16.7	59.3
Not satisfactory	8.3	7.7	2.8	6.2	4.5	-
Total percentage	100.0	100.0	100.0	100.0	100.0	100.0

Sources: Compiled from Rachmad, 1998; NTB Provincial Tourism Office, 2000; 2001.

tional political and economic crisis, Lombok was still perceived to be "safe." This perception of safety changed dramatically after the January 2000 riots, when the "good" rating by international tourists for safety and privacy dropped by almost 18 percent to 21.7 percent, lower than the rating by Indonesian tourists (see Table 4).

For the category "hospitality and friendliness of local people," Indonesian tourists were more critical than international tourists, but both groups recorded fewer "good" ratings for this category in 2000 than in 1997 (see Table 4). The Indonesians recorded an insignificant change in this rating between 1997 and 1999, but a 7 percent drop in 2000 to 33.6 percent. The foreigners' very high "good" rating of 78.8 percent dropped to 74.9 percent in 1999 and slumped a further 16.8 percent to 58.2 percent in 2000.

Foreign tourists are more likely to be visiting the island for holiday reasons and therefore are more likely to be more relaxed and more positively disposed towards the local people than domestic visitors. Additionally, as international visitors are more noticeable on Lombok due to their physical features and clothing, members of the local community, especially those involved in tourism, will make a special attempt to display friendliness towards foreigners to maximise levels of sales of souvenirs, food and services. Foreign tourists increased their "unsatisfactory" rating of hospitality by almost 4 percent from 4.5 percent in 1997 to 8.3 percent in 2000 after the Mataram riots, indicating that the riots impacted on perceptions of "friendliness." This compares to the Indonesian tourists' "unsatisfactory" rating of 7.7 percent in 2000. Improving visitor satisfaction ratings is a national as well as a local provincial concern.

TOURISM IN TRANSITION

Like many other tourism destinations in Asia, Lombok has a tourism plan prepared by foreign consultants, "seemingly to a common template: attract quality (read 'rich') tourists through the construction of opulent resort complexes" (Wall, 1998: 237). In the breathing space caused by interrupted tourism development since 1997, Lombok has had the opportunity to review plans, regulations and monitoring procedures for tourism development. This is happening in other Indonesian regions, for example, North Sulawesi (PATA, 2000). The PATA review team called for a new national sustainable tourism strategy. It also recognised that the international media, in portraying the country image, had a huge impact on the provincial image in the tourism marketplace. Until the "very challenging political, social, economic and military challenges currently facing the country are adequately addressed" (PATA, 2000: 8), the task of presenting a positive and safe image of tourism destinations across Indonesia is "enormously difficult." Professor Emil Salim, former Chairman of the President's Economic Advisory Council, commented at a meeting on transport and tourism and economic recovery in September 2000:

> Since Indonesia's crisis is not only an economic crisis but also that of politics and social issues, the likelihood of utilizing tourism to support economic recovery becomes even less feasible. Available funds must be allocated first towards more stabilizing factors in society over and above allocation for tourism promotion.
>
> In the world economy it has been proven that world travel follows economic growth. Travel does not precede growth. Therefore, the economy must first be stabilized . . . Only then can more normal conditions prevail, and only under normal conditions can tourism expect to thrive. (quoted in Sunario, 2000: 5)

The growth of international tourist arrivals for Indonesia has been dramatically revised from an overly optimistic 15 million to a more realistic 6.9 million arrivals for 2004 (Suniaro, 2000: 4). In the interim, it needs to be recognised that "tourism's impact is always played out in an already dynamic and changing cultural context" (Wood, 1993: 67-68) and that it is "always vulnerable to external factors which are beyond its control" (Wall, 1998: 237). Wall (1998) suggests that steps need to be taken to ensure that tourism is integrated with other economic activities to reduce the severity of the impact of a down-turn in numbers.

In this transitional time for tourism, the need to involve all stake-holders, including the local host communities has been increasingly recognised (BAPPEDA NTB, 2000; PATA, 2000; Tourism Resource Consultants, 2000). The Chair of the North Sulawesi Task Force, Steve Noakes, stated ". . . building a sustainable tourism strategy for North Sulawesi will have to involve all stakeholders in a continuous process of learning. It will not always be smooth sailing. It'll take leadership, commitment and a few sacrifices" (PATA, 2000: 19). These comments are equally applicable to Lombok.

There are many constraints that inhibit the involvement of local communities in tourism planning. These include the cultural and political legacy of decades of authoritarian rule; the lack of understanding by local communities; economic conditions; time factors; and the lack of collaboration skills by government officials (Timothy, 1998). However, as Pearce, Moscardo and Glenn (1996: 211-212) stress:

> It is likely to be more productive (for tourism business interests) to view community involvement as good business. The process of effective community involvement in tourism can generate ideas from extensive local knowledge, it can develop partnerships in the purchasing and production of tourism related goods, and it can be a first plank in the total marketing plan for the business.

If local communities are not involved, a backlash against tourism may develop (Pearce, Moscardo and Glenn, 1996) as experienced on Lombok in January 2000. These situations all contribute to reduced security for both local communities and tourists and combine to inhibit the growth of tourism. Local participation does not guarantee success. As Butler (1999b: 74) argues "the presence of local involvement does not guarantee successful integration, but one may argue strongly that its absence is very likely to result in *unsuccessful* integration" with other economic sectors.

There is evidence of some positive changes in tourism planning strategies and involvement of local communities in tourism projects on Lombok. For example, Gunung Rinjani National Park, at the end of a joint three-year project by the governments of New Zealand and Indonesia, has better environmental and visitor management and extensive community involvement (Fallon, 2002; Tourism Resource Consultants, 2000). In the south of Lombok at Kute, action by local communities has forced a change of plans for a Balinese Nusa Dua style luxury resort enclave to more appropriate smaller-scale tourism facilities that are more likely to be sustainable, in terms of the local economy, the community and the environment (Fallon, 2002). More recent full year visitor statistics for NTB in 2001 indicate a positive turn-around with an increase of 36.5 percent in the overall number of visitors to 319,028, including a 20.6 percent increase in international visitors (NTB Tourism Office, 2002). This represents a healthy return to pre-2000 riot visitor numbers. The "fast profit from up-market wealthy tourists" type of tourism planning has been superseded by a more carefully thought out integrated strategy with community involvement and sustainable development principles more firmly rooted at the core of planning. Together with the return of tourists, according to the 2001 visitor statistics, a more positive, upbeat attitude towards tourism was evident on Lombok island by mid-2002 (Lombok resident, personal communication, August 2002).

However, the tragic events of Bali on 12 October 2002 ("Bali 121002–Bali is wounded," 2002), if not a death knell, have created yet another severe shock for tourism, not only in Bali, but for Lombok and throughout Indonesia. In the short-term, as many as 2.7 million people may be unemployed directly and indirectly as a result of this incident, according to H.E. Mr. Gede Ardika, Indonesia's Minister for Culture and Tourism (WTO, 2002). Bali is the main gateway for tourists travelling to Lombok. With the increased threat of terrorist attacks and a volatile global situation, governments have been warning their citizens to stay out of Indonesia unless on essential business. Not only are tourists staying away, but also researchers, who have been refused permission by their universities to go as they would not be covered by insurance. Ross Gittens, the economics editor of *The Sydney Morning Herald* ("Summing up the damage," 2002) is quick to attempt to assess the economic loss for Indonesia overall as between 1 and 2 percentage points. He acknowledges that this is not good news, but that this is not the worst of Indonesia's problems. For Bali and Lombok, though, heavily dependent on tourism, the immediate future looks bleak. Kasman-Entus (2002, trinet discussion group, November 25), a researcher and resident of Bali, indicates that whilst there was an immediate reduction in tourist numbers, country travel warnings are beginning to soften, so that bookings are starting to increase again. The long-term effect cannot accurately be predicted, but the good news is that like Lombok, since 1998, serious discussions between tourism stakeholders are taking place to re-assess tourism activities to focus more consistently with local cultural values and to rethink strategies to integrate tourism more strongly with other industry sectors.

CONCLUSION

Like the Balinese, who see post-October 12 as a time to reassess tourism, the local communities on Lombok want tourism and they appreciate the economic benefits that can be derived from it. This paper has highlighted the devastating implications of widely reported rioting on both the local community and tourists for the island of Lombok. The value of tourism was keenly felt when the economic benefits disappeared after January 2000. All Lombok people, including *pamswakarsa* vigilante groups, are now fully aware of the importance of maintaining security to ensure a safe environment for tourists. This realisation will continue to deepen in the aftermath of the most recent Bali incident.

In the space caused by declining tourism numbers following the Indonesia-wide political and economic crisis in 1997 and the further critical fall-out resulting from the January 2000 riots, Lombok had a chance to review tourism planning and to involve local community members at a greater level that aims to integrate tourism with other industry sectors in a way that also aims to meet sustainable development principles. This was particularly evident in Gunung Rinjani National Park and at Kute, in the south of Lombok. Consultation with and involvement of local community members at many levels, training to develop human capacity, as well as encouraging appropriate tourism sensitive to local cultural values, are imperatives to building a secure environment for the healthy development of tourism. The challenge now remains to ensure consistent and sustained co-operation between different sectors and between key stakeholders in the tourism industry. By mid-2002, the likelihood of sustainable tourism development seemed more likely than in the different pre-1998 political era. Bali on 12 October 2002 and 9-11 have created a much tougher scenario. Tourism has been interrupted many times on Lombok since 1997. Each time, steps have been taken and the tourists began to return. The future seemed bright. There was time to make some structural changes to tourism and to allow a moderate amount of optimism, as advocated by WTO's tourism recovery committee (WTO, 2002). With the latest interruption to tourism, tourism stakeholders will be driven to work together creatively to make tourism less vulnerable to exogenous factors and to ensure it is better integrated with other industry sectors to ensure sustainable outcomes. A more than moderate amount of optimism and resilience will be required to ensure that this is merely another interruption, and does not spell the halt of tourism for Lombok.

NOTE

1. Since then, Bali's reputation as a "safe haven" has been shattered. After 11.30 p.m. on October 12, 2002, down-town Kuta resembled a war zone, when bombs exploded, blowing apart 2 nightclubs, 185 lives (42 bodies were still unidentifiable after six weeks) and injuring 324 people from 18 different countries ("Bali 121002," 2002).

REFERENCES

Aditjondro, G. (2000). Maluku: While elephants fight, the people of Maluku die. Asia-Pacific Network, January 27. Retrieved April 28, 2001, from *http://nuance. dhs.org/lbo-talk/0002/2173.html.*

After the riots, Lombok waits for the tourists. (2000, April 2). *The Jakarta Post*, Features. Retrieved April 4, 2000, from *www.thejakartapost.com.*

Alleged instigators of Lombok riots arrested. (2000, January 29). *The Jakarta Post,* National news. Retrieved January 30, 2000, from *www.thejakartapost.com.*

Australian tourists flee riot-torn Lombok. (2000, January 20). *The Sydney Morning Herald*, p. 1.

Bali 121002-Bali is wounded. (2002). Retrieved November 25, 2002, from *www.indo. com/bali/121002.*

Bali Update (2000). Electronic Newsletter No. 181, 6 March.

BAPPEDA NTB (2000). *Pokok-pokok rencana induk pengembangan pariwistata propinsi NTB* (Highlights of the tourism development plan for Lombok). Mataram: Author.

BPS NTB and BAPPEDA (Statistics Office of NTB Province and Regional Development Planning Board) (2000). *Nusa Tenggara Barat dalam Angka* (NTB in Figures). Mataram: Author.

Berno, T. (1996). Cross-cultural research methods: Content or context? A Cook Islands example. In R. Butler and T. Hinch (Eds.), *Tourism and Indigenous Peoples* (pp. 376-395). London: International Thomson Business Press.

Briguglio, L., Archer, B., Jafari, J., and Wall, G. (1996) (Eds). *Sustainable Tourism in Islands and Small States: Issues and Policies*. London: Pinter.

Butler, R. (1999a). Sustainable tourism: A state-of-the-art review. *Tourism Geographies*, 1(1): 7-25.

Butler, R. (1999b). Problems and issues in integrating tourism development. In D. Pearce and R. Butler (Eds.), *Contemporary Issues in Tourism Development* (pp. 65-80). London: Routledge.

Butler, R. (1998). Sustainable tourism–Looking backwards in order to progress? In C. M. Hall and A. Lew (Eds.), *Sustainable Tourism: A Geographical Perspective* (pp. 25-34). Essex: Addison Wesley Longman.

Butler, R., and Hinch, T. (1996). *Tourism and Indigenous Peoples*. London: International Thomson Business Press.

Calm returns to Lombok as death toll hits five. (2000, January 21). *The Jakarta Post*, National news. Retrieved January 21, 2000, from *www.thejakartapost.com.*

Cederroth, S. (1996). From ancestor worship to monotheism: Politics of religion in Lombok. *Temenos*, 32: 7-36. Retrieved August 3, 1999, from *www.abo.fi/comprel/ temenos/temeno32/cede.htm.*

Christians flee flame of Muslim fury on resort island. (2000, January 19). *The Australian*, p. 8.

Cukier, J. (1996). Tourism employment in developing countries: Analyzing an alternative to traditional employment in Bali, Indonesia. PhD thesis, University of Waterloo.

Fallon, F. (2002). Tourism interrupted: The challenge of sustainability for Lombok, 1987-2001. PhD thesis, Armidale, NSW: University of New England.

General disorder. (2000, January 24). *The Sydney Morning Herald*, p. 42.

Government ends bar on observing Chinese religions, traditions (2000). *The Jakarta Post*, National news. Retrieved January 20, 2000, from *www.thejakartapost.com*.

Hall, C. M. (2000). Tourism in Indonesia: The end of the New Order. In C. M. Hall and S. Page (Eds.), *Tourism in South and Southeast Asia: Issues and Cases* (pp. 157-166). Oxford: Butterworth-Heinemann.

Hall, C. M. (1994) *Tourism in the Pacific Rim: Development, Impacts and Markets.* Melbourne: Longman Cheshire.

Hall, C. M. and Lew, A. (1998). *Sustainable Tourism: A Geographical Perspective.* Essex: Addison Wesley Longman.

Hall, C. M. and Oehlers, A. (2000).Tourism and politics in South and Southeast Asia. In C. M. Hall and S. Page (Eds.), *Tourism in South and Southeast Asia: Issues and Cases* (pp. 77-93). Oxford: Butterworth-Heinemann.

Hall, C. M. and O'Sullivan, V. (1996). Tourism, political stability and violence. In A. Pizam and Y. Mansfield (Eds), *Tourism, Crime and International Security Issues* (pp.105-122). Chichester: John Wiley and Sons.

Hall, C. M. and Page, S. (2000). *Tourism in South and Southeast Asia: Issues and Cases.* Oxford: Butterworth-Heinemann.

Harrison, D. (1996). Sustainability and tourism: Reflections from a muddy pool. In L. Briguglio, B. Archer, J. Jafari and G. Wall (Eds.), *Sustainable Tourism in Islands and Small States: Issues and Policies* (pp.69-89). London: Pinter.

Indonesian time-bomb (2000, January 21). *The Sydney Morning Herald*, p. 1.

Islands of discontent. (2000, January 22). *The Australian*, p. 22.

Island rent by forces for hire. (2000b, January 22). *The Australian*, p. 11.

KMNK (Kantor Menteri Negara Kependudkan–Ministry of Population) (1999). *Population of Indonesia*, October 12, Jakarta: Author.

Lombok island post-riots devoid of tourism. (2000, January 30). *The Jakarta Post*, Features. Retrieved February 3, 2000, from *www.thejakartapost.com*.

Lombok remains tense. (2000, January 20). *The Jakarta Post*, National news. Retrieved January 21, 2000, from *www.thejakartapost.com*.

Lombok unrest: Description and analysis. (2000, January 19). Retrieved January 25, 2000, from *http://media.isnet.org/ambon/LombokUnrest.html*.

Lombok waits for tourists to return. (2000). *The Jakarta Post*, Features. Retrieved April 16, 2000, from *www.thejakartapost.com*.

Mataram refugees put heavy strain on Bali. (2000, January 23). *The Jakarta Post*, National news. Retrieved January 24, 2000, from *www.thejakartapost.com*.

Milne, S. (1998). Tourism and sustainable development: Exploring the global-local nexus. In C. M. Hall and A. Lew (Eds.), *Sustainable Tourism: A Geographical Perspective* (pp. 35-48). Essex: Addison Wesley Longman.

Mob burns 10 churches in Mataram. (2000, January 18). *The Jakarta Post*, National news. Retrieved January 20, 2000, from *www.thejakartapost.com*.

Mowforth, M. and Munt, I. (1998) *Tourism and Sustainability: New Tourism in the Third World.* London: Routledge.

NTB Tourism Office (2002). Tourism statistics. Mataram: Author.

NTB Tourism Office (2001). *Analisa Pasar Wisatawan NTB 2000* (Analysis of NTB Tourism Market 2000). Mataram: Author.

NTB Tourism Office (2000). *Analisa Pasar Wisatawan NTB 1999* (Analysis of NTB Tourism Market 1999). Mataram: Author.

NTB Tourism Office (1997). *Pariwisata dalam Angka* (Tourism in Figures). Mataram: Author.

One killed in Lombok as violence enters second day. (2000, January 19). *The Jakarta Post*, National news. Retrieved January 20, 2000, from *www.thejakartapost.com*.

Outsiders blamed for violence. (2000, January 22). *The Sydney Morning Herald*, p. 21.

PATA (Pacific Asia Travel Association) (2000, August 29-September 5). North Sulawesi Task Force Report: Charting a new direction for sustainable tourism in North Sulawesi, Indonesia. Bangkok: Author.

Pearce, D. and Butler, R. (1999). *Contemporary Issues in Tourism Development*. London: Routledge.

Pearce, P., Moscardo, G., and Ross, G. (1996). *Tourism Community Relationships*. Oxford: Pergamon.

Pizam, A., and Mansfield, Y. (1996). *Tourism, Crime and International Security Issues*. Chichester: John Wiley and Sons.

Pizam, A., Tarlow, P., and Bloom, J. (1997). Making tourists feel safe: Whose responsibility is it? *Journal of Travel Research*, 36 (1): 23-28.

Police shoot rioters as Lombok burns. (2000, January 20). *The Australian*, p. 1.

Rachmad, H. (1998). Tourism in Figures 1997 (*Pariwisata dalam angka 1997*). Report for the NTB Tourism Office (*Dinas Pariwisata Daerah Tingkat 1, NTB*), Mataram.

Racial conflicts may hamper tourism recovery. (2000, January 25). *The Jakarta Post*, Business news. Retrieved January 25, 2000, from *www.thejakartapost.com*.

Raging inferno. (2000, January 3). *Time*, pp. 56-61.

Refugees keep flowing out of Lombok island. (2000, January 22). *The Jakarta Post*, National news. Retrieved January 22, 2000, from *www.thejakartapost.com*.

Religious leaders join forces in preventing riots. (2000, January 23). *The Jakarta Post*, National news. Retrieved January 23, 2000, from *www.thejakartapost.com*.

Return to Lombok. (2000). *Travel Indonesia*, 22 (7): 19-24.

Rioters ignore threat to shoot on sight as Christian homes looted. (2000b, January 21). *The Sydney Morning Herald*, p. 9.

Robbed on Lombok: Bandits strike a group of travellers in the wilds of a remote Indonesian island. (1999, October 6). Retrieved November 20,1999, from *www.salon.com/travel/feature/1999/10/06/robbery*.

Sandiford, P. and Ap, J. (1998, August). The role of ethnographic techniques in tourism planning. *Journal of Travel Research*, 37: pp. 3-11.

Scene of the crime. (2000, January 27). *Far Eastern Economic Review*. Retrieved May 4, 2001, from *http://proquest.umi.com*.

Shadowplay. (2000, January 22) *The Australian*, pp. 17; 22.

Sirait, P. H. (2000, January). *Dari Maluku, kita ke Mataram*. (We go from Maluku to Mataram). *DR*, pp. 19-24.

Summing up the damage. (2002, November 2). *The Sydney Morning Herald*. Retrieved November 10, 2002, from *www.smh.com.au*.

Sunario, T. (2001, January 20). Political change, social change, and group psychology. *Indonesia Digest*, 91. Retrieved May 10, 2001, from *www.indonesiaku.web. id/docu . . . t/analysis*.

Sunario, T. (2000, September 10). The role of air transportation and tourism in economic recovery. *Indonesia Digest*, 74. Tourism and Business Communication Weekly newsletter.

Timothy, D. (1998). Participatory planning: A view of tourism in Indonesia. *Annals of Tourism Research*, 25, (2): 371-31.

Tourism Resource Consultants (2000). Gunung Rinjani National Park Project. Inception Report, Vols. 1 and 2, NZODA-Indonesia Programme of the Ministry of Foreign Affairs and Trade, New Zealand, and the Government of the Republic of Indonesia. Mataram: Author.

UN (United Nations) (2000). United Nations Commission on Human Rights Report on elimination of religious intolerance. Presented at the 55th session of the United Nations, September 8. Retrieved April 23, 2001, from *www.hri.ca/fortherecord2000/ vol3/indonesiatr/htm*.

USAID (United States Agency for International Development) (2000, December). Office of Transitions Initiatives Field Report: Indonesia. Retrieved April 25, 2001, from *gopher.info.usaid.gov/human_response/oti/country/indones/rpt1200.html*.

Van der Kraan, A. (1980a). *Lombok: Conquest, Colonization and Underdevelopment, 1870-1940*. Singapore: Heinemann Education Books, Asian Studies Association of Australia Southeast Asia Publications Series No. 5.

Van der Kraan, A. (1980b). Dutch rule in Lombok: The development of underdevelopment. Townsville: James Cook University South East Asian Monograph Series.

Van der Kraan, A. (1976). Selaparang under Balinese and Dutch colonial rule: A history of Lombok 1870-1940. PhD thesis, Canberra: Australian National University.

Violence traps Australian tourists. (2000a, January 20). *The Australian*, p. 7.

Wahab, S., and Pigram, J. (Eds) (1997). *Tourism, Development and Growth: The Challenge of Sustainability*. London: Routledge.

Wahid asks: Crisis, what crisis? (2000, January 20). *The Australian*, p. 7.

Wiranto linked to violence. (2000, January 19) *The Sydney Morning Herald*, p. 9.

Wall, G. (1998). Reflections upon the state of Asian tourism. *Singapore Journal of Tropical Geography*, 19 (2): 232-237.

Watson, D., Burke, C., and Harste, J. (1989). *Whole Language: Inquiring Voices*. Ontario: Scholastic Canada.

Weaver, D. and Lawton, L. (1999). Sustainable tourism: A critical analysis. Gold Coast: Cooperative Research Centre for Sustainable Tourism (Research report) No. 1.

Wood, R. (1993). Tourism, culture and the sociology of development. In M. Hitchcock, V. King and M. Parnwell (Eds.), *Tourism in Southeast Asia* (pp. 48-70). London: Routledge.

World Trade Organization (2002, November 19). Tourism between 'moderate optimism' and 'structural changes,' WTO tourism recovery committee says. Retrieved November 27, 2002, from *www.world-tourism.org/newsroom/Madrid_releases/ more_releases/November 2002/recovery-meeting.htm*.

Tourism Eclipsed by Crime: The Vulnerability of Foreign Tourists in Hungary

Gábor Michalkó

SUMMARY. This paper examines the relationships between crime and tourism in Hungary with special reference to spatial and temporal aspects, focusing on the main groups of offences committed against foreign tourists and the problem of crime prevention. The study shows that trends in criminality are closely related to the number of tourists arriving and staying in Hungary and are less associated with general criminal conditions. Most of the victims are Germans; their cars, valuables, and wallets are particularly vulnerable to criminal activity. The density of crime is highest in Budapest, the capital, and in the region surrounding Lake Balaton during the summer season when levels of tourism are at their highest. Tourist information and frequent police controls are considered the most effective measures for crime prevention. *[Article copies available for a fee from The Haworth Document Delivery Service: 1-800-HAWORTH. E-mail address: <docdelivery@haworthpress.com> Website: <http://www.HaworthPress.com> © 2003 by The Haworth Press, Inc. All rights reserved.]*

Gábor Michalkó is affiliated with the Geographical Research Institute, Hungarian Academy of Sciences, H-1112 Budapest, Budaörsi út 45, Hungary (E-mail: michalko@helka.iif.hu).

[Haworth co-indexing entry note]: "Tourism Eclipsed by Crime: The Vulnerability of Foreign Tourists in Hungary." Michalkó, Gábor. Co-published simultaneously in *Journal of Travel & Tourism Marketing* (The Haworth Hospitality Press, an imprint of The Haworth Press, Inc.) Vol. 15, No. 2/3, 2003, pp. 159-172; and: *Safety and Security in Tourism: Relationships, Management, and Marketing* (ed: C. Michael Hall, Dallen J. Timothy, and David Timothy Duval) The Haworth Hospitality Press, an imprint of The Haworth Press, Inc., 2003, pp. 159-172. Single or multiple copies of this article are available for a fee from The Haworth Document Delivery Service [1-800-HAWORTH, 9:00 a.m. - 5:00 p.m. (EST). E-mail address: docdelivery@haworthpress.com].

KEYWORDS. Hungary, tourism, public security, criminal offence, crime prevention

INTRODUCTION

According to the World Tourism Organization, Hungary is among the most visited countries in the world; in 2000, Hungary received 14 million tourists. Successive democratic governments following the change of political regime in 1990 have paid particular attention to the comprehensive development of tourism. Socio-economic changes, however, along with the transformation promoting this process, have generated negative trends as well. One of these is an increase in crime. As a consequence, crime has shown a tendency to expand; the crime rate rose from 34 per thousand inhabitants in 1990 to 45 in 2000. Most offences were committed in Budapest and other urban areas of the country most frequented by tourists. By now it has been realised that the security of tourists is mandatory for success in the tourism industry. Therefore, assuring the personal safety of visitors and security of their property has become a basic requirement. With high quality tourist information and the provision of assistance for tourists and orientation in an alien environment, the victimisation of foreigners can be reduced.

This paper aims to examine empirically the spatial and social relationships between crime and tourism in Hungary. The focus is on tourists as victims of crime and the locations and visitation patterns that contribute to this phenomenon.

CRIMINAL GEOGRAPHIC ASPECTS OF TOURISM

The interrelationships between the community environment and crime were among the earliest topics of studies in criminology. Criminal ecological surveys started in the 1920s and called attention to the fact that the scene of a criminal act or a series of offences is decisive with respect to relevant circumstances (Vág, 1982). Herold (1968) formulated his stance more cautiously, maintaining that only certain offence groups can be attributed to special spatial segments. In the opinion of geographers who deal with the spatial aspects of crime, in addition to investigations into the spatial order of crime, criminal geography should also study its social background in order to present a prognosis for future spatial changes (Herbert, 1982). Kovács (1990) emphasised that criminal geography should be aimed at the applicability of criminological research and the latter should focus on the explanation of criminality (e.g., frequency and character of crime) within a given area. In recent years, the range of studies has widened considerably and criminality was disclosed with the social status of the victimised person(s) duly taken into account (Pain, 1991; 1997), and social, economic and political backgrounds of a given offence group were analysed (Michalek, 1995). Geographical information systems (GIS) have become common in many disciplines for analysing situations and data of a spatial nature. The increase in use of GIS and the growing technology associated with it allows even smaller territorial units to be analysed and a basis established for noting trends in criminal activity (Ratcliffe and McCullagh 1998). Until now few researchers have focused on criminal geographical approaches to tourism except for the spatial presentation in studies dealing with the relationship between tourism and crime (Pizam and Mansfeld, 1996). However, among investigations focusing on urban tourism, a complex social geographical analysis of the vulnerability of tourists in Budapest was carried out by Michalkó (1996).

It should be acknowledged that the acquisition and supply of data for crime statistics are the responsibility of the police in Hungary, and the primary database for the present study was provided by the national police headquarters. Crime statistics suitable for international comparison are based on the moment investigations are completed and not on when the complaint is lodged. Thus, usually a criminal offence appears in the statistics not at the moment it is committed but several months later. It should also be noted that statistics contain only registered criminal offences or those discovered by the police and recorded. In the case of foreign victims it might be presumed that to avoid time loss involved in legal procedures they make complaints in serious cases only or in cases when a police record is necessary for insurance affairs or to replace missing documents.

Crime data in Hungary do not differentiate between foreign tourists and people from abroad who have residence permits or work visas. As a result, some criminal acts against tourists go unrecorded. In principle, statistics should contain criminal acts to the grievance of foreign citizens staying in Hungary illegally as well, but it is assumed that because of their underground lifestyle, members of this group rarely report incidents to the police. These circumstances pose somewhat of a hindrance to an objective evaluation of the problem. Nevertheless, it is probable that the majority of the foreigners victimised are tourists.

This analysis comprised the time interval between 1996 and 2000 in order to eliminate temporal distortions stemming from annual fluctuations in the number of foreign tourists and of criminal offences. The assessment included offences against foreigners and not those committed by them. It was assumed that tourism and crime are more closely associated with tourists as victims than with offenders; however, it should be noted that in some cases foreign tourists do commit minor offences, such as traffic violations. Foreign citizens staying in Hungary as a rule do not become offenders in the course of their activities, but most of the foreign victims are tourists.

Compared to crime statistics, official statistics on tourism offer more information promoting group-specific analysis. Statistics on border crossings provide data on the country of origin, but records of their stay (place, duration) are taken only at places of commercial and private accommodation. There is a tenfold difference between the number of foreigners crossing borders and those staying at official accommodations (i.e., of 31 million foreign visitors only 3.4 million spent at least one night in places of commercial and private accommodation in 2000). As each foreign guest can be victimised independent of his/her touristic behaviour, in the following evaluation crime data will be compared to border crossing data.

MEETING POINTS OF TOURISM AND CRIME

The problem of tourism security cannot be labelled as a novel social challenge of the post-modern era since travellers have always faced danger during their journeys. At no point in history could voyagers feel entirely safe, whether they travelled by horse, mail coach, or by car. Security issues in tourism have recently become a complex notion. This primarily refers to the personal safety of tourists and their property, but it includes an ability to become oriented in an alien environment, understand the local system of signs, indications and social conventions, and finally the security of shopping and consumer services (Michalkó, 2001). In this sense, the visited environment is alien, and the foreigner is exposed to a direct or indirect risk from the moment of arrival. Even though tourists rarely fall victim to violence, their personal security and the safety of their property are endangered directly. Events in the tense global political environment of the past few years, however, confirmed that brutal terrorism has extended to areas frequented by tourists as well (Hall, 1994; Wall, 1996). The recent bombings in Bali are a good example of this. Violence against tourists might occur at international sporting events in and around the stadiums when fans clash between themselves. In some cases demand by foreign tourists generates crime (e.g., in sex bars or drug dens), which can victimize tourists as conflict with persons of the underworld (Cohen, 1996).

While these events commonly receive media attention, violence against the person occurs less often than crime against property. In most cases the dress, communication, and behaviour of the tourist signpost the fact that he or she is a foreigner who possesses valuables (e.g., currency, credit cards, passports, and cameras). If tourists arrive by car it might be supposed they would not care much for crime prevention. Hotel rooms and apartment rentals occupied by tourists as a rule are empty during the day, and valuables left in the rooms can easily fall prey to burglars.

There is a significant difference between the internal structure of crime in various countries, so the state of public security cannot be generalized about what extent tourists are endangered by crime. INTERPOL data concerning criminal offences per 100,000 inhabitants of countries of Central Europe show that Germany is the "leader," while in Austria and Switzerland crime is on a level similar to that of Hungary. However, this cannot be accepted as a basis for comparison owing to the differences in legal regulations and related statistical systems of these countries (Table 1). Thus, without a thorough analysis of available data, it should be necessarily be concluded that tourists in Germany are more vulnerable to crime than tourists in Hungary.

In addition to the status of crime in developed and popular countries, the situation of public security in the developing world should be mentioned, as it gradually has become part of global tourism since the 1960s. The criminology literature, based on the postulate that social and economic development involves the expansion of crime, had long considered public security in developing countries inferior to that in developed countries. Actually, crime rates are lower in less-developed countries, even though they are increasing at a quicker pace than in the developed world. Moreover, the nature of criminal offences is becoming more brutal (McIlwaine, 1999). The presence of tourism contributes to the process because foreign guests arriving from Western societies with general behaviour and consumer habits strongly differing from those of destination residents, may easily become targets of crime.

The expansion of crime might lead to a decline in tourist arrivals with time although there are examples of cities (e.g., Naples and New York) where the thrill of danger has become part of the attraction. The tourist can actually turn

TABLE 1. Status of Crime in Some Central European Member States of INTERPOL, 1998

	Criminal offences	Criminal offences per 100 thousand inhabitants	Criminal offences committed by foreign citizens
Austria	479,859	5,940.0	19.4
Hungary	600,000	5,926.2	5.0
Germany	6,456,996	7,868.9	27.1
Switzerland	384,585	5,405.6	43.7

Source: Compiled from Hungarian National Police Headquarters (ORFK)

into a passive party of crime, while past criminal reputations can become tourist attractions (Tarlow and Muesham, 1996).

TOURISTS AS VICTIMS OF CRIME IN HUNGARY

Growing wealth is a notable indicator of individual success in present-day Hungary. While the range of available consumer products has grown considerably in recent years, they have remained largely inaccessible for some social classes. Consequently, some Hungarians are seeking to create a decent life by illegitimate means (Póczik, 1996). Following the change from state socialism, this process led to a rise in crime against property. Tourism contributes approximately ten percent to Hungary's gross domestic product, and although foreign tourists form a consumer group that should be protected, so far they have not been spared the effects of crime in Hungary. Between 1996 and 2000, three percent of the total number of criminal offences recorded in Hungary were committed against foreigners. Taking into account that during this period nearly 100 million tourists arrived in the country, the 80,000 registered offences might seem almost negligible. On average one in every 1,250 tourists falls victim to a crime. However, any foreign guest tends to create stereotypes under his or her own impressions about the country visited. In this sense, tourists are a kind of diplomat of their state and even a single incident is enough to form an unfavourable image of Hungary. Even if the offences committed against tourists are not too serious, they can be the focus of widespread publicity through the media, and resulting negative feedback might place competitor destinations in a more favourable position.

The general criminal environment and the number of tourists are two important variables in the commission of crimes against tourists. Presumably, a region with high numbers of foreigners will also become a region of higher levels of crime. Despite the growth of criminal offences in Hungary between 1997 and 1998, the ratio of victimised foreigners decreased because the total number of foreigners arriving in the country dropped (Table 2). However, when the number of foreign visitors showed an upward trend in 2000, there was an upsurge in crime against them even though the total number of offences continued to decrease. From this it may be concluded that criminal acts against foreigners are more closely correlated with increasing numbers of visitors than with general criminal activity. Tourists are likely to be victimized when their spatial and temporal concentration coincides with rising difficulties in safeguarding their valuables.

As far as the types of crime committed against foreigners are concerned, offences against property dominate (96.6%), and there is a minor proportion of

TABLE 2. Vulnerability of Foreigners to Crime in Hungary

Year	Criminal offences, total 1996 = 100% (466 thousand)	Ratio of criminal acts with foreign victims as percentage of the total offences	Foreigners arriving in Hungary 1996 = 100% (39,833 thousand)
1996	100	3.8	100
1997	110.4	3.3	93.7
1998	128.9	2.8	84.4
1999	108.5	2.6	72.3
2000	96.7	2.9	78.2

Sources: Compiled from ORFK, Central Statistical Office (KSH)

those against persons as well (1.5%). Of the former, motor vehicle related theft and burglary (50.1%), other forms of theft (23.1), pickpocketing (13.7%), and domicile burglary (9.4%) also prevail. Homicide (68 cases) and wilful bodily harm (643 cases) are rare. Of the total criminal offences, 33 percent involved the loss of money, securities and cheques, and in 11 percent of the cases, electronics or cameras were stolen. These figures corroborate the notion that valuables, documents, and cars are the primary targets. In light of criminal acts against property and tourism, the following statements can be made. Car theft represents a substantial share of motor vehicle-related crimes. There are relatively few guarded parking lots in the most popular destinations in Hungary, including the old city of Budapest. Foreigners must park their cars along the streets, putting them at risk of being stolen by gangs that specialize in the most fashionable cars. Besides car stealing and forced entry, stealing valuables from the cars is also typical. In the former case consumer electronics built in the car or personal belongings are the plunder. Some 17 percent of car-related thefts occur in cars that are left unlocked. Car wrecking is also frequent. In this case considerable harm is done by the offenders, who after having failed in car theft, break windows and force doors open. A classical relationship between tourism and crime is presented by pickpocketing. Nearly 87 percent of this category of offence occurs in Budapest, on vehicles of public transport, at railway stations, and at places of interest visited by dozens of tourist groups simultaneously. A basic precondition of pickpocketing is crowdedness and careless, absent-minded tourists, both typical in urban settings. Nearly always, the loss is realised by the tourist only after the perpetrator has disappeared.

Foreigners are victimised by burglary when they are absent from their accommodations. Taking into account that a mere 8.5 per cent of the foreigners staying in Hungary spend the night at commercial accommodation considered safer due to a permanent presence of servants, it is no wonder that this type of crime is also frequent.

Criminal acts that belong to the category of undistinguished theft prove best how vulnerable foreign visitors are to the potential danger and how clever the offenders are. Apart from cases considered traditional–stealing the luggage of a passenger waiting for a train at the railway station or sneak theft at hotels–criminals have recently begun to impersonate officials. Claiming to be police officers out of uniform, thieves stop tourists and pretend to carry out official duties, such as currency exchange controls and subsequently steal documents and valuables.

From an analysis of offences committed against foreign guests in Hungary it can be established that in most cases the victims are citizens of European countries (91.3%). They are followed by Asians (4.6%), Americans (3%), Australians (0.6%), and Africans (0.5%). Visitors from Germany comprise 43.7 percent of the victims in Hungary, Austrian visitors account for nearly 12 percent, while visitors from 13 other European countries comprise 30 percent of the victims. These figures are not surprising because the arrival of visitors is closely related to the geographical setting of Hungary. However, by examining Table 3, remarkable conclusions can be drawn. Group-specific investigations showed an increase in vulnerability among tourist from the EU and overseas countries. However, the rate of vulnerability/victimization among Hungary's Eastern European neighbour countries remained considerably far below that of visitors from Western Europe.

The rate of victimisation is considerably higher for visitors from the EU countries, particularly those nearest Hungary, than those arriving from other neighbouring nations. While Germans comprise 10.4 percent of visitors to Hungary, 43.7 percent of the total offences were committed against them, which means a fourfold level of vulnerability. This can be explained in part by the fact that guests from the more economically developed countries (i.e., those in Western Europe and North America) are in possession of more valuables, and they behave as tourists in a traditional sense. One-third (30%) of them stayed in registered commercial accommodation, while only two percent of those with lower rates of victimisation stayed in commercial lodging. Much of the problem can be attributed to their careless attitude, which may be a result of the fact that they come from places where levels of public safety are higher, and they are not warned about the status of crime in Hungary.

The primary motivation for residents of neighbouring countries to visit Hungary is shopping (Michalkó and Timothy, 2001). During their stay, which usually lasts only one or two days, they are victimised to a lesser extent. This may be because they are more resistant to crime (less naïve), possess fewer valuables, and in most cases, they speak Hungarian to some degree.

TABLE 3. Nationalities of Crime Victims in Hungary, 1996-2000

Country	Arrivals (% of total)	Rate of victimisation (% of arrivals)	Ratio of the group within total offences			
			Motor vehicle related crime	Theft undistinguished	Pickpocketing	Burglary
Austria	16.5	11.5	69.4	15.7	7.6	8.3
Belgium	0.3	1.0	45.6	21.0	27.3	5.5
France	0.6	2.0	42.4	25.9	27.3	2.9
Netherlands	0.7	3.4	35.4	35.1	23.2	6.5
Croatia	12.0	1.2	47.3	31.4	6.0	2.7
Yugoslavia	11.3	3.0	47.3	31.4	6.0	2.7
Germany	10.4	43.7	60.9	19.1	6.9	14.6
Great Britain	0.6	2.2	16.1	30.8	42.0	4.8
Italy	1.2	3.2	46.1	22.5	22.5	2.8
Romania	12.1	5.5	32.7	33.9	11.7	2.1
Switzerland	0.4	1.6	36.9	22.8	35.6	2.7
Sweden	0.4	1.6	36.9	22.8	35.6	2.7
Slovakia	13.6	1.7	59.0	21.8	5.7	3.5
Slovenia	3.1	0.4	61.9	22.8	35.6	2.7
Ukraine	6.1	0.9	27.0	27.3	12.6	4.4
China	0.0	1.3	24.1	22.2	14.4	18.9
USA	1.0	2.2	19.7	30.4	39.6	5.0
Rest of the world	9.5	13.1	25.0	31.1	26.4	4.7
Total	100	100	50.1	23.1	13.7	9.4

Sources: Compiled from ORFK, KSH

THE PRESENCE OF FOREIGNERS IN REGIONS OF HIGH CRIME

To establish the relationship between tourism and crime it is necessary to examine the spatial and temporal coincidence of the two. The spatial distribution of criminal acts against property is determined primarily by the accessibility and protection of valuables (Vavró, 1995). Figure 1 shows the distribution of criminal offences against foreigners by counties.

The national capital, Budapest (51% of the total number of cases), and the counties of Pest (4.5%), Somogy (12.2%), Zala (4.3%), Gyõr-Sopron Moson (6.0%), and Veszprém (5.7%) surrounding Lake Balaton, the largest natural lake in Central Europe, are the locations with the most occurrences of tourist-related crime. These regions with a high concentration of tourist attractions,

FIGURE 1. Spatial Distribution of Criminal Offences in Hungary (1996-2000)

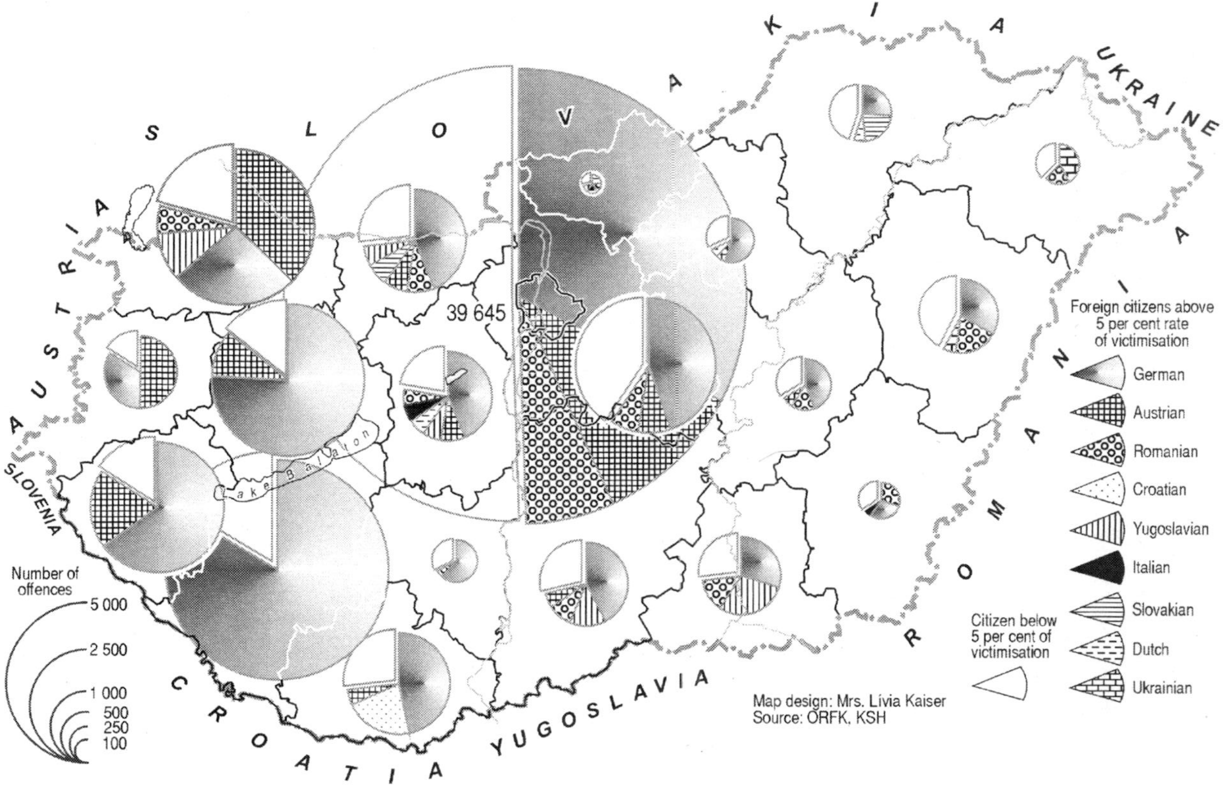

commercial accommodation facilities, international thoroughfares, and sites of multinational corporations, are visited by foreigners more than other regions of the country. When examining the victimisation of foreigners in relation to general criminal patterns context an earlier assumption about the massive influx of visitors as the primary cause of the high rate of victimisation seems to be confirmed. While approximately 31 percent of the crimes are committed in Budapest, however, the vulnerability of foreigners is higher by 20 percent as a result of their high concentration in the capital.

With regard to the spatial aspects of crime it is worthwhile to pay attention to the question of where the majority of criminal acts occur, because it may shed light on the activities of specific groups of foreigners. In most counties, the vulnerability of foreign visitors is close to the national average, but there are exceptions related to the geographical context. Thus, Romanians are clearly over-represented among the aggrieved persons in Békés County (30%), Yugoslavs in Csongrád (29.4%), Austrians in Vas (50.3%), Slovaks in Nógrád (23.1%), Ukrainians in Szabolcs-Szatmár-Bereg (41.7%), and Croatians in Baranya (21.5%). These figures show a close relationship with shopping tourism in the border zone (Michalkó and Timothy, 2001). In the two counties surrounding Lake Balaton, Germans appear to be disproportionately vulnerable to criminal acts (83.6% in Somogy County and 75.8% in Veszprém County) which is likely associated with their dominance in spending holidays along the lake.

Apart from the spatial aspects, the number of foreign visitors and the temporal distribution of criminal offences committed to their grievance also show a close relationship. As would be expected, in the off seasons, the number of offences is lower while in the high season, with the massive arrival of guests, the level of victimisation grows. Comparing monthly arrivals of people entering the country to their potential victimisation, a shift can be noted with criminal records taken at the moment of closing affairs with the end of investigations (Marosi, 1999). The spatial distribution by months, showing the most dangerous regions (Figure 2) proves that in the areas with high criminality the more frequently a certain attraction is visited, the higher the probability is of the occurrence of criminal offences. A clear example is counties surrounding Lake Balaton where after a negligible off-season, the vulnerability of foreigners as victims increases in July and August.

CONCLUSION:
THE ROLE OF CRIME PREVENTION IN TOURISM

Security is necessary for the successful growth of tourism. Thus, in the regions where there are high levels of tourism and crime, local government leaders, in addition to the operation of basic functions, should pay special attention

FIGURE 2. Temporal Distribution of Offences Committed Against Foreigners in Selected High-Crime Regions of Hungary with Increased Density of Crime (1996-2000)

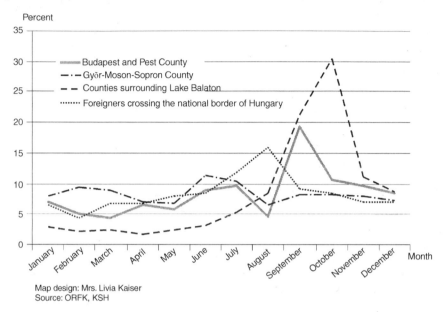

Map design: Mrs. Livia Kaiser
Source: ORFK, KSH

to the creation of a safe environment for their guests from abroad. Opinions are divided on how to relieve foreigners' fear of crime: by keeping secret the presence of crime or, on the contrary, by informing them about the possibility of being targeted and calling attention to appropriate actions that will lessen the chances of being victimized (Korinek, 1995).

To limit offences against foreign tourists, several measures have been taken recently. For example, financial support has been provided for the police by the authorities and organisations responsible for tourism (e.g., Ministry of Economy, regional commissions on tourism, local governments). The effects of criminal behaviour can be reduced by warnings addressed to the tourists or through increased police control. The police and tourist agencies ought to make tourists aware of danger by using leaflets printed in several languages and, by extension, the ways how to avoid criminal occurrences or report to the police in the case of incidents. Patrolling police create a calming effect both upon the local population and tourists; therefore, the number of police staff has been increased recently in the areas most frequented by tourists. In the frame of international collaboration, Hungarian police have begun to encourage the activities of colleagues from abroad in regions of touristic importance. Police officers wearing the uniforms of their home countries have begun to patrol together with Hungarian officers in an effort to curb intoxicated rowdy persons and limit unreasonable and fraudulent demands by entrepreneurs who claim losses. Space monitoring cameras brought into service recently have proven to be effective in tracing events at tourist centres, and the criminals' fear of getting caught will hopefully prevent them from committing future offences. In cases where the victims are foreigners, a rapid and professional administration of the European standard should follow. To attain this goal a 24-hour complaints center has been established in police stations with the involvement of student interpreters. In the city centre of Budapest there is a Tourinform bureau where police provide assistance to tourists in trouble. If measures based on crime prevention and on an efficient transaction of affairs prove to be fruitful not only for foreign visitors but also the local population, the status of public security in Hungary would improve.

REFERENCES

Cohen, E. (1996). Touting tourists in Thailand: tourist-oriented crime and social structure. In Pizam, A. and Mansfeld, Y. (Eds.), *Tourism, Crime and International Security Issues* (pp. 77-90). New York: Wiley.

Hall, C.M. (1994). *Tourism and Politics: Policy, Power and Place.* Chichester: Wiley.

Herbert, D.T. (1982). *The Geography of Urban Crime.* London: Longman.

Herold, H. (1968). *Kriminalgeographie, Ermittlung und Untersuchung der Beziengen zwischen Raum und Kriminalitat.* Hamburg: Steintor Verlag.

Korinek, L. (1995). Félelem a bünözéstől. (Fear of crime). Budapest: Közgazdasági és Jogi Könyvkiadó.

Kovács, Z. (1990). *A bünözésföldrajz szerepe a városi környezetminősítésben.* (Criminal geography in urban environment assessment). Budapest: MTA Földrajztudományi Kutatóintézet.

Marosi, L. (1999). A bûncselekmények gyakoriságának változása térben, időben. (Spatial and temporal variation in the frequency of crime). *Területi Statisztika,* 39 (1): 64-83.

McIlwaine, C. (1999). Geography and development: Violence and crime as development issues. *Progress in Human Geography,* 23 (3): 453-463.

Michalek, A. (1995). Spatial differentiation of criminality and chosen criminal acts in the Slovak Republic (on the level of districts). *Geograficky Casopis,* 47(2): 93-108.

Michalkó, G. (2001). Social and geographical aspects of tourism in Budapest. *European Spatial Research and Policy,* 8(1): 105-118.

Michalkó, G. (1996). A nemzetközi turizmus bünözésföldrajzi aspektusai Budapesten. (Criminal geographical aspects of international tourism in Budapest). *Belügyi Szemle,* 34(11): 12-30.

Michalkó, G. and Timothy, D.J. (2001). Cross-Border Shopping in Hungary: Causes and Effects. *Visions in Leisure and Business*, 20(1): 4-17.

Pain, R.H. (1991). Space, sexual violence and social control: Integrating geographical and feminist analyses of women's fear of crime. *Progress in Human Geography*, 15(4): 415-431.

Pain, R.H. (1997). Social geographies of women's fear of crime. *Transactions of the Institute of British Geographers*, 22(2): 231-244.

Pizam, A. and Mansfeld, Y. (1996). *Tourism, Crime and International Security Issues*. New York: Wiley.

Póczik, S. (1996). Rendszerváltozás és kriminalitás: Külföldiek és cigányok a bünpiacon. (Change of regime and criminality: Foreigners and Romas on the market of crime). *Valóság*, 39(6): 73-102.

Ratcliffe, J.H. and McCullagh, M.J. (1998). Aoristic crime analysis. *International Journal of Geographical Information Science*, 12(7): 751-764.

Tarlow, P. and Muehsam, M.J. (1996). Terrorism and tourism: An overview and Irish example. In Pizam, A. and Mansfeld, Y. (Eds.), *Tourism, Crime and International Security Issues* (pp. 11-22). New York: Wiley.

Vág, A. (1982). *Pillanatkép a nagyvárosi bünelkövetők makroszociológiájáról*. (Snapshot on macrosociology of urban offenders). Budapest: Közgazdasági és Jogi Könyvkiadó.

Vavró, I. (1995). A bünözési gyakoriság területi különbségei. (Spatial differences in the frequency of crime). *Statisztikai Szemle*, 73(4-5): 355-366.

Wall, G. (1996). Terrorism and tourism: An overview and an Irish example. In Pizam, A. and Mansfeld, Y. (Eds.), *Tourism, Crime and International Security Issues* (pp. 143-158). New York: Wiley.

A Local Reading of a Global Disaster: Some Lessons on Tourism Management from an *Annus Horribilis* in South West England

Tim Coles

SUMMARY. This paper describes the events of 2001 in South West England and explores their wider messages for the management of tourism in the region. The year 2001 was an *annus horribilis* for the region, witnessing as it did, first of all, an outbreak of Foot and Mouth Disease (FMD) and later, as the region began to emerge from its first crisis, the unfolding events of 09/11. This sequence of events is used as a lens through which to inspect the interaction of three sets of obviously overlapping tourism management approaches. This fusion reveals that important contradictions and tensions exist between the claims, assumptions and practices of contemporary tourism governance. A more strate-

Tim Coles is Lecturer in Human Geography and University Business Research Fellow, University of Exeter, Amory Building, Rennes Drive, Exeter, Devon, EX4 4 RJ UK (E-mail: t.e.coles@exeter.ac.uk.)

The author would like to thank Devon Books (Halsgrove Publishers) and the South West of England Regional Development Agency for their kind permission to reproduce the copyrighted material that appears in tables 3 and 5, 6 and 7 respectively.

The opinions expressed in this paper are the author's alone and the other usual caveats apply.

[Haworth co-indexing entry note]: "A Local Reading of a Global Disaster: Some Lessons on Tourism Management from an *Annus Horribilis* in South West England." Coles, Tim. Co-published simultaneously in *Journal of Travel & Tourism Marketing* (The Haworth Hospitality Press, an imprint of The Haworth Press, Inc.) Vol. 15, No. 2/3, 2003, pp. 173-197; and: *Safety and Security in Tourism: Relationships, Management, and Marketing* (ed: C. Michael Hall, Dallen J. Timothy, and David Timothy Duval) The Haworth Hospitality Press, an imprint of The Haworth Press, Inc., 2003, pp. 173-197. Single or multiple copies of this article are available for a fee from The Haworth Document Delivery Service [1-800-HAWORTH, 9:00 a.m. - 5:00 p.m. (EST). E-mail address: docdelivery@haworthpress.com].

10.1300/J073v15n02_10

gic approach to the concept of risk is required in the UK tourist "industry" since the prevailing principles and imperatives of tourism governance may have frustrated the response to events in 2001. *[Article copies available for a fee from The Haworth Document Delivery Service: 1-800-HAWORTH. E-mail address: <docdelivery@haworthpress.com> Website: <http://www.HaworthPress.com> © 2003 by The Haworth Press, Inc. All rights reserved.]*

KEYWORDS. 09/11, FMD, South West England, tourism, crisis, governance, management

09/11:
WHEN THE GLOBAL MET THE LOCAL

The world tourism industry is now beginning to turn the corner after the September 11th attack (hereafter "09/11"). According to the President of the WTTC, Jean-Claude Baumgartener, in May 2002, the world-wide industry has suffered badly due to the global impact of 09/11, with an accumulative loss of 7.4 per cent in travel and tourism demand, and the loss of 10 million job-equivalents in years 2001 and 2002. However, he expects the industry will rebound in 2003 with a growth rate of six per cent after a year of stabilisation and recovery in 2002 (Mills, S. 2002). The WTTC has not been alone in monitoring the effects of 09/11 on the tourism industry and publishing regular progress reports on the state of business. For instance, the Travel Business Partnership (2002a, 2002b) records that total visitor arrivals to New York and visitor spending dropped by 10% and 14% respectively. Similar gloomy prognoses are offered for other global destinations.

The result of such press releases and case-studies has been to develop a global narrative in which an orthodoxy of negative outcomes associated with 09/11 emerges. Of course, the power and veracity of such claims may be challenged by two immediate observations. The first is, as Stephen Smith (1998: 34-35) notes, that the WTTC is a pressure group whose role it is to project the image of tourism and to work towards the protection and advancement of its members' interests. On a less cynical note, it is clear to most observers that the situation at the local level has resolved differently to these "macro-prognostications," however subtle or radical that differentiation may be. Global signals impact upon, and are mediated by, local contexts, structures and processes (Hall, C.M. 2000; Milne and Ateljevic, 2001).

This second critique forms the basis for this paper. The year 2001 was an *annus horribilis* in South West England. Revulsion at the events of 09/11 was widespread but 09/11 happened two-thirds of the way through a year already atrociously blighted by the horror, distress and misery of a Foot and Mouth Disease (FMD) epidemic in the United Kingdom. First officially confirmed at an Essex abattoir in South East England on 19 February 2001 (Sharpley and Craven, 2001), the disease was rapidly transmitted throughout the country. The South West was soon affected. Devon, which trades on its attractive landscape, was one of the earliest and worst hit of the English counties (Mercer, 2002), second only to Cumbria in the number of confirmed cases (DCC, 2001). As will become apparent below, the FMD epidemic represented a major threat to the viability and vitality of the tourism industry as well as other sectors of the economy, not least agriculture. Recognising the gravity of this problem, local, regional and national government rallied to defend against the potentially ruinous effects of FMD on society and economy. Tourism was at the forefront of their actions in the South West in particular because of its value to the economy, its reliance on the environment in its destination marketing mix and promotional imagery, and because of the rural setting of many major attractions and accommodation units. Just as the South West started to free itself from the haunting spectre of FMD, the awful events of 09/11 unfolded. For tourism managers and producers, the central question became how would 09/11 impact on consumption: would it plunge the region back into a renewed period of depressed demand?

Events unfold at a variety of spatial scales that impact on local tourism sectors and can cause temporal market disturbances of varying duration. Moreover, the impacts of events are often felt in destinations far dislocated from where they take place. Such events take a variety of forms from natural landscape disasters to episodes of famine, disease and pestilence to wars, terrorist atrocities and political instability (Murphy, 1985; Murphy and Bayley, 1989; Poirier, 1997; Sönmez, 1998; Faulkner & Vikulov, 2001; Mazzocchi & Montini, 2001; Sharpley & Craven, 2001). As the pioneering work of Murphy (1985) suggests, such occurrences not only happen frequently, they do so with particular periodicities, almost to the point that they may be predicted (cf. McKercher, 1999; Faulkner, 2001). As work on crisis management advocates (WTO, 1998; McKercher, 1999; Boyd, 2000; Faulkner, 2001), an ideal tourism recovery scenario includes eventually returning at least to the routine (i.e., "normal") levels of production and consumption enjoyed before the "shock." Structured, deliberate planning responses such as Faulkner's (2001) "tourism disaster [survival] strategies" and Faulkner and Vikulov's (2001) "tourism management disaster plan" offer mechanisms by which equilibrium may be re-engineered.

This paper does not exclusively intend to extol the virtues of crisis management in tourism. That academic battle has been fought and largely won in theory at least (Murphy & Bayley, 1989; Hall, C.M., 1994; Poirier, 1997; McKercher, 1999; Faulkner, 2001). Unfortunately, the same cannot always be said of practice. Rather, this paper attempts to provoke wider academic debate by suggesting that mechanisms to engineer recovery should not be divorced from their wider political, intellectual, social and economic framing conditions. To a limited degree, this idea has already been floated in Poirier's (1997) exploration of political risk analysis by multi-national enterprises. However, all too often from a simple point of necessity the contextual focus of work on the impacts and management of crises, catastrophes and disasters is concentrated on the region itself and its immediate structural features and positions (Murphy & Bayley, 1989; Faulkner & Vikulov, 2001; Boyd, 2000). An inspection of the unfolding events and responses to the disasters to befall the South West in 2001 exposes limitations in the prevailing paradigm of tourism governance in the UK and other destinations subscribing to the same principles. Through the lens of the *annus horribilis*, the literature on the occurrence and outcomes of events will be coupled with the more mainstream corpus on governance. This fusion reveals that important contradictions and tensions exist between the claims, assumptions and practices of contemporary tourism governance. It becomes clear that a more strategic approach to the concept of risk is required in the UK tourist "industry." Furthermore, it proposes that the prevailing organisational principles and political imperatives of tourism governance may have conspired to frustrate the response to the events of 2001.

TERRORISM AND TOURISM, EVENTS AND RESPONSES

One of the saddest observations one can make is that 09/11 is not the first, and it will almost certainly not be the last, atrocity to have had an impact on global tourism. Without wishing to belittle the significance of this awful event, 09/11 does have to be seen in its wider historical context. As Sönmez's (1998) grim catalogue reveals, 09/11 is just one in a long line of terrorist events to befall the tourism industry. Increasingly, the relationship between tourism and terrorism is better understood. Sönmez's (1998) review reveals that the major themes to unite terrorism and tourism are the impacts of terrorism and political instability on tourism; using tourism as a political tool to advance the terrorists' agenda; the effects of political and terrorist violence on destination imagery; crisis management and recovery marketing efforts. Importantly, her review points to the differential influence and impact of individual terrorism episodes. She distinguishes between a protracted crisis as an event "which creates negative publicity and the period of time after a disaster occurrence which lasts until full recovery is achieved and pre-disaster conditions resume," while a disaster (more exactly) is "an event that abruptly causes loss of life, human suffering, public and private property damage, economic and social disruption." (Sönmez, 1998: 441). Irrespective of the gravity of the situation, she contends that the destination must manage the crisis, one pivotal element of which is the concerted marketing effort to recover lost tourism by rebuilding its positive image.

The precise nature of the marketing itself is not of interest here. Instead, the inherently cyclical nature of the recovery process is. Both Sönmez (1998) and Boyd (2000) offer conceptualisations of recovery in which, after falls induced by terrorism, tourism production and consumption levels come full circle back to those enjoyed before the event. Such expectations echo the advice offered by the World Tourism Organisation (WTO, 1998: 156) (Table 1). This pathway model is deliberately simplistic given its deployment. However, in an attempt to be accessible it glosses over important intricacies of crisis management. First, as Sönmez (1998) argues, the precise nature of, and pathways taken by, crises associated with terrorism are likely to be different to other forms of crisis. Second, the model's inherent linearity and the reduction of recovery to a set of practically automatic steps is stark. Finally, and most importantly, it views the events as

TABLE 1. The World Tourism Organizations' Advice on Crisis Management

CRISIS MANAGEMENT

An important management function is to respond rapidly and effectively to crisis situations. Crises in tourism in an area can result from many sudden problems: natural disasters such as high winds and flooding associated with major storms and earthquakes and seismic waves (tsunami) that strike tourism areas, epidemics of diseases such as cholera and hepatitis, political unrest and protests, ethnic conflicts and civil wars, violent acts of terrorism that affect tourists such as rape and murder. Typically the pattern of a tourism disaster is as follows:

- An incident occurs and the media describe the incident in [the] starkest terms, often but not always exaggerating the extent of the crisis.
- Tourists leave the area, tour operators cancel bookings and travel agents stop making sales.
- The destination suffers economically with reduced tourist arrivals and may continue experiencing poor press coverage that magnifies the effects of the incident.
- The destination commences its own media coverage, disseminating an accurate account of the situation.
- Vigorous and often expensive promotion is carried out over time and eventually tourists again visit the destination and tourism resumes its normal pattern.

Local authorities should have a disaster plan for general application in the area. The local tourism office should also have plans for action in the event of a major crisis affecting tourism. These plans should be co-ordinated with national and regional tourism disaster plans. In addition to responding to the crises with respect to health and safety of tourists, the media must be dealt with in an honest and accurate manner. . . .

Source: Abridged from WTO (1998: 156).

practically ring-fenced temporally so that there is a "normal pattern" to which production and consumption can return. Murphy's (1985: 84) work on economic cycles suggests that, rather than "steady state," fluctuating cycles of demand and consumption characterise sector performance. Similarly, in their invocation of chaos theory for crisis management in tourism, both McKercher (1999) and Faulkner (2001) note that, when not in crisis, destinations are in an extended programme of practically pre-event limbo, almost "waiting" for the important trigger event to take place which induces the need to deploy the tourism disaster strategy (cf. Faulkner, 2001). Thus, instead of being "freak," chance occurrences, crises are likely to be regular visitors in a destination's evolution, and should be factored into management plans.

According to McKercher (1999: 428), chaos theory "emerged from the realisation that many systems operated in a complex, non-linear, non-probabilistic, non-deterministic and systems manner and not as a machine." He continues to explain, "to the uninitiated, chaos implies a complete lack of order. In fact, while each element of the system may seem to act in an independent manner, collectively the entire system functions in an orderly manner that is governed by a number of underlying principles" (1999: 428). At the heart of the theory, according to Faulkner (2001: 135), is Edward Lorenz's (1993) "butterfly effect," whereby small changes or failures in the system can precipitate major displacement through mutually reinforcing positive feedback processes. Leaving aside the intricacies of chaos theory itself (see McKercher, 1999; Russell & Faulkner, 1999; Faulkner, 2001; Faulkner & Vikulov, 2001), McKercher (1999: 433) notes that one of the virtues of chaos theory is that it forces tourism managers to question the extent to which they exert "control" over the sector and they may predict future trends. By appreciating the chaotic nature of the system, he notes, tourism actors in the public and private sector may be better equipped to develop strategies and plans in response to disaster. Faulkner (2001: 143) clarifies the point by arguing that chaos theory may induce a series of events in which it may never be possible to return to the WTO's so-called "normal pattern." First, the loops and feedbacks may conspire to frustrate a return to pre-event status quo and, second, the chaos created in a crisis can be a creative process with the potential for innovative, new configurations to emerge from the ruins.

MARKET DISRUPTIONS AND THE GOVERNANCE OF TOURISM IN THE UK

Conceptualisations of responses to events sit comfortably with the management paradigm of "sustainable" (or "responsible") tourism. Over the past decade there has been a concerted global agenda to enshrine the principles of sustainable development into the production and consumption of tourism (Swarbrooke, 1999). Sustainable tourism has been become a central feature in recent UK tourism policy (DCMS, 1999; ETC, 2001). A pivotal philosophical concern, as the UK government advocates in its repackaging of the term, is to ensure "wise growth" (and hence management) of tourism now and in the future (DCMS, 1999; Church et al., 2000).

As countless authors have recognised, "sustainable tourism" represents a multi-faceted set of organising principles (see Swarbrooke, 1999). In spite of the inherent contestability of the concept, (Wheeller, 1993; Clarke, 1997; Butler, 1999), here a brief functional definition of sustainable tourism will be adopted as "tourism which meet[s] the needs of tourists, the tourism industry, and host communities today without compromising the ability of future generations to meet their own needs" (Swarbrooke, 1999: 13). According to Bramwell and Lane (1993, p. 2), sustainable tourism "is an approach which involves working for the long-term viability and quality of both natural and human resources. It is not anti-growth, but acknowledges that there are limits to growth." For them, four basic principles guide a sustainable tourism approach: holistic planning and strategy making; the importance of preserving ecological processes; the need to protect both human heritage and biodiversity; and the key requirement: to develop in such a way that productivity can be sustained over the long term for future generations (Bramwell and Lane, 1993: 2).

In the context of this paper, the first and fourth of these basic principles are most significant. The first implies that contemporary actions should be part of a more systemic programme of development which acknowledges the structures–spatial, temporal and political–in which local tourism development takes place, and which are reinforced by tourism development. With respect to the temporal, it warns against taking a very blinkered short-term approach to development. Rather, it hints that the future may not be taken for granted. Similar caution and respect for the temporal dimension is at the heart of the fourth principle. Once more this counsels prudence but preaches the gospel of inter-generational equity. This refers to the need to ensure that the legacies of a previous generation are not detrimental to its successor(s). Frequently the concept assumes environmental connotations. Contemporary tourism development in a destination must not be to the detriment of future residents' ability to make a livelihood from tourism, be it from the commodification of the natural environment or the cultural environment with its stock of heritage resources. However, unpromising inheritances are not solely a function of direct environmental defilement. Perception of environmental quality can be crucial. For instance, tourism producers and governors in post-socialist states have struggled to come to terms with enduring negative perceptions of their destinations

(Hall, D., 2000). Boyd (2000) describes how one legacy of "the troubles" in Northern Ireland has been to cast a long-term shadow over the province's image as a tourist destination, from which it is now emerging nearly five years after the 1998 "Good Friday Agreement" (cf. Sönmez, 1998). Finally, Urry (1990) cautions against the spatial fixity (and hence sunk costs) of capital invested in tourism infrastructure and accommodation only for the fickle, ephemeral tourist to switch spatial allegiances and visit destinations elsewhere (cf. Poirier, 1997).

In this context, chaos theory (or for that matter simpler conceptualisations) is usefully deployed to warn communities, especially in vulnerable destinations, against a complacent attitude towards the future. Community benefits from tourism should be secured immediately in the short term as well as into the longer term by the development of contingencies against particular occurrences which could have long and lasting impacts to the detriment of future generations. In short, the best form of attack is defence; to protect against being caught off-guard by events, and to have in place systems which allow a community to react to occurrences, but which are not so procrustean as to stifle the flexibility necessary to cater for different scenarios. Indeed, one of the appeals of disaster planning is its willingness to warn in an intelligent, yet non-alarmist manner about the future, its relative predictability, and the probable repetition of particular types of occurrences. They recognise the concerted capital, temporal and intellectual investments in the local tourism industry, their potential vulnerability to future events, and the need to act wisely to protect contemporary investments for future generations by developing practical insurances in the present.

In contrast with the obvious synergies between understanding events and sustainable tourism, the linkages between events and modes of governance remain under-explored. Within the United Kingdom as elsewhere in the western world (Harvey, 1989), more managerial modes of governance characteristic of modernity have been replaced by more entrepreneurial modes of governance which are characteristic of the (apparently) post-modern times we live in and the shift to post-Fordist patterns of production and consumption over the last three decades (Mowforth and Munt, 1998). As Michael Hall (2000: 17) outlines, within the western world in this time, there has been fundamental debate over the state's role in society and economy. As he notes, "at the national level policies of deregulation, corporatisation, privatisation, free-trade, the elimination of tax incentives and a move away from discretionary forms of macroeconomic intervention" have been the hallmarks of transition towards so-called "smaller" (central) government and reduced intervention. For Saxena (2002: 23), notable among these changes have been a blurring of the boundaries between the public and the private sectors, a shift in the public sector from direct service provision to an "enabling" function, and, as a result of these changes, the emergence of complex networks of agencies and partnerships (Rhodes, 1997; Goodwin, 1998). To this, it is important to note that localities have been forced to compete more ferociously with one another to secure investment from business and tourists (May & Newman, 1999).

In the UK this fundamental shift in the philosophy of governance has been accompanied by an emasculation of local government. Subsequent administrations in the 1980s and 1990s have cut the funding from central to local government. Furthermore, they have limited the ability of local government to raise revenue directly by local taxation. Declining contributions in relative and real terms have forced local authorities to act more proactively to discover new forms of revenue generation and to attract greater inward investment. In order to compensate for deficiencies in funding, public sector bodies have also been encouraged to develop partnerships with private sector actors, although the power relations and level of local participation have been subject to powerful critique (Goodwin, 1998; Prior, 1999; Bloomfield et al., 2001). If such reforms to local government were not enough, in the last decade government has been increasingly driven by the need to obtain "best value" in its operations (Church et al., 2000). Simply put, this mantra describes the responsibility of government agencies of all types and at all levels to find optimal solutions in terms of quality versus price for public capital investments. It reflects the ethos that government should be run as business in a strict cost-benefit manner to ensure greater efficiency and public accountability with the best returns for the tax payer. Of course, these have always been concerns of government. What has changed in the last decade has been the greater imperative to deliver efficiency in public services, given the simultaneous streamlining of government, its available resources, and its services at all spatial scales.

Tourism comes under the microscope of "best value" in several ways. Through regional tourist boards and local authorities, tourism administration represents an important generator of costs through such activities as destination marketing, spatial planning, day-to-day administration, and the delivery of tourist information, all of which have to be justified variously to management boards, politicians, tax payers and voters (Charlton & Essex, 1996; Agarwal, 1997; Godfrey, 1998; Meethan, 1998; May and Newman, 1999). Destination marketing, in particular, has been the focus of analysis in recent years. Marketing is viewed as necessary to raise awareness of destination brands and to ensure the local products remain fresh. However, marketing requires significant investment to function properly, budgets have been shrinking, and there have been increasing concerns as to whether it delivers value for money (Meethan, 1998, 2002). Further difficulties exist because the effectiveness of marketing campaigns is difficult to assess, and because even the best laid marketing plans are vulnerable to market vagaries, the inherent ephemerality of tourists, and untimely events.

In theory the three sets of concepts–crisis management planning, the sustainable approach to tourism management, and new modes of governance–would appear to be mutually inclusive and mutually reinforcing. For instance, the prudence, accountability, equity and inclusion associated with "sustainable" tourism would appear to reinforce, and should be endorsed by, the new modes of governance, the "best value" approach, and a strategic approach to risk and contingency against crises. The 'wise' use of resources advocated in 'best value' would appear to map closely with 'responsible' tourism management, and would appear to be both eruditely and logically informed by risk assessment and planning for contingencies to protect existing long term investments in the (local) "tourism industry." In what remains of this paper, the way in which these concepts resolved against one another "on the ground" during the *annus horribilis* will be sketched out.

2001 as **Annus Horribilis** *in the South West*

The South West of England comprises Cornwall, Devon, Dorset, Somerset, Bristol, Bath and North East Somerset, Wiltshire and Gloucestershire. As Meethan's (1998, 2002) work demonstrates, it is a region characterized by distinctive geographical variations in terms of product offerings and marketing mixes. In addition to traditional "bucket and spade" seaside, mass tourism resorts, the South West contains diverse cultural and heritage attractions, and is at the cutting edge of alternative modes of tourism consumption. Home to the Eden Project, the region has also recently developed a reputation as the "surf" capital of the UK, and for its Celtic culture and appeal to "new age" religions. In such a diverse region, it is difficult to establish common denominators. However, central to regional products is the environment. Coast and inland, rural areas are the most heavily commodified and consumed locations, and hence the quality of the environment–or the perception of it–in the South West is vital to commercial success. The basic dimensions of the tourism industry in the region are described in Table 2.

Administration and governance of tourism is ultimately a statutory responsibility for local authorities and the county councils (Meethan, 1998, 2002). Alongside, and often in collaboration with these agencies, functions South West Tourism (SWT), formerly the West Country Tourist Board (WCTB). In texts, regional tourist boards (RTB) are denoted in hierarchical organizational diagrams of UK tourism governance as below, and hence, by implication, connected and answerable to national tourist boards, in this case the English Tourism Council (ETC) (Holloway, 1994). In reality, while SWT may function as a

TABLE 2. The Basic Attributes of the Tourism Industry in South West England in 1997

- Accounts for one-sixth of all tourism spending in England.
- UK tourists made 21 million trips, stayed 97 million nights, and spent £3,200 million.
- Overseas guests made 2.2 million trips, stayed 19.9 million nights, and spent £728 million.
- 123 million day visits from home with associated spending of £1,826 million.
- Long holidays by UK tourists accounted for over half of nights (no growth).
- Growth of 21% in trips, 13% in nights, and 10% in real spending since 1989.
- Outperformed English average for nights and spend; loss share in trips.
- 612,000 bedspaces, 55% in caravans and 27% in hotels, guesthouses and B&Bs.
- Tourism spending accounts for 10% of GDP in region.
- Supports estimated 225,000 jobs.
- Tourism-dependent jobs account for 10% total employment in region.
- Tourism supports over 11,000 businesses, the great majority of which have under 10 staff.

Source: Compiled from WCTB (1999)

conduit for enacting ETC policies and management practices within the region, in fact it has become a private sector, non-statutory body; rather than being funded solely by direct government subvention it charges an annual membership fee and thus acts primarily to represent all its members' interests, both inside and beyond the region. With the exception of incorporating only West Dorset and South Gloucestershire, it has the same territorial coverage as the South West region as defined by central government and its Regional Development Agency (RDA).

Before proceeding, it is important to strike two short methodological notes. First, in view of the reticence of tourism stakeholders either to discuss the events of last year or to make public some of the more detailed commissioned research, it is difficult to present a very precise and intricate narrative of the South West tourism industry in 2001. Ironically (in keeping with the WTO's advice), it appears local actors were more prepared to talk to the media at the time than they are willing to talk to researchers a year on! Nevertheless, secondary sources in the form of newspaper articles, WWW archive pages, and research reports allow the salient features of 2001 to be uncovered, often by using the voices of those involved. The second is that the reader should be mindful of the positionality of many of the commentators and sources contributing to this paper, and hence the consistency and reliability of some of the data. Headline facts and figures become difficult to triangulate. Press releases, newspaper articles and research reports are not necessarily neutral, totally objective accounts, especially not when they refer to such inherently subjective and emotive experiences as crises and the efforts of regional stakeholders to develop solutions and represent their constituents.

According to Malcolm Bell, Chief Executive of SWT, the FMD outbreak had a practically immediate effect on the tourism industry in the South West (Table 3). Not only were rural attractions and farm accommodation closed for fear of transmission, coastal pathways and footways across areas without confirmed cases were closed as preventative measures against contagion. FMD decimated March and April bookings, in part because visitors believed the region, in particular Peninsula South West, was closed or they decided to go abroad because images of billowing funeral pyres stuck in their minds. Devon Farms, a private sector farm tourism marketing consortium, reported that, compared to March 2000, in March 2001 business was down by 83%, varying from 39% in the East of the County to 98% in central Devon. Overall, Easter was down by 74% (DCC, 2001).

Early research on behalf of Devon County Council points to the full magnitude of the unfolding catastrophe over the first two months (without extrapolating gross values) (Table 4). Almost a quarter of serviced accommodation had made redundancies in the face of lost bednights, while on Dartmoor a third of accommodation providers of all types had let staff go (DCC, 2001). Even locations without confirmed cases were hard hit in the early stages. Frustratingly for businesses in Exmoor National Park, 90% of accommodation establishments and 80% of retail outlets reported they were negatively affected by the outbreak. In the accommodation sector 53% of businesses recorded a loss of

TABLE 3. A Summary of the Unfolding Effects of FMD on the South West Tourism Industry

The impact of Foot and Mouth on the South West's tourism industry began towards the end of February and accelerated through March and April. The complete closure of many of the region's assets meant that all sectors of tourism suffered, albeit some suffered more than others, i.e., farm tourism, the Moors [esp. Dartmoor and Exmoor], Devon and the Forest of Dean.

This resulted in an average of 30% reduction in tourism bookings for March and more worryingly, a significant reduction in forward bookings for May, June and July. The loss of business in the South West has been calculated at £50-£60 million in March, together with a further £75 million lost in April.

The recovery commenced in May, but the losses continued to mount despite July and August having been relatively buoyant on the coast. It will not make up for the lost earnings earlier in the year. The total loss of business over the year is difficult to calculate but is likely to be in the range of £200-£300 million in the South West. The total impact is calculated by looking at the proportion of South West's tourism sector based on rural farm and moorland tourism (£2.3 billion per year).

Source: Malcolm Bell, Chief Executive of South West Tourism to the Devon FMD Inquiry. Comments quoted verbatim from Mercer's edit (2002: 65). Reprinted with permission.

TABLE 4. Selected Economic Impacts of FMD in Devon

	Camping & Caravan Sites		Serviced Accommoda-tion	Self Catering	Dartmoor*
Sample % of all in sector	8.4		7.7	12.8	30%
	Static (units)	Touring (pitch nights)	Bed nights	Unit nights	Bed nights
Cancellations by businesses	0	222	342	246	627
Cancellations by clients	232	894	5,935	1,643	3,052
Value of Lost Business	£11,700	£37,826	£576,820	£377,683	£331,699
% who have made staff redundant	27%		24%	13.2%	34%
No. of Jobs Lost	18		778	40	78

*Represents all types of accommodation.
Source: Abridged from DCC (2001) based on Tourism Associates report (18/04/01).

turnover of between 20-60%. Of greater significance was that many businesses operated across a number of sectors and as such their problems were compounded (Turner & Sheppard, 2001).

As Table 5 indicates, the effects of FMD were felt throughout the tourism sector. All forms of attractions, even those such as language schools which did not directly rely upon the landscape, were affected. Major established attractions such as those operated by the National Trust were hit hard as were the small corner shops; micro-accommodation providers were at the limits of existence, while larger accommodation providers bemoaned the decimation of their bookings; coasts, moor land, towns and cities felt the influence of FMD on arrivals and spending. Because of restrictions on activities, most tourism activity was concentrated in the coastal zones ("A story of two Easter weekends," 2002).

The South West tourism industry was unprepared for the outbreak of FMD. As far as this author can ascertain, there was no dedicated tourism crisis management strategy when the FMD crisis started. In spite of there not being structures in place to respond immediately, SWT, in particular its Chief Executive, has been singled out for praise for its response to the trying circumstances (Mercer, 2002). In keeping with standard prescriptions, marketing was ratcheted up to counteract the apocalyptic messages peddled in the media. In conjunction with SWT, the South West of England Regional Development

TABLE 5. 'Voices from Devon': Extracts of Evidence Submitted to the Devon FMD Inquiry 2001

The images of barbaric killing and primeval disposal of cattle and sheep carcasses have been transmitted around the world . . . People thought that they had gone back to the Dark Ages . . . I honestly believe we could get the business back next year with effective marketing . . . But it will not drift back on its own . . . The challenge for some businesses is to survive until Easter.

Malcolm Bell, Chief Executive, South West Tourism

The public got the idea that Devon and Cornwall was (sic.) closed....As far as the media and the public were concerned, it was essential to get the story over quickly and it was not done.

John Fowler, Chairman, John Fowler Holidays

The [National] Trust is still assessing the total cost of the outbreak on all its properties [major tourist attractions in the region] but our most up to date estimates indicate our loss to be approximately £800,000. If one uses the multiplier . . . the real loss to the economy in Devon is £5.2 million.

Mr. Cook, Devon Region, National Trust

General pattern: End February to Easter, enquiries stopped, cancellations flooded in. Cash flow dried up, so operators unable to advertise in 2002 brochures, and enhancement of facilities put on hold.
Summer: Farms near coasts, cities or with own web sites had a good July and August. Others had a patchy July, but generally a very good August.
Autumn: Very patchy. Some farms getting better bookings than last year. Others are well down. Things are well below normal for many farms and the feeling is that walkers and cyclists are not coming in their normal numbers.
Percentages by which bed and breakfast bookings were down in 2001 against the same month in 2000 for Dartmoor: March, 91% down, April, 81% down, Easter–77% down, May–65% down.

Mr. Head, Devon Farms Accommodation

Shop turnover is up to 30% down and diverse activities established to exploit tourism have all ceased.

Mr. Geeves, St Austell, Cornwall

We operate 14 self-catering holiday parks in Devon and Cornwall and accommodate in the region of 300,000 visitors each year. My company entailed approximately £1.5 million in unnecessary vacancies for accommodation compared to the previous three-year occupancy. The point I wish to make emphatically is despite Foot and Mouth there was no need for these visitors to have stayed away. When we were able to talk to clients who had booked it was easy to explain to them that Devon was not closed and seaside holiday parks continue to operate normally with virtually no inconvenience to our guests.

Mr. Fowler, Ilfracombe

We are a farm tourist attraction with over 400 animals feed and care for. We also have a caravan and camping site and a self-catering flat. Due to the Foot and Mouth crisis our business suffered substantial losses . . . We did have three camping rallies booked which should have brought us in an extra £3,500 but these were all cancelled by the Caravan and Camping Club.

Mrs. Harding, Farway

We run an English Language School for foreign adults and children. We spent a great amount of time on the phone and email informing and reassuring clients regarding the crisis . . . we had a great number of cancellations, particularly from junior groups, often as a request from their governmental authorities. Our overall bookings went down by 20% this year, going down nearly 800 student weeks . . ..

Ms. Borgen, Exeter

Source: Selected from Mercer (2002). Reprinted with permission.

Agency (SWRDA) developed a £990,000 strand devoted to "Selling the Region" as part of its £3 million programme of Action to Help Recovery in the South West which it launched on 9 April 2001 (SWRDA, 2001a). "Selling the Region" was primarily intended as a promotional action to rebuild domestic and international confidence in the South West as a destination (Tables 6 and 7). In May–that is, over two months since the first confirmed case in the UK– the SWRDA reported that brochures and newspaper supplements had been produced in advance of the Easter and Whit holidays, and that a national advertising campaign was intended for early June. (SWRDA, 2001a). When the detail emerged, "Selling the Region" entailed two phases of recovery work: an extensive first phase of marketing and promotional work; and a second, much smaller component comprising some marketing, but with an accent on assessing the penetration, power and hence value of the promotional work (SWRDA, 2001b).

"Selling the Region" comprised just under a third of the funding the SWRDA itself contributed towards recovery through its Action Plan. This was

TABLE 6. Basic Characteristics of the "Selling the Region" Strand.

	RECOVERY: PHASE ONE	RECOVERY: PHASE TWO
Approximate Time Line	TO END MARCH 2002	END SEPTEMBER 2003
Budget	£965k	£25k
Aim:	• To ensure the long-term and sustainable recovery of the region's image as a prime tourism and visitor destination.	
Objective:	• To continue to promote the *"South West of England is open for business"* message on a national and international stage.	
Delivery and contracting organisations: South West Tourism Sub-regional partnerships Devon Recovery Group Gloucester Tourism Association Farm Stay UK, Cartwheel Local business consortia	**Actions:** • Umbrella advertising; campaign addressing; tourism audiences across the UK. • PR activity to maximise media coverage. • Overseas and Internet marketing, including through sub-regional partnerships. • Devon and West Somerset to redress the damage done to the image of Devon, and specifically Dartmoor and Exmoor. • Gloucestershire promotion. Rebuild Cotswolds and Cheltenham Festival image (to Irish market).	Actions: • Farm Tourism through promotion at exhibitions, radio promotions and South West Farms web portal. • Undertake medium term intelligence research to ensure that the initiatives are delivering.

Source: SWRDA (2001b). Reprinted with permission.

TABLE 7. Detail of 'Selling the Region' Actions.

Action	Principal Features
UK-wide "Umbrella" Advertising.	• Strong national image-building campaign to combat the negative image arising from the Foot and Mouth crisis. • Uses large space newspaper advertising, billboard posters, advertising on the London Underground, third party promotions and exhibitions.
Public Relations.	• Ongoing PR support to include press visits to the region, regular media liaisons and interviews. • Specialist tourism journalists and general media.
Overseas and Internet Marketing.	• SWT will work with sub-regional partnerships to improve perception of region and win back press in major markets. • Use of Internet as a key communication to distant markets, including strengthening existing portals.
Devon and West Somerset Marketing.	• Redress the damage done to the image of Devon. • Provide specific marketing support to Dartmoor and Exmoor.
Gloucestershire Promotion.	• Strategy focusing to support Cotswolds brand in overseas markets (Northern Europe, Japan, USA and Australia). • Actions in Ireland for the 2002 Cheltenham Gold Cup. • Domestically, PR and promotions around short breaks markets, and help for walking and cycling tour operators.
Farm Tourism Promotion.	• Farm Stay UK and Cartwheel will work together to raise the profile of farm tourism • Attendance at exhibitions in 2002, radio promotions, a South West Farms web portal, promotions through gateway TICs and localised support for farm groups.
Medium Term Intelligence Research.	• Full impact of Foot and Mouth crisis on the tourism economy closely monitored to ensure money spent effectively and decline in visitor numbers is reversed. • Periodic surveys and other research will assess effectiveness and help report to funding sponsors.

Source: SWRDA (2001c). Reprinted with permission.

supplemented by a further £11 million Business Recovery Fund contributed by central government for the region and its overall economic resuscitation (SWRDA, 2002d). Put in context, according to some estimates, the tourism industry is estimated to be worth £2 billion to the regional economy, or £1,500 per resident ("A story of two Easter weekends," 2002). Tourism is clearly a key economic dynamo in the region and, when viewed in this light, on one hand it may be a little surprising that greater funding was not forthcoming to support it. On the other, given the diversity of "industry" producers, funding was available elsewhere in the wider set of recovery monies to address many of their particular needs. Questions also exist over the timing of the response. Certainly time had to be taken to appraise the situation carefully and to devise appropriate responses. Funding as well as partnerships and collaborations had to be assembled. However, throughout the intermission the tourism sector was haemorrhaging visitors and spending. Early estimates for Devon based on the situation prior to 19 March 2001 revealed that, were the FMD crisis to last for 12 months, damage to agriculture and tourism would force the local economy into recession. Nevertheless, the Devon Recovery Plan appeared in July 2001 with an impressive array of tourism measures (DCC, 2001, see also "Overhaul of tourism will help Devon," 2002). Despite the delays, the limited evidence available suggests that the crisis started to ameliorate in May and June with some, albeit limited, semblance of normality exhibited in July and August. As one commentator put it in a rather swingeing statement, "summer came and visitor numbers came back on track and eventually we managed to open rural areas and start the road to recovery" ("A story of two Easter weekends," 2002). The winners were the coastal resorts who retained visitors and benefited from trade diversion, while the rural, inland destinations still struggled to entice visitors back.

Reasons for this turnaround are difficult to assess; whether the return of visitors was a consequence of the marketing effort, or whether it was a function of the normalisation of consumer behaviour due to the gradual disappearance of the disease, or both, has unfortunately not been the subject of concerted research. Nor are they necessarily concerns for this paper. Rather, it is important to note that an event induced a significant loss of trade, significantly debilitated the sector, and exposed a lack of preparedness which reduced response. Furthermore, if the South West tourism industry was caught off-guard by FMD, it could not have anticipated it was going to face a second, potentially as damaging crisis within a year. 09/11 arrived at a pivotal moment in the recovery process. As Bell had warned (Table 5), the traditional "shoulder months" were going to be crucial if some businesses were to survive. The South West was beginning to emerge from crisis and to enjoy in some localities a relatively buoyant late season as compensation for early-season losses. In light of the perilous situations many businesses faced, and the need to pick up trade in Autumn to sustain operations through the winter, 09/11 assumed the potential to compound the impacts of FMD and threaten many enterprises with failure.

There is no doubt that 09/11 had an effect on tourism in the region (Clough, 2002); what is less clear is the precise magnitude and duration of its effects. In contrast to and perhaps because of the costs of FMD, there has been much less comment about 09/11 in the media and relatively little detailed research on its consequences has appeared regionally. A survey of business confidence in Bath, Bristol, Gloucestershire, Somerset and Wiltshire carried out shortly after 09/11 revealed that 45% of businesses enjoyed an increase in the number of domestic visitors, while conversely a half of businesses experienced a decline in visitor numbers (SWT, 2001). Anecdotal evidence privately from several tourism producers hints that 09/11 in fact offered many businesses if not a life-line then a helpful late season fillip. Although no exact data exists, it appears that visitor numbers were boosted by increases in domestic arrivals, especially from the region's core market areas of the Midlands, South and South East. Many people were deterred from taking even relatively short flights and decided not to go abroad, instead venturing to the South West for their autumn short breaks and school half-term holidays in October. Less convincing is that the region attracted some European visitors looking for longer, late holidays. Also deterred from flying, they travelled by car, ferry and/or Eurotunnel to the South West.

Unlike FMD, which has disappeared from media scrutiny, 09/11 and the war on terrorism has continued to be headline news throughout the last year. Anxiety over travelling persisted in altering demand into the first half of 2002. SWT noted in its regular review of bookings that increased bookings for the first quarter of 2002 on the previous year (i.e., just before FMD took hold) was an encouraging sign ("Bright tourism forecast with surge in bookings," 2002). However, this appears to have been predicated on domestic and short-haul demand. Tourism managers in Bath, for instance, noted during this period the benefits of a combination of domestic visitors' prolonged fear of flying and a release of pent-up demand from European visitors, with German and Spanish visitors singled out for their strong interest in the product ("Welcomed back with open arms," 2002). Unfortunately, although there were some signs of North American visitors, this sector remained stagnant ("Welcomed back with open arms," 2002). Coastal resorts such as Lyme Regis enjoyed similarly strong early season demand because, as the Leader of West Dorset District Council candidly explained, "September 11 has had a lingering effect and a lot of people are less enthusiastic about travelling abroad' ("Oh we do like to be beside the seaside," 2002). Finally, far from mere substitution and diversion, changes in consumption patterns were precipitated. Simon Bradley, Head of Operations at SWT, noted in May 2002 that more "people are booking one- and two-week stays in Devon and Cornwall, a shift away from weekenders and day trippers . . . .That is a direct result of events like September 11–confidence has been knocked and people [i.e., the domestic market] are now looking at taking their big holidays in the UK rather than abroad" ("Bright tourism forecast with surge in bookings," 2002).

Thus, three sets of outcomes from this global event are visible in the South West. The first has been an uneven decline in the number of overseas visitors to the region. The absence of long haul visitors, in particular from North America, has been felt keenly in destinations such as Bath and the Cotswolds which in the past have greatly benefited from such segments ("Britain missing out on foreign tourists," 2002). Second, in many coastal and rural destinations, anxieties over flying have manifested themselves in trade diversion as domestic visitors have returned to the region, while for short haul European visitors the region has become a more realistic and feasible option in the current geopolitical circumstances. Finally, there have been signs in 2002 of increases in the average durations of stays in the South West and hence enhanced sector performance. What remains unclear, however, is whether these outcomes represent short term adjustments or long-term, enduring changes to the region's visitor market profile and consumption. Similarly, it is difficult to gauge what has been the most significant consequence of 09/11: geographical trade diversions may have saved some businesses and induced longer stays in some destinations, but the loss of overseas visitors, especially from North America, represents a major threat to several destinations' performances and many individual businesses' profitability since such visitors are among the highest per capita spending segments. Moreover, they take considerable investments of time and finance to entice back.

DISCUSSION AND CONCLUSION

In the case of the unfolding events of 2001 one is reminded of Lady Bracknell's acerbic observation in Oscar Wilde's (1895) *The Importance of Being Earnest*: "To lose one parent, Mr Worthing, may be regarded as a misfortune; to lose both looks like carelessness." To be caught off-guard by one major disaster was bad enough, but a second could have been potentially ruinous. By the time that the 09/11 crisis was unfolding, the South West had endured and started to emerge from the FMD crisis. The full impacts of FMD and, more especially, 09/11 have not yet fully worked their way through the regional tourism sector. Although the 09/11 atrocity presented difficulties for the region, it also provided some destinations limited release from the worst pressures of the preceding months. From a chaos theory perspective, there may have been some creativity in the form of placing the South West prominently as a candidate for domestic and short-haul European vacations as well as the signs of changes in consumptive practices. Nevertheless, it has to be hoped that 09/11– with its deep impact on North American visitors' willingness to fly–does not also represent an irreversible shock; rather, the more simplistic, cyclical predictions hold true and the "normal position" is reassumed for long haul markets.

Although the recovery of English tourism is "still fragile" (ETC, 2002a), the effectiveness of the responses to 2001 have not been the central concern here (see SWRDA, 2002a). Of far greater relevance have been the manner of the responses, the sector-wide lack of preparedness, and the broader conceptual debates to which these observations speak. To bring the various strands together, it is clear through the lens of 2001 that there exists serious practical tensions and inherent contradictions between the three sets of approaches and concepts to tourism management. Given sustainable (or responsible!) tourism's interest in future outcomes and the wise use of resources, as well as best value's fascination with ensuring high quality, yet cost-efficient returns, it is disappointing that little attention has been paid to insuring contemporary investments into the future. Within the UK, there was practically no formal contingency planning in place for the tourism industry *per se* to respond to a crisis of the gravity of FMD or 09/11, nor has this featured in subsequent discussions (Morris, 2002: D26). Notwithstanding the preparation of contingency plans for future FMD outbreaks (DEFRA, 2002a, 2002b), disappointingly they only recognise the dualities between tourism and rural activities in the broadest sense. Similarly, an advisory role has been played by RTBs in the RDAs' recovery plans which themselves have economy- and society-wide remits (DCMS, 2001: 10). Such an absence of tourism-dedicated, forward thinking is at odds with the confessed "wise growth" approach at the heart of the Blair government's tourism policy (DCMS, 1999; Church et al., 2000).

Indeed, it is possible that, in spite of the theoretical synergies between the three sets of approaches, the cultures of accountability and responsibility that stem from 'best value' and, to a lesser extent, sustainable tourism may have conspired to frustrate the response to events. Best value's fascination with cost, the perceived relative infrequency of such catastrophic events, and narrow interpretations of sustainable tourism and wise use of resources, all appear to have mediated against crisis management planning. However, cost and accountability are the key issues. Budgets to RTBs have been cut in relative terms over the past decade and their roles have been reduced to ones primarily of marketing, quality assurance, enhancing competitiveness, and information provision (Agarwal, 1997; Meethan, 1998; Church et al., 2000). In 2001, SWT received £3.55 million to support its operations, comprising £0.5 million from central government, £0.75 million from the RDA, and £2.3 million from "the industry" through members' subscriptions ("Tourism boss wants fair competition deal," 2002). For the SWRDA (2002b), this level of support effectively represents a significant level of under-funding in its own right. The amount of money the region gets to support tourism is much less than given to Scotland and Wales which respectively receive £3.77 and £4.03 per head of population for tourism from government. The equivalent spend for all the English regions is £0.20.

As SWT's major priorities are the promotion of the region; quality assurance; enhancing resources, competitiveness and the skill base; understanding the visitor; and market intelligence (WCTB, 1999; see SWT, 2002), there is little slack to afford contingency planning. Moreover, at the moment it does not appear to form part of SWT's operating remit and, as Meethan (1998) notes, SWT's members have parochial interests (marketing) and very instrumental reasons for subscription (to increase turnover). Thus, from a perspective of relatively frugal resourcing and "best value," it is understandably very difficult for managers to justify any investment in, or requests to funding agencies to support, "tourism management disaster plans" (and the like) which *may never* in fact be invoked. This is in contrast to other actions which may be able to offer more tangible, immediate outcomes; which are going to be of a high quality and high level of cost-effectiveness; which are commensurate with the relatively short term nature of many funding windows; and hence which are more likely to have a greater chance of receiving support. Furthermore, the provisional nature of contingency plans is difficult to defend to subscribing industry members, many of whom are small- and medium-sized enterprises, who wish to see solid, immediate returns and value for money for their membership fees. For many, in early 2001 before FMD such planning would have been viewed dimly as luxury rather than necessity, a point exacerbated by their challenging economic circumstances.

In 2001 South West England lurched from crisis to crisis and, in a similar vein to Abraham Lincoln writing in 1864, tourism producers and governors could "claim not to have controlled events, but [had to] confess plainly that events have controlled [them]." The way forward is clear. It is imperative that the role and significance of events and their management is acknowledged by tourism governors at all levels. Readings of "best value" and "wise growth" have to integrate the temporal dimension and the likelihood of events in a more intelligent manner. Dedicated tourism crisis management strategies are required. Further research is clearly required to determine whether these should be locally-focused (cf. Agarwal, 1997; Meethan, 1998) or regionally administered (cf. Hall and Jenkins, 1995). The latter would appear to be the more attractive option given RTBs' abilities to bring together stakeholders, to access regional and central government, and to influence resource allocation. This, though, is unlikely in the short term since the position and funding of the RTBs is changing (SWRDA, 2002a, 2002c), other priorities are set to dominate the RTBs' agendas, a new lead body for tourism in England is in prospect with an as yet unresolved relationship with the RDAs and RTBs (ETC, 2002b), and there is a belief that tourism has been adequately addressed in wider recovery programming (DCMS, 2001: 10). Until this policy issue is addressed seriously, as Malcolm Bell commented in July 2002 of the recovery, "We are quite quietly confident but we are still in the hands of the weather and events" ("Welcomed back with open arms," 2002).

AUTHOR NOTE

Tim Coles' current research concerns the restructuring and political economy of the tourism sectors in South West England and Eastern Germany. He is director of Tourism Associates, a major tourism consultancy in South West England, which has had a long-standing involvement in shaping the future of the regional tourism industry. He is also Honorary Secretary of the Geography of Leisure and Tourism Research Group of the Royal Geographical Society in London, which is a new speciality group for academic research workers.

REFERENCES

A story of two Easter weekends. (2002). *North Devon Journal*. 01/04/02 [On-line edition].

Agarwal, S. (1997). The public sector: planning for renewal? In G. Shaw and A.M. Williams (Eds.), *The rise and fall of British coastal resorts* (pp. 137-158). London: Mansell.

Bloomfield, D., Collins, K. & Munton, R. (2001). Deliberation and inclusion: Vehicles for increasing trust in UK public governance? *Environment and Planning C*, 19: 501-513.

Boyd, S. (2000). Heritage tourism in Northern Ireland: Opportunity under peace. *Current Issues in Tourism*, 3(2): 150-174.

Bramwell, B. & Lane, B. (1993). Sustainable Tourism: An Evolving Global Approach. *Journal of Sustainable Tourism*, 1(1): 1-5.

Bright tourism forecast with surge in bookings. (2002). *North Devon Journal* [On-line Edition] 04/05/02.

Britain missing out on foreign tourists. (2002). *The Bath Chronicle*. 01/07/02 [On-line edition].

Butler, R. (1999). Sustainable Tourism: A State-of-the-Art Review. *Tourism Geographies*, 1(1): 7-25.

Charlton, C. & Essex, S. (1996). The involvement of district councils in tourism in England and Wales. *Geoforum*, 27(2): 175-192.

Church, A., Ball, R., Bull, C. & Tyler, D. (2000). Public policy engagement with British tourism: the national, local and European Union. *Tourism Geographies*, 2(3): 312-36.

Clarke, J. (1997). A Framework of Approaches to Sustainable Tourism. *Journal of Sustainable Tourism*, 5(3): 224-233.

Clough, M. (2002). Tourism could be set for new high. *North Devon Journal* [On-line Edition] 23/02/02.

Department of Culture, Media and Sport–Tourism Division (DCMS). (1999). Tomorrow's Tourism: A Growth Industry for the New Millennium. London: DCMS.

Department of Culture, Media and Sport–Tourism Division (DCMS). (2001). Tourism–The hidden giant–and Foot and Mouth. Government Response to the Fourth Report from the Culture, Media and Sport Select Committee, Commons Session 2000-2001. London: HMSO (CM5279).

Department for Environment, Food and Rural Affairs (DEFRA). (2002a). FMD interim contingency plan: work in progress. News Release 12 March 2002. Online available from: www.defra.gov.uk/news/2002/020312c.htm. Last accessed: 27 November 2002.

Department for Environment, Food and Rural Affairs (DEFRA). (2002b). Interim Foot and Mouth Contingency Plan (Version 2.3). London: DEFRA. Online pdf edition available from: www.defra.gov.uk/news/2002/020312c.htm. Last accessed: 27 November 2002.

Devon County Council (DCC). (2001). Devon Recovery Plan. An Integrated Plan to Help the Economy and Community Recover from the Effects of Foot and Mouth Disease. Exeter: Devon County Council.

English Tourism Council (ETC). (2001). National Sustainable Tourism Indicators. Monitoring Progress towards Sustainable Tourism in England. London: ETC.

English Tourism Council (ETC). (2002a). Recovery in English tourism 'still fragile.' Press Release 9 September 2002. Online available from: www.englishtourism. org.uk. Last accessed: 27 November 2002.

English Tourism Council (ETC). (2002b). New lead body for tourism–The process for detailed proposals begins. News Briefing 26 November 2002. Online available from: www.englishtourism.org.uk. Last accessed: 27 November 2002.

Faulkner, B. (2001). Towards a framework for tourism disaster management. *Tourism Management*, 22: 135-147.

Faulkner, B. & Vikulov, S. (2001). Katherine, washed out one day, back on track the next: A post-mortem of a tourism disaster. *Tourism Management*, 22: 331-344.

Godfrey, K. (1998). Attitudes towards 'sustainable tourism' in the UK: a view from local government. *Tourism Management*, 19(3): 213-224.

Goodwin, P. (1998). 'Hired hands' or 'local voice': Understandings and experiences of local participation in conservation. *Transactions of the Institute of British Geographers New Series*, 23: 481-499.

Hall, C.M. (1994). *Tourism and Politics· Power, Policy and Place.* Chichester: Wiley.

Hall, C.M. (2000). *Tourism Planning: Policies, Processes and Relationships.* Harlow: Prentice Hall.

Hall, C.M. & Jenkins, J. (1995). *Tourism and Public Policy.* London: Routledge.

Hall, D. (2000). Destination branding, niche marketing and national image projection in Central and East Europe. *Journal of Vacation Marketing*, 6(2): 227-237.

Harvey, D. (1989). From managerialism to entrepreneurialism: the transformation in urban governance in late capitalism. *Geografiska Annaler*, 71B: 3-17.

Holloway, J.C. (1994) *The Business of Tourism.* London: Pitman (4th Edition).

Islam, F. (2002). Take tourism seriously, say chiefs. *The Observer.* 8 September 2002. Online available from: www.guardian.co.uk. Last accessed: 27 November 2002.

Lorenz, E. (1993). *The Essence of Chaos.* Washington: The University of Washington Press.

May, J. & Newman, K. (1999). Marketing: A new organising principle for local government? *Local Government Studies*, 25: 16-33.

Mazzocchi, M. & Montini, A. (2001). Earthquake effects on tourism in central Italy. *Annals of Tourism Research*, 28(4): 1031-1046.

McKercher, B. (1999). A chaos approach to tourism. *Tourism Management*, 20: 425-434.

Meethan, K. (1998). New tourism policy for old? Policy developments in Cornwall and Devon. *Tourism Management*, 19(6): 583-593.

Meethan, K. (2002). Selling the difference: tourism marketing in Devon and Cornwall, South-west England. In R. Voase (Ed.), *Tourism in Western Europe: A Collection of Case Histories* (pp. 23-42). Wallingford: CAB International.

Mercer, I. (2002). Final Report. Crisis and Opportunity. Devon Foot and Mouth Inquiry 2001. Tiverton, UK: Devon Books.

Mills, S. (2002). Tourism leaders meet in Paris to develop future for industry. Press Release circulated, World Travel and Tourism Council, 10th May 2002.

Milne, S. & Ateljevic, I. (2001). Tourism, economic development and the global-local nexus: theory embracing complexity. *Tourism Geographies*, 3(4): 369-394.

Morris, H. (2002). Rural tourism: Post FMD, will they come flocking back? *Insights*, January 2002: D21-D26.

Mowforth, M. and Munt, I. (1998) *Tourism and Sustainability: New Tourism in the Third World*. London: Routledge.

Murphy, P.E. (1985). *Tourism: A Community Approach*. London: Routledge.

Murphy, P.E. & Bayley, R. (1989) Tourism and disaster planning. *Geographical Review*, 79(1): 36-46.

Oh we do like to be beside the seaside. (2002). *The Bath Chronicle*. 10/06/02 [On-line edition].

Overhaul of tourism will help Devon. (2002). *North Devon Journal*. 15/05/02 [On-line edition].

Poirier, R. (1997). Political risk analysis and tourism. *Annals of Tourism Research*, 24(3): 675-686.

Prior, D. (1999). 'Working the network': Local authority strategies in the reticulated local state. *Local Government Studies*, 25: 93-104.

Rhodes, R. (1997). *Understanding Governance*. Buckingham: Open University Press.

Russell, R. & Faulkner, B. (1999). Movers and shakers: Chaos makers in tourism development. *Tourism Management*, 20: 411-423.

Saxena, G. (2002). An examination of relationships and networks in sustainable tourism: issues related to tourism provision in the Peak District National Park. University of Staffordshire, UK: Doctoral dissertation.

Sharpley, R. & Craven, B. (2001). The 2001 Foot and Mouth crisis–Rural economy and tourism policy implications: a comment. *Current Issues in Tourism*, 4(6): 527-537.

Smith, S. (1998). Tourism as an industry: Debates and concepts. In D. Ioannides & K. Debbage (Eds.), The Economic Geography of the Tourist Industry (pp. 31-52). London: Routledge.

Sönmez, S.F. (1998). Tourism, terrorism and political instability. *Annals of Tourism Research*, 25(2): 416-456.

South West Regional Development Agency (SWRDA). (2001a). Action to help recovery in the South West. Press Release update May 2001. Online available from: www.southwestrda.org.uk. Last accessed: 11 July 2002.

South West Regional Development Agency (SWRDA). (2001b). Selling the Region. Press Release update 22 June 2001. Online available from: www.southwestrda. org.uk. Last accessed: 11 July 2002.

South West Regional Development Agency (SWRDA). (2001c). Selling the Region. Press Release update May 2001. Online available from: www.southwestrda. org.uk. Last accessed: 11 July 2002.

South West Regional Development Agency (SWRDA). (2001d). Action Plan–Responding to the Economic and Social Impact of FMD in the South West of England. Press Release update 18 July 2001. Online available from: www.southwestrda. org.uk. Last accessed: 11 July 2002.

South West Regional Development Agency (SWRDA). (2002a). South RDA and South West Tourism welcome new future for tourism. Press Release 31 October 2002. Online available from: www.southwestrda.org.uk. Last accessed: 27 November 2002.

South West Regional Development Agency (SWRDA). (2002b). Welcome for new regional tourism role. Press Release 14 May 2002. Online available from: www. southwestrda.org.uk. Last accessed: 27 November 2002.

South West Regional Development Agency (SWRDA). (2002c). A new future for tourism. Press Release 22 October 2002. Online available from: www.southwestrda. org.uk. Last accessed: 27 November 2002.

South West Tourism (SWT). (2001). Final Report into the Immediate Effect on the Tourism Industry in Bath, Bristol, Gloucestershire, Somerset and Wiltshire of the September 11th Tragedy. Exeter: South West Tourism.

South West Tourism (SWT). (2002). About South West Tourism: Aims of South West Tourism. Online available from: www.swtourism.co.uk. Last accessed: 27 November 2002.

Swarbrooke, J. (1999). *Sustainable Tourism Management*. Wallingford: CAB International.

Tourism boss wants fair competition deal. (2002). *North Devon Journal* [Online Edition]. 01/05/02.

Travel Business Partnership. (2002a). New York City. *City Profiles*, 1 (March): 12-14.

Travel Business Partnership. (2002b). Comment: Measuring the real impact of September 11. *Travel Market Monitor*, 1 (April): 3-4.

Turner, M. & Sheppard, A. (2001). *The Economy of Exmoor National Park: A Brief Review of the Impact of the FMD Epidemic*. Exeter: University of Exeter–Agricultural Economics Unit.

Urry, J. (1990). The *Tourist Gaze: Leisure and Travel in Contemporary Societies*. London: Sage.

Welcomed back with open arms. (2002). *The Bath Chronicle*. 05/05/02 [Online edition].

West Country Tourist Board (WCTB). (1999). *Towards 2020. A Tourism Strategy for the South West*. Exeter: WCTB.

Wheeller, B. (1993). Sustaining the Ego. *Journal of Sustainable Tourism*, 1(2): 121-9.

World Tourism Organization (WTO). (1998). *Guide for Local Authorities on Developing Sustainable Tourism*. Madrid: WTO.

Crisis Communication and Recovery for the Tourism Industry: Lessons from the 2001 Foot and Mouth Disease Outbreak in the United Kingdom

Brent W. Ritchie
Humphrey Dorrell
Daniela Miller
Graham A. Miller

SUMMARY. As the number of disasters and crises affecting the tourism industry increases, it is becoming necessary to understand the nature of these disasters and how to manage and limit the impacts of such incidents. This paper defines crises and disasters before discussing the area

---

Brent W. Ritchie is Senior Lecturer, School of Service Management, University of Brighton, 49 Darley Road, Eastbourne, BN20 7UR, United Kingdom (E-mail: b.ritchie@bton.ac.uk) and Tourism Program, University of Canberra, ACT 2601, Australia. Humphrey Dorrell and Daniela Miller are former Honour Students, School of Service Management, University of Brighton, 49 Darley Road, Eastbourne, BN20 7UR, United Kingdom. Graham A. Miller is Senior Lecturer, Centre for Tourism, University of Westminster, London, United Kingdom (E-mail: G.Miller01@wmin.ac.uk).

The authors wish to thank the participants from the organisations that were directly involved in the research projects. However, as always the interpretation of data collected and any omissions are the responsibility of the authors alone.

[Haworth co-indexing entry note]: "Crisis Communication and Recovery for the Tourism Industry: Lessons from the 2001 Foot and Mouth Disease Outbreak in the United Kingdom." Ritchie, Brent W. et al. Co-published simultaneously in *Journal of Travel & Tourism Marketing* (The Haworth Hospitality Press, an imprint of The Haworth Press, Inc.) Vol. 15, No. 2/3, 2003, pp. 199-216; and: *Safety and Security in Tourism: Relationships, Management, and Marketing* (ed: C. Michael Hall, Dallen J. Timothy, and David Timothy Duval) The Haworth Hospitality Press, an imprint of The Haworth Press, Inc., 2003, pp. 199-216. Single or multiple copies of this article are available for a fee from The Haworth Document Delivery Service [1-800-HAWORTH, 9:00 a.m. - 5:00 p.m. (EST). E-mail address: docdelivery@haworthpress.com].

of crisis communication management and crisis communication in the tourism industry. The paper then applies the foot and mouth disease (FMD) which occurred in the United Kingdom to crisis communication theory at a national level (by examining the response of the British Tourist Authority) and at a local level (by examining the response of a District Council). The response was limited in part because of a lack of preparedness, but also due to the nature of the foot and mouth outbreak, and the speed and severity of international media coverage. Action was taken in the emergency phase of the crisis and was reactive involving inconsistency in developing key messages to stakeholders, partly due to confusion and a lack of information at the national level. Recovery marketing was also limited due to the length of time of the disease outbreak. This paper provides lessons for destinations and organisations are discussed which may help develop crisis communication strategies for tourism organisations. *[Article copies available for a fee from The Haworth Document Delivery Service: 1-800-HAWORTH. E-mail address: <docdelivery@haworthpress. com> Website: <http://www.HaworthPress.com> © 2003 by The Haworth Press, Inc. All rights reserved.]*

KEYWORDS. Tourism, disaster, crisis, communication, United Kingdom, foot and mouth

INTRODUCTION

In February 2001, the first case of Foot and Mouth Disease (FMD) was confirmed in the UK since an outbreak of the disease in 1967. A total of 2,030 cases of the disease were identified and a total of over 4 million animals were culled during the crisis with worldwide media broadcasts showing burning carcasses of culled animals. The English Tourism Council (ETC) predicted that losses to English tourism in 2001 would be £5bn, while in 2002 and 2003 reductions would total £2.5bn and £1bn respectively (ETC, 2001a). On January 15, 2002, government officials announced that the disease had finally been defeated after 11 months of battling the outbreak. Despite the end of the disease, the outbreak has deeply affected the farming and tourism industry and raised questions concerning government policy toward the farming and tourism industry. Questions have been specifically raised concerning the responsiveness and preparedness of the tourism industry for the FMD and the ability of tourist promotion agencies to reduce the negative media coverage due to slow response time. Although the outbreak was not expected, Faulkner (2001) notes there are an increasing number of disasters and crises which affect the tourism industry, ranging from natural to human influenced disasters. This has been made most evident since the events of September 11, 2001, which dramatically impacted upon the tourism industry illustrating the need to understand and effectively manage such incidents, with crisis communication an important part of this management.

Faulkner (2001) argues that there is a lack of research on disaster phenomena in the tourism industry, on the impacts of such events on both the industry and specific organisations, and the responses of the tourism industry to disasters. Yet Lee and Harrald (1999:184) note that crisis management, disaster recovery, and organisational continuity are important competencies for managers in both the public and private sector. This paper aims to address these deficiencies as well as to consider FMD in the light of crisis communication, as it appears that communication is an important aspect of effectively and efficiently dealing with crisis situations. An examination of the management of the FMD and the crisis communication strategies employed may assist other destinations and organisations in developing crisis management and crisis communication strategies to deal with unforeseen events. First a discussion of crisis management definitions and crisis communication theory takes place prior to discussion of crisis communication specifically for the tourism industry. Then the paper outlines the research methods and research findings related to crisis communication and the FMD outbreak in the UK.

CRISIS AND DISASTER DEFINITIONS

A number of authors have attempted to define a crisis to help improve their understanding of this phenomenon. Pauchant and Mitroff (1992:15) believe that a crisis is a "disruption that physically affects a system as a whole and threatens its basic assumptions, its subjective sense of self, its existential core." Selbst (1978 in Faulkner, 2001:136) defines a crisis as "any action or failure to act that interferes with an organisation's ongoing functions, the acceptable attainment of its objectives, its viability or survival, or that has a detrimental personal effect as perceived by the majority of its employees, clients or constituents." Selbst focus on perceptions implies that if an organisation's publics or stakeholders perceive a crisis, a real crisis could evolve from this misconception, illustrating that perception management is a key activity in managing crises.

Faulkner (2001) considers the principal distinction between what can be termed a "crisis" and a "disaster" to be the extent to which the situation is attributable to the organisation itself, or can be described as originating outside the organisation. Thus, a "crisis" describes a situation "where the root cause of an event is, to some extent, self-inflicted through such problems as inept management structures and practices or a failure to adapt to change," while a "disaster" can be defined as "where an enterprise . . . is confronted with sudden unpredictable catastrophic changes over which it has little control" (Faulkner, 2001:136).

Crisis Management and Control

Lee and Harrald (1999:184) state that "natural disasters can disrupt the supply and distribution chains for even the best prepared businesses . . . service businesses are increasingly vulnerable to electrical, communication and other critical infrastructure failures." Kash and Darling (1998:179) agree, and claim that it is no longer a case "if" a business will face a crisis; it is rather a question of "when," "what type" and "how prepared" the organisation is to deal with it. Both statements illustrate that although organisations are able to design pre-crisis strategies to help with crisis management they are often unable to prevent a crisis from occurring. However, the real challenge is to recognise crises in a timely fashion and implement coping strategies to limit their damage (Darling et al., 1996). Authors such as Burnett (1998) and Kash and Darling (1998) note that decisions undertaken before a crisis occurs will enable more effective management of the crisis, rather than organisations being managed by the crisis and making hasty and ineffective decisions. Proactive planning through the use of strategic planning and issues management will help reduce risk, time wastage, poor resource management and reduce the impacts of those that do arise (Heath, 1998).

Coombs (1999) notes that all crises are different and crisis managers need to tailor responses to individual crises rather than try to plan for every individual situation. Heath (1998:272) agrees and states that "no crisis has exactly the same form, the same time limitations, the same demand for resources . . . or the same temporal, social and economic threats." In addition crises are indefinite, numerous, unexpected and unpredictable (Parsons, 1996; Williams et al., 1998). Authors such as Kash and Darling (1998) believe that although crisis management is a requirement for organisations, and although business leaders recognise this, many do not undertake productive steps to address crisis situations.

Other crisis management research has focussed on the stages of crises to assist in understanding crisis phenomenon and assist in proactive and strategic management of crises (see Richardson, 1994; 1995). Fink (1986) and Roberts (1994) both developed slightly different models to explain the lifecycle of crises (see Table 1). Faulkner (2001) developed the first tourism specific disaster

TABLE 1. The Crisis and Disaster Lifecycle

Faulkner's (2001) stages	Fink's (1986) stages	Robert's (1994) stages
1. Pre-event		*Pre-event:* where action can be taken to prevent disasters (e.g., growth management planning or plans aimed at mitigating the effects of potential disasters)
2. Prodromal	*Prodromal stage:* when it becomes apparent that the crisis is inevitable	
3. Emergency	*Acute stage:* the point of no return when the crisis has hit and damage limitation is the main objective	*Emergency phase:* when the effects of the disaster has been felt and action has to be taken to rescue people and property
4. Intermediate		*Intermediate phase:* when the short-term needs of the people must be dealt with– restoring utilities and essential services; the objective at this point being to restore the community to normality as quickly as possible
5. Long term (recovery)	*Chronic stage:* clean-up, post-mortem, self-analysis and healing	*Long-term phase:* continuation of the previous phase, but items that could not be addressed quickly are attended to at this point (repair of damaged infrastructure, correcting environmental problems, counselling victims, reinvestment strategies, debriefings to provide input to revisions of disaster strategies)
6. Resolution	*Resolution:* routine restored or new improved state	

Source: Reprinted from *Tourism Management*, 22 (2), Faulkner, B., Towards a framework for tourism disaster management, page 140, copyright (2001) with permission from Elsevier Science.

management framework and subsequently applied this framework to the Katherine Floods in Australia (see Faulkner & Vikulov, 2001).

Although understanding the nature of crises is important, understanding how to manage crises is more critical. In particular, managing communication and perceptions through a crisis communication strategy can limit the negative media coverage and manage perceptions both during a crisis or disaster and at the recovery/resolution stage. Crisis communication and marketing is important to provide information to key publics and to help tourism destinations limit the impact of a crisis as well as help them recover from incidents by safeguarding the destination image and reputation which is of immense value to tourism destinations. The development of crisis communication and marketing strategies by organisations is therefore a critical competency for tourism managers.

Crisis Communication and Crisis Marketing

Crisis management literature emphasises the need to have a detailed communication strategy as the media can encourage the flow and the intensity of a crisis or even turn an incident into a crisis (Keown-McMullan, 1997). Barton (1994) believes that a strategic crisis plan can help limit the damage from a crisis and allow an organisation to concentrate on dealing with the crisis at hand. Marra (1998:461) notes that poor communication strategies can often make the crisis worse as a deluge of questions is often asked from a wide range of stakeholders including reporters, employees, stockholders, government officials and public residents. The initial response is important and Table 2 illustrates five main considerations for responding to crises.

Responding quickly to demands of the media and publics is important as the media have deadlines to work to and are looking for quick sources of information. If the crisis team does not fill the void, someone else will (Coombs, 1999). Zerman (1995:25) agrees stating that "the mass media has the power to make a break a business." Sensationalist media coverage of the 1980 Mt. St. Helens disaster and the 1985 East Kootenay forest fires were noted as contributing to confusion during the emergency phase as the media were blamed for misleading public opinion concerning the severity of the disasters. This also impacted upon the long term recovery phase for the destination (see Murphey and Bayley, 1989). However, difficulties have been noted in managing the me-

TABLE 2. Five-Point Crisis Communication Plan

Point	Action
1.	Respond quickly. Develop two-way communication with the media to provide accurate information to key stakeholders. This will reduce misinformation and help develop a consistent message.
2.	Give instructing information such as what happened, when it happened, where it took place, and how it occurred. Also discussion of the precautions stakeholders should take and what corrective action is being undertaken.
3.	Consistency in developing the communication plan and key messages including discouraging any unofficial spokespersons.
4.	Openness and accessibility including availability of spokespersons and generating a willingness to disclose information and being honest.
5.	Express sympathy to victims.

Source: Adapted after Berry (1999) and Coombs (1999:114).

dia as it is unlikely that there will be a time delay between the start of any crisis and media coverage (Ashcroft, 1997).

Crisis communication is mainly concerned with providing correct and consistent information to the public and enhancing the image of the organisation or industry sector faced with a crisis. An emphasis on communication and public relations is required to limit harm to an organisation in an emergency that could ultimately create irreparable damage. Co-operation with the media is considered vital because the media provides information to the public (Berry, 1999), illustrating the need to keep the media briefed frequently so misinformation is reduced. Regular two-way communication is the best way of developing a favourable relationship with publics (Coombs, 1999:134). Consistency of response is also noted as a key element in crisis communication. The ability to provide a consistent message to all stakeholders will build credibility and preserve the image of an organisation instead of tarnishing reputations through providing inconsistent messages (Coombs, 1999). Barton (1994) believes that many issues are overlooked by crisis managers regarding crisis communication, namely to focus on identifying the audience, developing goals for communicating effectively and creating strong positive messages.

Marketing and advertising is also noted as an important part of crisis communication, especially during the long term recovery stage of a crisis or disaster. As Heath (1998:26) notes "crisis management is as much about dealing with human perceptions about the crisis as it is about physically resolving the crisis situation." This suggests that crisis communication is an essential part of managing crises and disasters and will be an important consideration for the tourism industry.

Crisis Communication in the Tourism Industry

Despite the susceptibility of the tourism industry to external and internal crises and disasters, and the importance of destination image and marketing, little research has been undertaken concerning crisis communication for the tourism industry. As Beeton (2001:422) notes:

> crises occur at all levels of tourism operations with varying degrees of severity, from much publicised environmental economic and political disasters through to internally generated crisis such as accidents and sudden illness.

Crises can impact negatively upon destination image, especially if it is dramatised or distorted through rumours. Henderson (1999:108) states that "National Tourist Organisations with their responsibility for general destination marketing, research and development have an important role to play in the process of travel and tourism crisis management, representing and acting on behalf of the industry as a whole." This quote emphasises the importance of a national tourist organisation in responding to crises, implementing crisis communication strategies and designing recovery marketing campaigns. However, Henderson (1999) found that in the case of the Asian Economic Crisis, the Singapore Tourist Board implemented reactive strategies which took time to implement reducing their effectiveness.

Sönmez et al. (1999) noted the importance for marketers to have a prepared crisis communication and marketing plan, as the cost of this will be far less than the costs associated with a downturn in visitor confidence and visitation due to a slow response. Sönmez et al. (1999) suggest several ways to improve crisis communication for tourism crisis management including the preparation of a task force involving the private and public sector including a PR team, recovery marketing team, information coordination team and a finance and fund raising team.

The development of Fiji's Tourism Action Group (TAG) during the military coups illustrates the advantages of forming such as group. Fiji's tourist industry responded faster than expected because of the implementation of a task force combined with target marketing to restore confidence. As Sönmez et al. (1999:8) note "it is imperative for destinations to augment their crisis management plans with marketing efforts, to recover lost tourism by rebuilding a positive image."

RESEARCH METHODS

Research was carried out to examine the effectiveness of the crisis communication of the British Tourist Authority at the national level and an unnamed District Council at the local level in England. This research was carried out by two separate yet linked research projects that explored similar themes concerning crisis communication specifically associated with the FMD in the United Kingdom.

Secondary and Primary Research Strategy

Throughout both pieces of research, the researchers undertook thorough secondary data analysis of press releases, newspaper articles, position statements and relevant marketing documents and policies related to the FMD and the organisations under study. Primary research was carried out in both pieces of research through the use of in-depth semi-structured interviews to supplement the secondary data collected. All interviews were undertaken in January and February 2002 and the following outlines the procedures undertaken for each project.

In the study at the national level, tourism representatives were selected judgementally from the British Tourist Authority (BTA) and key industry sector groups that represent the national interests of tourism and hospitality businesses. These representatives were interviewed for between 45 minutes and an hour and a half, and a tape recorder was used to record the interviews for later transcription. All were interviewed concerning the response of the British Tourist Authority to the crisis and their effectiveness in implementing crisis communication strategies. Although the BTA was the focus of the study, in order to avoid bias other tourism organisations were selected on the basis of their ability to judge the effectiveness of BTA's crisis marketing and communication strategy. Representatives from the various industry organisations were elite interviews at the managerial or CEO level and were well informed and had a high level of expertise and knowledge. Something which Saunders et al. (2000) note is important in undertaking a judgmental sample selection. Confidentiality was provided to all respondents and therefore no respondents are identified in this paper. From the literature several themes were investigated within the interviews and corresponded with Coombs' (1999) themes for responding to crises through communication. The researcher classified the data into emerging themes based upon Coombs' (1999) classification and transcribed, read and re-read the transcriptions before placing comments into themes which are discussed in the results below.

In the study at the District Council level tourism representatives were selected judgementally from the District Council and also included 5 representatives from the accommodation industry, local tourism attraction and visitor group, the National Trust, and an individual operator. They were interviewed for between 45 minutes and an hour and a half while Faulkner's (2001) disaster response grid and disaster framework were used as a guide to the semi-structured interviews. The representative of the District Council was interviewed first and then industry representatives were interviewed. Similar to the national level study the researcher tape-recorded and transcribed the interviews and placed them into themes based on Faulkner's (2001) tourism disaster framework model and relating them to crisis communication theory and literature where applicable.

Potential Limitations and Bias

Although relevant industry and government representatives were interviewed concerning crisis communication strategies implemented by the BTA and the District Council, these representatives do not represent the views of industry who do not belong to these organisations or who do not share their view. The BTA and the District Council avoided answering some questions directly in relation to its activities. Although other organisations were able to examine the role of the BTA and District Council, as Alreck and Settle (1997) note, affinity bias may exist as some of these representatives have a close working relationship with the organisations under study. Some respondents may have been concerned that their comments would make their way back to these organisations, despite assurances of confidentiality.

Interviewer bias is possible but was reduced through the use in both instances of semi-structured techniques and a set of themes developed from the literature which were used to structure the interview. Researchers did not make any personal opinions during the interviews and used a similar tone of voice and dress throughout, which have been noted to minimise interviewer bias (Saunders et al., 2000).

RESULTS AND DISCUSSION

Due to space constraints not all results can be presented in this paper. The following section first outlines the development of a crisis response strategy, before discussing respondents response time, the consistency of crisis communication strategies, access to information, and finally, the implementation of recovery marketing strategies. Where applicable the results are compared and contrasted with literature and theory discussed earlier in the paper.

Crisis Response Strategy

At the national level tourism industry representatives believed that the BTA failed to react sufficiently and effectively, as they did not appear to have a crisis management strategy in place prior to the outbreak. Nevertheless, the BTA stressed that they did have a "fairly basic crisis management strategy in place" although the British Hospitality Association believed that it was too little too late (Cotton, 2001). Having an established and formal crisis communication strategy may have reduced the response time and developed quicker communication channels to facilitate the distribution of information and the reduction in inconsistent messages (discussed later). The BTA excused the insufficiency by explaining that the intensity of the FMD could not be forecast. Nevertheless, they acknowledged that the FMD has taught them "how to have an even better crisis response strategy (in the future)."

Similar findings were discovered at the local level with the District Council noting that "there was something on file from the previous foot and mouth outbreak but not much . . . there was only a rumour that there was one (a disaster plan) lying around." Although they did have one regarding foot and mouth it was last examined briefly after the 1967 outbreak. Furthermore, from industry representatives interviewed none had a crisis plan in place for their own business before the outbreak. Perhaps more surprisingly the tourism industry seemed to have learnt little from their experience at the local level. According to one representative "I don't know whether people would have (a plan) in the future because I think that people felt that it has happened once and couldn't happen again." Only two people expressed an interest in developing a crisis management plan in the future, because crises are seen as infrequent and that little can be done to alter their impacts. The only contingency considered was setting aside money and resources to deal with unforeseen events. However, crisis management theory suggests that established plans can limit the severity of crises and disasters through proactive contingency planning (Kash and Darling, 1998; Heath, 1998).

Response Time in the Emergency Phase

Because of a combination of a delay in identifying foot and mouth, a disbelief of the severity of such a crisis and a lack of proactive planning, there was a delay in reacting to the crisis by the tourism industry at both a national and local level. Both the BTA and industry at the national and local level only accepted the implications of the outbreak at the emergency phase and reacted only due to negative publicity. The BTA in their media releases noted this in a statement issued by the head of EU Affairs in Brussels which stated "in dealing with the Belgian media, the current tactics are more reactive than proactive" (BTA 2001a). Although in the personal interview the BTA insisted that they reacted within the first three days of the outbreak it was not until 28 March (one month later) that a BTA board meeting took place to co-ordinate communications and prepare a recovery plan for England. Industry representatives at the national level agreed that the response of the tourism sector generally had been slow and the power and effect of the media had been under-evaluated. However, the response of the BTA was to attempt to market and improve the image of the UK to target markets but this process was hampered by the ongoing outbreak and continued spread of the disease throughout the UK.

At the local level, the majority of respondents did not believe the implications of the outbreak until the emergency phase. According to one respondent "we knew what was going on, but we were trying not to think about it." Furthermore, another respondent described decision making as "mainly stabbing in the dark." This slow response could be because the initial outbreaks were in other districts and there seemed to be confusion about the potential impacts and what should be done about them. Little communication was occurring between decision makers at the national level and the local level. A lack of knowledge of the disease and its implications meant that footpaths and attractions were closed and the District Council sought advice over what to do as they did not want to put tourism businesses at risk. This decision making was further complicated by mixed messages at the national level by government over whether the countryside was closed or actually open for business, illustrating that consistency in responding to the crisis and communicating positive messages to key audience groups was lacking.

Inconsistency of Responses

This inconsistency of messages sent out by tourism organisations and other government agencies involved in handling the disease impacted upon the dissemination of facts and figures concerning the disease, but more importantly confused potential tourists' and the tourism industry. Coombs (1999) suggests that consistency is important to avoid speculation and confusion. In the case of the FMD both were evident at the national and local level. The international market confused the outbreak with the BSE disease and some had the perception that it was deadly to humans. The domestic public was unsure whether they should try and help rural economies by visiting such areas or whether they could best help by staying home and not spreading the disease. This statement is supported by market research conducted by the English Tourism Council (2001b) that showed consumers were still confused in June 2001, several months after the outbreak. Contradicting statements were being published and this was even more confusing by the fact that many areas were totally unaffected by the disease. The BTA representative interviewed noted that there was no united approach and that different messages and statements were provided by different tourism and hospitality organisations.

Another potential problem which resulted in inconsistency in messages was the encroaching deadline for the government to announce a general election. The government held a strong lead over political rivals in the polls and had made little secret of its desire to face a spring election. However, the images of burning cows saturating news coverage meant an early election was impossible unless the disease could be eradicated without risking the rural vote that was heavily influenced by the farmers. Yet, the crisis/disaster conflict reflects the multi-sectoral nature of industry in rural areas, and there was disagreement over how the emergency stage should be handled and whether vaccination would be a better strategy than burning animals. This debate was held during the emergency phase of the outbreak which suggests that decisions may not have been made with thorough consideration for their impacts. It was the policy of slaughter and burn that ensured a negative media coverage and images, severely damaging the tourism industry.

Inconsistency also occurred at the local level according to respondents. The District Council felt that in hindsight a more consistent approach was required. The Council stated "we were all calling for consistency at the same time, but the situation was moving so fast that no one seemed to be able to do it. I received 145 e-mails during this period, a lot of these were policy documents, technical specifications and general advice that would change day by day and area by area." This lack of consistency was not the fault of the District Council but their inability to answer queries created an information void and created what one respondent termed a "knee jerk response." The combination of resources between the District Council (local level) and the County Council (regional level) also caused inconsistency and contradictory advice. As the District Council respondent noted, "the County Council had put notices and signposts at the local level which stated that most footpaths in the County are closed, which was not effective when at the local level we were trying to encourage people to come to the area." It was not until after April 2001 and the immediate phase of the crisis that co-ordination between the two bodies led to more consistency, but by then rumour and confusion had a damaging effect. One of the major reasons for this lack of consistency according to local level respondents was a lack of access to relevant information.

Access to Information

The BTA felt that the media was very intense for the first three months and at times their reporting was hostile, sometimes neutral but rarely friendly leading to misinformation (BTA 2001b). The BTA set up an Immediate Action Group (IAG) consisting of internal BTA staff from a range of departments to help implement strategies regarding the outbreak. The BTA also implemented a number of other measures to provide better access to information and provide consistent and positive messages which are outlined in Table 3.

Initially access to information was difficult due to uncertainty and slow response of the national government. Although the development of communication channels was created by the BTA as information and policy was developed, many industry operators were simply unable to access some of the information due to a lack of e-mail and Internet facilities. For instance, in the South East of England only 60% of Tourist Information Centres had e-mail facilities and prior to the outbreak only six out of ten Regional Tourist Boards had web sites (DCMS 2001). The web site, however, was useful for providing information to potential overseas visitors.

TABLE 3. British Tourist Authority Aim and Major Strategies to Limit Severity of the Foot and Mouth Outbreak

Aim	• To correct misleading information in their overseas markets concentrating on the ones that had been most severely hit by the crisis.
Strategies	• They employed a global PR agency to manage the negative perceptions of Britain overseas. • A new web site provided information on whether attractions and events were open and showed that by Easter 80% of attractions were actually open. • The development of media bulletins and newsletters were also used to facilitate the exchange of information.
Aim	• To assure summer holiday bookings and provide correct and consistent messages.
Strategies	• Including market research and tactical advertising to assure summer holiday bookings. • An e-mail campaign to 10 million people world wide. • A number of trade and press trips.
Aim	• To re-brand and re-market Britain as a tourist destination to aid in the recovery of the tourism destination.
Strategies	• UK OK and "Only in Britain: Only in 2002" campaign

At the local level access to information was difficult and the District Council were unsure what to do and what the risks were to local farmland. As one respondent noted the "attractions were seeking advice as they did not know how they were going to be affected" and were passed to different national organisations in search of information which was described by an industry respondent as "frustrating." Sources of information followed a long chain of command from national government, regional tourist boards, county councils to the local level. At the local level consistent messages were created by press and media contacts as well as briefing Tourist Information Centre staff regarding what attractions and footpaths were open. However, research indicated that staff had detailed information concerning attractions, but little knowledge of footpaths which attract a number of hikers to the local region and are a major tourist asset.

Recovery Marketing Strategies

As noted earlier, tourism organisations, especially NTOs, are in a position to assist with the marketing and recovery of destination image or reputation that may have been damaged through a crisis or disaster. Recovery marketing at the national level was complicated by the fact that not all regional areas were affected by the outbreak and thus wondered what all of the fuss was about. As mentioned above some areas actually improved their situation as holiday markers changed their travel patterns from rural or countryside areas to coastal resorts (Wright, 2002). Certain attractions also benefited as visitors changed from outdoor activities to indoor activities such as museums and galleries.

There were no tourism resources damaged by FMD to be repaired and the blackened image of the UK could not be repaired until the disease had been defeated, despite many areas of the UK having never been affected by the disease. Thus, the nature of the disaster meant that there was no "turning point" when a town was re-opened, or a building restored or re-built, instead areas of the country gradually tried to persuade visitors that it was safe to visit, while other areas of the UK continued to suffer with new outbreaks of the disease. Such a scenario led to calls from some sectors of the tourism industry to proceed with advertising campaigns encouraging visitors to the countryside, while for others, such confidence-building campaigns were misplaced until the problem had universally been removed.

The English Tourism Council (ETC) was given £3.8m to promote tourism to a domestic audience in April 2001, which was spent on specific market campaigns, coupled with developing web sites to inform potential visitors of where was safe to visit. The ETC calculated that this financial aid generated 766,000 additional visits and produced a return on investment of £27 for each £1 spent (ETC, 2001c). In May, a further £12m was given to the BTA for international marketing, while no further finance was available for the ETC and the domestic market (ETC, 2001c). The BTA started planning in September 2001 to re-brand and re-image Britain through a new £5 million campaign called UK OK which was implemented in January 2002 to attract the visiting friends and relatives market. This was targeted at seven selected key markets (USA, Canada, Germany, France, Belgium, Netherlands, the Republic of Ireland). However, industry representatives believed that it was not enough for such a large target audience. Further funding for marketing of Britain overseas was secured in April 2002 with £20m contribution from the government, £5m cash from industry and a further £15m of collateral marketing by the campaign partners (BTA, 2002). This money will be spend on the "Only in Britain: Only in 2002" campaign which is expected to attract an extra one million visitors in 2002 and generate £0.5b for the national economy (BTA, 2002).

At the local level recovery was undertaken from the intermediate phase of the crisis onwards as the area did not have any confirmed cases of the foot and mouth disease. A publicity campaign was implemented to attract tourists back to the local area but representatives felt that it was difficult to get the interest of the media who were more interested in "mountains of cows in Cumbria (being burned)." The recovery strategy was also limited by budget constraints and a reluctance to put large amounts of money towards a recovery strategy when the disease was not yet defeated at the national level. According to the District Council this "would have been a waste of money." The ETC helped later in the long term recovery stage by providing money for publicity campaigns and publicity work was conducted in conjunction with county councils. Recovery was quick at the local level under study, partly due to good weather and also because major competitors such as Cumbria and the South West of England were still battling the outbreak throughout the recovery phrase.

CONCLUSION

This paper has outlined the importance of crisis management, and in particular crisis communication for tourism organisations. Tourism is highly susceptible to external crises and disasters, yet even after the foot and mouth outbreak few lessons appear to have been learnt by some parts of the industry. At the national level a greater number of changes have been implemented and the BTA are constantly refining their crisis management strategies and plans. The BTA did the best they could under the circumstances, yet the nature of the FMD meant that recovery marketing was considered wasteful until after the outbreak had been defeated and a lack of a crisis management and communication strategy prior to the outbreak hampered recovery.

The absence of a crisis communication or management strategy at the local level was evident and yet it appears doubtful if one will be created at all due to the perceived uniqueness of individual disasters and crises. Yet as Kash and Darling (1998) and Beeton (2001) note all organisations and tourism organisations suffer from external or internal crises of varying magnitudes. In particular, this paper has noted that a lack of crisis management strategy combined with a slow response time, inconsistent communication strategies and poor access to information limited the effectiveness of crisis communication for the tourism industry. In particular, access to information was critical for consumers, industry and local regions. Recovery marketing has been implemented, and in the case of the local level recovery was rapid as they appear to have benefited at the expense of other regions. Yet, at the national level recovery marketing is still continuing and the success of which is yet to be evaluated. The FMD outbreak was chaotic as noted by Fink (1986). The fragmentation of the tourism industry did little to alleviate this confusion with decisions being made in the heat of the crisis, illustrating the need planning before such incidents occur.

Greater research and understanding is required in the field of crisis communication and theory to help improve the understanding of such incidents. This understanding will hopefully aid the development of suitable crisis communication models for managers to implement which can be varied depending on the scale and type of crisis or disaster encountered. Faulkner's (2001) model is a useful start; however, more research is needed into disaster phenomena and crisis communication in the tourism industry. The cost of developing a crisis management strategy would be far less than the cost of not having one and a key aspect to any crisis strategy is crisis communication. It is hoped that this paper has contributed in some way to the field of crisis communication in tourism through evaluating the FMD outbreak in the UK.

REFERENCES

Alreck, P. & Settle, B. (1997). *The Survey Research Handbook*. (2nd Ed). Chicago: Irwin.

Ashcroft, R. (1997). Crisis management: Public relations. *Journal of Managerial Psychology*, 12 (5): 325-332.

Barton, L. (1994). Preparing the marketing manager for crisis: The use and application of new strategic tools. *Marketing Intelligence and Planning*, 12 (11): 41-46.

Becton, S. (2001). Horseback tourism in Victoria, Australia: Cooperative, proactive crisis management. *Current Issues in Tourism*, 4 (5): 422-439.

Berry, S. (1999). We have a problem . . . call the press! (crisis management plan). *Public Management*, 81 (4): 4-15.

British Tourist Authority (BTA). (2001a). MEMO. Brussels: British Tourist Authority.

British Tourist Authority (BTA). (2001b). BTA corporate information. London (online). Available at: http.//www.tourismtrade.org.uk/corporate_info.htm (Accessed 02 January 2002).

British Tourist Authority (BTA). (2002). Media releases. London (online). Available at: http://www.tourismtrade.org.uk/pdf/PPR_MVC_OnlyBritain.pdf (Accessed 28 April 2002).

Burnett, J. (1998). A strategic approach to managing a crisis. *Public Relations Review*, 24 (4): 475-488.

Coombs, T. (1999). *Ongoing Crisis Communication: Planning, Managing and Responding*. Thousand Oaks, CA: Sage.

Cotton, B. (2001). Foot and mouth: The lessons we must learn. *Tourism: Journal of the Tourism Society*, Autumn, 110: 5.

Darling, J., Hannu, O. & Raimo, N. (1996). Crisis management in international business: A case situation in decision making concerning trade with Russia. *The Finnish Journal of Business Economics*, Vol. 4, np.

Department of Culture, Media and Sport (DCMS). (2001). Press releases. London (online). Available at: http://www.culture.gov.uk/tourism/search.asp?Name=pressreleases/tourism/2001/dcms (Accessed 02 January 2002).

English Tourism Council (ETC). (2001a). Press briefing. London: ETC, 25th July.

English Tourism Council (ETC). (2001b). NewsETCetra. London (online). Available at: http://www.englishtourism.org.uk/webcode/common/middle_page_nav.asp?ID=S217 (Accessed 02 January 2002).

English Tourism Council (ETC). (2001c). English Tourism Council. London (online). Available at: http://www.englishtourism.org.uk/ (accessed 21 December 2001).

Faulkner, B. (2001). Towards a framework for tourism disaster management. *Tourism Management*, 22 (2): 135-147.

Faulkner, B. & Vikulov, S. (2001). Katherine, washed out one day, back on track the next: A post mortem of a tourism disaster. *Tourism Management*, 22 (4): 331-344.

Fink, S. (1986). *Crisis Management: Planning for the Inevitable*. New York: American Association of Management.

Heath, R. (1998). *Crisis Management for Managers and Executives*. London: Financial Times Management.

Henderson, J. (1999). Tourism management and the Southeast Asian economic and environmental crisis: A Singapore perspective. *Managing Leisure*, 4: 107-120.

Kash, T. & Darling, J. (1998). Crisis management: Prevention, diagnosis and intervention. *Leadership and Organisation Development Journal*, 15 (4): 179-186.

Keown-McMullan, J. (1997). Crisis: When does a molehill become a mountain? *Disaster Prevention and Management*, 6 (1): 4-10.

Lee, Y. & Harrald, J. (1999). Critical issue for business area impact analysis in business crisis management: Analytical capability. *Disaster Prevention and Management*, 8 (3): 184-189.

Marra, F. (1998). Crisis communication plans: Poor predictors of excellent crisis public relations. *Public Relations Review*, 24 (4): 461-474.

Murphey, P. and Bayley, J. (1989). Tourism and disaster planning. *The Geographical Review*, 79: 26-46.

Parsons, W. (1996). Crisis management. *Career Development International*, 1 (5): 26-28.

Pauchant, T. & Mitroff, I. (1992). *Transforming the Crisis Prone Organization*. San Francisco, CA: Jossey-Bass Publishers.

Richardson, B. (1994). Crisis management and management strategy–Time to "loop the loop?" *Disaster Prevention and Management*, 3 (3): 59-80.

Richardson, B. (1995). Paradox management for crisis avoidance. *Management Decision*, 33 (1): 5-18.

Roberts, V. (1994). Flood management: Bradford paper. *Disaster Prevention and Management*, 3 (3): 44-60.

Saunders, M., Lewis, P., & Thornhill, A. (2000). *Research Methods for Business Students*. (2nd ed). Harlow: Pearson.

Sönmez, S., Apostolopoulos, Y., & Tarlow, P. (1999). Tourism in crisis: Managing the effects on tourism. *Journal of Travel Research*, 38 (1): 3.

Williams, D. & Olaniram, B. (1998). Media Relations: Powerful Tools for Achieving Service Quality. *Managing Service Quality*, 9 (4): 246-256.

Wright, R. (2002). Crisis, what crisis? An examination of the foot and mouth outbreak in Eastbourne, UK. Unpublished BA Honours Dissertation. School of Service Management, University of Brighton.

Zerman, D. (1995). Crisis communication: Managing the mass media. *Information and Computer Security*, 3 (5): 25-28.

Malaysia's Response to the Asian Financial Crisis: Implications for Tourism and Sectoral Crisis Management

Nicolette de Sausmarez

SUMMARY. Tourism is a fragile industry and the damage caused by a crisis may have serious implications for a national economy. Crisis management is the means by which the impact of a crisis may be minimised and recovery assisted. This paper analyses the Malaysian response to the Asian financial crisis in the context of tourism and considers whether there is the potential for crisis management at a sectoral level, and if so how it should be developed and implemented. It concludes that although both the public and private sector recognise the need for such a measure, issues such as funding and the identification of appropriate indicators need to be resolved. *[Article copies available for a fee from The Haworth Document Delivery Service: 1-800-HAWORTH. E-mail address: <docdelivery@ haworthpress.com> Website: <http://www.HaworthPress.com> © 2003 by The Haworth Press, Inc. All rights reserved.]*

KEYWORDS. Tourism, Malaysia, Asian financial crisis, crisis management, private sector

Nicolette de Sausmarez is Lecturer in Tourism Management, Lancashire Business School, University of Central Lancashire, Preston PR1 2HE, UK (E-mail: ndesausmarez@ uclan.ac.uk).

[Haworth co-indexing entry note]: "Malaysia's Response to the Asian Financial Crisis: Implications for Tourism and Sectoral Crisis Management." de Sausmarez, Nicolette. Co-published simultaneously in *Journal of Travel & Tourism Marketing* (The Haworth Hospitality Press, an imprint of The Haworth Press, Inc.) Vol. 15, No. 4, 2003, pp. 217-231; and: *Safety and Security in Tourism: Relationships, Management, and Marketing* (ed: C. Michael Hall, Dallen J. Timothy, and David Timothy Duval) The Haworth Hospitality Press, an imprint of The Haworth Press, Inc., 2003, pp. 217-231. Single or multiple copies of this article are available for a fee from The Haworth Document Delivery Service [1-800-HAWORTH, 9:00 a.m. - 5:00 p.m. (EST). E-mail address: docdelivery@haworthpress.com].

INTRODUCTION

Although said to be the world's largest industry, tourism is vulnerable to the economic climate as well as to changes in public perception in both the destination and generating countries, so that a crisis in one may have considerable impact on the other. In addition, improvements in technology and a global media mean that no crisis is restricted to its immediate vicinity but can cause global repercussions. Because of the economic importance of tourism, it is crucial that swift action be taken in the event of a crisis. Crisis management offers the possibility of restoring the status quo promptly, minimising any economic losses resulting from a crisis and at the same time bolstering public confidence. However, the preparation of a crisis management plan requires not only substantial time and effort to identify objectives and priorities and to rationalise operations but there may also be a considerable financial cost involved. Failure to manage a crisis may lead to bankruptcy of suppliers, job and financial losses, or at worst the collapse of the tourism sector which, particularly in the case of developing countries, may be a major contributor to the economy.

The aim of this study is to examine the response of Malaysia to the Asian financial crisis and to consider the potential for crisis management at a sectoral level and the means by which it may be effected. Although during the same period the country suffered from several other lesser crises, in particular the Southeast Asian haze, only the economic dimension of crisis management is addressed in this paper, as this had by far the greatest national significance. With tourism increasingly threatened by international terrorism, as shown by the recent targeting of tourists in Bali, Indonesia and Mombasa, Kenya in October and November 2002 respectively, this research offers the opportunity of learning from the Malaysian experience.

THE CONTEXT

Crisis management has been a recognised concept since the 1962 Cuban missile crisis although it has been practised for much longer. There is an extensive literature dating back to the 1970s with classics such as Fink (1986) and Meyers and Holusha (1986) and more recently Mitroff, Pearson and Harrington (1996) and Heath (1998). However, almost all of this literature is devoted to crisis management in developed rather than developing countries, principally the United States, and most of the studies relate to crisis management at a corporate level, often in the pharmaceutical or engineering industries, rather than at a national or federal level. The exceptions are instances where national security is threatened, such as by a nuclear disaster (Williams, 1976; Willby and Potter, 1995) or an international conflict (Frei, 1978; Clutterbuck, 1993).

Tourism growth has been continuous over the last 40 years and yet there has been relatively little research into crisis management in this context. This is strange, particularly in view of the increase not only in the length and frequency of journeys and thus a greater chance of serious accidents, but also in the number of developing country destinations where there is a higher risk of natural disasters occurring (World Tourism Organization/World Meteorological Organization, 1998). Here again, much of the research that has been done is at a micro level, focussing on a particular organization or destination (Barton, 1994; Durocher, 1994). Whilst the value of crisis management at this organizational level is not disputed, two recent crises have highlighted the necessity for some form of crisis management provision for the tourism sector itself. Neither the British foot and mouth crisis in 2001 nor the terrorist attacks in New York and Washington, D.C. on September 11, 2001 had anything to do with tourism initially and yet both had a devastating impact on the tourism sectors of the respective countries.

There have been a number of case studies of national responses to crises affecting the tourism industry. In the field of conflict and political turmoil, Richter (1999), Mansfeld (1999) and Ioannides and Apostolopoulos (1999) consider the management of tourism in three Asian countries, in Israel, and in Cyprus respectively. In such situations, however, the climate of danger imposes on tourism recovery very different parameters from in the wake of an economic crisis. Of much greater relevance to this paper is Henderson's (1999) comparison of the response of Thailand and Indonesia to the Asian financial crisis although their recovery was still in the early stages. None of these studies, however, considers crisis management in very much detail. In contrast, Cassedy (1991) tackles the issues around developing a crisis management plan with the aid of three case studies, one of which is of Fiji's response to the 1987 coup. This again is a political scenario but greater relevance is added by Berno and King's (2001) examination of the recovery of the Fijian tourism industry after the subsequent coup in 2000, in the light of previous experience.

It can be assumed that the crisis period can be divided into three stages: the pre-crisis stage leading up to the climax, which may vary in length depending on the crisis; the crisis itself which usually lasts a relatively short time; and the post-crisis period which again may last for a considerable period (Meyers and Holusha, 1986). Most crisis management is concerned with the post-crisis period when the immediacy of the crisis is past and steps can be taken to restore normality; once a crisis strikes there is little that can be done other than contain it. But the crisis management which offers the greatest potential benefit but also the greatest challenge addresses the pre-crisis period and focuses on the detection of indicators that herald the approach of a crisis and the subsequent measures taken to minimise or deflect the crisis altogether. There are two major difficulties here. Firstly, the identification of appropriate indicators may not be easy; in a tourism context consumer confidence may be rocked by a crisis anywhere in the world, as was seen in the crisis following the September 11 tragedy. Secondly, there must be a sufficiently long pre-crisis period for these indicators to be picked up and preventative action taken.

Both the formulation and the evaluation of a crisis management plan may be a source of difficulty, especially so in tourism given the fragmented nature of the industry. At an organizational level, decisions as to the nature and funding of a plan will rest with the management who will consider it to have been successful or effective if in the first instance the organization survives the crisis, or when profits return to pre-crisis levels. However, at sectoral level it may not be so straightforward. Where the responsibility for developing and implementing a plan lies will depend on the economic and political climate and how the tourism sector is organised. Measures of a plan's effectiveness may also be complicated; changes in indicators such as tourism arrivals or receipts may be simplistic and, together with regional differences, may obscure the true situation.

The analysis of the response to a crisis, known as pre- and post-crisis auditing, is considered in some detail by Mitroff et al. (1996) who stress the benefits that this practice may confer on crisis management planning. With this in mind, Malaysia's experience of the Asian financial crisis and its aftermath was explored in detail by way of semi-structured interviews with 18 senior public and private sector officials during July and August 2001, in order that the measures taken could be evaluated with the benefit of hindsight. Rather than merely looking at Malaysian strategies in the post-crisis period, this research also explored pre-crisis "proactive" management possibilities, eliciting suggestions as to possible indicators to monitor and the means by which a programme to deal with future crises might be prepared and implemented.

The 1997 Asian crisis started as a financial crisis in Thailand but spread through most of Southeast Asia and developed into an economic crisis of serious proportions. A wealth of information about the crisis may be found on the website of Roubini (2002). Chote (1998) offers an economic perspective and Prideaux (1999) analyses the causes and interprets the crisis in a tourism context. Over the 30 years prior to the financial crisis, the Asia Pacific region had shown unprecedented economic growth, with GDP per capita in Thailand, Malaysia, South Korea and Indonesia increasing consistently at 5% or more annually (Stiglitz 1998). The onset of the crisis is generally considered to be the collapse of the Thai baht on 02 July 1997 when its value fell 60% overnight;

this was followed by the spread of currency instability to neighbouring countries. Although recovery was initially slower than anticipated, the region overall has recovered more quickly than anyone predicted, as measured by changes in GDP shown in Table 1. Tourism had also been thriving prior to the crisis but as the disposable income of those living in the region was severely reduced so too was intra-regional travel; greater detail of the impact of the crisis on tourism in the region is provided by Muqbil (1998) and the World Tourism Organization (1999).

The financial crisis had a major impact on the Malaysian economy and the tourism industry did not escape undamaged. Tourism had been growing rapidly in Malaysia in the 30 years prior to the crisis and had become a major source of foreign exchange and employment. Table 2 shows the growth in tourist arrivals and receipts 1990-2001 and the more recent factors shaping tourism development are summarised by the World Tourism Organization (2000). A comprehensive summary of the growth and diversity of the Malaysian tourism industry is provided by Khalifah and Tahir (1997) and McVey (2001) and the effect of the crisis is covered in considerable detail by Musa (2000). The current performance indicators showing the extent of the recovery of the sector can be found in Tourism Malaysia (2002).

Prior to the crisis Malaysia was aiming to become fully industrialised by the year 2020 but this vision has had to be modified significantly; not only was there the financial crisis during 1997-98 but Malaysia also suffered outbreaks of Japanese encephalitis and Coxsackie virus as well as the haze from the Indonesian forest fires in Sumatra and Borneo and some political unrest. To a greater or lesser extent all affected the tourism sector even though none started specifically as a tourism crisis. The lowest point for Malaysia is generally considered to have been January 1998 when the National Economic Action Coun-

TABLE 1. Growth of GDP (%) in Selected Southeast Asian Countries

Country	1996	1997	1998	1999	2000	2001
Brunei	1.01	3.60	−3.99	2.56	2.83	1.47
Indonesia	7.82	4.71	−13.13	0.79	4.90	3.32
Malaysia	10.00	7.32	−7.36	6.14	8.33	0.45
Philippines	5.85	5.19	−0.59	3.41	4.01	3.40
Singapore	7.71	8.54	−0.09	6.93	10.25	−2.04
Thailand	5.90	−1.38	−10.57	4.50	4.67	1.73

Source: Adapted from ASEAN Surveillance Coordinating Unit (Table 2.1. Growth of Gross Domestic Product; http://www.aseansec.org/macroeconomic/GDPgrowth.htm).

TABLE 2. Tourist Arrivals and Receipts: Malaysia 1990-2001

Year	Total tourism receipts (RM million)	Tourist arrivals
1990	7,446	1,667
1991	5,847	1,530
1992	6,016	1,768
1993	6,504	2,050
1994	7,197	3,440
1995	7,469	3,909
1996	7,138	4,447
1997	6,211	2,702
1998	5,551	2,456
1999*	7,931	3,242
2000*	10,222	4,562
2001*	12,775	6,374
2002*	13,292	6,785

Source: Compiled from Tourism Malaysia (2003); World Tourism Organisation (2003)

cil (NEAC) was set up as a consultative body to the Malaysian cabinet to deal with the crisis (NEAC, 2002). The NEAC, whilst not focusing on the tourism sector itself, did have input from a tourism sub-committee representing both the private and public sectors.

POST-CRISIS STRATEGIES

The initial response to the crisis by the Malaysian government was a call for retrenchment and a reduction in spending which did little to diminish the effects of the crisis. Subsequently a number of strategies were implemented with the broad aims of stabilising the national economy and promoting Malaysia at home and abroad.

In September 1998 the government imposed capital controls and pegged the ringgit to the US dollar. This latter was a bold step and there were predictions that it would end in disaster but although GDP fell in 1998 by 7.5%, the following year there was growth of approximately 5% (*The Economist*, 1999). The pegging stabilised the ringgit but made it vulnerable to fluctuations in the value of the dollar, considered at the time the lesser of two evils. Although these measures had a number of implications for tourism (Sadi, 1999), they were not strategies for tourism itself and a detailed treatment is outside the scope of this paper. Although the pegging placed Malaysia somewhat at a disadvantage as a destination compared to other competing Southeast Asian countries with free floating currencies, its relative stability was of considerable benefit to the Malaysian travel trade, especially those involved in dollar transactions. However, the majority of those interviewed felt that it was time to return to a free-floating currency, particularly in view of the recent recession in the United States and the uncertainty in the value of the dollar.

Once the worst of the crisis was over the government started to promote domestic tourism as a means of supporting the hotel sector, which was suffering badly from the fall in intra-regional arrivals. In January 1999, to boost the short break market, public sector employees were given the first Saturday of each month off and a year later this was increased to include the third Saturday; the banks and private sector were called upon to follow suit. The *Cuti Cuti Malaysia* campaign was launched in September 1999 with the two aims of developing a holiday culture and informing Malaysians of the attractions of their own country (Malaysian Tourism Promotion Board). This initiative was reinforced by daily television exposure and supported by city hotels hoping to attract visitors from the provinces by developing a variety of short packages which included excursions to local attractions and visits to theme parks rather than merely offering shopping vouchers.

It is difficult to assess how successful *Cuti Cuti Malaysia* has been. The government claims that domestic tourism trips increased from 8.32 million trips between August 1997 and July 1998 to 15.8 million trips in 1999, an increase of 89.9%. Figures for domestic hotel guests increased by 46% from 698,000 in March 1998 to 1.02 million in March 2000 (Economic Planning Unit, 2001). However, the representatives of the private sector who were interviewed were rather more sceptical. As Malaysians traditionally go back to their hometown or the beach when they have time off, not only may a two-day break be too short a time but also city hotels will derive little benefit. In addition, because it is the first and third rather than any two weekends per month, there are the inevitable problems of congestion that may prove a disincentive to travel.

The promotion of Malaysia abroad was a two-pronged campaign. Firstly, a special promotional budget of RM150 million (approximately USD 39.5 million) was approved for Tourism Malaysia in 1999, a fourfold increase on previous funding (Economic Planning Unit, 2001). This was spent partly in the traditional regional markets, which had rather been taken for granted before the crisis and partly on emerging markets such as India and China as well as the Middle East. The untapped potential of the regional markets was only realised when efforts were made to develop them further and arrivals increased from 1998 to 1999 by 62.9% from Singapore, 9.6% from Thailand and 95.3% from Indonesia (McVey, 2001). A Tourism Malaysia representative observed that before 1997 they had been complacent and allowed advertising and promotion to lapse; the crisis had taught them not to underestimate the importance of marketing even while there is a healthy market and sustained growth.

The promotion in the newer markets has also been very successful and has resulted in the fastest growth rates in tourist arrivals, with an average annual rate of 34.6% from India and 32.4% from China (Economic Planning Unit, 2001). Concurrent with this increased promotion the immigration department empowered Tourism Malaysia, Malaysia Airlines offices and certain leading Indian and Chinese travel agents to issue Malaysian tourist visas at the request of the Ministry of Culture, Arts and Tourism. This move was welcomed by the travel trade who anticipated an increase in arrivals of 500% as a result (Nithiyananthan, 2000).

Malaysian marketing is now much more culture-based than before the crisis and a larger budget is allocated to developing links and communicating the image of Malaysia through visits to overseas events, rather than through buying expensive air time for advertising. A public relations strategy, the Mega Fam campaign, offered familiarisation trips to Malaysia to 500 foreign tour operators and media representatives each month. This is considered to have been very cost effective and has gone a long way towards correcting the distorted image of the country which the Malaysians felt was created by the international media during the crisis period.

In tandem with the government's focus on overseas promotion there was a shift by the Malaysian travel trade in favour of inbound tourism, which was encouraged by the government as a means of keeping the currency at home and, more importantly, attracting foreign exchange. Inbound agents, which depended on the regional markets, had been badly affected as visitor arrivals from ASEAN countries (82% of total arrivals) fell by 14.6% and from East Asia by 28% between 1997 and 1998 (Tourism Malaysia, 1998). Early currency fluctuations meant that a number of smaller travel agents involved in ticketing had been unable to pay the airlines on time so were delisted and as a result had gone out of business. In contrast, those dealing with Europe or North America and those involved with domestic tourism did comparatively well. The net result was fewer players; the number of registered tour and travel agencies in Malaysia fell from 2,562 in 1997 to 2,050 in 1998, a drop of 19.5% (Tourism Malaysia, 1998). The experience of the crisis has resulted in a widespread recognition of the importance of diversification. Traditionally Malaysians felt that to build a successful business it was necessary to specialise into a niche market. Certainly with regard to the travel trade, those operators who had diversified into a variety of markets and/or tourism products were in a stronger position to withstand the damage inflicted by the crisis and continue trading.

There were a number of other strategies introduced, which were of lesser importance nationally, or were complementary to those outlined above. Malaysia has been promoting itself as a shopping haven and there have been initiatives such as the thrice-yearly Mega Sale Carnival that aimed to attract both domestic and regional visitors. The government also imposed a moratorium on the building of 4- and 5-star hotels in Kuala Lumpur and the Klang valley because of overcapacity resulting from the sharp fall in regional business traffic. Ironically many of these hotels had been built to service the participants and spectators at the Commonwealth Games and other international sporting events held in 1998 which, although helping to attract visitors in the immediate post-crisis period, had been planned long before the crisis.

PRE-CRISIS CONSIDERATIONS

Although those interviewed felt that the Malaysian government had done a good job since 1997 in restoring normality to the tourism sector, there was some concern expressed over how long this had taken and the initial delay in responding to the crisis. It was not until September 1998 that the ringgit was pegged, 14 months after the collapse of the baht and eight months after the worst of the Malaysian crisis. The *Cuti Cuti Malaysia* and *Malaysia Truly Asia* campaigns were launched even later, in 1999. The explanation given by Tourism Malaysia was that for the first two years after the crisis priority was given to re-establishing the national economy as a whole rather than paying special attention to any particular sectors. In view of the fact that tourism is Malaysia's fourth largest generator of foreign exchange, this might appear to have been rather misguided. The general impression to emerge from the interviews was that there was chaos during this period, with both public and private sectors trying desperately to keep afloat and taking each day as it came, with no co-ordination, nothing resembling a plan of action and no means of monitoring the success or otherwise of any measures taken. All those interviewed felt that a plan of any sort would have provided direction and a framework on which to develop strategies appropriate to the crisis itself and would be of great value in the event of another crisis occurring.

There appears to be a real desire in both the private sector and the government to develop together some means by which future crises might be anticipated and managed but no consensus on what form such an initiative should take, how it should be implemented, who should lead it and how it should be funded. Public sector representatives interviewed were of the opinion that the government already does enough for tourism and that this would be a suitable instance where the private sector could play a major part, not only in developing a strategy but also in funding it, as they would be major beneficiaries. In addition it was felt that the private sector should be prepared to supply the data which could be used for monitoring the situation and would act as indicators of an approaching crisis. There was some doubt about how likely the private sector would be to participate and contribute such information. The reason given for this lack of optimism was that the private sector seldom see the wider picture but instead focus on their immediate environment and operation. They would be reluctant to divulge information about their transactions that could be leaked to their competitors. In addition, as tourism players are often small and medium enterprises, it would be difficult to orchestrate a significant and cohesive response.

The private sector was enthusiastic about the idea of developing a crisis management procedure but felt that the government was in the best position to lead such a programme, as they have the power to demand participation by all the relevant parties and are in a position to make the submission of certain data a requirement. As far as funding was concerned, they felt that as a result of the intense pressures of the last four years their profit margins were so low that they could ill afford to contribute to a scheme that might never be needed. With tourism so important to Malaysia and as it would be a national initiative they saw funding as the responsibility of the government. Over the question of supplying figures for monitoring, they supported the idea that the data should be collected but were unhappy about submitting any additional information to the government; the involvement of an independent third party was felt to be an acceptable option.

With respect to indicators of an approaching crisis threatening to affect the tourism sector, when asked for suggestions as to what data might be appropriate there were few ideas forthcoming. It is difficult to identify data that can be obtained sufficiently far in advance as to allow it to be analysed, and measures enacted in response, as for example in the case of the information obtained by the immigration department from the cards filled out on arrival in Malaysia. One possibility suggested was that advance bookings for tour groups should be obtained from inbound tour agents, although it was pointed out that the lead time is often very short, with bookings made only a few weeks before groups arrive.

DISCUSSION

On balance the strategies that were introduced in Malaysia's response to the crisis have been effective as figures for tourist arrivals and receipts indicate, although factors such as the disappearance of the haze, the strengthening economy and the fact that Malaysians have increasingly more disposable income may have played some part in the recovery. Similar strategies, namely the promotion of domestic tourism together with increased marketing overseas focusing on new markets or the expansion of existing ones, with relaxed immigration regulations, employed by Thailand and Indonesia are considered by Henderson (1999) also to have had varying degrees of success. Indonesia, too, had other political and social problems, which compounded the damage caused by the financial crisis. Malaysia differed from the other two countries in imposing exchange rate controls rather than accepting International Monetary Fund (IMF) help, which may have conferred an unforeseen advantage. The feeling of "going it alone," together with a new awareness of the country resulting from the domestic tourism promotions, has reinforced national identity and cannot but help strengthen the image of Malaysia as a tourist destination both at home and abroad.

There can be no doubt that, especially in the case of the tourism sector which is so diverse and the different sub-sectors so closely interrelated, a single sectoral crisis management policy would facilitate the monitoring of tourism demand and world events and the response to a crisis. However, in a country the size of Malaysia the impact of a crisis on tourism may not be consistent throughout the country. This was seen in the Asian financial crisis, when the southern state of Johor as a cheap destination for Singaporeans suffered less from the crisis than did Kuala Lumpur and the Klang valley which is much more dependent on business tourism, while the northern island of Langkawi which caters for the international market experienced a 15% increase in business out of Europe in 1997 (Hiebert, 1998). This would suggest that a federal crisis management plan may not be the best option but instead a regional or state approach might be more appropriate. A regional response to a crisis could not only be more prompt but also better tailored to suit the immediate requirements locally. However, research into the German response to the nuclear fallout from the Chernobyl explosion (Czada, 1990; König, 1990) suggest that while this approach has advantages, in times of crisis there are potential problems in the communication of information between different regions as well as co-ordination of their responses.

Henderson (1999) concludes from her study that there is a need for some strategy to assist in the management of crises but does not make any suggestions as to the format of such a strategy. It is clear from the interviews carried out in Malaysia that both private sector and public sector feel it would be a good idea but it is questionable whether there is enough commitment to develop and fund a plan which may never be needed. While a government may accept that it should initiate such a scheme, neither the public nor the private sector may feel that responsibility for its funding lies with them, especially when the tourism sector is relatively healthy and there may exist a false feeling of security. In addition, because there is so great a range of tourism products and the tourism sector is so diverse, it is possible that any sectoral crisis management provision would have be so general as to be of little value.

Reactive crisis management, the planning of a response to a crisis and the strategies to be employed in this response, is relatively straightforward. As discussed earlier, the anticipation of a crisis is a much greater challenge but much more valuable. In order to take even preliminary steps in this direction it is necessary to address the issue of indicators. A vast number of crises may strike at any time and many crises occur with next to no warning but often there is time to detect the signals if they have been identified previously. Traditional indicators such as tourist arrivals and length of stay may not be appropriate for use in the context of crisis management but instead it may be necessary to use completely different figures or more likely a combination of both. What is recognised, however, is the importance of monitoring performance consistently.

CONCLUSION

It can be concluded from this study that crisis management at sectoral level is certainly desirable but whether or not it is achievable is still open to debate. There is little doubt that because the return on investment in tourism is faster than in other sectors, the tourism sector should be accorded special consideration in terms of crisis management and as Sharpley and Craven (2001) illustrate in their analysis of the response to the British foot and mouth outbreak, the tourism sector may be of much greater real value to an economy than the perceived value of other sectors. It is surely therefore important that resources are focused on managing the successful recovery of a specific sector rather than being less effective through being spread thinly throughout the economy as a whole. But whilst crisis management at sectoral level may be feasible in the more homogenous and discrete sectors of an economy, one factor to emerge from this research is the difficulty of formulating crisis management provision for the tourism sector because it is so fragmented and so diverse.

As regards the manner in which a crisis may be managed so as to be of greatest benefit to the tourism sector, the experience of Malaysia has shown reactive strategies to be effective. Initially the stabilisation of the economy was the primary objective of the government and once this had been achieved, international and domestic marketing of tourism together with the easing of financial constraints on the private sector and facilitation of international tourism movement were all major contributors to the recovery of the tourism sector. However, it is more difficult to draw conclusions about the potential for pre-crisis management in general and public/private sector co-operation in particular; competition in the industry is intense and there is considerable reluctance in the private sector to spend hard-earned profits on making provision for a hypothetical crisis that may never materialise. In addition, the format of a crisis management plan and the most appropriate indicators to be monitored all remain unresolved and more research is needed in this area. Because tourism is so vulnerable to such an enormous number of possible crises in so many different scenarios, the identification of an approaching crisis by monitoring appropriate indicators in sufficient time to take remedial action becomes so complex as to be unrealistic. It may be the case that less ambitious and regular monitoring of tourism trends will keep the industry healthy, diversified and well regulated and consequently more resilient in periods of adversity.

Whilst regional crisis management initially appears to be a serious option, it is hard to envisage the extent to which this could be implemented. The most successful strategies for Malaysia after the financial crisis included the international marketing promotions and the measures taken both to boost domestic tourism and to facilitate travel from new markets, which required substantial funding, and government action in terms of the collection of statistics or legislation; none could have been effected on a regional or state basis. However, the proximity of the state public sector to the private sector tourism players does suggest that some involvement at a regional level would be advantageous. It might be that the direction of the crisis management should be at a national level but its interpretation and feedback should be regional so as to be tailored to suit local requirements.

Due to the absence of appropriate data, this research neither considers the environmental or political dimensions of the Malaysian experience, nor does it make a distinction between the impacts of the several crises that occurred in Malaysia in 1997. Because the economic dimension overshadowed other considerations, the changes in tourist arrivals have been attributed to the impact of the financial crisis, which in turn has been considered the focus of the crisis management measures introduced. In fact, it has been suggested that media coverage of the haze may have affected tourist arrivals from outside the East Asia Pacific region to a much greater extent than the financial crisis; further research in this area would be of considerable interest.

Although there remain a number of unresolved issues, this research offers a foundation on which to base further study. Through an examination of Malaysia's response to the Asian financial crisis in the context of tourism, it is hoped that issues emerging may be useful to other countries facing a crisis situation and offer possible strategies by way of which the tourism sector may be restored.

REFERENCES

Barton, L. (1994). Crisis management: Preparing for and managing disasters. *The Cornell HRA Quarterly*, 35 (2): 59-65.

Berno, T. and King, B. (2001). Tourism in Fiji after the coups. *Travel and Tourism Analyst*, 2: 75-92.

Cassedy, K. (1991). *Crisis Management Planning in the Travel and Tourism Industry*. San Francisco: Pacific Asia Travel Association.

Chote, R. (1998). Financial crises: The lessons of Asia. In Centre for Economic Policy Research, Conference Report No. 6: Financial Crises and Asia (pp. 1-34). London: Centre for Economic Policy Research.

Clutterbuck, R.L. (1993). *International Crisis and Conflict*. Basingstoke: MacMillan Press Ltd.

Czada, R. (1990). Politics and administration during a 'nuclear-political' crisis: The Chernobyl disaster and radioactive fallout in Germany. *Contemporary Crises*, 14: 285-311.

Durocher, J.F. (1994). Recovery marketing: What to do after a natural disaster. *The Cornell HRA Quarterly*, 35 (2): 66-71.

Economic Planning Unit (2001). Eighth Malaysia Plan 2001-2005. Kuala Lumpur: Economic Planning Unit.

Economist, The (4 December 1999) Odd man in. http://www.economist.com/

Fink, Steven (1986). *Crisis Management: Planning for the Inevitable*. New York: Amacom.

Frei, D. (1978). International crises and crisis management: An East-West symposium. International Crises and Crisis Management Conference held at University of Zurich. Farnborough: Saxon House.

Heath, R.L. (1998). *Crisis Management for Managers and Executives*. London: Financial Times Management.

Henderson, J.C. (1999). Southeast Asian tourism and the financial crisis: Indonesia and Thailand compared. *Current Issues in Tourism*, 2(4): 294-303.

Hiebert, M. (1998, July 23). Paradise lost. *Far Eastern Economic Review*, pp. 56-57.

Ioannides, D. and Apostolopoulos, Y. (1999). Political instability, war, and tourism in Cyprus: Effects, management, and prospects for recovery. *Journal of Travel Research*, 38 (1): 51-56.

Khalifah, Z. and Tahir, S. (1997). Malaysia: Tourism in perspective. In F.M. Go and C.L. Jenkins (Eds.), *Tourism and Economic Development in Asia and Australasia* (pp. 176-196). London: Cassell.

König, K. (1990). Comments on 'The Chernobyl disaster and nuclear fallout.' *Contemporary Crises*, 14: 313-319.

Malaysian Tourism Promotion Board–Event Promotion. URL: http://www.tourism.gov.my/Activities/events_promotions.asp [12 May 2002].

Mansfeld, Y. (1999). Cycles of war, terror, and peace: Determinants and management of crisis and recovery of the Israeli tourism industry. *Journal of Travel Research*, 38 (1): 30-36.

McVey, M. (2001). Malaysia. *Travel and Tourism Intelligence Country Reports*, 1: 63-79.

Meyers, G.C. and Holusha, J. (1986). *When It Hits the Fan: Managing the Nine Crises of Business.* London: Unwin Hyman.

Mitroff, I.I., Pearson, C.M., and Harrington, L.K. (1996). *The Essential Guide to Managing Corporate Crises.* New York: Oxford University Press.

Muqbil, I. (1998). The fall-out from the Asian economic crisis. *Travel and Tourism Analyst,* 6: 78-95.

Musa, G. (2000). Tourism in Malaysia. In C.M. Hall and S. Page (Eds.), *Tourism in South and Southeast Asia: Issues and Cases* (pp. 144-156). Oxford: Butterworth-Heinemann.

NEAC (2002). National Economic Action Council–NEAC. URL: http://www.neac. gov.my [10 May 2002].

Nithiyananthan, N. (2000 August 11-17). Visa authority in trade hands. Travel Trade Gazette Asia. URL: http://www.ttg.com.sg/ [12 November 2002].

Prideaux, B. (1999). Tourism perspectives of the Asian financial crisis: Lessons for the future. *Current Issues in Tourism,* 2 (4): 279-293.

Richter, L.K. (1999). After political turmoil: The lessons of rebuilding tourism in three Asian countries. *Journal of Travel Research,* 38 (1): 41-45.

Roubini, N. (2002) Global macroeconomic and financial policy site: The Asian crisis. URL: http://pages.stern.nyu.edu/~nroubini/asia/ [15 June 2002].

Sadi, M.A. (1999). Responding to the Asian financial crisis: Malaysian capital controls and their implications for tourism. *The Journal of Hospitality Financial Management,* 7 (1): 87-98.

Sharpley, R. and Craven, B. (2001). The 2001 foot and mouth crisis–Rural economy and tourism policy implications: A comment. *Current Issues in Tourism,* 4 (6): 527-537.

Stiglitz, J. (1998). Macroeconomic dimensions of the East Asian crisis. In Centre for Economic Policy Research, Conference Report No. 6: Financial Crises and Asia (pp. 54-62). London: Centre for Economic Policy Research.

Tourism Malaysia (1998). Annual Tourism Statistical Report. Kuala Lumpur: Malaysia Tourism Promotion Board.

Tourism Malaysia (2002). Tourism in Malaysia: Key Performance Indicators 2001. Kuala Lumpur: Malaysia Tourism Promotion Board.

Willby, C.R. and Potter, C. (1995). Planning for potential nuclear accidents. In Institution of Mechanical Engineers, Conference on Emergency Planning and Management. Bury St Edmunds: Mechanical Engineering Publications.

Williams, P. (1976). *Crisis Management: Confrontation and Diplomacy in the Nuclear Age.* London: Martin Robertson and Co Ltd.

World Tourism Organization (1999). *Impacts of the Financial Crisis on Asia's Tourism Sector.* Madrid: World Tourism Organization.

World Tourism Organization (2000). *Tourism Market Trends: East Asia and Pacific, 2000 Edition.* Madrid: World Tourism Organisation.

World Tourism Organization/World Meteorological Organization (1998). *Handbook on Natural Disaster Reduction in Tourist Areas.* Madrid: World Tourism Organization and World Meteorological Organization.

The Importance of Food Safety in Travel Planning and Destination Selection

Tanya L. MacLaurin

SUMMARY. This study investigates the strength of the relationship between the destination choices of respondents and the perceived risk of food-borne illnesses, as well as respondents' sources of information regarding food safety prior to traveling. Results indicate that food safety was of secondary importance to respondents with frequent travelers more willing to discount the use of food safety in their travel decisions. Female respondents were likely to regard food safety as more important than their male counterparts. Africa was the top region that most respondents would avoid due to food safety concerns. Friends and relatives, travel agents, and magazines and newspapers were the most common sources turned to for health and food safety information. Travel agents were not perceived as a reliable source of food safety information. *[Article copies available for a fee from The Haworth Document Delivery Service: 1-800-HAWORTH. E-mail address: <docdelivery@haworthpress.com> Website: <http://www.HaworthPress. com> © 2003 by The Haworth Press, Inc. All rights reserved.]*

KEYWORDS. Risk perception, destination choice, food safety, safety information

Tanya L. MacLaurin is affiliated with the School of Hospitality and Tourism Management, University of Guelph, Guelph, Ontario N1G 2W1, Canada (E-mail: tmaclaurin@ uoguelph.ca).

The author would like to gratefully acknowledge the research contributions of Foo Woei Kuan, Boey Mun Joon, and Wong Bee Bee toward this paper.

[Haworth co-indexing entry note]: "The Importance of Food Safety in Travel Planning and Destination Selection." MacLaurin, Tanya L. Co-published simultaneously in *Journal of Travel & Tourism Marketing* (The Haworth Hospitality Press, an imprint of The Haworth Press, Inc.) Vol. 15, No. 4, 2003, pp. 233-257; and: *Safety and Security in Tourism: Relationships, Management, and Marketing* (ed: C. Michael Hall, Dallen J. Timothy, and David Timothy Duval) The Haworth Hospitality Press, an imprint of The Haworth Press, Inc., 2003, pp. 233-257. Single or multiple copies of this article are available for a fee from The Haworth Document Delivery Service [1-800-HAWORTH, 9:00 a.m. - 5:00 p.m. (EST). E-mail address: docdelivery@ haworthpress.com].

INTRODUCTION

Travel, whether for business or pleasure, can offer people a chance to get away and experience a different culture or relax. Yiannakis and Gibson (1992) found that relaxation needs were a major motivation for traveling. However, travel also possesses risks, which range from the life threatening (e.g., political instability) to those of a minor inconvenience (e.g., travel delays).

As the decision to travel can be complex, the topic of travel decision making is widely researched in the tourism literature. Studies have addressed various aspects of the travel decision-making process, including decision-making models (Corey, 1996; Sirakaya et al., 1996), the types of participants in the decision-making process and their roles (Zalatan, 1998; Zimmer et al., 1995; Gitelson and Kerstetter, 1994; Madrigal, 1993; Fodness, 1992), and the types of risks involved in traveling (Sönmez and Graefe, 1998a; Sönmez, 1998; Page and Meyer, 1996; Cossens and Gin, 1994). Additional studies have been conducted on the effect of travel distance (McKercher, 1998; Ankomah et al., 1996), nationality (Pizam and Sussmann, 1995), destination image (Milman and Pizam, 1995), and religion (Cohen, 1998) on travel planning.

The literature about the impacts of risk on travel decision-making has focused primarily on two main forms of risk when travelling: security and health. Security risks (e.g., terrorism) have a significant impact on travel decision-making and have the ability to alter travel plans (Sönmez, 1998). The effect of health risks on travel decision-making is less clear, owing to a lack of prior research in this area. Cossens and Gin (1994) found that, although HIV infection was a serious health risk, the majority of New Zealanders surveyed would not be affected in their choice of destination by perceived risk of HIV infection.

The most frequent complaint among world travelers is diarrhoea. Travelers to Asia, Latin America and Africa are at greatest risk with diarrhoea affecting approximately 30% of visitors to these regions (Johns Hopkins Health Information 2000). There is clear evidence that traveling to developing countries in the tropics may cause diarrhoea (Cossar, 1996, Cartwright, 1996, 1992). Physical pain and discomfort and problems of finding suitable medical treatment, especially when there are language barriers, may spoil the entire vacation experience.

Few studies have been done on the impact of food safety in travel decision-making, and tourism providers have often overlooked the area of food safety. Handszuh (1991) noted that handbooks on tourism marketing tend to mention many tourist assets such as beautiful scenery, shopping opportunities, and the attitudes of local people, but not safe food.

A survey of travel brochures in Scotland found 38% carried no general health advice, 80% carried no specific health information and 18% carried neither general nor specific health advice (Cossar et al., 1993). One study of Australian travelers found that 51% of respondents had not been given any health and safety information prior to departure (Peach and Bath, 1998), and in another study, the researchers covertly visited travel agencies in the United Kingdom and requested package holidays in Kenya or flights to India. No spontaneous health warnings were given in 61% of the consultations even though both countries were high-risk destinations in health terms (Grabowski and Behrens, 1996).

Food-borne diseases account for nearly 5,000 deaths each year, an estimated 76 million illnesses, and 325,000 hospitalisations in the United States alone, according to the Centers for Disease Control and Prevention (CDC) (2002). The World Health Organization (WHO) has also acknowledged that contaminated foods are one of the principal threats to tourists traveling abroad. According to the World Tourism Organization's (WTO) estimates, 660 million people traveled internationally in 2000. Growth in global travel has significant implications for the spread of food-borne infections. Diarrhoea and vomiting caused by contaminated foods may damage the reputation of a country as a tourist destination (World Health Organization, 2000).

The proportion of travelers not receiving health and safety information should be a concern to the tourism industry. Ensuring freedom from risk and danger is an important dimension in delivering quality service (Handszuh, 1995; Wilks and Oldenburg, 1995). Travelers can be expected to search for reliable information from different sources to reduce risk in their travel decision-making. Risk perception and information-search are important factors influencing travel planning (Maser and Weiermair, 1998; Sönmez and Graefe, 1998b). Holidaymakers use information searches to help them choose a destination and enhance the quality of their trip by decreasing the level of associated uncertainty (Fodness and Murray, 1997).

The present study examines the importance of food safety to Singaporeans in relation to travel destination decision-making and the type and reliability of information sources used prior to traveling. This study also examines potential food safety importance differences during travel between two sub-samples: respondents who had attended a travel fair and those who did not.

METHODOLOGY

Sample Selection

Residents of Singapore formed the population of the study. Based on the 2000 Census, 76.8% of Singaporeans were Chinese, 13.9% Malay, 7.9% Indian and 1.4% other races (Singapore Department of Statistics, 2002). To obtain a heterogeneous population based on the above demographics, six areas were sampled across Singapore. Two samples of data were collected: Singaporeans living in housing estates (Sample 1) and attendees at a travel fair held in Singapore (Sample 2). Respondents for Sample 1 were selected randomly at six town centers and mass rapid transit (MRT) stations in the same six neighborhoods. Respondents for Sample 2 were attendees at the SIA (Singapore International Airlines) Travel Fair at Suntec City Convention Centre. Respondents were selected randomly for both sub-samples.

Two sets of questionnaires were adapted from a similar study by Sönmez and Graefe (1998b). Questionnaire 1 was used for town centre respondents (Sample 1). The survey had four types of questions: traveler profile, the importance of food safety in travel decisions, information search and reliability prior to traveling, and demographics. Food safety importance was measured by perceptions of food safety, priority of food safety in travel decisions, and world regions avoided due to food hygiene concerns.

Perceptions were measured by asking participants to respond to a set of statements related to food safety and travel on a 5-point agreement scale (1 = strongly agree, 2 = agree, 3 = neutral, 4 = disagree, 5 = strongly disagree). Respondents were asked to indicate eight factors they considered prior to traveling: price, health and food safety, political stability, social (e.g., friendliness of the people), attractions, amenities, accessibility and security. Respondents were also asked to indicate regions they would avoid with respect to food safety concerns, and regions they had previously visited and number of visits over their lifetime.

Respondents were asked to indicate the reliability of ten types of health and food safety information sources they might have used for pre-trip information. These sources were: travel agents, the Internet, magazines and newspapers, medical practitioners, friends and relatives, business associates, television and radio news, travel guides, government agencies and others. Respondents who had not researched any pre-trip health and food safety information were asked why they had not done so. The reliability of various information sources used prior to traveling was measured using a 5-point reliability scale.

Questionnaire 2 was used for travel fair attendees (Sample 2) and was a shortened version of Questionnaire 1. Traveler profiles were measured by purpose of trip, frequency of travel in a year, and food poisoning experiences. The importance of food safety in travel decisions was measured by respondents' perceptions of food safety while traveling. Participants were also asked about their preferred information sources for health and travel safety.

A pilot study was conducted to obtain an indication of the usability and to assess evidence of reliability and validity. The original questionnaire was shortened and revisions were made in wording and layout to improve comprehension. The final instrument required an average of eight minutes to complete based on a second pilot study conducted.

Data for Sample 1 were collected over a period of six weeks at the town centers and MRT stations. The questionnaires were self-administered and resulted in 334 useable responses. Data for Sample 2 were collected over the three-day duration of the travel fair. Again, the questionnaires were self-administered and resulted in 380 useable responses.

Data were analysed using the Statistical Package for the Social Sciences. The number of respondents varied by item. Descriptive statistics were calculated for all survey items. Differences in responses on the importance of food safety in travel decisions, owing to different demographic groups and traveler profiles, were determined by using cross-tabs.

For Questionnaire 1, one-way analysis of variance (ANOVA), t-tests and Bonferroni's multiple comparison were used to determine the ranking of food safety in the travel decisions of Singaporeans and the ranking of the reliability of the information sources Singaporeans used prior to traveling. Only nine reliability of information sources were used in the statistical tests as the category of "other" was excluded because very few respondents selected this option. Independent sample t-tests were run for common questions in the two sets of questionnaires to compare the effects of travel fair attendance on the perception of importance of food safety among respondents during travel and in developing and developed countries.

RESULTS AND DISCUSSION

Demographic characteristics of respondents are shown in Table 1. The 380 travel fair attendees were evenly distributed between men and women. Two-thirds (67%) were between 18 and 39 years old, 36% had at least tertiary education, and 62% of attendees had monthly incomes of $2000 and above. Ninety-two percent of fair attendees were Chinese.

The 334 town centre respondents consisted of 67% females and 33% males. Over half (53%) were between 18 and 29 years of age and one out of four (25%) had at least tertiary education. More than half of the respondents (58%) had monthly incomes below $2,000 and 75% were Chinese.

The travel fair sample respondents were older, with 12% more in the 40-49 age group. They were better educated and had higher income levels. Ten percent more had at least tertiary education and 20% more had monthly income levels of $2,000 and above.

TABLE 1. Demographic Characteristics of Respondents

	Travel Fair (n = 380)		Town Centres (n = 334)	
	Number	Percentage	Number	Percentage
Gender				
Male	190	50.0	109	32.6
Female	190	50.0	225	67.4
Age				
18-29	151	39.7	176	52.7
30-39	102	26.8	87	26.0
40-49	97	25.5	45	13.5
50-64	30	8.0	21	6.3
>65	-	-	5	1.5
Status				
Singaporean	328	86.3	297	88.9
Permanent resident	52	13.7	21	6.3
Others	-	-	16	4.8
Education Level				
O Levels or below	117	30.8	122	36.5
A Levels or diploma	114	30.0	116	34.7
Vocational/technical school	14	3.7	12	3.6
Graduate degree and above	135	35.5	83	24.9
Others	-	-	1	0.3
Income				
<$1,500	80	21.0	140	41.9
$1,500-$1,999	65	17.1	51	15.3
$2,000-$4,999	175	46.1	131	39.2
$5,000-$9,999	48	12.6	12	3.6
> $10,000	12	3.2		
Race				
Chinese	349	91.8	250	74.9
Malay	13	3.4	48	14.3
Indian	17	4.5	31	9.3
Others	1	0.3	5	1.5

Travel Profiles of Respondents

The travel profiles of respondents are shown in Table 2. Two-thirds of travel fair attendees (67%) traveled for vacation purposes only, and 73% traveled less than 2 times per year. Twenty-seven percent had food poisoning experiences in Singapore, while 16% had food poisoning overseas.

TABLE 2. Travel Profiles of Respondents

Characteristic	Travel Fair (n = 380)		Town Centres (n = 334)	
	Number	Percentage	Number	Percentage
Purpose of travel				
Business only	13	3.4	6	1.8
Vacation only	253	66.6	275	82.3
Both	114	30.0	53	15.9
Frequency of travel per year				
1 to 2 times	278	73.2	264	79.0
3 to 5 times	60	15.8	43	12.9
> 5 times	42	11.0	27	8.1
Food poisoning in Singapore				
Yes	102	26.8	93	27.8
No	278	73.2	241	72.2
Food poisoning overseas				
Yes	62	16.3	44	13.2
No	318	83.7	290	86.8
Length of stay				
1-5 days	-	-	130	38.9
6-10 days	-	-	152	45.5
11-15 days	-	-	30	9.0
> 15 days	-	-	22	6.6
Companionship during traveling				
Alone	-	-	23	6.9
Couple	-	-	32	9.6
Group of friends	-	-	182	54.5
Group of relatives/family members	-	-	97	29.0
Arrangements by travel agents				
Never	-	-	53	15.9
Sometimes	-	-	135	40.4
Often	-	-	78	23.4
Always	-	-	68	20.3

Note: Some of the traveler profile characteristics for Questionnaire 1 (town centres) were omitted for Questionnaire 2 (travel fair).

The majority of respondents from town centers (82%) traveled for vacation purposes only. Seventy-nine percent traveled less than 2 times per year with 84% spending a maximum of 10 days abroad. Twenty-eight percent had incurred food poisoning experiences in Singapore, while 13% had the same experience overseas. The majority of respondents preferred to travel with friends (55%) or family members (29%), and 84% had used a travel agent (Table 2).

Almost twice as many travel fair attendees (30%) traveled for both vacation and business purposes compared to town centre respondents (15.9%). Fair attendees also traveled more frequently. Sixteen percent of fair attendees and 13% of town centre respondents reported food poisoning when traveling overseas. These were significantly lower percentages than reported by *Travel Weekly* (1998) in a study of 1,000 adult travelers in the United States, which found that 35% had experienced food poisoning-related illnesses during overseas travel.

Food Safety in the Travel Planning Process of Town Centre Respondents by Frequency of Travel

Differences in respondents' food safety perceptions were examined by demographic characteristics and travel profile. Significantly different results were not found among demographic characteristics. Significant differences were found for travel profile, frequency of travel, frequency of usage of travel agents, and overseas food poisoning experiences.

Approximately half (48%) of frequent travelers (> 5 times per year) disagreed that food safety was important in their travel decisions (Table 3). One in four (25%) of less frequent travelers (1-2 times per year) disagreed that food safety was important. This finding indicated that a higher percentage of the frequent travelers would not consider food safety an important consideration in trip planning.

Seventy-four percent of frequent travelers (> 5 times per year) disagreed that other people's negative food safety experiences would influence their travel decisions. Only 35% of less frequent travelers (1-2 times per year) shared the same response. Other people's negative food safety experiences were more likely to influence the plans of less frequent travelers (Table 3).

Food safety and other people's negative experiences with food might not influence the travel decisions of frequent travelers as much owing to their extensive travel experience, which conditions them to minimize travel-related risks. For less frequent travelers, food safety issues might be an unfamiliar risk necessitating the reliance on another person's experiences with food safety to help them in their travel decisions.

TABLE 3. Food Safety in the Travel Planning Process by Frequency of Travel in Town Centre Respondents

Characteristic	Variable			Chi-Square
	Frequency of travel			
Food safety is important in making travel decisions	1-2 times per yr	3-5 times per yr	≥ 5 times per yr	
Agree	142 (53.8%)	22 (51.2%)	12 (44.4%)	
Neutral	56 (21.2%)	4 (9.3%)	2 (7.4%)	11.789
Disagree	66 (25.0%)	17 (39.5%)	13 (48.2%)	(p = .019)
	Frequency of travel			
Other people's negative food safety experiences influence travel decision	1-2 times per yr	3-5 times per yr	≥ 5 times per yr	
Agree	96 (36.4%)	12 (27.9%)	6 (22.2%)	
Neutral	75 (28.4%)	14 (32.6%)	1 (3.7%)	17.622
Disagree	93 (35.2%)	17 (39.5%)	20 (74.1%)	(p = .001)

Food Safety Perceptions by Frequency of Use of Travel Agents

Approximately one-third (32%) of respondents who never used travel agents agreed that nothing could prevent them from going abroad (Table 4). Only 13% of respondents who always used travel agents shared the same response. This finding indicated respondents who used travel agents more often were less enthusiastic about traveling. Approximately one-third (36%) of respondents who never used agents indicated that food safety was unimportant in their travel decisions. Only 24% of participants who always used travel agents shared the same response. Increased frequency in use of travel agents was an indicator that respondents would consider food safety important in their travel decisions. This finding could be influenced by increased purchase of tour packages, which include meals, from travel agents where travelers had less choice on their meal selection.

Half (51%) of respondents who never used travel agents indicated that they would not be influenced by other people's negative food safety experiences (Table 4). Only 32% of respondents who always used agents shared the same response. It appears that increased use of travel agents impacted the importance of respondents' reliance on other people's negative food safety experiences.

Results suggest that heavy users of travel agents, compared to light users, tended to be less enthusiastic about traveling. This finding contradicts the results of a study done by Goldsmith and Litvin (1999) on Singaporean heavy users of travel agents. They found that, compared to light users, Singaporean

TABLE 4. Food Safety Perceptions of Town Centre Respondents by Frequency of Use of Travel Agents

Characteristic	Variable				Chi-Square
	Frequency of use of travel agents				
Nothing can prevent international travel	Never	Sometimes	Often	Always	
Agree	17 (32.0%)	39 (28.9%)	8 (10.3%)	9 (13.2%)	
Neutral	3 (5.7%)	34 (25.2%)	18 (23.0%)	16 (23.5%)	11.615
Disagree	33 (62.3%)	62 (45.9%)	52 (66.7%)	43 (63.3%)	(p = .020)
	Frequency of use of travel agents				
Food safety is important in making travel decisions	Never	Sometimes	Often	Always	
Agree	30 (56.6%)	59 (43.7%)	43 (55.1%)	44 (64.7%)	
Neutral	4 (7.6%)	29 (21.5%)	21 (26.9%)	8 (11.8%)	19.356
Disagree	19 (35.8%)	47 (34.8%)	14 (18.0%)	16 (23.5%)	(p = .004)
	Frequency of use of travel agents				
Other people's negative food safety experiences influence travel decisions	Never	Sometimes	Often	Always	
Agree	17 (32.1%)	34 (25.2%)	35 (44.9%)	28 (41.2%)	
Neutral	9 (17.0%)	44 (32.6%)	19 (24.3%)	18 (26.5%)	15.038
Disagree	27 (50.9%)	57 (42.2%)	24 (30.8%)	22 (32.3%)	(p = .020)

heavy users of travel agents were more enthusiastic about traveling. One possible explanation for this was that the present sample of respondents was taken from town centres, whereas Goldsmith and Litvin's (1999) sample was taken from a travel fair and furniture show. The earlier comparison of the traveler profile between fair attendees and town centre respondents suggested that fair attendees traveled more often than town centre participants and a higher frequency of travel may have caused fair attendees to be more enthusiastic about travel.

Food Safety Perceptions from Overseas Food-Borne Illness Experiences

Almost one-third (30%) of respondents who had experienced food-borne illness when traveling disagreed that negative food safety news would discourage them from traveling (Table 5). Only 14% of respondents who were not food-borne illness victims shared the same response. This finding may be attributable to victims of overseas food poisoning knowing proper future precautions while traveling. Negative news would not effect their travel decisions. Powell (1999) suggested that people were more concerned about unfamiliar

TABLE 5. Food Safety Perceptions Across Food-Borne Illness Experiences of Town Centre Respondents

Characteristic	Variable		Chi-Square
	Victim of food poisoning when traveling		
Negative news discourages international travel	Yes	No	
Agree	29 (65.9%)	197 (67.9%)	
Neutral	2 (4.6%)	52 (17.9%)	9.866
Disagree	13 (29.5%)	41 (14.2%)	(p = .007)
	Victim of food poisoning when traveling		
Food safety is important in making travel decisions	Yes	No	
Agree	28 (63.6%)	148 (51.0%)	
Neutral	1 (2.3%)	61 (21.0%)	8.900
Disagree	15 (34.1%)	81 (28.0%)	(p = .012)
	Victim of food poisoning when traveling		
Possibility of food poisoning discourages international travel	Yes	No	
Agree	19 (43.2%)	166 (57.2%)	
Neutral	7 (15.9%)	57 (19.7%)	6.403
Disagree	18 (40.9%)	67 (23.1%)	(p = .041)
	Victim of food poisoning when traveling		
Own negative food safety experiences influence travel decisions	Yes	No	
Agree	10 (22.7%)	139 (47.9%)	
Neutral	7 (15.9%)	52 (17.9%)	13.035
Disagree	27 (61.4%)	99 (34.2%)	(p = .001)
	Victim of food poisoning when traveling		
Other people's negative food safety experiences influence travel decisions	Yes	No	
Agree	7 (15.9%)	107 (36.9%)	
Neutral	12 (27.3%)	78 (26.9%)	9.102
Disagree	25 (56.8%)	105 (36.2%)	(p = .011)

risks (e.g., terrorism) than familiar risks (e.g., food poisoning). Negative news may not discourage people from traveling, except to an area that travelers were unfamiliar with and did not know how to take precautions for (e.g., terrorism).

Approximately two-thirds (64%) of respondents who had experienced food-borne illness overseas agreed that food safety was important in their travel decisions (Table 5). However, only 43% agreed that the possibility of food-borne illness would discourage them from traveling. Respondents who had experienced food-borne illness overseas would not be discouraged from traveling. Food poisoning victims would instead take more precautions by including food safety considerations in their travel plans.

Sixty-one percent of victims of overseas food-borne illness indicated that they would not let their negative experiences in a country influence their decision to revisit that country. Similarly, 57% of food poisoning victims indicated that their travel decisions would not be affected by other people's negative experiences (Table 5).

Food Safety Perceptions of Travel Fair Attendees

Differences in food safety perceptions among travel fair attendees were examined based on demographic characteristics and travel profile. Gender, frequency of travel and overseas food-borne illness experiences were significantly related to food safety perceptions among travel fair respondents.

Forty-one percent of male respondents disagreed that nothing could prevent them from international travel, and 31% of female attendees shared the same response (Table 6). This finding indicated that female attendees were more enthusiastic about traveling despite the risks involved. Three-quarters (75%) of female attendees agreed that food safety was an important factor in their travel

TABLE 6. Food Safety Perceptions Across Gender of Travel Fair Respondents

Characteristic	Variable		Chi-Square
	Gender		
Nothing can prevent international travel	Male	Female	
Agree	91 (47.9%)	90 (47.4%)	
Neutral	21 (11.0%)	41 (21.6%)	9.092
Disagree	78 (41.1%)	59 (31.0%)	(p = .011)
	Gender		
Food safety is important in making travel decisions	Male	Female	
Agree	116 (61.0%)	142 (74.7%)	
Neutral	30 (15.8%)	16 (8.4%)	8.776
Disagree	44 (23.2%)	32 (16.9%)	(p = .012)
	Gender		
Will not travel to country that had food safety problem	Male	Female	
Agree	106 (55.8%)	130 (68.4%)	
Neutral	30 (15.8%)	26 (13.7%)	7.272
Disagree	54 (28.4%)	34 (17.9%)	(p = .026)

decisions while only 61% of male attendees shared the same response. Food safety was more likely to influence the travel decisions of females compared to males.

More female respondents (68%) would not travel to countries with food safety problems compared to males (56%). Females indicated a higher enthusiasm for traveling, but had greater concern for travel safety than males. Females were more likely than males to consider food safety in their travel decisions and took precautions by not traveling to countries that had experienced food safety issues.

Food Safety Perceptions by Frequency of Travel

Fifty-two percent of frequent travelers (>5 times per year) agreed that nothing could prevent them from traveling internationally (Table 7). Only 45% of less frequent travelers (1 to 2 times per year) shared the same response. Frequent travelers may have perceived themselves to be more experienced with unexpected situations due to their vast travel experience. They were less cautious about risks and hence more enthusiastic to travel compared to less frequent travelers.

Three out of four (73%) less frequent travelers (1 to 2 times per year) agreed that food safety was important in their decisions compared to 57% of frequent travelers (>5 times per year). Similarly, 70% of the less frequent travelers agreed that they would not visit countries that had experienced food safety problems. Only 43% of frequent travelers shared the same response. This finding indicated that food safety was more important to less frequent travelers. These respondents took precautions by visiting countries where food safety problems exist (Table 7).

Almost half (47%) of less frequent travelers (1 to 2 times per year) indicated that their own negative experiences with food safety in a country would influence their travel decisions to that particular country. Only 38% of frequent travelers (>5 times per year) indicated the same response. Less frequent travelers were more likely to let their negative experiences with food influence their travel decisions compared to frequent travelers. Less frequent travelers were not as enthusiastic about traveling and more likely to let food safety factors or their negative experiences with food safety influence their decisions and avoid countries that had experienced food safety problems. Frequent travelers were more enthusiastic about traveling and were not likely to let food safety concerns or their negative experiences with food influence their travel decisions.

The lack of influence of food safety in decisions of frequent travelers and their willingness to visit countries that had experienced problems could be partly explained by the results of a similar study done by Sönmez and Graefe

TABLE 7. Food Safety Perceptions by Frequency of Travel for Travel Fair Respondents

Characteristic	Variable			Chi-Square
	Frequency of travel			
Nothing can prevent international travel	1-2 times per yr	3-5 times per yr	≥ 5 times per yr	
Agree	126 (45.3%)	33 (55.0%)	22 (52.4%)	
Neutral	50 (18.0%)	2 (3.3%)	10 (23.8%)	11.615
Disagree	102 (36.7%)	25 (41.7%)	10 (23.8%)	(p = .020)
	Frequency of travel			
Food safety is important in making travel decisions	1-2 times per yr	3-5 times per yr	≥ 5 times per yr	
Agree	202 (72.7%)	32 (53.3%)	24 (57.1%)	
Neutral	28 (10.0%)	12 (20.0%)	6 (14.3%)	11.638
Disagree	48 (17.3%)	16 (26.7%)	12 (28.6%)	(p = .020)
	Frequency of travel			
Will not travel to country that had food safety problems	1-2 times per yr	3-5 times per yr	≥ 5 times per yr	
Agree	194 (69.8%)	24 (40.0%)	18 (42.9%)	
Neutral	36 (12.9%)	12 (20.0%)	8 (19.0%)	27.689
Disagree	48 (17.3%)	24 (40.0%)	16 (38.1%)	(p = .000)
	Frequency of travel			
Own negative food safety experiences influence travel decisions to particular country	1-2 times per yr	3-5 times per yr	≥ 5 times per yr	
Agree	130 (46.8%)	23 (38.3%)	16 (38.1%)	
Neutral	56 (20.1%)	4 (6.7%)	8 (19.0%)	12.9
Disagree	92 (33.1%)	33 (55.0%)	18 (42.9%)	(p = .012)
	Frequency of travel			
Safe and hygienic to eat in rural areas in developing countries	1-2 times per yr	3-5 times per yr	≥ 5 times per yr	
Agree	31 (11.2%)	9 (15.0%)	10 (23.8%)	
Neutral	88 (31.7%)	12 (20.0%)	4 (9.5%)	13.487
Disagree	159 (57.1%)	39 (65.0%)	28 (66.7%)	(p = .009)

(1998b). Their study found that past travel experiences to specific regions both increased the intention to travel there and decreased the intention to avoid risky areas. Applying their results to the present study, respondents who traveled more often and had more travel experience would still travel to countries that had experienced food safety problems if they had traveled to that country before.

Frequent travelers had stronger views about food in rural areas of developing countries than less frequent travelers (Table 7). One third (32%) of less frequent travelers (1 to 2 times per year) were neutral about the hygiene of food found in the rural areas of developing countries, while only 10% of frequent travelers (>5 times per year) expressed the same opinion. The proportion of frequent travelers who either agreed or disagreed with the view that food in rural areas was safe and hygienic was higher than that of less frequent travelers.

Food Safety Perceptions by Overseas Food-Borne Illness Experiences

Eighty-four percent of travel fair attendees who had previously experienced food poisoning when traveling believed it was unsafe and unhygienic to eat in rural areas in developing countries (Table 8). Only 55% of attendees who were not victims of food poisoning when traveling shared the same response. Respondents who had experienced food poisoning while traveling were significantly more concerned about the level of food safety standards in rural areas than respondents who had not experienced food poisoning. Victims of overseas food poisoning may have been more sensitive toward food safety to avoid a recurrence of the incident.

Seventy-one percent of the victims of food poisoning also agreed that it was safe and hygienic to eat in urban areas in developed countries compared to travelers who had not experienced food poisoning while traveling (56%) (Table 8). Victims of food poisoning when traveling did not perceive food safety problems to be an important consideration in urban areas in developed coun-

TABLE 8. Food Safety Perceptions by Food-Borne Illness Experiences of Travel Fair Respondents

Characteristic	Variable		Chi-Square
	Victim of food poisoning when travelling		
Safe and hygienic to eat in rural areas in developing countries	Yes	No	
Agree	4 (6.5%)	46 (14.5%)	
Neutral	6 (9.6%)	98 (30.8%)	18.420
Disagree	52 (83.9%)	174 (54.7%)	(p = .000)
	Victim of food poisoning when travelling		
Safe and hygienic to eat in urban areas in developed countries	Yes	No	
Agree	44 (71.0%)	177 (55.7%)	
Neutral	12 (19.4%)	113 (35.5%)	6.264
Disagree	6 (9.8%)	28 (8.8%)	(p = .044)

tries, even though they had previously fallen ill. A possible reason might be that these respondents had the perception that food in developed countries was generally safer and more hygienic than food found in developing countries. Their food poisoning incidents might have occurred predominately in developing countries. Another reason might be due to respondent beliefs that developing countries' health and food safety standards were lower than that of the developed countries.

Effects of Travel Fair Attendance on the Food Safety Perceptions of Singaporeans

Independent samples *t*-tests were conducted to examine the effect of travel fair attendance on the food safety perceptions of respondents. In comparing the mean response on an agreement scale of 1 = *Strongly Agree* to 5 = *Strongly Disagree*, travel fair attendees were found to be more willing to travel compared to town centres respondents (Table 9). Travel fair attendees (mean response of 2.77) tended to agree that nothing could prevent them from traveling compared to town centres respondents who had a mean response rate of 3.70.

Despite their willingness to travel, travel fair attendees also disagreed that food safety was not an important consideration when they traveled (mean response of 3.96). Town centre respondents (mean response of 3.48) slightly disagreed that food safety was not an important consideration (Table 9). This finding indicated that for travel fair attendees food safety was more important than for town centre respondents.

Significant differences were also found among perceptions of food safety standards of urban areas in developing countries. Town centre respondents (mean response of 4.05) perceived that food found in urban areas in developing countries was safe and hygienic compared to expressions by travel fair participants (mean response of 3.17). Travel fair attendees, with a mean response

TABLE 9. Effects of Travel Fair Attendance on Food Safety Perceptions

Food Safety Perceptions	Mean Response		p-value
	Travel Fair	Town Centres	
Nothing can prevent traveling	2.77	3.70	0.00
Food safety not important to travel decision	3.96	3.48	0.00
Food in urban area of developing countries not safe	3.17	4.05	0.00
Food in hawker stalls in developed countries not safe	4.24	3.58	0.00

Note: Scale for mean response: 1 = strongly agree, 2 = agree, 3 = neutral, 4 = disagree, 5 = strongly disagree.

of 4.24, felt more strongly than town centre respondents (mean response of 3.58) that food found in hawker stalls in developed countries was safe and hygienic (Table 9).

Importance of Food Safety in Travel Decisions

The eight factors in the travel decisions of town centre respondents were ranked according to their mean response of agreement of 1 = *Strongly Agree* to 5 = *Strongly Disagree* (Table 10). Security, political stability and attractions were the three most important factors that respondents considered prior to traveling. The highest mean response score was 2.34, indicating that all eight factors were important to town centre respondents (Table 10).

One-way ANOVA and Bonferroni's multiple comparison tests were used to determine the relative importance of each travel factor. These tests indicated that all eight factors could be divided into two distinct groups. The primary factors considered by respondents in their travel decision-making process were security, political security and attractions. The other five factors were of a secondary nature–health and food safety, price, amenities, accessibility and social factors. Political stability and security were important to respondents because they were life-threatening risks that visitors have little control over.

Results were consistent with a similar study by Sönmez and Graefe (1998a) of U.S. residents. Their study found that terrorism risk was an important factor for American respondents in their travel decisions. Although unclean food could be a life threatening risk (e.g., food poisoning, viruses, infection), travelers often had more control over these risks by simply avoiding a particular

TABLE 10. Mean Ranking of Factors Affecting Travel Decisions of Respondents

Travel Factor	Mean Importance	Rank
Security	1.76a	1
Political Stability	1.79a	2
Attractions	1.89ab	3
Price	2.06b	4
Amenities	2.16bc	5
Accessibility	2.20bc	6
Health/Food safety	2.22bc	7
Social (Friendliness of the people)	2.34c	8

Note: Means followed by different lower case letters were significantly different at $p < .05$.

food or by bringing their own food and medication. Security risks and political instability were often factors that travelers could not take precautions against.

Regions Avoided Due to Food Safety Concerns

Africa was the most common destination that respondents would avoid due to food safety concerns (Figure 1). Approximately one-third (126 out of 334) of town centre respondents indicated that they would avoid Africa. Central/South America and Asia were the second and third most avoided regions. Not surprisingly, given Singapore's location, Asia was the most visited region, with 312 out of 334 town centre respondents traveling in the region. The Pacific islands (i.e., Australia, New Zealand) and North America were the second and third most visited regions (Figure 1).

Regions commonly avoided by respondents were usually also the least visited destinations generally. Only 12 participants indicated that they had visited Africa while the figure for Central and South America was nine. The South Pacific had 136 visitors with only six avoiders. North America had 81 visitors with only five avoiders. As would be expected, Asia was the most visited region, but also the third most avoided destination. A lack of familiarity of Africa and Latin America might have explained why they were the two most avoided regions owing to food safety concerns (Figure 1).

FIGURE 1. Regions Avoided Due to Food Safety Concerns

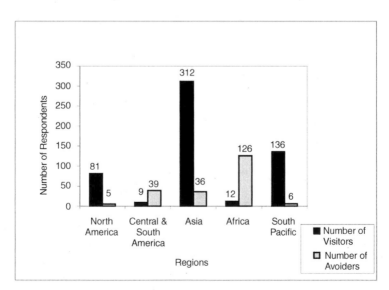

Information Sources Used by Respondents Prior to Traveling

Ten different sources of information selected by all respondents are profiled in Figure 2. Friends and relatives, magazines and newspapers, and tour agents were the three most popular information sources. Most town centre respondents (54%) looked for health and food safety information by asking their own friends and relatives in contrast to travel fair attendees who relied more on newspapers and magazines (55%). Travel fair respondents were better educated in terms of tertiary education (36%) compared to town centre participants (25%) (Table 1). This might explain their increased preference for newspapers and magazines for travel information.

More town centre respondents used travel guides (36%) compared to travel fair attendees (25%) (Figure 2). Travel fairs and travel guides essentially offer similar types of information. Travel fairs do not occur frequently; therefore, travel guides can be an information substitute. Eighteen percent of town centre respondents and eight percent of travel fair respondents did not take any action searching for health and safety information prior to traveling. Most participants did not consider this information important or relevant to their travels.

FIGURE 2. Information Sources Consulted Prior to Traveling

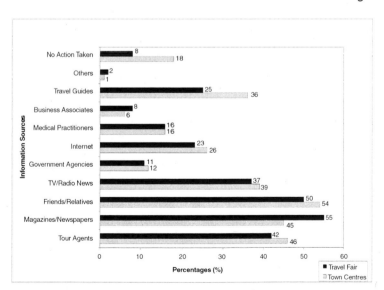

The Internet was used by approximately one-quarter of travel fair attendees (23%) and town centre (26%) respondents for health and food safety information even though there were numerous Web sites on health and food safety. Weber and Roehl (1999) found that, compared to other Internet users, those who search for or purchase travel on-line tended to have more years of experience on-line. Although the present study did not explore respondents' number of years of on-line experience, e-commerce is still relatively new in Singapore. The lack of experience on-line might explain why people were not using the Internet to search for health and food safety information.

Reliability of Information Sources Used

The nine information sources used by respondents prior to traveling were ranked according to their mean response of reliability (Table 11). Town centre participants considered all nine sources to be reliable. Medical practitioners were viewed as the most reliable information source.

The one-way ANOVA test and Bonferroni's multiple comparison were used to indicate the relative reliability of each information source. Results indicated that the nine information sources could be divided into three groups. Medical practitioners, government agencies, TV and radio news, and magazines and newspapers were the most reliable information sources perceived by respondents. Friends and relatives and travel guides were moderately reliable, while tour agents, business associates and the Internet were the least reliable.

Tour agents were the third most consulted information source (Figure 2). More than 40% of travel fair (42%) and town centre respondents (46%) indicated they would use tour agents as an information source, even though agents

TABLE 11. Ranking of Information Sources Consulted Prior to Traveling

Information Source	Mean Reliability	Rank
Medical practitioners	2.08a	1
TV\Radio news	2.11a	2
Government agencies	2.16a	3
Magazines\Newspapers	2.19a	4
Friends and relatives	2.42b	5
Travel guides	2.42b	5
Tour agents	2.52bc	6
Business associates	2.55bc	7
Internet	2.62c	8

Note: Means followed by different lower case letters were significantly different at $p < .05$.

were also perceived as one of the least reliable sources compared to friends and relatives and travel guides. Medical practitioners and government agencies were the most reliable, but less than 20% of respondents consulted these sources (Figure 2). Some travel agents may not always provide an accurate picture of their tour packages to clients, as they may have a tendency to emphasize more the attractions of their tours rather than the risks involved.

Travel agents were also not viewed as experts in the provision of health and food safety advice, as respondents perceived that the information provided was unreliable. This finding was similar to the results of a study done by Lam and Zhang (1999) on the service quality of Hong Kong travel agents (see also Lovelock, this volume). According to Lam and Zhang (1999), customer perceptions of travel agents' service quality fell short of expectations, with the reliability dimension having the largest gap. Customers perceiving reliability problems with travel agents might also be less likely to view travel agent health advice as reliable.

Respondents might find that consulting government agencies or medical practitioners was expensive or inconvenient. These sources were viewed as experts for health and food safety information, but were not widely used. Sharpley et al. (1996) postulated that governments might not always be impartial providers of travel advice, since they may use the opportunity to achieve political ends. Encouraging citizens not to visit a particular country could be an attempt to use travel advice as a method of imposing a form of tourism embargo on another country.

CONCLUSIONS

Food Safety Perceptions of Travel Fair Respondents

The findings suggest that travel fair and town centre respondents had different views about travel and food safety. Those at the fair were more enthusiastic about taking trips and the importance of food safety than town centre participants. Overseas food poisoning experiences did not influence the importance of food safety among travel fair attendees but did influence their perceptions of food safety in developing and developed countries. Food safety in decision-making was critical among town centre participants who were victims of overseas food poisoning. They were more reluctant to travel but less likely to let food safety influence their travel decisions.

Travel fair respondents perceived that food in developed countries was safer than it is in developing countries. Town centre participants were more willing to eat in urban areas (e.g., restaurants) than at hawker stalls, and to them the type of eating outlet was more important in determining whether the food was safe to be consumed than the level of host country development.

Frequent traveling females were more willing to travel. They were also more likely to consider food safety in their travel decisions and took precautions by not visiting countries where food safety is a concern. This finding indicated that female respondents were more risk-averse and preferred to travel safely.

Frequent travelers were more willing to discount the importance of food safety in their travel decisions. They also more likely not to let other people's negative food experiences influence their decisions and were more willing to visit countries that had experienced food safety problems. The same cohort also had stronger and more objective views on the food safety standards in rural areas of developing countries.

Food safety was more important to heavy users of travel agents than light users. Experiences with food-borne illness increased the importance of food safety in travel planning, but would not discourage people from travelling or influence their decision to travel to a country where they had experienced food poisoning in the past. Africa and Latin America were the two most avoided regions as a result of health and food safety concerns. While Asia was the most visited region, it was also the third most avoided region for the same reason. This finding indicates that Singaporeans perceived other Asian countries to have different food safety standards and would generally avoid the destinations that did not meet their expectations.

Friends and relatives, newspapers and magazines, and travel agents were the most common sources of health and food safety information. Travel fair attendance motivated many to travel and raised their awareness of food safety issues. Fair participants tended to judge the safety standards of a country by its stage of development rather than the type of eating establishment.

Recommendations

The low reliability accorded to travel agents by respondents should be a concern to the travel industry. Travel agents, facing increasing pressure from other channels of distribution, could use information dissemination about food safety issues as a value-added service while counselling their clients. This could also provide travel agents with a competitive product and service advantage, compared to non-traditional channels of distribution.

Few respondents consulted medical practitioners before they traveled despite this being the most reliable source of health and food safety information. This should be a concern to public health officials as people may be traveling to risky destinations without knowledge of health risks and proper precautions.

Education programs may help travelers judge levels of food safety at a food service outlet by its hygiene conditions, rather than level of national development.

This study investigated the impact of food safety on the travel decisions of Singaporeans. Results should not be generalised to other populations, as Pizam and Sussmann (1995), for instance, noted that nationality can affect tourist behaviour. This study was biased toward a younger sample with older persons (>50 years) comprising 7.9% of the travel fair and 7.8% town centre sample. Singapore has a rapidly aging population (International Association of Gerontology, 2000). To add a balanced perspective, further research should be conducted into the travel decision-making processes of older Singaporeans. Food safety is only a small part of the overall health risks to which travellers are exposed. Other health risks include malaria, AIDS and other infectious diseases transmitted by means other than food. Future studies ought to consider the impacts of health risks on consumer travel behaviour.

REFERENCES

Ankomah, P. K., Crompton, J. L., and Baker, D. (1996). Influence of cognitive distance in vacation choice. *Annals of Tourism Research*, 23(1): 138-150.

Cartwright, R. (1996). Travelers' Diarrhoea, in S. Clift and S. Page (Eds.), *Health and the International Tourist* (pp. 44-66). London: Routledge.

Cartwright, R. (1992). Epidemiology of travelers' diarrhoea in British package holiday tourists. *PHLS Microbiology Digest*, 9(3): 121-124.

Centers for Disease Control and Prevention (2002). Food-related illness and death in the United States. http://www.cdc.gov/ncidod/eid/vo15no5/mead.html (November 11).

Cohen, E. (1998). Tourism and religion: A comparative perspective. *Pacific Tourism Review*, 2: 1-10.

Corey, R. J. (1996). A drama-based model of traveler destination choice. *Journal of Travel and Tourism Marketing*, 5(4): 1-22.

Cossar, J. H. (1996). Traveler's Health: A Medical Perspective. In S. Clift and S. Page (Eds.), *Health and the International Tourist* (pp. 23-43). London: Routledge.

Cossar, J. H., McEachran, J., and Reid, D. (1993). Holiday companies improve their health advice. *British Medical Bulletin*, 306 (6884): 1070-1071.

Cossens, J. and Gin, S. (1994). Tourism and AIDS: The perceived risk of HIV infection on destination choice. *Journal of Travel and Tourism Marketing*, 3(4): 1-20.

Fodness, D. (1992). The impact of family life cycle on the vacation decision-making process. *Journal of Travel Research*, 31(2): 8-13.

Fodness, D. and Murray, B. (1997). Tourist information search. *Annals of Tourism Research*, 24: 503-523.

Gitelson, R., and Kerstetter, D. (1994). The influence of friends and relatives in travel decision-making. *Journal of Travel and Tourism Marketing*, 3(3): 59-68.

Goldsmith, R. E., and Litvin, S. W. (1999). Heavy users of travel agents: A segmentation analysis of vacation travelers. *Journal of Travel Research*, 38(2) (November): 127-133.

Grabowski, P. and Behrens, R. H. (1996). Provision of health information by British Travel Agents. *Tropical Medicine and International Health*, 1(5): 730-732.

Handszuh, H. F. (1995). Developing Quality in Tourism Services: A Brief Review. In G. Richards (Ed.), *Tourism in Central and Eastern Europe: Educating for Quality* (pp. 225-240), Tilburg: Tilburg University Press.

Handszuh, H. F. (1991). *Food and the Quality of Tourism. Food Safety and Tourism Proceedings 1991*. Madrid: World Tourism Organization.

International Association of Gerontology (2000). 1997 World Congress of gerontology aging beyond 2000: One world one future. [On-line] http://www.cas.flinders.edu.au/iag/proceedings/proc0006.htm

Johns Hopkins Health Information (2002). Stemming the Tide: Coping with Traveler's diarrhea. [On-line] http://www.intelihealth.com/IH/ihtIH?t=20886&c=229773&p=~br,IHW|~st,408|~r,WSIHW000|~b,*|&d=dmtContent, November 16.

Lam, T., and Zhang, H. Q. (1999). Service quality of travel agents: The case of travel agents in Hong Kong. *Tourism Management*, 20: 341-349.

Madrigal, R. (1993). Parents' perceptions of family members' relative influence in vacation decision making. *Journal of Travel and Tourism Marketing*, 2(4): 39-57.

Maser, B., and Weiermair, K. (1998). Travel decision-making: From the vantage point of perceived risk and information preferences. *Journal of Travel and Tourism Marketing*, 7(4): 107-120.

McKercher, B. (1998). The effect of market access on destination choice. *Journal of Travel Research*, 37(3): 39-47.

Milman, A., and Pizam, A. (1995). The role of awareness and familiarity with a destination: The Central Florida Case. *Journal of Travel Research*, 33(3): 21-27.

Page, S. J. and Meyer, D. Y. (1996). Tourist accidents: An exploratory analysis. *Annals of Tourism Research*, 23: 666-690.

Peach, H. G., and Bath, N. E. (1998). Australians traveling abroad without health and safety information: How many and who are they? *Asia Pacific Journal of Tourism Research*, 3(1): 64-74.

Pizam, A. and Sussmann, S. (1995). Does nationality affect tourist behaviour? *Annals of Tourism Research*, 22(4): 901-917.

Powell, D. (1999). An introduction to risk communication and the perception of risk. [On-line] http://www.oac.uoguelph.ca/riskcomm/rc-basics/risk-review/risk-review.htm, (July 23): 1-19.

Sharpley, R., Sharpley, J., and Adams, J. (1996). Travel advice or trade embargo? The impact and implications of official travel advice. *Tourism Management*, 17: 1-7.

Singapore Department of Statistics. (2002). Key Stats: Census of population 2000. [On-line] http://www.singstat.gov.sg/keystats/c2000/wallchart.html, (November 10).

Sirakaya, E., McLellan, R. W. and Uysal, M. (1996). Modelling vacation destination decisions: A behavioural approach. *Journal of Travel and Tourism Marketing*, 5(1): 57-75.

Sönmez, S. F. (1998). Tourism, Terrorism and Political Instability. *Annals of Tourism Research*, 25: 416-456.

Sönmez, S. F. and Graefe, A. R. (1998a). Influence of Terrorism Risk on Foreign Tourism Decisions. *Annals of Tourism Research*, 25: 112-144.

Sönmez, S. F. and Graefe, A. R. (1998b). Determining future travel behaviour from past travel experience and perceptions of risk and safety. *Journal of Travel Research*, 37(2): 171-177.

Travel Weekly (1998). Have you been ill on vacation? *Travel Weekly*, (July 30): 18.

Weber, K., and Roehl, W. S. (1999). Profiling people searching for and purchasing travel products on the World Wide Web. *Journal of Travel Research*, 37: 291-298.

Wilks, J. and Oldenburg, B. (1995). Tourist health–The silent factor in customer service. *Australian Journal of Hospitality Management*, 2(2): 13-23.

World Health Organization. (2000). Food safety: An essential public health issue for the new millennium. [On-line] http://www.who.int/fsf/brochure/foodsafety/fdbroe1.pdf, (February 22).

Yiannakis, A., and Gibson, H. (1992). Roles tourists play. *Annals of Tourism Research*, 19: 287-303.

Zalatan, A. (1998). Wives' involvement in tourism decision processes. *Annals of Tourism Research*, 25: 890-903.

Zimmer, Z., Brayley, R. E., and Searle, M. S. (1995). Whether to go and where to go: Identification of important influences on seniors' decisions to travel. *Journal of Travel Research*, 33(3): 3-10.

New Zealand Travel Agent Practice
in the Provision of Advice
for Travel to Risky Destinations

Brent Lovelock

SUMMARY. Travel agents are one of the most important influencing factors in the travel decision-making process. In terms of safety, there is a growing expectation that travel agents should, as do tour operators, assess destination safety even more critically than a member of the general travelling public. However, the provision of safety advice by travel agents is challenged by the increasingly complex and competitive environment in which they work. Travel safety, while looming large in the thoughts of the general travelling public, may not be a high priority function for travel agents. This paper reports on research undertaken into the attitudes and behaviours of travel agents in New Zealand. A nationwide survey attempts to discern the personal and employment related characteristics of travel agents that may be important influences upon agents'

Brent Lovelock is affiliated with the Department of Tourism, University of Otago, P.O. Box 56, Dunedin, New Zealand (E-mail: blovelock@business.otago.ac.nz).

The author wishes to acknowledge the support of University of Otago through its Otago Research Grant programme, and the research assistance of Caroline Higham, Department of Tourism, University of Otago.

[Haworth co-indexing entry note]: "New Zealand Travel Agent Practice in the Provision of Advice for Travel to Risky Destinations." Lovelock, Brent. Co-published simultaneously in *Journal of Travel & Tourism Marketing* (The Haworth Hospitality Press, an imprint of The Haworth Press, Inc.) Vol. 15, No. 4, 2003, pp. 259-279; and: *Safety and Security in Tourism: Relationships, Management, and Marketing* (ed: C. Michael Hall, Dallen J. Timothy, and David Timothy Duval) The Haworth Hospitality Press, an imprint of The Haworth Press, Inc., 2003, pp. 259-279. Single or multiple copies of this article are available for a fee from The Haworth Document Delivery Service [1-800-HAWORTH, 9:00 a.m. - 5:00 p.m. (EST). E-mail address: docdelivery@haworthpress.com].

perceptions of destination risk, and on their behaviour in terms of selling products for "risky" destinations. *[Article copies available for a fee from The Haworth Document Delivery Service: 1-800-HAWORTH. E-mail address: <docdelivery@haworthpress.com> Website: <http://www.HaworthPress.com> © 2003 by The Haworth Press, Inc. All rights reserved.]*

KEYWORDS. Travel agents, travel decision-making, New Zealand, risk communication, risk assessment

INTRODUCTION

Travel agents are an important source of information and advice on many aspects of holiday planning. However, their abilities and responsibilities in the provision of travel advice are challenged by an increasingly complex operating environment. The traditional travel agency functions in an increasingly competitive sector, with challenges from the relentless expansion of e-commerce, reduced commissions, along with rationalisation and globalisation of the industry. Furthermore, travel agents are now operating in an increasingly complex legal environment where there are very real legal implications and repercussions of providing inappropriate or incomplete travel advice regarding health and safety issues. This legal environment is changing due to an expanded awareness and growth of individual consumer rights, which has brought about changes to legislation, sometimes in distant parts of the world (for example the European Community Directive on Package Travel (EEC, 1992)), that have implications for travel agents worldwide.

These challenges are being faced by the industry at a time when their potential clients are becoming increasingly concerned about personal safety issues, and about the security of destinations. The terrorist events of September 11th, 2001 in the United States and October 12th, 2002 in Bali have reverberated around the world, to an extent that the general travelling public's sense of personal safety may never again be the same. Travellers are also becoming increasingly well-informed through an enhanced destination information-base, contributed to by a range of media, and most notably the Internet. These trends make it necessary now, more than ever before, that travel agents demonstrate appropriate knowledge and practices with respect to the issues that arise in destinations, which may ultimately impact upon the personal safety of their clients.

This paper presents the findings of research that has built upon work undertaken within New Zealand and abroad focussing upon health advice provided by travel agents (e.g., Lawton and Page, 1997). While there has been an emphasis on health, to date there has been little empirical research (especially in New Zealand, but abroad too) that has examined the political and safety aspects of travel advice. This paper aims to redress this gap by examining the way in which the tourism industry perceives and responds to safety issues at the point of sale of tourism products. In particular, it seeks, through the provision of empirical data, to further the debate surrounding the role of the travel agency sector in providing safe tourism experiences.

THE ROLE OF THE TRAVEL AGENT

Travel agents are an important source of information and advice on many aspects of travel planning (e.g., McGuire et al., 1988; Roehl, 1990; Mitchie and Sullivan, 1990). Hsieh and O'Leary's (1993) research in the United Kingdom revealed travel agents to be the most frequently used communication channel as a source of travel information. Similar research undertaken in other parts of the world reinforces the importance of the travel agent in destination choice and travel panning (Gitelson and Crompton, 1983; Snaepenger et al., 1990; Wilks and Atherton, 1994). This role continues despite the growth of other forms of interaction between the client and the supplier of tourist products, for example use of the Internet for direct booking (Lawton and Page, 1997). As Lawton and Page note, travel agents are opinion formers, and "their opinions and the level of information they impart should not be underestimated in terms of their impact on an intending traveller's holiday decision-making process" (1997:100-101).

However, despite their undisputed role in informing the traveller, there is a paucity of research on the finer details of how travel agents fulfil their role in the tourism distribution chain (Lawton and Page, 1997). This particularly applies to the provision of advice regarding general safety issues, an area increasingly advocated by interests such as the World Tourism Organisation (1996: 138), which views safety and security as an integral part of a "tourism quality product." But only one aspect of safety, namely health, has been examined to any great extent. A number of useful articles have been published on the role of the travel agent in providing health advice (e.g., Grabowski and Behrens, 1996; Lawton and Page, 1997; Lawlor et al., 2000; Lee and Spisto, 2001). Sadly, however, much of this research is fairly damning of travel agents in this respect. For example, Lawton and Page's (1997) research into travel agents in New Zealand revealed that the level of health advice given is extremely low, and moreover is not very accurate or reliable. Similar results are evident in the United Kingdom, where travel agents fail to provide simple health advice, despite recommendations by their professional bodies that they do so (Lawlor et al., 2000). Grabowski and Behrens (1996) describe travel agents' health advice in the United Kingdom as inconsistent, noting that agents only mention health risks when prompted.

A number of important issues have been identified that help explain why travel agents provide such poor advice. Some researchers argue that many travel agents lack the training or experience to be able to advise on health risks, and furthermore that they rely on sources of information that are unreliable (Dawood, 1989; Grabowski and Behrens, 1996). Other research points to the changing work environment of travel agents, who in an increasingly competitive sector may not have the resources to offer travel health advice. Lawton and Page (1997) consider that travel agents are already overloaded and that economic pressures make the provision of health advice a burden that many are unwilling to take on. This is illustrated by the high proportion of agents in their study who indicated that they would not be willing to use a health database if one was available.

A common theme across research into travel health advice is the argument used by travel agents that they are not doctors and it is not their business to provide detailed health information (e.g., Dawood, 1989; Lawton and Page, 1997). A similar argument could be applied by agents in terms of general travel safety advice–although certainly in some generating regions, and for some destinations, travel agents have been reluctant to send their clients off into possible danger. For example, during the Kosovo conflict in 1999, many agents in Europe discouraged travel to nearby Croatia and were "not willing to risk the problems their customers might face" (Cavlek, 2002: 482).

But further weight is leant to the agents' case for not providing specific safety advice when consideration is given to the often-murky legal context in which travel advice is given. While Lawton and Page (1997) recommend that agents become more aware of their legal responsibilities, the actual extent of this responsibility is disputed in a number of jurisdictions. Although travel agents do not generally accept liability for services offered by the principal (Witt et al., 1991), they operate in an increasingly litigious environment in many countries, with "increasing civil and criminal liability of travel agents" (Wilks and Atherton, 1994). Often the legal environment in which agents provide advice may be downright confusing. There is, for example, in New Zealand, a distinct lack of legislation directly and specifically relevant to the provision of health advice to travellers (Lee and Spisto, 2001). Moreover, Lee and Spisto (2001: 17) note that despite an ethical responsibility to provide sound advice, "it is sometimes more beneficial for a travel provider to not provide any [health] travel advice at all, than to take risks in providing advice which may subsequently be found to be inaccurate or inadequate."

But while the business environment, training and legal responsibilities of travel agents have been broadly addressed in terms of how they impact the level and accuracy of advice given to clients, research has yet to focus on the personal characteristics of the travel agents themselves. The personal attitudes of agents may predispose them to advise on health and safety issues in predetermined ways. For example, an agent with an allergy to sheep may think twice before sending clients off to a holiday in New Zealand. Or, similarly, an agent who was mugged the last time he or she visited Bogota may think again before sending clients there. Although such personal attitudes and experiences have been widely recognised to play an important role in the travel decision-making behaviour of tourists, they have been relatively unexplored in travel agents; therefore, a significant research gap exists, considering the acknowledged importance of agents in the holiday decision-making process.

Research into tourists' decision making behaviour is well progressed. However, in terms of travel to destinations with a higher degree of risk, for example through terrorism or political instability, the work of Sönmez and Graefe (1998) stands out. Based upon their model of the international tourism decision-making process, Sönmez and Graefe identify a number of internal, external and demographic factors that may influence travellers' decision to travel and their destination choice. Internal factors include travel experience, travel attitude, risk perception level and traveller personality type (e.g., Plog's (1974) psychocentric-allocentric tourist personality continuum). External factors include media coverage of destinations and associated safety issues, and travel advice from a range of sources (for example from travel agents, friends and family, or from government travel advisories). Demographic factors influencing travel decisions are said to include age, gender, income, education and the presence of children in the household. A combination of these factors potentially influences key stages of travel decisions, namely the initial decision to travel, the extent of information searches undertaken concerning destinations, the evaluation of alternative destinations, and ultimately the destination choice.

Sönmez and Graefe's empirical testing of the model revealed that although a number of the above variables contributed indirectly or in a minor way to decision-making, the variables of attitude toward foreign travel, risk perception level and income emerged as the strongest predictors of travel decisions involving terrorism risk or political instability. However, Sönmez and Graefe's (1998) model was developed for tourists, rather than for the advisors of tourists. To consider the role of travel agents as providers of safety advice, a number of the issues discussed above need to be incorporated, which could result in a model such as that illustrated in Figure 1, a basic Travel Agent Safety Advice Model, showing the potential influences on and of travel agents in the provision of safety advice.

FIGURE 1. Travel Agent Safety Advice Model

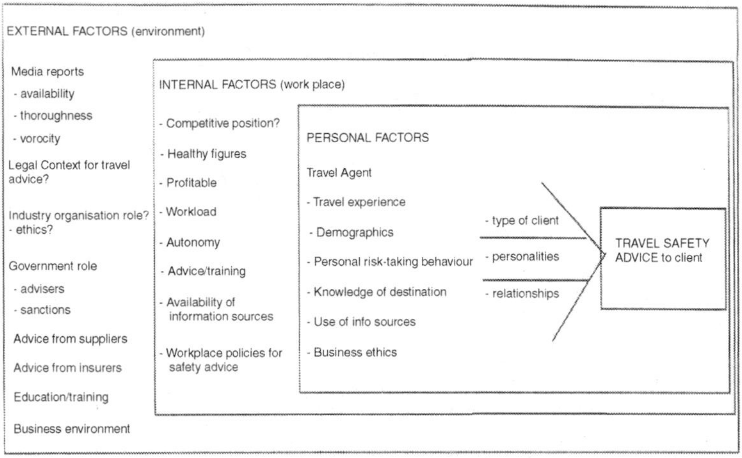

This model identifies external factors acting upon individual agents, but distinguishes between the influence of media and other sources of information, legal and/or ethical considerations and the business environment. These factors collectively act upon and are filtered through the travel agent's personal characteristics and experiences, which may include training, travel experience, knowledge of destinations, and past exposure to risk, along with demographic and psychographic variables (such as personal risk-taking behaviour).

This paper reports upon one aspect of the travel agent safety advice model, that is their personal characteristics, including demographic and psychographic variables, their knowledge of destinations, and previous travel experience. Data on these variables and their effect on how agents perceive destinations in terms of their safety, and also upon their behaviour with respect to selling products for "unsafe" destinations, were gathered through a nationwide survey of travel agents in New Zealand. The research attempts to draw links between consultants' personal attitudes towards risk and their perceptions of travel risk to various destinations, and also gauges their responses to clients, in terms of advice given and products sold. The paper also draws attention to some of the contextual issues in which travel advice is given–for example, the place of safety and security within the training and education of travel agents, the business environment in which travel agents operate, and the industry guidance available in this area.

THE SURVEY

A questionnaire survey was developed to generate data on travel agents. At this stage it is pertinent to note that the questionnaire addressed two main areas of interest, that is safety advice and also ethical considerations for travel advice to "politically unsustainable" destinations. The information presented in this paper is drawn from the items in the questionnaire addressing safety advice.

The questionnaire comprised two sections, the first of which dealt with ethical and safety issues of travel advice, the second seeking data on the travel agents, their personal details, travel experience and leisure choices. Section one contained three questions that ascertained the frequency of which advice was given for travel to unstable and unsafe destinations. Two further items provided a list of destinations and asked agents to report on their safety and ethical perceptions for each, along with the agents' actual behaviour in terms of selling products for the destinations. Another item required agents to identify how often they use a range of information sources. Two final items in this section asked agents for their responses to two actual scenarios of travel to potentially dangerous situations, one past, one current. Section two collected demographic information on the respondents in terms of age, gender, ethnicity, education, and professional position and experience. One item inquired about work place policies for safety advice. Respondents were then asked about their travel experience and whether or not they had felt unsafe in overseas destinations, and why. A further two items sought information on personal risk-taking behaviour through respondents identifying their participation in a range of leisure pursuits.

The questionnaires were mailed to travel agents identified from a membership list obtained with the permission of the Travel Agents Association of New Zealand (TAANZ), in combination with a web site search and use of the Yellow Pages. An explanatory letter was enclosed with each questionnaire outlining the purpose of the survey, together with a reply-paid envelope. A total of 510 questionnaires were mailed out in June 2002, with a follow up letter three weeks later, and then follow up e-mails and telephone calls to non-respondents two weeks after that. Questionnaires were addressed to one individual travel agent responsible for international travel, in each agency in New Zealand. A small incentive (prize draw for duty-free travel vouchers) was offered to encourage participation. A total of 136 questionnaires were completed and returned. Taking changes of address and staff departures into account, the effective response rate was 26.7%. In order to investigate the possibility of non-response bias, telephone calls to a large sample of non-respondents were made. These indicated that "too busy" was the main reason for non-response rather than any inherent aversion to the topic of the questionnaire, or particular views on safety issues.

RESULTS

Travel Agent Characteristics

In terms of numbers, respondents were mainly female (61.7% 38.3% male), and within the 41-50 year age group (30.6%) (Table 1). Most respondents (81.3%) were between the ages of 31 and 50 years, with relatively few younger than 31 years, and even fewer older than 60 years (3%). The group was dominated by agents of New Zealand European or Pakeha[1] descent (84.3%) with Asians being the next most represented ethnic group (8.2%).

Vocational or trade qualification was the predominant highest level of education (49.6%), with about an equal portion having a lower level of education (high school (23.7%) or a higher level (degree or post-graduate (26.7%)). In terms of professional experience, very few had been employed as a travel agent for five years or less (17.9%) with a significant number (61.2%) having been in the sector for longer than ten years. A high proportion (40.1%) of respondents were either owner or part-owner of their business, reflecting the large number of small owner-operated agencies in New Zealand. The mean number of agents working in agencies represented in the study was 6.7, with a mode of 3. Most agents in the study worked mainly in international travel, with 73.3% of agents reporting that over three-quarters of their clients travelled overseas.

Advice to Unsafe Destinations

Most respondents (85.7%) had at some stage given advice to clients about travel to politically unsafe destinations. However agents encountered such clients relatively infrequently, with a high proportion of respondents saying that they saw such clients only "once or twice a month" (36.6%) or "once or twice a year" (45.5%).

Respondents were given a list of countries and asked to rate their safety using a five-point Likert-type scale ranging from "Very safe" to "Very risky" (Table 2). The list of countries that respondents were required to rate for safety is by no means comprehensive. Rather, it is just a list that includes within it a number of countries that have had media coverage of politically related vio-

TABLE 1. Characteristics of Respondents

Characteristics	Frequency (n = 136)
Gender	
Male	38.3%
Female	61.7%
Age	
<20 years	1.5%
21-30 years	14.2%
31-40 years	26.1%
41-50 years	30.6%
51-60 years	24.6%
61 or over	3.0%
Ethnicity	
NZ European/Pakeha	84.3%
Non-NZ European	4.5%
Maori	1.5%
Asian	8.2%
Other	1.5%
Education	
Secondary school	23.7%
Vocational/Trade	49.6%
Degree	20.6%
Post-graduate	6.1%
Length of time travel agent	
0-1 year	4.5%
2-5 years	13.4%
6-10 years	20.9%
11-20 years	33.6%
Over 21 years	27.6%
Position in organisation[a]	
Travel agent	10.4%
Senior travel agent	30.6%
Manager	29.1%
Owner/part owner	47.0%

[a] Percentage values may not sum to 100% owing to multiple responses to this item.

TABLE 2. Safety Ratings for Countries

Country	Mean score, all respondents (1 = very safe; 5 = very risky)	Agents sold products for destination in last year (% respondents) (n = 136)	Would participate in a familiarisation tour (% respondents) (n = 136)
Iraq	4.09	7.8	13.8
Israel	3.96	31.8	31.7
Pakistan	3.94	23.3	17.9
Zimbabwe	3.77	37.2	35.0
Sudan	3.72	2.3	18.7
Iran	3.68	15.5	19.5
Colombia	3.37	16.3	23.6
Nigeria	3.36	11.6	25.2
Solomon Islands	3.25	28.7	28.5
North Korea	3.20	16.3	39.8
Sri Lanka	3.20	31.8	32.5
Myanmar	3.14	24.8	50.4
Kenya	2.99	35.7	49.6
India	2.98	77.5	55.3
Guatemala	2.92	11.6	36.6
Tibet	2.87	23.3	46.3
Cuba	2.65	27.9	52.0
Yugoslavia	2.52	51.2	56.9
Philippines	2.52	55.0	46.3
Russia	2.23	58.1	69.9
Indonesia	2.20	82.9	78.9
Turkey	2.09	71.3	85.4
Malaysia	1.58	89.9	81.3
United States	1.55	92.2	87.0
Fiji	1.39	93.8	88.6
Thailand	1.37	92.3	85.4
Australia	1.11	93.8	85.4

lence over the previous year, and some countries that have totalitarian leadership and/or non-democratically elected governments. A number of "neutral," "safe" countries are also included.

Predictably, respondents' ten most "risky" countries from the selection provided featured countries that had gained much media coverage as stated above. Iraq, Israel, Iran and Pakistan are typical of this group (see Table 3).

TABLE 3. Media Mentions and Ethical Rankings for the Ten Most Risky Countries

Top ten most "risky" countries (1 = "most risky")	Number of times mentioned in a regional newspaper in New Zealand (Sept. 2001- Aug. 2002)[a]	Ethical ranking for countries–mean for all respondents (1 = least ethical destination)
1 Iraq	101	1
2 Israel	387	3*
3 Pakistan	352	2
4 Zimbabwe	57	3*
5 Sudan	10	6
6 Iran	95	5
7 Colombia	37	10*
8 Nigeria	26	10*
9 Solomon Islands	26	10*
10 North Korea	59	7

[a]The *Otago Daily Times* was searched using its own search engine and website (www.odt.co.nz).
*Indicates a "tie."

The first three in particular have a long history of terrorism and/or war. Pakistan has more recently been associated with the Afghanistan war on terrorism.

The Solomon Islands and Zimbabwe both undoubtedly pose risks to travellers, but are anomalies in this study in that they began to feature in the media only in the latter stages of the survey. However, the top ten also includes Sudan, Colombia, Nigeria, and North Korea–none of which had featured very highly on the news in New Zealand over the previous year. However, although they did not attract much press coverage for violence, they are all linked with larger political issues: Sudan is linked with Islamic fundamentalism, as a suspected refuge for terrorists; Colombia is linked with corruption and drugs; Nigeria is linked with ethnic violence and corruption; and North Korea has a totalitarian state. So even though there is no absolute evidence that these countries pose risks to travellers, respondents still ranked them as risky.

Confirmation of the link between safety considerations and ethical considerations for destinations is provided by the ethical rating that respondents were required to give for the same list of countries (Table 3). Agents were asked on *ethical grounds* (not safety) if they would send clients to the destination. The six least desirable destinations on ethical grounds correlate fairly nicely with the six most risky destination for traveller safety.

Information Sources

Still, the question remains, where do agents obtain their information that informs them on safety and related issues? This is particularly intriguing for countries such as Sudan, Nigeria and Colombia, which do not feature highly in the media–at least not in New Zealand. Respondents were asked to indicate the frequency with which they used various sources of information on destinations (Table 4). Newspapers and television news and documentaries are the most commonly used sources of information on international destinations. Travel magazines were also highly used. Although travel advisories and foreign embassies come well down the list in terms of regularity of use, travel insurance companies are regularly used sources for agents when judging the relative safety of destinations. This may explain why countries such as Sudan are considered unsafe destinations, although they do not feature highly in the news–because they have poor insurance ratings. Presumably, insurance companies base their safety ratings on objective data gained from on-the-ground reports and government advisories in combination with statistics from actual

TABLE 4. Use of Various Information Sources

Information source	Ranking (1 = most used; 15 = least used)
Newspapers	1
TV news and documentaries	2
Travel insurance companies	3
Travel magazines	4*
Colleagues	4*
Internet	6
Standard publicity material	7
Ministry of Foreign Affairs travel advisory	8
Familiarisation trips	9
Friends and family	10
Public talks/visits by reps	11
Foreign embassies	12
Other travel advisories	13
Tourism academic journals	14
Movies	15

*Indicates a "tie."

insurance claims. However, one agent commented that travel insurance companies seem to act only in crisis situations and lack "finesse" in discerning the risks of destinations on a regular everyday basis.

Statistical testing revealed no association between frequency of use of information sources and destination safety perception, nor with selling behaviour for products to the ten most risky destinations. In other words, there was no difference in perceptions or behaviour between those respondents who frequently use a wide range of information sources, and those who use a more limited range of sources, and less frequently.

For the list of countries provided, respondents were asked to record if they had sold products for these countries within the previous twelve months (Table 2). The ten most risky destinations offer some interesting juxtapositions. Although Iraq and Sudan were not especially popular destinations in terms of travel products sold, significant sales of products were recorded for Israel, Pakistan, Zimbabwe and the Solomon Islands. Nearly one-third (31.8%) of respondents had sold products to Israel, nearly one-quarter of respondents (23.2%) sold products for Pakistan, and 37.2% had sold products for Zimbabwe. This is despite these countries being rated as the second, third and fourth most risky destinations on the list. And also despite these countries' ranking as the second and third (equal) least ethical international destinations on the list. This gap between travel agent attitudes concerning safety and/or ethics and their behaviour in practice is also reflected in the small number of agents who say that they would refuse (on ethical grounds) to sell products for those destinations (Israel 6.0%; Pakistan 8.3%; Zimbabwe 4.5%).

Workplace Factors

About a third of respondents (32.3%) reported that their workplaces had policies about advice for travel to risky destinations, although the nature of those policies was not revealed in this stage of the study. The existence of a travel-safety policy in the workplace did not influence respondents' selling behaviour for travel products associated with the top ten most risky destinations. Other workplace factors such as size and format of the agency appeared to have no influence on risk perceptions of respondents, nor upon selling behaviour for risky destinations.

Personal Travel Experience and Advice Given

Respondents were asked to indicate if they had ever felt unsafe in an overseas destination, and were asked to identify the cause of this feeling. Just under half (46.3%) of respondents had felt unsafe. Statistical tests (Chi-Square) revealed no discernible links between demographic or work experience data (age, gender, ethnicity, education, having lived overseas, length of time in service as a travel agent, and position in the agency) and respondents having felt unsafe in an overseas destination.

The most commonly experienced scenario when feeling unsafe was respondents feeling in danger of becoming a potential victim of a crime (45.2%)–although only 17.7% had actually fallen victim to crime (see Table 5). Interestingly, a relatively high 33.9% of respondents for this item reported "political unrest" as a cause for their feeling unsafe, and even war or threat of war was significant in 12.9% of cases.

One could assume that those respondents who had experienced danger overseas, and who had been exposed to a wider range of dangerous situations may have different perceptions of the safety of places or behave differently in terms of selling travel products for the more dangerous destinations. However, this was not the case. Statistical tests revealed that there was no difference in the perceptions of destinations or in the selling behaviour of products (for the top ten most risky destinations) between respondents who had felt unsafe overseas and those who had not. Similarly, the number of dangerous travel situations that respondents had encountered had no discernible influence upon the perceptions of destinations, nor upon the selling behaviour for risky destinations.

One item of the questionnaire addressed the travel experience of respondents, in terms of the number of overseas trips they had made in their lifetime, and the regions they had visited. Statistical tests revealed that there was no association between the total number of trips taken by respondents and their feeling unsafe in overseas destinations. Also, the number of trips taken had no

TABLE 5. Experience of Danger Overseas

Danger scenario	Percent of cases (multiple responses (n=136))
Potential victim of a crime	45.2
Motor vehicle or traffic	43.5
Political unrest	33.9
Health (disease/poisoning/animal attack)	30.6
Actual victim of a crime	17.7
War or threat of war	12.9
Air travel	12.9
Physical activity or sport	4.8

discernible influence upon selling behaviour nor upon the perception of destination safety. For the item addressing regions visited, each region was given a score based upon common perceptions of danger (the researcher's judgement–e.g., Australia = 1, South America = 3), thus each respondent was assigned a total travel diversity score. Respondents who had travelled to a broader range of regions did not perceive destinations differently in terms of safety or behave differently in selling products to risky destinations.

Personal Risk-Taking in Leisure Activities

Data on personal risk-taking behaviour were gathered through the inclusion of two items that required respondents to indicate which of a range of outdoor recreational activities they actively engaged in (e.g., bungy-jumping, hang-gliding, water-skiing). Participation in these activities was converted into a physical risk taking score, which was then related to respondents' perceptions of safety. However, participation in these activities was not associated with respondents having felt unsafe in an overseas destination. It did not have a discernible effect upon destination safety perceptions, nor upon respondents' selling behaviour for travel to the ten most risky destinations.

Risk Scenarios

In addition to asking respondents about their sales of products to risky destinations, respondents were given two specific "real-life" travel risk situations, one historic and one contemporary, and asked to describe their sales behaviour for these scenarios. The first situation concerned the most recent Fiji coup, where the Prime Minister of Fiji and a number of other political figures were held hostage by coup leaders from May to June 2000. This coup received a great deal of media coverage in New Zealand. Over the period of the coup, Fiji gained an image of being a volatile and dangerous country, with one tourist resort even being taken over by Fijians in support of the coup. The New Zealand Government issued warnings against travel to Fiji. Respondents were asked whether or not they continued to sell Fiji-related products during the period of the coup. More than half (54.8%) of respondents continued to sell Fiji products. Respondents who ceased selling Fiji products were then asked the main reason why they had done so, 62.3% citing safety of clients as the main reason. However, the most important reason for a large portion of respondents ceasing to sell products was simply the lack of demand.

The second situation concerned India and Pakistan, which during the time of the survey were being portrayed in the media as being on the brink of war–possibly nuclear. There were many media illustrations of extreme violent events occurring over this period, and the major travel advisories were warning against travel to the sub-continent. Respondents were asked what their response would be to a client who came in wishing to travel to India or Pakistan at that time (Table 6).

Overwhelmingly the largest proportion of respondents said that they would advise their clients of the safety issues surrounding travel to India or Pakistan at that time. However, relatively few (only 6.9% of cases) respondents would actually discontinue with the sale. Alarmingly, a small number of respondents even indicated that they would say nothing (in terms of the safety issues) and continue with the sale. A significant percentage of respondents would seek ethical advice from their supervisor, industry association or other source on this issue.

DISCUSSION

This study showed, as to be expected, that travel agents, like the general travelling public, have differing perceptions of the safety of different destinations. Some places are seen as very risky, while others are seen as being quite safe. However, the study did not identify personal or work-related characteristics of travel agents that could be considered good predictors of agents' perceptions of safety. This is in contrast to the travelling public, for which a range of variables (e.g., age, gender, income, children in household) have been demonstrated to contribute toward perceptions of risk and decision-making (Sönmez and Graefe, 1998). In the current study, even variables such as travel experience, in terms of the number of trips made by travel agents, and the diversity of regions they visited were not linked with their perceptions of safety.

TABLE 6. Response to Request to Travel to India or Pakistan

Response to client	Percent of cases (multiple responses (n=136))
Advise the client of the safety issues surrounding travel to India or Pakistan	86.9
Advise client of the safety issues surrounding travel to India or Pakistan and discontinue with sale	6.9
Seek ethical advice from another source (e.g., supervisor, TAANZ)	20.8
Say nothing and continue with sale	4.6

Sönmez and Graefe (1998) demonstrated a tangible link between attitudes and behaviour for the travelling public in terms of the destinations they ultimately choose. For example, their study found that risk perception level was a strong predictor for travel decision-making. This study, however, did not discern any link between risk perception and travel agent behaviour, in terms of selling products for risky destinations. Although travel agents rated countries differently for risk, this had no significant influence upon their decision whether or not to sell clients a product for a risky destination.

This point was further amplified by the results of the Fiji and the India/Pakistan travel scenarios in the questionnaire. In the Fiji situation, there was a very real, highly publicised danger to tourists. Yet over half of the respondents in the study continued to sell products for the destination. In the India/Pakistan scenario, two countries came as close as any to the brink of nuclear war, yet despite the demonstrated violence in the subcontinent, relatively few respondents said they would discontinue a sale to a client wishing to travel there.

The fact that travel agents' perceptions of destination safety are not reflected in their behaviour with respect to selling products may be attributed to a number of reasons. First, of course, the travel agents themselves would not be travelling to those potentially dangerous destinations, so the personal risk factor does not exist as it does for their clients. Second, as illustrated in the Travel Agent Safety Advice Model, a number of external, environmental and work-place factors come into play, along with personal factors. The relationship between the agent and the client, and the type of clients are also likely influences on the level of action taken regarding their travel safety.

This study demonstrated that personal factors, such as demographics, risk perceptions, personal risk taking, leisure behaviour and travel experience are not significant influences upon travel agent behaviour. This would imply, then, that external environmental and work place factors may be more important in shaping travel agent responses. These external and work place factors can be seen as either influencing factors or as filters that modify the normal risk perception-decision making link that has been observed in the general travelling public (e.g., Sönmez and Graefe, 1998).

A major external factor is the "information environment" in which agents develop their risk perceptions for destinations and then make decisions regarding the sale of products. The influence of information sources on travel agent behaviour may be observed on a number of levels; external, workplace and personal. It is observed in the external environment, in terms of the availability of information on certain destinations, and also in terms of the credibility of this information. While the present study showed that travel agents tend to utilise a wide range of information sources, the emphasis is on what Gartner and Shen (1992:47) would term "autonomous" or second-party sources, mainly the media. This study revealed that travel agents' top two sources of information on destinations are newspapers and TV news and documentaries. This is alarming if the "credibility" of these sources is considered to include coverage and thoroughness as well as voracity. For example, both of these sources can have regional and ethnic biases in their coverage of events. New Zealand, for instance, tends to get a reduced coverage of events in Central and South America and sub-Saharan Africa.

The frequent use of travel magazines as a source of information on safety (or ethics) by travel agents in the study is also somewhat of concern, as this type of publication tends to downplay or neglect political and ethical issues. In a feature article (Myers, 2002) on travel to Sri Lanka in a recent volume of a major industry magazine, for example, there is not one mention of the Tamil Tiger issue and possible related travel security matters. This is despite there being extensive current warnings in travel advisories about the risks to tourists from terrorism and land mines in Sri Lanka (e.g., U.S. Department of State, 2002).

The workplace is also important in the ways it may influence the use of information sources, especially in terms of making them available to their travel agent employees, for example by subscribing to various publications, by making time for employees to consult relevant websites, or by regularly circulating travel advisories. Ultimately, however, the use of these information sources is up to the individual travel agent. This study indicated that no matter how motivated (or indolent) the travel agent is with respect to the use of information sources, this did not alter the way travel safety advice was given or that products were sold for risky destinations, nor did the use of specific information sources, such as government travel advisories, influence perceptions of risk or selling behaviour. Thus, ultimately no matter what information is made available to travel agents it appears to have little influence on their behaviour with respect to safety issues.

While this research did not focus upon the complete range of external environmental and work-place factors, a small number were investigated. These included factors such as the agent's position in the agency and the presence or absence of a workplace policy on travel safety advice. Neither of these, however, were predictors of travel agent behaviour. Obviously a range of workplace factors may influence travel agent behaviour, including the company's profitability, employee workload, the degree of employee autonomy, and the availability of advice and ongoing training (some of the larger travel agent chains in New Zealand have in-house training programmes). Business-related factors may be particularly important.

The gap between how travel agents feel about the safety of destinations and their sales of products for risky destinations is likely linked to two fundamental influences in the travel agents' decision-making process. First, agents are in a highly competitive sector and need to generate business; they may not have the luxury of turning clients away. Second, agents may feel that they have an ethical duty to meet the needs of clients, wherever they may wish to go, no matter how dangerous or politically unattractive the destination may be.

The Travel Agents Association of New Zealand *Code of Ethics and Practice* reveals that agents do not have to follow their clients directions blindly, although "members will treat their clients' interests as paramount" (TAANZ, 2002: 50). This clause of the code is seemingly written with the financial interests of the client in mind. But even if interpreted more broadly, it is confusing in terms of the agent being required to balance the need to fulfil clients' personal motivations for travel with the need to keep them from harm–both valid "interests." The TAANZ code also states that agents should ascertain "all pertinent facts" concerning destinations "so that they may fulfil their obligation to inform their clients accurately about the services they sell" (TAANZ, 2002: 50). Presumably this would include advice on safety issues that may influence the client's ability to partake of and enjoy those services. Although clear guidance may not be forthcoming from travel agent associations, some workplaces do have policies regarding safety advice. But as indicated above in the survey, this did not appear to influence sales of products to risky destinations.

So the travel agent is therefore trapped in a situation of "ethical dissonance." This term has been used to describe tourism managers who experience conflict between the stronger ideological aspect (what they believe) and the operational aspect (what they practice) of their ethical philosophy (Whitney, 1990: 58). In the travel safety advice scenario, the magnitude of the "dissonance" is influenced by a range of external, workplace and personal characteristics interacting in ways that may be difficult to quantify or predict. Furthermore, travel agents are trapped between two sets of ethics–the humanitarian ethic that says fellow human beings should not be sent off into potential danger, and the business ethic that says the customer is always right (and so is the boss–we need the business!). In New Zealand the business ethic or drive is possibly felt more strongly owing to the structure of the industry which still has a high proportion of small owner-operated agencies, who operate in a highly competitive sector that has undergone some substantial changes in recent times, not the least of which has been reductions in commissions for air travel.

CONCLUSION

In contrast to the experience in some parts of the world where there has been some reluctance on the part of travel agents to send their clients into potentially dangerous destinations, in New Zealand travel agents seem hesitant about taking special action in such scenarios. The findings of this study on travel safety advice mirror that of previous research into health advice (e.g., Lawton and Page, 1997) where generally poor (or lack of) advice is given by travel agents. This is attributable to a wide range of external environmental and workplace factors such as incomplete training, a confusing legal context and a competitive business environment that possibly fails to encourage the provision of travel safety action. These factors are largely outside of the control of individual agents and need to be addressed by industry in co-operation with government. The large number of ongoing conflicts throughout the world, the seeming growth in the use of tourists as political pawns, coupled with the large number of tourists forever "pushing the frontiers" dictate that the current approach is no longer acceptable. In the final analysis, this study revealed more about the importance of sector-wide issues in travel safety advice than about the personal factors that were initially investigated. This suggests that further research is needed, not only on the interpersonal relations between travel agent and client, but on the broader sector-wide issues that influence travel safety advice.

NOTE

1. "Pakeha" is a Maori term generally used to describe Caucasian residents of New Zealand.

REFERENCES

Cavlek, N. (2002). Tour operators and destination safety. *Annals of Tourism Research*, 29(2): 478-496.

Dawood, R. (1989). Tourists' health–Could the travel industry do more? *Tourism Management*, 10(4):285-287.

EEC (1992). Council directive on package travel, package holidays and package tours. 90/314 *EEC Official Journal of the European Communities* No. L 158/59/23/6/90.

Gartner, W.C. and Shen, J. (1992). The impact of Tiananmen Square on China's tourism image. *Journal of Travel Research*, 30(4): 47-52.

Gitelson, R. and Crompton, J. (1983). The planning horizons and sources of information used by pleasure vacationers. *Journal of Travel Research*, 22(2): 2-7.

Grabowski, P. and Behrens, R.H. (1996). Provision of health information by British travel agents. *Tropical Medicine and International Health*, 1(5): 730-732,

Hsieh, S. and O'Leary, T. (1993). Communication channels to segment pleasure travellers. *Journal of Travel & Tourism Marketing*, 2(2/3): 57-75.

Lawlor, D.A., Burke, J., Bouskill, E., Conn, G., Edwards, P., and Gillespie, D. (2000). Do British travel agents provide adequate health advice for travellers? *British Journal of General Practice*, 50: 567-568.

Lawton, G. and Page, S. (1997). Evaluating travel agents' provision of health advice to travellers. *Tourism Management*, 18(2): 89-104.

Lee, C. and Spisto, M. (2001). The provision of travel advice to tourists and travellers: The legal implications in New Zealand. *Asia Pacific Journal of Tourism Research*, 6(1): 12-19.

McGuire, F., Uysal, M. and McDonald, G. (1988). Attracting the older traveller. *Tourism Management*, 9(2): 161-163.

Mitchie, D. and O'Sullivan, G. (1990). The role of the international travel agent in the travel decision making process of clients' families. *Journal of Travel Research*, 29(2): 30-33.

Myers, P. (2002). Beauty and the beasts. *PATA Compass*, July-August: 26-27, 35.

Plog, S.C. (1974). Why destination areas rise and fall in popularity. *The Cornell Hotel and Restaurant Administration Quarterly*, 14(9): 55-58.

Roehl, W.S. (1990). Travel agent attitudes toward China after Tiananmen Square. *Journal of Travel Research*, 29(2): 16-22.

Snaepenger, D., Meged, K., Snelling, M. and Worral, K. (1990). Information search strategies by destination-naïve tourists. *Journal of Travel Research*, 29(1): 13-16.

Sönmez, S.F. and Graefe, A.R. (1998). Influence of terrorism risk on foreign tourism decisions. *Annals of Tourism Research*, 25(1): 112-114.

TAANZ (2002). *TAANZ Handbook 2002*. Wellington: Travel Agents Association of New Zealand.

U.S. Department of State (2002). Sri Lanka Consular Information Sheet 11/4/02. [Online] Available at: *http://travel.state.gov/sri_lanka.html* (August 2002).

Whitney, D. (1990). Ethics in the hospitality industry: With a focus on hotel managers. *International Journal of Hospitality Management*, 7(1): 59-68.

Wilks, J. and Atherton, T. (1994). Health and safety in marine tourism: A social, medical and legal appraisal. *Journal of Tourism Studies*, 5(2): 2-16.

Witt, S., Brooke, M. and Buckley, P. (1991). *The Management of International Tourism*. London: Unwin Hyman.

World Tourism Organisation (1996). *Tourist Safety and Security*. Madrid: World Tourism Organisation.

The Need to Use
Disaster Planning Frameworks
to Respond to Major Tourism Disasters:
Analysis of Australia's Response
to Tourism Disasters in 2001

Bruce Prideaux

SUMMARY. This paper looks at the Australian federal government's response to a series of tourism disasters and crises that affected the Australian tourism industry in 2001 and measures these impacts against the response mechanism suggested in the Tourism Disaster Framework Model developed by Faulkner (2001). The paper finds that as shocks often occur with little warning, the establishment of a formal disaster management framework should be given a high priority by government and receive support from the private sector. Had such a mechanism been in place in Australia prior to 2001, the government may have been able to respond to the disasters in a more considered manner. *[Article copies available for a fee from The Haworth Document Delivery Service: 1-800-HAWORTH. E-mail address: <docdelivery@haworthpress.com> Website: <http://www. HaworthPress.com> © 2003 by The Haworth Press, Inc. All rights reserved.]*

Bruce Prideaux is affiliated with the School of Tourism and Leisure Management, The University of Queensland, 11 Salisbury Road, Ipswich, Queensland 4307, Australia (E-mail: b.prideaux@mailbox.uq.edu.au).

[Haworth co-indexing entry note]: "The Need to Use Disaster Planning Frameworks to Respond to Major Tourism Disasters: Analysis of Australia's Response to Tourism Disasters in 2001." Prideaux, Bruce. Co-published simultaneously in *Journal of Travel & Tourism Marketing* (The Haworth Hospitality Press, an imprint of The Haworth Press, Inc.) Vol. 15, No. 4, 2003, pp. 281-298; and: *Safety and Security in Tourism: Relationships, Management, and Marketing* (ed: C. Michael Hall, Dallen J. Timothy, and David Timothy Duval) The Haworth Hospitality Press, an imprint of The Haworth Press, Inc., 2003, pp. 281-298. Single or multiple copies of this article are available for a fee from The Haworth Document Delivery Service [1-800-HAWORTH, 9:00 a.m. - 5:00 p.m. (EST). E-mail address: docdelivery@haworthpress.com].

10.1300/J073v15n04_04

KEYWORDS. Disaster, policy, terrorism, Tourism Disaster Framework Model, planning, September 11, 2001

INTRODUCTION

As a sector, tourism has repeatedly demonstrated sensitivity to disruptions to the political, economic, military and cultural affairs of nations. Surprisingly, few tourism scholars have conducted research into methods and frameworks that allow ordered and measured responses to disasters and crises (Prideaux and Master, 2001). From a theoretical perspective, Faulkner (2001) explored a number of issues associated with the impact of unexpected events on the tourism industry and, finding that existing models (for example, Cassedy, 1991; Drabek, 1995) failed to provide an effective conceptual framework for responding to tourism crises and disasters, developed the Tourism Disaster Management Framework (TDMF). While Faulkner's framework offers a significant advance over previous models, the only test of the framework to date has been its application to a relatively small scale disaster. Although the TDMF has significant operational capability, adaptability to specific types of disasters and inbuilt flexibility, the need for adapting the framework as a management tool for large scale crisis and disasters has not been previously addressed.

This paper examines the issue of disaster management in the tourism industry following unexpected shocks and crises. The September 11, 2001 terrorist attack on the US has highlighted the vulnerability of the tourism industry to unexpected disasters in a dramatic manner. Disasters of this magnitude are relatively rare but when they occur, they create considerable problems for the tourism industry that, unfortunately, continues to ignore the need for developing mechanisms to cope with the unexpected. History tells us that disasters and crises are usually unforseen, occur regularly, act as a shock on the tourism industry and are almost always poorly handled. In the decade prior to the September 11 attacks, major tourism disasters included the Foot and Mouth outbreak in the UK, earthquakes in recent years in Taiwan and Japan, a major war in the Persian Gulf, the Asian Financial Crisis and many other disasters and crises of smaller magnitude. The need for a well planned disaster response mechanism is apparent but many countries, including Australia, have yet to develop appropriate response mechanisms for their tourism industries. This stands in stark contrast to the response by governments to other forms of disaster that cause injury to citizens or damage to property and infrastructure.

To develop the Tourism Disaster Management Framework, Faulkner (2001) drew on existing tourism research and insights gained from research into disaster management reported in journals such as *Disaster Prevention and Management*, *Risk Management* and the *International Journal of Mass Emergencies and Disasters*. By synthesising previous research, Faulkner was able to develop the Tourism Disaster Management Framework as an aid for managing disasters and crises that affect tourism. Faulkner's framework is based on three principal components; firstly, an anatomy of the disaster process is outlined commencing with a Pre-event phase and concluding with a Resolution phase; secondly, Elements of the disaster management responses are detailed; and thirdly, Principal ingredients of the disaster management strategies are outlined. Of the three components of the framework, the Phases in Disaster process (Column 1) and the Principal Ingredients of the Disaster Management Strategies (Column 3) are generic to most disasters while the Elements of the Disaster Management Responses component (Column 2) is more specific to the type of disaster being managed. In a subsequent paper, Faulkner and Vikulov (2001) investigated the response of the tourism industry to a real disaster by applying the TDMF to the 1998 Australia Day Flood in Katherine, Australia. In this test, the TDMF demonstrated a capability to be used as both a preventative planning tool and as a template for real-time disaster management. The framework's usefulness in larger disasters and crises has yet to be tested although the need for a development of this nature became apparent in the aftermath of the September 11 terrorist attack. The capability of the TDMF to cope with large-scale disasters has yet to be conceptualised and incorporated into a modified framework. Beyond single large scale disasters there is also a need to develop a capability to deal with multiple crises and disasters of the type that affected the Australian tourism industry during 2001.

This paper will focus on events in Australia to highlight the range and scope of events that may face the tourism industry as it attempts to cope with disaster and crisis on a front that is broader than a single incident at a single point in time. While specifically focusing on Australia, findings from this research are applicable to all national tourism industries. Following a discussion of the impact of the disasters and crises (collectively described as shocks) experienced during 2001 by the Australian tourism industry, the response of the government will be analysed and measured against the TDMF. Deficiencies in the government response will then be identified and suggestions for appropriate modification of the TDMF to cope with large scale disasters and crises will be incorporated into a revised framework. The paper identifies both short term and long term elements of public sector response with the major area of focus being on the short term.

THE TOURISM DISASTER MANAGEMENT FRAMEWORK

It is useful to briefly review the literature used by Faulkner to develop the TDMF. Drawing on the well established disaster management literature (particularly Fink, 1986; Keown-McMullan, 1997; Weiner and Kahn, 1972) Faulkner (2001) identified the key characteristics of disasters and crises as:

- A triggering event,
- A high threat environment with short response times,
- A perception of an inability to cope by those directly affected, at least in the short term,
- A turning point where the situation is responded to, and
- Characterised by "fluid, unstable, dynamic" situations (Fink, 1986: 20).

Faulkner (2001) then examined the immediate responses to disaster situations from a sociological perspective (see Arnold, 1980; Booth, 1993), finding that the initial shock of the event may impair adaptive responses in some situations while acting as a mobilising factor in other situations. Ultimately, the community will accept the reality of the change that has occurred and at this turning point will develop adaptive responses to cope with new realities and enter into a rebuilding phase.

The manner in which the tourism industry is affected during the immediate post-disaster period will depend on a range of factors, including: the internal cultures and modus operandi of organisations responding to the disaster; the ability of various organisations to work cooperatively to solve the problem; the ability of normally bureaucratic hierarchical organisations to respond swiftly and decisively; the manner in which the media cover the situation; the resources available to the public sector to respond to the disaster; and the ability of the private sector to continue to trade during and after the disaster. There is also a long term aspect to disaster response that should be considered when short term response strategies are being developed. Drawing on elements of the disaster response stages suggested by Fink (1986) and Roberts (1994), Faulkner postulated six stages that a community may pass through during a disaster. To these stages Faulkner added disaster survival strategies based on previous research by Turner (1994) and Quarantelli (1984) and the ingredients of tourism disaster strategies developed by Cassedy (1991) and Drabek (1995) to develop the TDMF illustrated in Figure 1.

FIGURE 1. Tourism Disaster Management Framework

Phase in disaster process	Elements of the disaster management responses	Principal ingredients of the disaster management strategies
1. *Pre-event* When action can be taken to prevent or mitigate the effects of potential disasters.	*Precursors* • Identify relevant public/private sector agencies/organizations • Establish coordination/consultative framework and communication systems • Develop, document and communicate disaster management strategy • Education of industry stakeholders, employees, customers and community • Agreement on, and commitment to, activation protocols • Establish a joint industry/government disaster coordination committee	*Risk assessment* • Assessment of potential disasters and their probability of occurrence • Development of scenarios on the genesis and impacts of potential disasters • Develop disaster contingency plans • Develop a forecasting capability • Identify possible public sector policy responses
2. *Prodromal* When it is apparent that a disaster is imminent.	*Mobilisations* • Warning systems (including general mass media) • Establish disaster management command centre • Secure facilities	*Disaster contingency plans* • Identify likely impacts and groups at risk • Assess community and visitor capabilities to cope with impacts • Articulate the objectives of individual (disaster specific) contingency plans • Identify actions necessary to avoid or minimise impacts at each stage • Devise strategic priority (action) profiles for each phase
3. *Emergency* The effect of the disaster is felt and action is necessary to protect people and property.	*Action (will depend on type of disaster)* • Rescue/evacuation procedures • Media campaigns to reassure or capture new markets • Determine level of government assistance required • Additional security measures	° Prodromal ° Emergency ° Intermediate ° Long-term recovery • On-going review and revision in the light of ° Experience ° Changes in organisational structures and personnel ° Changes in the environment • Review of risk assessment after event
4. *Intermediate* A point where the short-term needs of people have been addressed and the main focus of activity is to restore services and the community to normal.	*Recovery* • Damage audit/monitoring system • Clean-up and restoration • Media comunication strategy	
5. *Long-term (recovery)* Continuation of previous phase, but items that could not be attended to quickly are attended to at this stage. Post-mortem, self-analysis, healing.	*Reconstruction and reassessment* • Repair and rehabilitation of damaged areas and infrastructures • Counselling victims • Restoration of business/consumer confidence and development of investment plans • Debriefing to revise strategies • Public sector funding requirements	
6. *Resolution* Routine restored or new improved state establishment.	*Review* • Review of policy successes and failures and rectify any short comings	

Source: Adapted from Faulkner (2001).

BACKGROUND TO MAJOR SHOCKS IN 2001

Following the success of the Sydney Olympics in 2000, the Australian tourism industry was expecting an increase of approximately 6.6% per annum in arrivals during 2001 (Tourism Forecasting Council, 1999). However, three unrelated events individually and collectively, severely disrupted domestic and international tourism flows during the course of 2001. In March 2001, HIH Insurance, Australia's leading provider of public liability insurance, ceased trading, leading to significant increases in public liability insurance premiums. In September the Al-Qaeda terrorist attack on the US had major ramifications for global tourism flows leading to a fall in inbound tourism that had not recovered by late 2002. Three days after the US incident and in an unrelated event, Ansett Airlines, Australia's second largest domestic airline, ceased trading, severely disrupting domestic aviation as well as disrupting the travel plans of international visitors who used Ansett's Star Alliance affiliations for the domestic component of their journey.

The response to these "shocks" by the national government was vigorous but not as considered as would be expected given the status of Australia's tourism industry as the nation's fourth largest export industry (11.2% of total export receipts in 1998). At the time that vigorous government action was sought by the tourism industry, the Federal Government was simultaneously: preparing to fight a federal election; dealing with a major political crisis that emerged from the government's handling of illegal refugee arrivals in Northern Australia; determining its response to a US request for Australia to join the international collation of nations committing troops to Afghanistan to combat Taliban and Al-Qaeda forces; and organising the annual Commonwealth Heads of Government Meeting (CHOGM) that involved the Prime Ministers or senior leaders of over 50 British Commonwealth countries as well as Queen Elizabeth II, of the UK. Security fears eventually saw the CHOGM meeting cancelled and rescheduled to February 2002. The following sections will summarise the immediate impact of each shock followed by an assessment of the public sector's response.

Impact of the Collapse of HIH Insurance

On March 15, 2001 HIH Insurance was placed into receivership after accumulating trading losses in excess of AUD$5.3 billion. At the time of its collapse, HIH was Australia's major provider of public liability insurance with approximately 40% of the market ("Post-HIH Premium Spike," 2002). The impact of the collapse on the tourism industry began to emerge within weeks. One of the causes of the companies' collapse was HIH's deliberate strategy of using low premiums to capture a major share of the domestic public liability insurance market. As a result of HIH's business strategy, the national insurance industry collected AUD$803.5 million in premiums in 2000 but paid out AUD$1.009 billion in claims ("Post-HIH Premium Spike," 2002). Losses of this magnitude were not sustainable in the long run and the remaining insurance companies commended increasing premiums on Public Liability Insurance shortly after HIH ceased trading. Premiums increased by between 25%

and 1,000% ("Premiums Soar," 2002: 135). The September 11 attack created a new difficulty for the insurance industry. Following that attack, premiums were again increased substantially as reinsurance pools worldwide were exhausted and risk factors escalated rapidly.

The impact of premium rises on the tourism industry was substantial. In one representative example, the Big Banana, a themed tourist attraction in Coffs Harbour, New South Wales, was faced with a 359% increase in public liability insurance with annual premiums rising from AUD$39,000 to AUD$140,000. Two further examples (of many) illustrate the impact on events. The annual Thorpedale Potato Festival in Victoria faced a 1,000% increase in the cost of its public liability insurance cover while in Tumbarumba, New South Wales, the Easter Tooma Gymkhana was cancelled because the public liability insurance premium increased from $1,600 to $10,000 ("Give Back our Source of Funds," 2002). Most tourism businesses and festivals experienced similar premium increases, leading to the cancellation of many events.

Impact of September 11 on Australian Tourism

The terror factor created by the graphic images of passenger aircraft flying into New York's World Trade Centre Towers and the following lock down of all US air services for 3 days caused an immediate decline in global departures. In Australia, this shock had two consequences. International arrivals and departures declined immediately and had not return to pre-September 11 levels by late 2002. The ensuing rumours of war and threat of additional terrorist attacks in many popular international tourist destinations exacerbated this situation. Afraid to travel overseas, many Australians cancelled their overseas holidays and substituted domestic locations as an alternative. However, the collapse of Ansett limited the ability of many people to substitute domestic travel for international travel during the period it took for remaining domestic carriers Qantas and Virgin Blue to increase capacity.

The impact of the events of September 11, 2001 caused a severe decline in inbound travel from all of Australia's major markets. Compared to the same month in 2000, inbound travel in 2001 declined by 12% in September, 16.2% in October, 20.5% in November and 10.7% in December. By September 2002 the inbound market had not recovered and compared to the preliminary figures for January to August 2001, the preliminary figures for same period in 2002 were down 4% (Australian Tourist Commission, 2002). A 2002 survey of Australian inbound operators conducted by the Australian Tourism Export Council ("Tourism Feels the Chill Wind," 2002) found that in the June quarter of 2002 group travel remained subdued and discounting had become widespread as inbound operators attempted to stimulate travel to Australia.

Collapse of Ansett

For several months prior to September 11, Ansett appeared to be in financial trouble. By the time of its collapse Ansett's market share had eroded to 35% of the domestic market with Virgin Blue accounting for approximately 10% of the market and Qantas accounting for the remaining 55%. Air New Zealand had built up 100% equity in Ansett to give it a significant presence in the large Australian domestic market with the aim of growing the enlarged and merged airline into a major regional carrier. However, financial problems experienced by both Air New Zealand and Ansett forced Air New Zealand to walk away from its investment in Ansett and on 14 September, the airline was placed into receivership. This decision had a major impact on the domestic tourism industry, particularly in regional areas where Ansett's regional subsidiaries provided substantial capacity. While the remaining domestic carriers rapidly increased capacity, the demand for seats exceeded supply for several months. After six weeks, the airline's receivers returned the airline to partial operations as a European style no-frills airline but with a substantially reduced network and fleet size, in the hope that a buyer could be found.

This strategy was not successful and the restructured airline only managed to recapture 5% of the market and accumulated additional losses of AUD$50 million (Buffini, Evans and Hepworth, 2002). Plans to relaunch Ansett as a full service airline were announced in December 2001; however, significant shortcomings in the bid made by the Tesna consortium; including its business plan (Boyle, 2002), an inability to secure the leasehold of the Ansett domestic terminals at Sydney and Melbourne Airports and problems with leasing sufficient aircraft caused the bid to collapse.

Major implications of the failure of Ansett for the Australian tourism industry were the loss of tourists from New Zealand, disruption of services to rural areas and the loss of the ability for customers of Star Alliance partner airlines to use frequent flyer points for travel to and within Australia. The impact on tourism flows from New Zealand was particularly severe. With the collapse of Ansett, Air New Zealand lost its domestic airline network in Australia and faced considerable difficulty moving passengers from many Australian ports to connect with Air New Zealand's international flights.

GOVERNMENT RESPONSE

The following discussion examines the manner in which the government responded to these shocks. Each shock was handled using existing government administrative and policy frameworks. Contingency planning, as a mechanism for preparing the apparatus of government for dealing with the unexpected, is not part of the normal framework for dealing with matters effecting tourism. Responses to issues that arose were generally made on an ad hoc basis and without the benefit of a previously determined response protocol. This was surprising though not unexpected as the lessons of the Asian financial crisis of 1997-98 (Prideaux, 1999) had been forgotten and no ongoing disaster mechanism had been established.

The HIH collapse was the first shock felt by the tourism industry. From a government perspective, it appears that the legislative framework designed to prevent collapses of this nature was ineffective. As a first step, the government established a Royal Commission of Enquiry into the collapse and from the findings of this Commission it may be anticipated that there will be recommendations for enhancing the role of the Australian Securities and Investment Commission and the Australian Prudential Regulatory Authority (APRA). Concurrently, the Federal Government commenced investigating alternative methods of dealing with public liability claims but little was done to assist tourism SMEs (Small to Medium Enterprises) suffering from substantial increases in premiums on the grounds that it is not possible to isolate one industry from many which face increased premiums. The issue of corporate governance and public accountability is global in importance and the recent problems experienced in the US with Enron and WorldCom indicate the dangers that can occur when governments do not take strong proactive leadership to prevent corporate financial malpractice.

Dealing with the many complexities generated by the ongoing problems caused by HIH as well as September 11 and the Ansett collapse was a difficult task for the Federal Government and was compounded by other events including the looming Federal election (held in October 2001) and the war in Afghanistan. The problem was made more difficult by the international aspect of actions required to respond to these shocks. The Ansett collapse was particularly challenging as the Federal Government was forced to commence high-level negotiations with the New Zealand Government over claims that Air New Zealand had stripped Ansett of cash and sold off aircraft to provide cash to enable Air New Zealand to continue to operate (Sandlands, 2002). The role of the partially Singaporean Government-owned carrier, Singapore Airlines, as a significant share holder in Air New Zealand added a further layer of complexity to attempts to resolve the problem.

During periods of crisis it is usual for government to seek advice from industry bodies; however, the previous collapse of the Tourism Council of Australia (TCA), the tourism industry's peak industry lobbying group, reduced the government's ability to gauge industry reaction to policy proposals. A second body, the Tourism Task Force which represents many of the nation's large corporations involved in tourism, did not expand its brief to incorporate the views of the small business sector. To canvas industry views about the impact of the Ansett collapse and September 11, the Government established the Tourism Industry Working Group (TIWG, 2001), but only on an ad hoc basis. Membership consisted of representatives from Government and the tourism industry. Research undertaken by the Working Group was extensive and included:

- A survey of tourism businesses throughout Australia. This resulted in 5,000 responses (2,800 in an on-line survey conducted by the Australian Tourist Commission and 2,200 in a telephone survey);
- An evaluation of the economic impact on the Australian economy of the recent tourism-related events; and
- Consultations with more than 1,000 members of the industry in regional areas into the impacts of September 11 and the Ansett collapse.

Recommendations of the Committee were only partly implemented and after presenting its report, the Tourism Industry Working Group was disbanded.

The ad hoc nature of the Government's response was demonstrated by its response to demands by Ansett employees for the payment of outstanding wages and entitlements claims. In the normal course of events, employee entitlements (wages, superannuation and redundancy payments) are funded by the proceeds of the sale of company assets; however, the size of Ansett's 15,000 workforce and the generous redundancy benefits trade unions had previously won from Ansett, combined with the militancy of the work force who staged many mass public protests, created a situation that could not be ignored by a Government then in election mode. Although creating a potentially expensive precedent for dealing with future corporate collapses, the government agreed to partially fund workers' entitlements. To recover its expenditure, the Government imposed a AUD$10 levee on all domestic air travel. The Government also made representations to Air New Zealand for funds to cover debts that were claimed to be Air New Zealand's responsibility as the owner of Ansett. However, shortly after its divestment of Ansett, Air New Zealand encountered significant cash flow problems and would have followed Ansett into receivership if the New Zealand Government had not intervened and purchased most Air New Zealand shares at a token price and injected a substantial amount of cash into the nearly bankrupt airline. To avoid a lengthy court case, Air New Zealand agreed to make a one-off cash payment of AUD$150 million to the Ansett receivers to cover ongoing claims against Air New Zealand for its part in Ansett's collapse.

An analysis of the events surrounding the Ansett collapse indicates the complexity of the problems that shocks can cause for government and the need for a whole-of-government response with appropriate follow-up action by the many branches of government. Elements of the Government's response to the Ansett collapse included the following:

- High-level negotiations with a foreign corporation and governments.
- Involvement of many government organisations including the Departments of Treasury, Foreign Affairs, Tourism, Industrial Affairs, Transport, Justice as well as civil aviation authorities.
- Negotiations with unions, potential purchasers of the airline, airport owners and Ansett's receivers.
- A range of action taken in the Courts.
- Discussions with many pressure groups and lobbyists, as well as the tourism industry.
- Discussions with State Governments many of which instituted their own schemes to assist Ansett regional subsidiaries to resume limited services to remote regional areas.

The Government's response was directed towards restoration of air services and the then imminent federal election provided the Government with an incentive to rapidly restore air services to regional communities. In a free market economy there is always the possibility that commercial collapses will occur and it becomes a matter of ideology as to the degree that governments should intervene in the market place. In a major collapse where there are numerous losers there is often considerable support for government assistance, usually at taxpayers' expense. If governments step in, there is always the possibility that inefficient companies or outdated technologies will be supported on grounds of sentiment or as a means of gaining or retaining voter favour. Government allocation of resources to corporate rescues of this nature reduces funding available for other sometimes more pressing or deserving areas of need, or necessitates imposition of additional taxes. Whether governments should intervene in the free market to prop up inefficient companies is a deeply ideological issue. If intervention occurs for one company there may be support for intervention in many or all corporate collapses. Social justice questions, such as the plight of the redundant Ansett workers' access to their legal redundancy payments, must also be examined in parallel to questions of the role of the government in the operation of the free market.

In its dealing with the problems arising from the Ansett shock and to a lesser degree with HIH and September 11, the Government viewed the shocks as more than a tourism industry problem because of the wider implications for all Australians. As a consequence, the Department of Transport became the lead agency for many of the issues connected with aviation. This was made easier because the Transport Minister was a member of Federal Cabinet. Responsibility for tourism and sport resided with a junior Minister who reported to Cabinet through a senior Minister, the Minister for Industry, Science and Resources. As a consequence, the concerns of the tourism industry were to some extent filtered through the bureaucracy compared to those of the aviation industry because of the ranking of the respective Ministers.

Adequacy of Government Response

The adequacy of government response must be measured in a number of ways: its short term response and the success of these responses; the success of long term responses; and the disaster time frame from the onset of the crisis to the point where both short and long term impacts have been dealt with. The Government's preference for using existing disaster response mechanisms reveals a number of shortcomings. Often, responses were made without full knowledge of the problems being encountered and without consideration of longer term implications. Several deficiencies are highlighted in the following discussion on the response by government to these shocks.

Within the structure of the Australian Federal Government there is a well-established framework for responding to the wide range of problems that almost daily confront government. Responses normally occur in three stages. In the first instance the Department that has administrative and legislative responsibility for policy administration in the area where the shock was experienced is required to assess the extent of the problem and, based on this assessment, develop possible responses. If administrative responsibility for areas affected by the shock is shared by two or more departments, an inter-government committee will be given the task of examining the problem and recommending policy responses. In the second stage, recommendations developed either at departmental level or as the result of interdepartmental consultations are taken to cabinet which decides on the level of response. The third stage describes the implementation of cabinet decisions by the department or departments involved. This may include using existing legislation or passing new legislation.

Compared to the suggested response pattern of the TDMF, the response mechanisms currently in place lack a clearly defined Pre-event stage, including the capability to undertake risk assessment. Moreover, the Government's response lacked many of the elements of the Prodromal stage which suggests that contingency plans based on identified likely risks and groups at risk should be in place. The absence of a fully representative national tourism peak body able to advise government during all stages, but particularly in Stages One to Three, is also a major problem. From the forgoing analysis, it is also apparent that many of the public organisations that should have responded during Stage One failed to undertake adequate risk assessment and many did not act until the Ansett and HIH collapses had entered the third stage described by the TDMF.

Legal and policy mechanisms already in place failed to: undertake the type of risk assessment that is a key element of Stage One; failed to identify likely impacts (Stage Two); and were only able to respond with any level of effectiveness in Stages Three and Four. In the case of HIH Insurance, a Royal Commission of Enquiry was established to investigate the causes of the problem and identify deficiencies in the existing regulatory. A more effective investigation into the needs for a mechanism to strengthen capabilities to undertake Stage One risk assessment and Stage Two disaster contingency planning would give the government better intelligence on emerging disasters in this area of the corporate sector. Similarly, the enhancement of the capabilities of corporate watchdogs such as the APRA may give an early indication of the problems encountered by Ansett.

Development of capabilities of this nature requires additional and ongoing funding and maintenance of this may become difficult, particularly where the threat has passed. One problem encountered is an inability to measure the success of policies because of their preventive nature. For example, the inclusion of armed Air Marshals and increased airport security may deter would-be highjackers who would have undertaken action in the absence of such security measures. The absence of other forms of attacks may also be attributed to expeditious policy implementation. The success of preventive measures can be demonstrated in the aviation industry by the falling incidence of air crashes due to more rigorous aircraft safety regimes. The danger is that the success of preventive measures is not readily quantifiable or obvious and therefore may be the subject of later cost cutting because of the apparent lack of a problem.

To reduce the level of risk in the future, the role of watchdog and regulatory organisations may need to be strengthen to give them Stage One and Two capabilities similar to those outlined in the TDMF. If this does not occur it is likely that the Government will again be forced to make hasty policy decisions and assume the role of corporate saviour. Early evidence at the HIH Royal Commission points to a failure of regulatory watchdogs, in this case the Australian Prudential Regulatory Authority and the Australian Securities and Investment Commission, to monitor the market and undertake preventative actions designed to avert a future corporate collapse.

The model adopted by aviation regulatory bodies for the monitoring of training and maintenance standards in civil aviation exhibit capabilities that are found in Stages One and Two of the TDMF. The success of aviation regulatory bodies in reducing accidents illustrates the success of this type of disaster prevention planning. In the case of HIH, recognition that premiums were not matching payments should have alerted the Australian Prudential Regulatory Authority that problems were developing. Ansett's problems were also apparent to many commentators but because it was a wholly owned offshore company the ability of regulators to investigate problems other than the issue of safety was diminished and the ability of the share market to voice it approval or disapproval of management through the share price was muted. While it may not always be possible or even wise to avert corporate collapses, and collapses of this nature are an expected feature of the free market, it may be possible to identify companies at risk and issue timely advisory warnings. Action of this nature may be one measure to avert the type of sudden yet long lasting impact of the shocks that were generated by HIH, September 11 and Ansett. From the Government's perspective most of the problems arising from the shocks experienced during 2001 were dealt with by existing administrative structures and arrangements and by 2002 a sense of normality had returned. There was little ongoing analysis of continuing effects of the crisis or the success of failure of policy measures implemented. As the level of threat reduced and then passed, the justification for establishment of new Stage 1 and 2 capabilities was lessened and other issues emerged to occupy the attention of government, until the next disaster. Sadly, by late 2002 new policy measures to avert a similar collapses had not been developed.

ADAPTING THE TDMF

It is apparent from this brief analysis that the TDMF offers a range of capabilities that are currently lacking in the Government's ability to effectively manage disasters in the tourism industry. With a range of modifications, particularly in the Precursors component of Stage One of Column 2 (Elements of the Disaster Management Responses) and the Review component also of Column 2, the TDMF will have the added capabilities required to assist the authorities respond to single or multiple disasters. In Column 3 of Stage 1 there is a need for a specific forecasting element to be included. If an expanded version of the TDMF had been in place prior to 2001 there may have been some warning of the problems being experienced by HIH and Ansett giving the government the opportunity to initiate appropriate policy responses and possibly avert or mitigate the negative impacts experienced after the firms collapsed. Similarly, risk analysis would have indicated that there was a possibility that a major unanticipated international disaster would affect global tourism flows. Rather than the ad hoc response that occurred, more effective containment and recovery plans could have been developed and, with appropriate modifications, implemented. An important element of the success of the TDMF is the incorporation of a forecasting element that allows the authorities to develop contingency plans, based on generating a series of scenarios for a range of possible risks or threats. The need for a forecasting capability of this nature falls outside of the perimeters of existing forecasting tools and is discussed by Prideaux, Laws and Faulkner (2003).

Specific modifications required to adapt the TDMF to large scale disaster include the following:

- Elements of the Disaster (Column 2)

Stage 1 Precursors. This element requires expansion to incorporate joint industry/government standing disaster coordination committee, designation of specially trained liaison officers to coordinate between the various organisations responding to disasters, consideration of emergency funding arrangements, enacting legislation that will enable rapid responses to be made to emergent disasters and, importantly, the establishment of a permanent Disaster Control Organisation able to mobilize and control the combined response of all public and private sector organisations involved in any aspect of disaster response through to Stage 6 Resolution.

Stage 6 Review. In this phase there is a requirement to assess the success of all policy and other responses to identify shortcomings that can be rectified in future crisis situations. This action must include analysis of policy, administrative frameworks and legislative arrangements.

Stage 5 Reconstruction and Reassessment. For recovery from large scale disasters there is a need for the implementation of appropriate funding mechanisms, rebuilding if required and mounting of promotion campaigns in major markets. This will require significant input from the public sector.

- Principle ingredients of the Disaster Management Strategies (Column 3)

Stage 1 Risk Assessment. This element requires a forecasting capability in addition to a risk assessment capability.

Stage 2 Disaster Contingency Plans. The TDMF requires a capability to review risk assessment following the lessons learnt from handling large scale disasters. This new capability can then be lined back to the development of risk assessment in Stage 1.

The need for a formal response mechanism of the capability of the TDMF was demonstrated on 12 October 2002 when at least 190 persons, including 88 Australian tourists, were killed during a terrorist bombing of a Bali night club. While government agencies responded swiftly by providing aero medical evacuations and specialist police investigators to assist the Indonesian authorities, there was no overall disaster framework in place. At the time of writing the authorities suspected that elements of the Al Qeada terrorist network were behind the bombing and, following a warning apparently given by Osama bin Laden that Australia was a future terrorist target, a number of countries issued general travel warnings about travel to Australia. If a disaster management organisation had been in place the Australian tourism industry may have been in a better position to respond to these concerns and deal with a major terrorist incident should one occur.

CONCLUSION

From the evidence outlined in the preceding discussion it is apparent that the shocks felt during 2001 were unexpected and little prior disaster planning was evident. Given that shocks often occur with little warning, the establishment of a formal disaster management framework should be given a high priority by government and receive support from the private sector. Had such a mechanism been in place in Australia prior to 2001, the Government may have been able to respond to the disasters in a more considered manner. Faulkner's TDMF is one disaster management tool that holds considerable promise for enabling both the public and private sectors to develop contingency plans for more effective disaster management. The ability of the TDMF to be employed in a wide range of disaster situations is a major strength of the framework. It is also apparent that long term implications should be considered as an integral part of any response. Unfortunately, once new issues arise there is a tendency for earlier issues to be forgotten.

In the future, as in the past, new and unexpected disasters will continue to disrupt the tourism industry. Without the establishment of a formal framework of the type suggested by Faulkner, the tourism industry will continue to suffer unnecessary disruption. Valuable lessons are often learnt during the disaster, only to be forgotten because of the failure of organisations in both the public and private sectors to incorporate a mechanism for retaining and updating corporate knowledge.

For governments, any action that can minimize the impact of disaster has a direct monetary consequence. If inbound arrivals fall the government suffers reduced taxation revenue as company profits decline, reduced sales tax revenue, less personal income tax as the tourism workforce contracts and added welfare payments to retrenched tourism workers. Measured against these revenue criteria, governments that fail to development a disaster response mechanism of the nature suggested by the TDMF incur substantial financial penalties.

REFERENCES

Arnold, W. (1980), in Booth, S. (1993), *Crisis Management Strategy: Competition and Change in Modern Enterprise*, New York, Routledge.
Australian Tourist Commission, (2002), ATC Online Research, http://atc.australia.com/research.asp visited 1 November.
Booth, S. (1993), *Crisis Management Strategy: Competition and Change in Modern Enterprise*, New York, Routledge.
Boyle, J. (2002), Forget all the Bleating–it's a Search for a Scapegoat, *The Australian Financial Review Weekend*, March 2-3, pp. 6.
Buffini, F. Evans, S. and Hepworth, A. (2002), Wisdom of Keeping Carrier Flying Queried, *The Australian Financial Review*, 28 February, p. 12.
Cassedy, K. (1991), *Crisis Management Planning in the Travel and Tourism Industry: A Study of Three Destinations and a Crisis Management Planning Manual*, San Francisco, Pacific Asia Travel Association.
Drabek, T. E. (1995), Disaster Responses Within the Tourism Industry, *International Journal of Mass Emergencies and Disasters*, 13(1), 7-23.
Faulkner, B and Vikulov, S. (2001). Katherine, Washed Out One Day, Back on Track the Next: a Post-mortem of a Tourism Disaster. *Tourism Management*, 22, Issue 4, pp. 331-344.
Faulkner, B. (2001). Towards a Framework for Tourism Disaster Management. *Tourism Management*, 22, 135-147.
Fink, S. (1986), *Crisis Management*, New York, Association of Management.
Give Back our Source of Funds, and Fun, *The Australian*, March 26, p. 11.
Keown-McMullan, C. (1997), Crisis: When does a Molehill Become a Mountain? *Disaster Prevention and Management*, 4(2), 20-37.
Post-HIH Premium Spike Inflates Insurers' Profits, *The Weekend Australian*, February 23-24, p. 3.
Premiums Soar as Insurers Fear Backing the Wrong Horse, *The Weekend Australian*, 26 January, p. 55.
Prideaux, B. (1999), Tourism Perspectives of the Asian Financial Crisis, *Current Issues in Tourism*, 2(4), 279-293.
Prideaux, B. and Master, H. (2001), Health and Safety Issues Effecting International Tourists in Australia, *Asia Pacific Journal of Tourism*, Vol. 6(2), 24-32.
Prideaux, B. Laws, E. and Faulkner, B. (2003), Events in Indonesia: Exploring The Limits to Formal Tourism Trends Forecasting Methods in Complex Crisis Situations, *Tourism Management*, 24(4) 475-87.
Quarantelli, E. L. (1984), Organisational Behaviour in Disasters and Implications for Disaster Planning, *Monographs of the National Emergency Training Centre*, 1(2), 1-13.
Roberts, V. (1994), Flood Management: Bradford Paper, *Disaster Prevention and Management*, 3(2), 44-60.
Roux-Dufort, C. (2000), Why Organisations Don't Learn for Crises: The Perverse Power of Normalisation, *Review of Business*, pp. 25-30.
Sandlands, B. (2002), Stopovers on the Runway to Ruin, *The Australian Financial Review*, 28 February, p. 13.

Tourism Feels the Chill Wind of Post-September 11 World, *The Courier Mail*, 1 August, pp. 23.

Tourism Forecasting Council (1999), Forecast. Vol. 5, Issue 1, Canberra: Sport and Tourism Division, Commonwealth Department of Industry, Science and Resources.

Tourism Industry Working Group (2001), Report on the Implications of the Ansett Collapse and US Terrorist Attacks for Australia's Tourism Industry, www.indus. gov.au/library/content_tiwgFINALREPORT.doc visited 20 March 2002.

Turner, D. (1994), Resources for Disaster Recovery, *Security Management*, 57-61.

Weiner, A. J. and Kahn, H. (1972), Crisis and Arms Control. In C. F. Hermann (Ed.), *International Crises: Insights from Behavioural Research* (p. 21), New York, The Free Press.

Crisis Management and Tourism: Beyond the Rhetoric

Gui Santana

SUMMARY. Undoubtedly, the tourism industry is one of the most susceptible and vulnerable industries to crises. Recent major events that had devastating impacts on the industry ranges from natural disasters to epidemics, and from mismanagement to terrorist attacks. These kinds of episodes are not confined to any geographical region, as crises respect no political or cultural boundaries. Two major recent events illustrate this point: the BSE crisis in the UK in the 1990s, which was followed by the foot and mouth disease in 2000 and 2001, crippled the industry in several regions of England. Most recently, the events of September 11th in New York and Washington changed the way the industry operates forever. Crises are not new to the tourism industry. However, it has been observed that tourism management capability and ability to deal with complex and critical situations are limited.

This paper discusses the concept of crisis management and its relevance to tourism. It presents an overview of the general trends in tourism crises events of the last two decades, assesses the impacts of major man-made crises on the industry, and argues for the importance of crisis management in tourism management. The paper also discusses the

Gui Santana is affiliated with Centro de Ciências Tecnológicas da Terra e do Mar–CTTMar, Universidade do Vale do Itajaí, Rua Uruguai, 458–Itajaí, Santa Catarina–88.302-202, Brazil (E-mail: gui@cttmar.univali.br).

[Haworth co-indexing entry note]: "Crisis Management and Tourism: Beyond the Rhetoric." Santana, Gui. Co-published simultaneously in *Journal of Travel & Tourism Marketing* (The Haworth Hospitality Press, an imprint of The Haworth Press, Inc.) Vol. 15, No. 4, 2003, pp. 299-321; and: *Safety and Security in Tourism: Relationships, Management, and Marketing* (ed: C. Michael Hall, Dallen J. Timothy, and David Timothy Duval) The Haworth Hospitality Press, an imprint of The Haworth Press, Inc., 2003, pp. 299-321. Single or multiple copies of this article are available for a fee from The Haworth Document Delivery Service [1-800-HAWORTH, 9:00 a.m. - 5:00 p.m. (EST). E-mail address: docdelivery@haworthpress.com].

10.1300/J073v15n04_05

complex issue of crisis definition and its implications for organizations, and provides an operational definition of crisis management. Critical issues in crisis management, such as crisis anatomy, crisis incubation, risk perception in tourism and destination image, are discussed. Finally, the paper explores and analyses, in the context of crisis anatomy, the public sector handling of a major resort pollution crisis in Southern Brazil.

KEYWORDS. Crisis management, tourism impacts, crisis definition, crisis anatomy, crisis management model, destination image, terrorism

TOURISM AND CRISIS

It is not common to think about tourism and disaster/crisis in the same light. Enjoyment, pleasure, relaxation, and safety are embodied in the concept of tourism, whereas crises/disasters bring distress, fear, anxiety, trauma, and panic. Unfortunately, the issues of crises and disasters are real ones and have to be acknowledged by all involved in any tourism activity. Regardless of the unpleasantness of the topic, it has also to be acknowledged that crises (whether natural or man-made) have been and continue to be a part of organizational operations and directly or indirectly affect all concerned (communities, visitors, regulators, promoters, and so forth). Where tourism destinations and/or communities have considerable economic dependence on tourism related activities, their vulnerability to crisis occurrence is significantly increased, given that they need to maintain a positive image of attractiveness for continued success. As noted by Pearce (1992), Woodside and Lyonski (1990), and Gooddrich (1978), destination image is a key factor in tourists' buying behaviour. Research conducted by the above scholars clearly demonstrates that there is strong correlation between a positive perception of a destination and a positive purchase decision. Likewise, a negative image, even if it is unjustified, inhibits potential tourists and results in negative buying behaviour. As a voluntary, peacetime activity, tourism is very sensitive to variations in external conditions that may compromise the travel experience.

The tourism industry has experienced a series of catastrophic incidents in the past, which have raised public consciousness of the risks associated with activities and sectors within the industry. Some well-publicized tourism related crises in the last decade include various terrorist attacks directed at both tourism premises/facilities and tourist themselves in many parts of the world (notably those in Egypt), violent crime involving tourists (Brazil, the United States, Italy and others), several airplane disasters, hotel fires, tourist kidnapping, overcrowding, food poisoning, product boycott, civil unrest, tourist victimization and so on (Santana, 2001). In general, it can be said that there are a few generic factors that may cause or contribute towards the development of crisis in tourism. Figure 1 illustrates how crisis can be categorized in clusters. It is also possible to establish a cause-effect relationship between clusters or individual crisis. For example, a major industrial accident may result in pollution or contamination, or false advertising can compromise destination image. In addition, crisis can move from normal to severe, depending on how it evolves. In real situations, crisis moves around within the framework, resolving itself or generating new ones. The attributions given to the axis are just for purpose of illustration.

The devastating effect of these issues is evidenced by the performance of the industry in countries where major crises have occurred. Most recently, the

FIGURE 1. A Framework of Generic Causes of Crises in Tourism

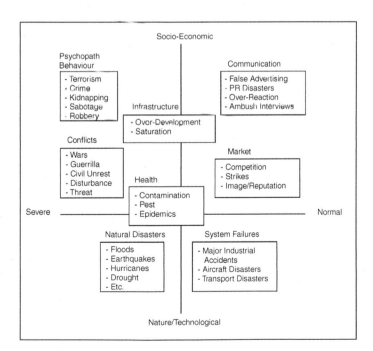

world witnessed a series of large-scale crises that had unprecedented negative impact in several economic activities in the world, generating lack of confidence in some sectors, and that had specifically severe detrimental effects on the tourism industry. The terrorist attacks in the United States in September 2001 reversed a long-term growth trend in the tourism industry. It had been growing at a yearly average rate of 5% since World War II and had registered a negative growth of 0.4% only in 1982 (with contributing factors including the Falklands war, martial law in Poland, and the conflict between Israel and Lebanon) (WTO, 2002a). The industry had a positive result in terms of arrival of 1.2% even in the 1991 Gulf War (WTO, 2002b). As a consequence of the terrorist attacks, and considering a combination of other negative factors, 2001 registered a negative growth of 0.6% (WTO, 2002b). These events at the beginning of 2001 challenged the reputation of resiliency of the tourism industry. Considering only a couple of them, the foot and mouth disease in the UK and the terrorism attacks in the USA, it is possible to understand the magnitude and potential of such situations.

The foot and mouth disease in 2000 and 2001 crippled the industry in several regions of England and Ireland and resulted in a reduction of 5-6% in the number of arrivals during the first eight months in the UK (WTO, 2002b; see also Coles, this volume). As to the other event, it had a more profound effect on the industry and was not bounded by any geographical or cultural barrier: the terrorist attacks of September 11, 2001 in New York City and Washington. The consequences of the reduction in the number of visitors are far-reaching and had not been confined to one specific geographical region either. Several airlines had filed bankruptcy (Sabina, Swissair, US Airways, and others around the world) after the attacks, and thousand of jobs had been lost in the tourism industry. This event had also a severe psychological and emotional effect on travellers. Virtually the entire world was, for several weeks, exposed to graphic images of the destruction caused by the attacks and to the suffering of the families and friends that lost loved ones in the tragedy. Combined with other factors, this exposure heightened the perception of travel risks. The security measures that followed the events and the uncertainty about the engagement of the United States in a conventional war had also contributed to this perception. Perhaps, the overall ignorance of the population and the lack of understanding of the media of the new element of bio-chemical terrorism had the largest contribution to the perception of risk in relation to travelling. Over the years, travellers had learned to live with the reality of certain travel risks such as aircraft disasters, the eventual violence (tourist victimization), etc., but the threat of a biological attack was a new, totally unknown component of reality. Adding to the points mentioned above, a series of corporate America accounting scandals in 2002 had not contributed positively to the general scenario of uncertainty, lack of confidence and trust. Overall, the floods of summer 2002 in Europe, the worst experienced by the continent in 200 years, the Al Qaeda terrorist attack at a night club in Bali aimed at international tourists, and other episodes of the kind, have been also hampering tourism recovery.

THE INEVITABILITY OF CRISIS AND MANAGEMENT CAPABILITY

Human-induced crises today have the potential to rival natural disasters in both scope and magnitude. The devastation caused by some recent crises included loss of hundreds of human lives as well as immeasurable damage to future generations and to the environment. However, the stereotype of crises, spectacular explosions, large-scale chemical releases, big fires, devastating natural disasters and so forth, account for a very small part of the crises experienced by modern organizations. The vast majority of identified organizational crises in the last few years had to do with issues such as white-collar crimes (extortion, fraud, etc.), human resources crises (sexual harassment, discrimination, labour disputes, etc.), and bad administration (negligence, violation of norms and legislation, scandals, etc.) (Institute for Crisis Management, 1997). The effects of these organizational dysfunctions were manifested in various forms, usually in crises of large proportions that proved devastating to the organizations involved.

An organizational crisis can occur today with little warning, anywhere, any time. A crisis can also happen to any organization, large or small, public or private, regardless of its management style. Regrettably, the prospects of organizations having to face some form of major crisis are greater than ever before. Crises usually occur as a consequence of the dysfunctional nature of an organization's culture, core beliefs, values and the basic assumptions of decision-makers and the approach taken to both external and internal communication. Moreover, most of the current knowledge in designing innovative and high-performing organizations tends to increase their degree of complexity and fragility (Pauchant and Douville, 1993).

The failure of the methods currently used by organizations in attempting to avoid and resolve organizational crises, such as risk analysis and contingency planning, only partially justify the disastrous ways in which organizations have been responding to the emergency of crises. Other explanations may be found in the systems themselves and their properties. Indeed, as argued by Mitroff and Pearson (1993), Perrow (1994), Reason (1997) and others, the potential negative effects of technology exceed the ability of our organizations and management structures to control them. Unfortunately, crisis management is still considered peripheral to the core activities of the day-to-day operations of organizations. Research on crisis management has been largely overlooked in comparison to other issues that promote "success." The net result of such emphasis is that managers are not prepared technically, psychologically, and emotionally to deal with a common feature of business operations and management today: crisis. As suggested by Booth (1993), "most executives are not used to tacking the complex set of internal and external issues that are thrown up by crisis." Managers are often seen as lacking in confidence or a pessimist when contemplating a down turn in their business.

If decision-makers acknowledge that in these complex and unpredictable times in which we live and operate, anything is possible, including a major crisis that may prove devastating to their organizations, management will be in the "right frame of mind" to accept the contention that forms the basic foundation of crisis management: proper advance planning. Only then, there can be a positive side to a crisis. It is no longer enough for managers to consider "if" a system will fail but rather "when" that failure will occur, "which type," "how" it will develop, "where" in the system, and "who" and "how" it will affect. Therefore, organizations should strive to have the frameworks and capabilities to cope with high levels of uncertainties and the seemingly increasing magnitude of crises events.

CRISIS MANAGEMENT:
AN ESSENTIAL TOOL FOR THE TOURISM INDUSTRY

Despite the fact that there is enough evidence to suggest that the tourism industry is one of the most vulnerable industries to crisis (Brownell, 1990, argues that the very nature of the tourism industry makes it both susceptible and vulnerable to crisis), crisis management is an issue that has been largely overlooked by the industry and tourism scholars alike. Considering that perception is reality in the tourism industry (Wahab, 1996; Pizam et al., 1997; Sönmez, 1998; Wall, 1996) it is not difficult to realize how sensitive the industry is to changes in its operational environment. A study of three major tourism offices dealing with major crises which affected their destination (Hong Kong, after the Tiananmen Square student massacre in China; Fiji, after a bloodless military coup in 1987; and San Francisco, after the Loma Prieta earthquake in 1989) revealed that a crisis can very quickly cripple the travel industry (Cassedy, 1992). In these cases the crises were ones of perception and it was observed that they could be just as devastating, if not more so, than crises that actually cause physical damage. In each of the cases, the crises were the perception of instability and danger by the travelling public. The industry suffered because people lost confidence in the destination as an attractive and safe place to visit and stay in. Safety misperception can indeed be a dangerous issue for destinations. The tourism industry in Florida underwent a phase of decline in visitor arrivals following a series of crimes against tourists. The negative effect on Florida's tourism industry, it is argued, was caused by distorted and extensive media coverage of incidents of crime against tourists and an overestimation of tourists' real risk and victimisation (Crystal, 1993). Other evidence suggests that the real risks for tourists were substantially smaller than public perception would suggest (Brayshaw, 1995). Despite the arguments, Florida, as a destination, experienced a real crisis.

The case of Florida is not an isolated one. While it can be argued that the likelihood of being involved in acts of violence and other incidents at home are statistically greater than the chances of being mugged on a London street or murdered in Egypt, the reality, however, is that tourists travel in order to experience travelling attributes such as relaxation, pleasure, peace, tranquillity, enjoyment, comfort, etc. These are all concepts conveyed by the concept of tourism. Anything that might suggest a move away from achieving them is not part of most travellers' equation. The main problems are that not only are tourists' logical base for fear often poor but also that their perception of risk usually has little to do with logic. The media plays an important role in travel patterns since it has the power to shape the public's perception of a destination or issue. With advances in telecommunication technology, many events today are covered live, or by amateur video cameras and shown later to a worldwide audience. Usually, graphic scenes or pictures are presented which have profound effect on the public (major recent events include the fire in a tunnel in the resort sky of Kaprun, Austrian Alps–2000; the plight of Concord flight in France–2000; the unveiling terrorist attacks and the full tragedy that followed the attacks in the USA–2001; the coverage of the world's worst air-show disaster, where a jet aircraft crashed at a Ukrainian air show, killing over 80 spectators and injuring 120 more–2002; and the devastation of tourist monuments and facilities in several European cities by the floods of summer 2002). Moreover, as far as tourism is concerned, security issues (real or perceptive) always have a spillover effect. That is, tourists tend to associate a security incident with an entire region. For example, during the Gulf War North-American tourists avoided the entire region, including Europe, and preferred Caribbean destinations (Wall, 1996; Sönmez, 1998). Tourists are deterred from travelling to perfectly safe places because they assume the entire region to be risky (Vukonic, 1997; Mansfeld, 1995; Sönmez, 1998; Richter and Waugh, 1986; Wall, 1996).

Given that tourism activities are interrelated and there is a great deal of dependence on transportation, exchange rates, political and social structures in both destination and origin, weather, and so forth, the tourism industry is highly vulnerable to variations in any, or a combination of these factors. Organizations responsible for tourism should, therefore, have in place mechanisms and expertise to deal with both real and perceived issues.

THE NATURE OF CRISIS AND CRISIS MANAGEMENT– A BRIEF OVERVIEW

Crises have some distinct characteristics. They are usually new situations to the organization, often defined as unexpected, definitely unstructured situations and outside the typical operational framework of the organization. As such, crises require a non-programmed response. Routine solutions applied to an abnormal situation tend to aggravate rather than alleviate a problem. They are also characterized by an excessive amount of incomplete and conflicting information. Usually, crises are highly emotional situations that exert a great amount of emotional and psychological pressure on decision-makers. These attributes (high emotional and psychological toll) make both quality decision-making and strategy implementation very difficult and vulnerable to malfunctions. Creative decisions, therefore, become more desirable and less likely.

Defining Crisis and Crisis Management

The term "crisis" is among one of the most misused terms within the management literature. The word "crisis" is derived from the Greek "Krisis," meaning "decision" (Pauchant and Douville, 1993). Another meaning was the "turning point" of an illness "in which it is decided whether or not the (individual) organism's self-healing powers are sufficient for recovery" (O'Conner, 1987: 54-55).

Considering that the concept of crisis is used in many different fields, the definition of crisis as well as the attributions of its causes are often highly diversified as well as strongly biased by the particular field in which they are studied (Pauchant and Douville, 1993). The literature is also split on the issue of crisis sources (Mitroff et al., 1992). Some researchers have labelled crises as "normal accidents," that is, as emerging naturally from the complexity and tight-coupling embedded in modern technologies (Perrow, 1984); others have emphasized that crises are the results of "wrong" decisions made by policy-makers (Janis, 1989); others have suggested that the emergence of crises is to be seen in the complex interrelations existing between humans and technologies, embedded in the "causal texture" of both environments and organizations (Shrivastava, 1992; Pauchant and Mitroff, 1992); while others have attributed crisis to repeated successes and gradual acclimatization (Starbuck and Milliken, 1988). It can be concluded then that there is indeed a problem of construct. The literature provides no generally accepted definition of crisis and attempts to categorize types or forms of crises have been sparse. Although some researchers have explored multiple forms of crises (Meyers and Holusha, 1986; Fink, 1986; Mitroff et al., 1989), others have examined crisis as a single phenomenon (Nystrom and Starbuck, 1984; Smart and Vertinsky, 1984) or have concentrated on only one manifestation of crisis (Billings et al., 1980). The issue of construct has been further complicated by the use of various different terms in the literature as synonyms for crisis, such as disaster, catastrophe, jolt, problem and turning point.

Not surprisingly, the tourism literature provides very few attempts to define crisis management. Definitions of tourism crisis (and for that matter, tourism-related crisis) are extremely rare and those that do appear in the literature are contextualized and reflect one single purpose, usually explaining a particular crisis phenomenon. Sönmez et al. (1994: 2.2 in Sönmez and Tarlow, 1997) define tourism crisis in general as:

> ... any occurrence which can threaten the normal operation and conduct of tourism-related businesses; damage a tourist destination's overall reputation for safety, attractiveness, and comfort by negatively affecting visitor's perception of that destination; and, in turn, cause a downturn in the local travel and tourism economy, and interrupt the continuity of business operations for the local travel and tourism industry, by the reduction of tourist arrivals and expenditures.

One of the serious results of the lack of a widely accepted crisis definition is that it is hampering the development of the field.

Crisis Management Defined

As seen above, crises are generally distinguished from routine situations by a sense of "urgency" and a concern that problems will become "worse" in the absence of action. Action can then be seen in a broader sense, not only reactive. Indeed, crisis management starts well before any event boils into a full-blown crisis (Fink, 1986; Santana, 1999). It is important to understand that, unlike risk, uncertainty can never be completely controlled or eliminated (Courtney et al., 2001). As the external environment (and to a certain degree the internal environment) becomes increasingly uncertain, the ways in which organizations minimize the risks of and capitalize on the opportunities presented by that uncertainty become correspondingly important.

Crisis management can be defined as an ongoing integrated and comprehensive effort that organizations effectively put into place in an attempt to first and foremost understand and prevent crisis, and to effectively manage those that occur, taking into account in each and every step of their planning and training activities, the interest of their stakeholders (Santana, 1999) (Figure 2).

Anatomy of a Crisis–The Case of Balneário Camboriú

Understanding how a crisis develops and evolves, and being familiar with all phases management needs to control, is a critical knowledge for effective crisis management. This paper draws from the experience of Balneário Camboriú, Santa Catarina, Brazil, where severe water and beach pollution caused a major decrease in the number of visitors to the resort. A brief background of Balneário Camboriú is discussed first and explores the public sector handling of the crisis within the framework of crisis anatomy. Through this process, one can understand how a crisis develops and the implications the dynamics of each phase pose to management.

Located in the central-north coast of the state of Santa Catarina, Balneário Camboriú is not a typical Brazilian tourist resort. It has evolved from just a few fishing huts to one of the most important tourist destinations in the Southern Cone of the Americas in just over 30 years. The seven-kilometre beachfront and its clear, calm water make it the ideal destination for families. With a fixed population of 77,000 inhabitants, Balneário Camboriú swells to become a busy resort of over 1.5 million tourists in the summer season. The whole economy of the city is heavily dependent on tourism flow and expenditure.

In 1999, Balneário Camboriú received over 1.5 million tourists (SANTUR, 1999; Secretaria de Turismo e Desenvolvimento de Balneário Camboriú, 1999). Brazilians, mainly from the southern states, accounted for 89% of all tourists, and foreign tourists accounted for 11% of the total. Argentineans, Uruguayans, Germans, and Chileans are the main foreign market to the town. Brazilian and South American tourists reach the town mainly by road and when at the resort the vast majority stay in rented houses and flats (38%), or with friends and relatives (23%) (Secretaria de Turismo e Desenvolvimento de Balneário Camboriú, 1999). Although the number of hotel beds is relatively high for a small town, over 18,000, hotels catered for only 16% of all tourists in 1999. On average tourists spent six days in Balneário Camboriú in 1999 (SANTUR, 1999).

Families are the predominant market; accounting for over 64% of all tourists, and the beach is the main attraction for over 90% of tourists. An interesting feature of this market is that the vast majority of tourists are frequent visitors. Over 24% of them have been visiting the town for more than five

FIGURE 2. Operational Definition of Crisis Management

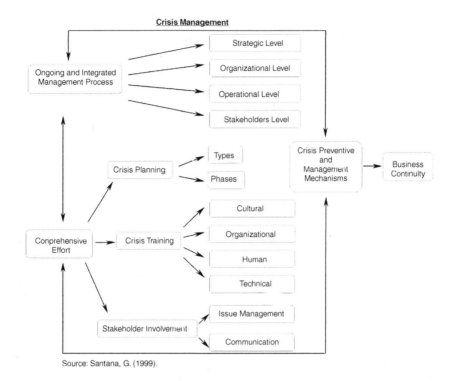

Source: Santana, G. (1999).

years. More than 36% came to the town every year for the last five years, and only 6% were in the town for the first time in 1999 (Santana, 2000). In 1996, however, a series of public health and environmental issues started to be linked to the organic pollution of the water and beach of the resort. Reports from local hospitals, and indeed from other regions of the country, clearly identified beach related diseases on patients that visited the beach. This generated national and international negative publicity and developed into a full-blown tourism crisis for this tourism-dependent city. The situation was aggravated considerably due to the way in which the public sector has managed the issue.

Understanding Crisis Anatomy–The Case of Balneário Camboriú

A crisis has some distinct phases that, in turn, require distinct management approaches. A crisis follows a consistent pattern of at least 3 (three) distinct phases: the pre-crisis period, the crisis itself, and the post-crisis period. Nearly all crises pass through the following phases: from early warning signals to prevention, through damage containment and business recovery, to organizational learning. Different dangers and opportunities are inherent in each phase. However, a crisis does not necessarily follow all the crisis phases. A crisis can, although extremely rarely, occur without warning. If the organization is prepared, a crisis can go directly from the warning signal phase to the learning phase. It is important to observe that the learning phase should be a continuum. Organizations can only increase their ability to manage crises if they properly understand and manage each phase of the process (Fink, 1986). Figure 3 sets out in a systematic fashion the phases that need to be managed before, during, and after any major crisis.

Warning Signals/Preparation and Prevention

The first phase of a crisis is where warning signals can be detected. In many instances, this is a real turning point. If the turning point is missed, the next phase (the crisis itself) can strike with such swiftness that the so-called after the fact crisis management is, in reality, merely damage control. However, if it is identified corrective action (preparation) can be implemented.

The aim of crisis management in this stage is not the prevention of all crises as they cannot all be prevented. The aim is to do as much as possible to prevent crises from occurring in the first place and to effectively manage those which still happen despite best efforts. In other words, the degree to which management heeds the warning signals and prepares the organization will determine how well it responds to the impending crisis (Figure 4).

Balneário Camboriú–The Warning Signals

As mentioned above, Balneário Camboriú is a resort that has developed very rapidly. This process has caused many problems of both environmental and urban nature. Some contextual issues, such as lack of legislation, local government corruption, lack of planning, land speculation and pressure from the construction industry, among others, have contributed to a disorderly development.

Tourism is an activity that relies on a number of services, many of them provided or controlled by the public sector (e.g., public utilities). In the case of Balneário Camboriú, the water and sewage services are provided by the state company CASAN (Companhia de Água e Saneamento), it is not a municipal controlled service. CASAN has been unable to follow the pace of development and basic infrastructure is poor and inadequate. The demand on water supply and drainage/sewage systems is extremely high during the summer season and

FIGURE 3. The Crisis Management Phases

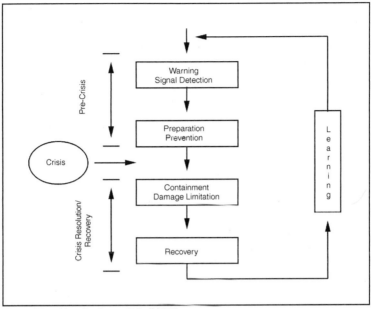

Crisis Management Phases

Source: Adapted from Pauchant and Mitroff (1992).

it is not uncommon for both systems to collapse during periods of peak demand, with the consequence that some are left without running water or raw sewage is discharged directly onto the beach. There are also several hundred illegal drainage/sewage systems polluting the beach from both private apartment blocks and commercial buildings.

The city has an added problem with regard to the sewage system. The terrain is flat and all sewage and other effluents have to be pumped to the treatment station outside the town. The main problem is that the system was designed many years ago to cope with a given volume. As the town has expanded and the system has not been upgraded, it is inevitable that a certain amount of raw sewage will end up on the water and beach. Moreover, the city's rainwater drainage system is also inadequate and both the inhabitants and businesses suffer serious consequences during the rainy season, which coincides with the summer season. Both systems run in parallel, which means that every time one of them overflows, contamination is inevitable. That is, when the rain drainage system overflows, the surplus water drains into the sewage system, putting pressure on a system that is unable to cope with large volumes. On the other hand, when the sewage

FIGURE 4. Effective Management of Warning Detection and Preparation/Prevention Phases

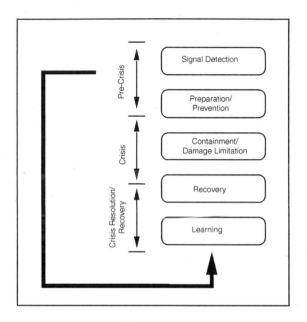

system overflows, it flows into the rainwater drainage system, which runs straight to the beach, depositing raw sewage on the beach environment.

Following these contextual explanations, other direct warning signals were evident from summer 1996:

- The population started complaining about unpleasant smells.
- Visual evidence of raw sewage on the beach.
- FATMA (Fundação do Meio Ambiente de Santa Catarina), the official state environmental agency that controls water quality in the state and conducts year-round weekly tests, reported that Balneário Camboriú's beach was unsuitable for public use at several points. The local government has always contested the results of the tests.
- Other analyses from independent laboratories have also indicated that some points are unsuitable for swimming. However, as the beach points identified by the laboratories did not match with those first mentioned by FATMA, the local government concluded that they were both mistaken and designed a public relations campaign to discredit the evidences. In reality, the points did not match because of several obvious reasons:

beach dynamic and morphology, currents, tide and the methodologies applied, among others. This, however, does not invalidate the analyses. On the contrary, it could also be argued that the beach was polluted in many other points or under different natural conditions. Or, one could actually argue that the beach was so polluted that not even different tides, currents and other natural conditions were able to disperse the pollution.

- Several NGOs (local and national) began campaigning on many fronts, such as warning the public of the risks associated with using the beach through media talk shows and interviews, distributing leaflets at hotels and on the beach, circulating reports of independent analyses to the media, picketing in front of the Prefeitura Municipal de Balneário Camboriú (Council), and other means.
- The local and regional electronic media and press dedicated unprecedented space to debating the issue. The issue was featured on several occasions in talk shows with the participation of experts in different fields such as biologists, medical doctors, public health officials, politicians, city planners, architects and engineers. Adult entertainment programs featured the issue for months during and outside the summer period.
- In summer 1996, the Argentinean press reported cases of skin diseases and associated the cases to the pollution in Balneário Camboriú.
- After the reported cases in Argentina, the local and regional media began to report skin diseases and cases of diarrhoea and other symptoms of pollution.
- The municipal health department issued a health warning relating to beach usage.
- The judicial department, after a public hearing, determined that the local government should place warning signs on the beach, identifying the points unsuitable for bathing. This was contested by the public authorities and the Secretaria do Planejamento (Municipal Planning Secretary) refused to implement the measures. The city was fined for disobeying the ruling. This episode attracted a large amount of media attention in Brazil and in other South American countries.
- Local authorities blamed CASAN (the state public utilities company) for the problems and for the lack of investment in the services, and accused the directors of plotting against the city.

Containment/Damage Limitation

Despite signal detection and preparation programmes, some crises will inevitably occur. As mentioned previously, crises are inevitable due to, among other reasons, the complexity of systems and the impossibility of perfect control. In many ways, this is the point of no return. Once the warning has ended and the transition from one crisis stage to another is consummated, it is virtually impossible to recover the ground already lost. At this point, some damage has already been done; how much additional damage occurs depends on management. The intention of this phase is to limit the effects. Limitation mechanisms prevent the damage from engulfing other parts of the organization or its environment. That is, effective management of this phase will keep the crisis localized.

This phase is characterized by disruption and confusion. Usually a single dramatic event signals the onset of the crisis and draws increased attention to the problem, but it is too late to do much about it. As Meyers and Langhoff (1987: 21) put it, ". . . at this stage, the old rules of business and behaviour no long apply. The degree of damage depends on management's preparation to the crisis." Fink (1996) observes that this phase is the shortest of all. However, because of its intensity, it often feels as though it is the longest phase.

Balneário Camboriú–The Crisis and Containment/Damage Limitation

During the pre-crises period, and despite all the warning signals, not much was done to resolve the problem. The authorities were busy fending off the media onslaught, assigning blame to all those involved (FATMA, NGOs, State Health Authority and the State Government), which in fact had the effect of generating other types of crises, and designing and launching a national and international advertising campaign emphasizing the natural attributes of the town, including its "clear and transparent" water.

A documentary on the beach pollution aired by *"Fantástico"* (one of the most watched TV programs in the country) caused major holiday cancellations to the town in 1998. The report emphasized that the problem had been well known to the authorities since 1995 but the public sector had not acted upon the evidence. A series of medical cases on beach-related diseases were shown and the general feeling of discontent of both the population and those representing the tourism trade in Balneário Camboriú were also focused on. In addition, the weekly national magazine *"VEJA"* published an article that featured the pollution problems in Balneário Camboriú. The magazine also published the rainfall in the region, which is considerably higher than in other holiday destinations such as the Northeast. As a result of these media reports, tourist arrivals fell by 40% compared to 1997 and tourism receipts dropped 41.4% in the same period (SANTUR, 1999; Secretaria de Turismo e Desenvolvimento de Balneário Camboriú, 1999).

However, other issues could have contributed to the depressing tourism performance and figures. In 1997 the town was rated by the Brazilian Government as the city with the highest incidence of HIV positive and AIDS in the country. The neighbouring town of Itajaí, which has one of the major sea ports in the country, has a high rate of drug trafficking and was constantly in the national news due to drug-related crimes and activities in 1997.

In general, most of the responses from the local government offices had the effect of exacerbating the problem instead of resolving it:

- Denial of the allegations and evidence.
- Accusing the national media of plotting against the southern states.
- Threatening to sue laboratories.
- Refusing to talk to the electronic media (playing preference with the media).
- Fending off the media by "counter-attacking" with promotions and advertising.

Perhaps, the most damaging episode was an "off the record" comment by the Mayor arguing that "as long as people would come to the city, leave their money, and get sick after they are back home, that is fine." The literature on crisis management leaves no doubt that all systems have a propensity for failure. Moreover, the nature and mechanism of error are imbedded in all kinds of organizational processes, which generally end up in a collapse of the natural and technical systems. However, the starting point is still the belief and the total confidence in the invulnerability of the human construct. The phrase of the mayor above is a reflection of this kind of situation.

Recovery Stage

It is during this phase that organizations seek to repair the damage to their images (and very likely their financial well-being) caused by crises. This is sometimes called the clean-up phase, or post-mortem. It is also the phase when organizations have the chance to reorganize vital organizational aspects and attempt to resume normal operations. However, "business as usual" is not always possible, depending on the nature of the crisis and on the effectiveness of the planning and handling of the crisis. Nevertheless, the main purpose of the recovery stage is to recover normal business operations as soon as possible so that strategic goals are not further distorted or damaged.

Balneário Camboriú–Recovery Stage

The public sector response to the pollution crisis created more problems than solutions. The town image was tarnished and the response from its traditional market was unmistakable. Data from the Secretaria de Turismo de Balneário Camboriú (1999) have clearly demonstrated that the profile of visitors changed in the 1999 season, following the trend started in 1998. Accommodation prices halved and visitor expenditures declined. Restaurant and commerce revenues also suffered. As mentioned above, Balneário Camboriú is a traditional destination, with a loyal market. After the pollution episode, and as a consequence of the reduced prices exercised by the tourism trade, it became very attractive to lower spending segments. This, apparently, is further aggravating the situation as it creates an image clash between the visiting groups. One could say that the new segments are alienating the old ones. An indication is the high number of houses and flats for sale in the town and the increased demand for plots of land and houses on nearby beaches. It can be also observed that unemployment in the sector has risen since 1998 (Secretaria de Turismo e Desenvolvimento de Balneário Camboriú, 1999).

Therefore, the original crisis (as it was inappropriately handled) has set off a chain of other crises for which there is no probable outcome, apart from the realization that Balneário Camboriú is increasingly losing its prestige as a holiday destination for its traditional market and that any attempt towards reverting the situation will be extremely costly with no immediate results.

Even with all the evidence, the official position still is one of defiance and arrogance. Despite this, a series of concrete steps were announced in 1999 and are underway. However, the proposed solutions had been of a structural nature rather than, unfortunately, of a revision of the institutional attitude and position. Thus, although the proposed solutions may provide practical results, i.e., solve the pollution problem, the critics and the public opinion of the local government may not change.

Among the measures taken by the local government in attempting to resolve the pollution problems are:

- The application of robotic technology to identify illegal effluent discharges.
- A series of new legislation regarding residential and commercial waste discharges.
- The beginning of a major re-structuring of the city's drainage and sewage system, which is being funded by the InterAmerican Development Bank and the Brazilian Government through PRODETUR SUL (Tourism Development Program).
- Beach nourishment–also funded by the InterAmerican Development Bank and the Brazilian Government through PRODETUR SUL (Tourism Development Program).

It can be concluded that the crisis has evolved from a tangible issue (environmental pollution) to an intangible one (image and reputation). The failure to understand this crisis dynamic caused the public sector to propose the right solution to the wrong problem. In this sense the crisis has been further aggravated. The continuous lack of understanding of the situation by the public officials is creating an ever-widening gap between all the stakeholders involved. Since no one is prepared to view the issue from the other's perspective, the players are unlikely to share the same definition of the problem. In such a situation, it is also unlikely that they will share the same solutions. It can be envisaged, given the way this process has been developing, that the parties involved will continue to propose perfectly reasonable solutions to the wrong problem.

Learning Stage

Learning is a continuous process. Therefore, while the recovery takes place, it is also the time to assess what happened, a period of "self-analysis." It is also a time for further crisis management planning–analyzing what went right and/or what went wrong and taking appropriate action. Ideally, the primary goal of the learning stage should be to review and critique, without assigning blame, so as to learn what was done well and what was done poorly so that the organization can handle crises better in the future.

Balneário Camboriú–Learning Stage

As can be deducted from the above discussion, the Mayor's office has been wasting the opportunity of learning with the process. Instead, every episode is a motif for the group to reinforce their beliefs and to justify them through measures that to the outside observer appears totally inappropriate, disproportionate and absurd. Janis (1972) identified this process as the great danger of "groupthink." Janis analysed teams of political decision makers such as Kennedy's advisers before the disastrous Bay of Pigs invasion (see also Janis, 1989).

Perhaps the most striking feature of this case is the lack of perception of public managers to understand complex systems. In an earlier stage of this paper, the issue of crisis definition was extensively discussed. It can be seen now why the process of crisis definition is so important in any circumstances. As a short cut solution to this crisis, considering that all necessary measures proposed will take several years to be completed, the local government decided to use a bactericide to decrease the level of pollution (since the system cannot cope with actual volumes). The result, from the point of view of the council, has been extremely successful. Indeed, the seawater in Balneário Camboriú since 2001 has acceptable levels of pollution and the council has flooded the national press with details of its incredible achievement. The point, however, is that although there is no pollution, there is not much left either since the substance applied was strong enough such that it has created an even more serious environmental problem than the original one.

Finally, an observation of the literature relating to system failures, human error and crisis management leaves no doubt that most of the disastrous events of the last decades have similar underlying structures and characteristics. Moreover, the contributing factors for their emergency also share common patterns. The striking point, however, is the remarkable reluctance of our society to learn from these events. However, it is perfectly conceivable, and perhaps even logical, that we will continue to experience complex and critical crisis situations and their impacts.

CONCLUSION

There is no doubt that the tourism industry is one of the most vulnerable industries to crises. Moreover, there is evidence to suggest that recovery is complicated in the industry due partially to the poor logic of tourists' risk perception. There is in general ready availability of a substitute–other destinations/products to which the market can shift.

A crisis is not an event. It is a process that develops in its own logic. One's ability to deal and manage crisis depends greatly on one's understanding of the phases a crisis evolves and the implications each one of these stages pose to management. The case of a beach pollution crisis in Brazil was used in this paper to present the model of crisis anatomy. The inappropriate response by the public sector generated other crises that created uncertainty as to the future of the destination, despite the fact that several practical measures had been taken to solve the pollution problem. As perception *is* reality in tourism, even if the tangible issues are resolved, Balneário Camboriú might still have to engage in the usually expensive and lengthy process of trying to change public's perception. The community is economically dependent on tourism-related activities and there is a need to maintain a positive image of attractiveness for its survival and prosperity. Finally, it has been argued that crises are becoming more frequent and complex and that tourism destination as well as businesses should be better prepared to deal with this phenomenon.

REFERENCES

Billings, R. S., Milburn, T. W., and Schaalam, M. L. (1980). A Model of Crisis Perception. Administrative Science Quarterly, 25: 300-316.

Booth, S. (1993). Crisis Management Strategy–Competition and Change in Modern Enterprises. London: Routledge.

Brayshaw, D. (1995). Negative Publicity About Tourism Destinations–A Florida Case Study. Travel & Tourism Analyst, 5: 62-71.

Brownell, J. (1990). The Symbolic/Culture Approach: Managing Transition in the Service Industry. International Journal of Hospitality Management, 9 (3): 191-205.

Cassedy, K. (1992) Preparedness in the Face of Crisis: An Examination of Crisis Management Planning in the Travel and Tourism Industry. World Travel and Tourism Review, 2: 169-174.

Courtney, H., Kirkland, J., and Viguerie, S. (2001). Strategy Under Uncertainty. The McKinsey Quarterly, 4-December: 5-14.

Crystal, S. (1993). Welcome to Downtown U.S.A. Meetings and Conventions, 28 (3): 42-59.

Fink, S. (1986). Crisis Management–Planning for the Inevitable. New York: American Management Association.

Institute for Crisis Management (1997). Significant Trends in News Coverage of Business Crisis Events During 1996. Louisville: The Institute for Crisis Management.

Janis, I. L. (1989). Crucial Decisions–Leadership and Policymaking and Crisis Management. New York: The Free Press.

Janis, I. L. (1972) The Victims of Groupthink: A Psychological Study of Foreign-Policy Decisions and Fiascos. Boston: Houghton Mifflin.

Mansfeld, Y. (1995). Wars, Tourism and the 'Middle East' Factor. Proceedings of the First Global Research and Travel Trade Conference on Security and Risks in Travel and Tourism, Östersund, Sweden, pp. 109-128.

Meyers, G. C. and Holusha, J. (1986). When It Hits the Fan: Managing the Nine Crises of Business. Boston: Houghton Mifflin Company.

Meyers, G. C. and Langhoff, P. (1987) Expecting the Unexpected. New Management, 5 (1): 20-23.

Mitroff, I., Pearson, C. and Pauchant, T. (1992). Crisis Management and Strategic Management: Similarities, Differences and Challenges. In Shrivastava, P.; Huff, A.; Dutton, J. (Eds.)–Advances in Strategic Management, V. 8. JAI Press Inc.

Mitroff, I. and Pearson, C. (1993). From Crisis-Prone to Crisis Prepared: A Framework for Crisis Management. Academy of Management Executive, 7 (1): 48-59.

Mitroff, I., Pauchant, T., Finney, M. and Pearson, C. (1989). Do (Some) Organizations Cause Their Own Crisis? The Cultural Profiles of Crisis-Prone vs. Crisis-Prepared Organizations. Industrial Crisis Quarterly, 3: 269-283.

Nystrom, P. and Starbuck, W. (1984). To Avoid Organizational Crises, Unlearn. Organizational Dynamics, Spring: 53-65.

O'Conner, J. (1987). The Meaning of Crisis: A Theoretical Introduction, New York: Basil Blackwell.

Pauchant, T. and Mitroff, I. (1992). Transforming the Crisis-Prone Organization: Preventing Individual, Organizational, and Environmental Tragedies. San Francisco: Jossey-Bass Publishers.

Pauchant, T. and Douville, R. (1993). Recent Research in Crisis Management: A Study of 24 Authors' Publications from 1986 to 1991. Industrial and Environmental Crisis Quarterly, 7 (1): 43-63.

Pearce, P. (1982). Perceived Changes in Holiday Destinations. Annals of Tourism Research, 9: 145-164.

Perrow, C. (1984). Normal Accidents: Living with High-Risk Technologies. New York: Basic Books.

Pizam, A., Tarlow, P., and Bloom. J. (1997). Making Tourists Feel Safe: Whose Responsibility Is It? Journal of Travel Research, Summer: 23-28.

Reason, J. (1997). Organizational Accidents: The Management of Human and Organizational Factors in Hazardous Technologies. London: Ashgate.

Richter, L. K. and Waugh Jr., W. L. (1986). Terrorism and Tourism as Logical Companions. Tourism Management, 7 (4): 230-238.

Santana, G. (2001). Globalisation, Safety and National Security. In: Wahab, S. and Cooper, C. (Editors), Tourism in the Age of Globalisation. London: Routledge (pp. 213-241).

Santana, G. (2000). Criminalidade, Segurança e Turismo: A Imagem de Balneário Camboriú Segundo as Perspectivas dos Turistas e da Comunidade Receptora. Estudios y Perspectivas en Turismo, 10 (3/4): 267-289.

Santana, G. (1999). Understanding Crisis and Crisis Management: Towards a Model. In Eco-Terrorism: Chemical and Biological Warfare Without Chemical and Biological Weapons, Proceedings of the Chemical and Biological Medical Symposium, CBMTS–Industry I, Portland, Maine–USA, Applied Science and Analysis, Inc. (pp. 285-292).

SANTUR–Santa Catarina Turismo S.A. (1999).

Secretaria de Turismo e Desenvolvimento de Balneário Camboriú (1999).

Shrivastava, P. (1992). Bhopal–Anatomy of a Crisis, London: Paul Chapman Publishing Ltd., 2nd Edition.

Smart, C. and Vertinsky, I. (1984). Strategy and the Environment: A Study of Corporate Response to Crisis. Strategic Management Journal, 5: 199-213.

Sönmez, S. (1998). Tourism, Terrorism, and Political Instability. Annals of Tourism Research, 25 (2): 416-456.

Sönmez, S., F. and Tarlow, P. (1997). Managing Tourism Crises Resulting from Terrorism and Crime. Paper presented at the International Conference on "War, Terrorism, Tourism: Times of Crisis and Recovery," Dubrovinik, Croatia (September 25-27, 1997).

Starbuck, W. H. and Milliken, F. J. (1988). Challenger: Fine-Tuning the Odds Until Something Breaks. Journal of Management Studies, 25 (4): 319-330.

Vukonic, B. (1997). Tourism in The Whirlwind of War. Zagreb: Golden Marketing.

Wahab, S. (1996). Tourism and Terrorism: Synthesis of the Problem with Emphasis on Egypt (pp. 175-186). In Pizam, A. and Mansfeld, Y., Editors (1996) Tourism, Crime and International Security Issues. New York: John Wiley & Sons.

Wall, G. (1996). Terrorism and Tourism: An Overview and an Irish Example (pp. 143-158). In Pizam, A. and Mansfeld, Y., Editors (1996) Tourism, Crime and International Security Issues, New York: John Wiley & Sons.

Woodside, A. and Lyonski, S. A. (1990). General Model of Traveller Destination Choice. Annals of Tourism Research, 17: 432-448.

WTO (World Tourism Organization) (2002a). *http://www.world-tourism.org/newsroom/Releases/more_releases//june2002/data.htm* 26/08/2002.

WTO (World Tourism Organization) (2002b). *http://www.world-tourism.org/newsroom/Releases/more_releases//january2002/data.htm* 26/08/2002.

Crisis Management
in Small-Scale Tourism

Gavan Cushnahan

SUMMARY. Since the events of September 2001, many tourism academics, analysts, and corporations have displayed attention toward crises in the tourism industry. Most attention has focussed on how nations and large tourism corporations cope with unforseen crises. However, when crisis strikes, it is indiscriminate, affecting small-scale tourism businesses also. This article analyses some popular crisis management models, and their applicability to smaller scale businesses. The small island of Gili Air in Indonesia is examined, and the crisis management techniques employed by owners and operators of small and micro tourism businesses. The results indicate that while these businesses face similar issues resulting from crises, they are ill equipped to produce long-term solutions. *[Article copies available for a fee from The Haworth Document Delivery Service: 1-800-HAWORTH. E-mail address: <docdelivery@ haworthpress.com> Website: <http://www.HaworthPress.com> © 2003 by The Haworth Press, Inc. All rights reserved.]*

KEYWORDS. Prolonged crises, small-scale tourism, Indonesia, resource-poverty

Gavan Cushnahan is a PhD Candidate, Department of Anthropology, The University of Western Australia, Nedlands 6907, Western Australia, Australia (E-mail: gcushnah@ cyllene.uwa.edu.au).

[Haworth co-indexing entry note]: "Crisis Management in Small-Scale Tourism." Cushnahan, Gavan. Co-published simultaneously in *Journal of Travel & Tourism Marketing* (The Haworth Hospitality Press, an imprint of The Haworth Press, Inc.) Vol. 15, No. 4, 2003, pp. 323-338; and: *Safety and Security in Tourism: Relationships, Management, and Marketing* (ed: C. Michael Hall, Dallen J. Timothy, and David Timothy Duval) The Haworth Hospitality Press, an imprint of The Haworth Press, Inc., 2003, pp. 323-338. Single or multiple copies of this article are available for a fee from The Haworth Document Delivery Service [1-800-HAWORTH, 9:00 a.m. - 5:00 p.m. (EST). E-mail address: docdelivery@haworthpress.com].

INTRODUCTION

Crisis management in the tourism sector tends to focus on large hotels, airlines, and tour companies, and how they cope with unforseen crises. However, when crisis strikes, it is indiscriminate, affecting small-scale tourism businesses also. More traditional crisis management techniques may not necessarily be applicable to small or micro tourism businesses, especially in the developing world.

Several times in the last five years foreign tourists have either left or avoided Indonesia. In mid-1997 there were several plane crashes, and parts of Indonesia were blanketed in thick smoke. In the same year, the Asian financial crisis struck Indonesia badly, eventually leading to the resignation of President Suharto, and outbreaks of ethnic, religious, and political strife in 1998. Presidential elections in 2000, and the replacement of President Wahid in 2001 arguably created as much uncertainty as stability. Protracted ethnic, religious, and political strife in at least four outlying provinces, and occasional flare-ups in large parts of the country have continued, culminating in the bombing of two nightclubs in Bali in October 2002.

During this protracted crisis rated hotels have been faced with single digit occupancy rates, and many have drastically reduced their prices to attract customers. The government has engaged in a number of campaigns to promote the country as a safe and pleasant travel destination, although the results were largely undermined as the crisis continued.

The owners and managers of small-scale tourism businesses have been faced with the same crisis, but they are often ignored as it is believed that they can simply close for the bad times, and return to farming, fishing, or other economic activities. This article will examine the small or micro tourism businesses on the island of Gili Air, near Lombok, Indonesia. While some owners and managers of the businesses on this island can turn to other sources of income, the generally depressed state of the economy, coupled with heavy debt burdens, has forced many of those operating even the smallest forms of accommodation into a similar situation to their larger colleagues. This paper will examine what options they have realistically had, what measures they have taken as part of their crisis management in this situation, and the implications this has for crisis management among small tourism businesses elsewhere.

Indonesia's Crisis

In 1997 South-East Asia experienced the El Niño weather phenomenon, with drier than usual conditions across the region. Many parts of Indonesia, which usually receive several metres of rain per annum, experienced a severe drought. This drought, coupled with opportunistic forest-clearing practices in the west of the country, created ideal conditions for devastating forest fires in Kalimantan and Sumatra in 1997. The smoke from these fires blanketed the region in thick smoke, from August to December 1997. The effect on tourism was devastating in Indonesia, Singapore, Malaysia, and Brunei, despite the fact that Java and Indonesia's eastern islands were smoke free (Henderson, 1999).

Although not as a direct result of the smoke in the region, in September 1997 a passenger jet in northern Sumatra crashed. This came at a time when the world's media was giving the region considerable attention as a result of the smoke. In the same year rioting between ethnic groups in Ujung Pandang, a city in Sulawesi, erupted. This turned out to not be an isolated event, but symptomatic of the political and ethnic problems facing the country; problems largely suppressed by the government of 32 years (Eklof, 1998:22).

In 1997 the Southeast Asian region experienced the now famous currency crisis, bringing the region's rapid growth economies to a halt. The crisis appears to have begun with the float of the Thai Baht in July 1997, and spread within a month to Malaysia and Indonesia. As a result of the crisis, the Indonesian Rupiah lost 80% of its nominal value, and other affected currencies lost 38% or more of theirs (Bank of England Quarterly Bulletin August, 1999).

In Thailand and Malaysia, and to a lesser extent Singapore, the currency crisis led to self- and IMF-imposed austerity programmes, and lower economic growth figures. In Indonesia it was much worse, leading directly to a political crisis. This culminated in May 1998 in violent rioting, the resignation of the president of 32 years, and outbreaks of political, ethnic and religious strife across the country. Violence accompanied the March 1999 general election and the October 1999 presidential ballot. The East Timor ballot in August 1999, and the subsequent violence in September and October 1999, was reported across the world, with boycotts of Indonesia and generally negative coverage of the country. For the next two years the political and economic situation reached comparative stability. The events surrounding the September 11 events in the United States, and subsequent war against the Taliban and Al Qaida, produced a sentiment among some in Indonesia that the West was at war with Islam. Threats of violence toward Westerners, and in particular Americans, in late 2001 resulted in Britain and American missions warning their citizens to avoid travel to Indonesia. The bombing of two nightclubs in Bali filled with foreign visitors resulted in even sterner travel warnings. Several provinces continue to experience political, ethnic, and religious violence, although the levels of violence vary considerably. The currency continues to languish, at just over one-third of pre-crisis levels, and the economy will take several years to recover the losses of the last five years.

Several times between 1997 and 2002 the above events caused the majority of foreign tourists either to leave Indonesia, or change their travel plans to avoid the country. The fall in value of South-East Asian currencies forced many potential tourists from the region itself to cancel trips, the effects of which have been felt not only in the region, but also as far away as Hong Kong and Hawaii (Economist, 1998; Klara, 1998; "Warm climate and white sand equal gold," 1999). Additionally, persistently bad press has led to a more chronic fall in tourist numbers to Indonesia, which continued in 2002, five years after the crisis first began. This has had a devastating effect on the developing tourism industry in Indonesia. Large rated hotels in the major cities have been faced with single digit occupancy rates. Resort hotels were faced with bad outcomes also, and many drastically reduced the room rates they charge tour companies, to attract some customers. The government and large hotels subsequently engaged in campaigns to promote the country as a safe and pleasant travel destination. In one case the chief of police of the province of Bali travelled to Australia to reassure potential visitors that the island was safe. Any positive results were largely undermined by the international media, as the crisis has continued.

The owners and managers of small-scale tourism businesses have been faced with the same crisis as their star-rated counterparts, but they are often ignored in analysis and government crisis management. Many in government and tourism promotion bodies assume that small tourism operators can simply turn to farming, fishing, or some other economic activities until the crisis passes. The author's research has shown that while there is some capacity for turning to other sources of income, the generally depressed state of the economy, coupled with high relative debt burdens, has forced many of those operating even small *pondok*-style hotels (up to five rooms) into the same situation as their larger colleagues. In order to remain in business many of these operators have employed a number of tactics such as staff shedding, closing their businesses temporarily, attempting to sell or lease their businesses to foreigners, supplementing their income through other work or business activities, and lastly living off savings.

BACKGROUND ON CRISIS MANAGEMENT

Before focusing on crisis management it is important to examine what is meant by the term crisis. Booth (1993:85-86) covers a number of definitions of crisis in an organisational context, and concludes with the definition of "A situation faced by an individual, group or organisation which they are unable to cope with by the use of normal routine procedures . . . " Crises therefore require management procedures outside of those which are normal.

Not all crises have the same structure, and Booth (1993:87) defines three major types. The first is a gradual external erosion or internal decline which threatens the organisation. The second is a periodic threat or loss to part of the organisation. Finally, there is a sudden threat or loss to the whole organisation. The crisis in Indonesia clearly falls into the last category, as the crisis developed suddenly, and it affects not only entire organizations, but also whole sectors of the economy.

Fink (1986) breaks crises into four stages. The first is the prodromal crisis stage, where the warning signs of an impending crisis begin to become clear. In Indonesia this stage occurred in early to mid-1997. The second stage is the acute crisis stage, where the crisis is unavoidable, and often occurs very quickly. This occurred in Indonesia from mid-1997 onwards. The next stage is the chronic crisis stage, which is essentially where the situation is cleaned up. Indonesia is currently in the chronic crisis stage, where industry and government are pursuing solutions. The final stage is that of crisis resolution, where the situation moves from a crisis back to that of normal operations. Indonesia has yet to reach this stage, as the crisis has entered its sixth year, with no clear signs of abating.

With these definitions of crises in mind, it is possible to now examine what is meant by crisis management. Littlejohn (1983:11) defines crisis management as essentially that which provides an organisation with a systematic, orderly response to crisis situations. Important in this definition is the understanding that crisis management is not something which can be completed within a short amount of time.

Crisis management can be separated into three parts. The first is the estimation of the various risks to a particular business. Booth (1993) covers the four broad areas of social, technological, political, and economic sectors as important external factors. These factors could be termed "normal" as they occur within typical and expected parameters. Andriole (1985) focuses on terrorism, foreign and domestic political instability, international conflict, and monetary and trade instability as primary sources of what he calls "high order," or abnormal, corporate crises.

Once the crises are estimated, the next steps most analysts and consultants encourage are the formation of a crisis management team, and crisis management plan. Many larger corporations now employ people to deal specifically with the planning, revising, testing, and execution of crisis situations (Littlejohn, 1983).

Fink (1986) states that every business, regardless of size, should have a crisis management plan. He claims the virtues of the crisis management plan as enabling a crisis manager to focus on the content of the crisis, while allowing the crisis management plan to deal with the mechanical aspects of the crisis, claiming that these aspects are often predictable and similar for many businesses and organizations.

Risk assessment and crisis management planning as outlined above assume that organizations have the skills and resources to access the correct types of data, conduct such analysis on that data, and produce reports, which would form the basis of later aspects of crisis management planning. Most crisis management books and advice are directed toward medium to large corporations, where resources and skills are most readily available to be put into crisis management. Most best practice examples are of large trans-national corporations. Also, this advice is most notably directed toward corporations in developed countries, where crises are less pandemic, and stability the norm rather than the exception. The author will now examine contemporary crisis management in the context of the crisis affecting tourism, on the small Indonesian island of Gili Air.

The research findings presented in this paper are the result of the author's 14-month doctoral research on Gili Air from May 1998 until July 1999. The author has also kept in contact with informants on the island, which has enabled the data to be updated to early-2002. This research represents the first long-term investigation into tourism on the three so-called Gili Islands off Lombok. This research consisted of structured interviews with local people (n = 150), including all tourism-oriented businesses on the island. Unstructured interviews were conducted with local people (n = 50), including tourism owners and managers. Finally, participant-observation data allowed for both cross-checking of data, the elicitation of non-solicited data, and importantly, the feelings of local people involved in the tourism industry.

BACKGROUND TO THE CRISIS ON GILI AIR

The island of Gili Air covers an area of just two square kilometres. While not a true coral atoll, the highest peak is only 13 metres above sea level. Gili Air lies approximately 2 kilometres off the northwest coast of Lombok, in the province of West Nusa Tenggara, with views of the popular tourism destination of Bali from some beaches. The climate is tropical, with a marked wet season and a comparatively long dry season. The island's soils are nutrient poor, with thin topsoil above a subsoil of coral grit. There is no surface water, and artesian water varies from brackish near the coast and in some of the interior, to drinkable fresh water in a few localised areas. Extensive stands of coconut trees give the island the "pleasant rural character" espoused not only by the

Lonely Planet guide books (Lyon and Wheeler, 1997:404), but also by numerous visitors.

Approximately half of the island is surrounded by a fringing reef. In the past this supported seagrass, colonies of fish, dugong, and shellfish, but most has now died. Some of the other reefs near the island continue to support colonies of soft and hard corals, coral fish, and reef sharks.

The three islands of Gili Air, Gili Meno, and Gili Trawangan were permanently settled relatively recently. Problems obtaining fresh water, combined with comparatively poor land quality made the islands unattractive to potential immigrants from nearby Lombok. Evidence indicates that the islands' inhabitants first came from southern Sulawesi around 100 years ago. There are currently 1,100 local residents on the island, with a further 200-300 new arrivals, and anywhere from 10-350 tourists at any time. Most local people live in the main village in the south of the island, and in a series of hamlets scattered throughout the central, eastern, and northern parts of the island.

For current purposes, the economy of Gili Air can be roughly divided into more traditional and more overtly tourist industries, although there is sometimes considerable overlap between them. Traditional industries have existed for several decades, and the capital and income patterns have allowed the industries to evolve and expand slowly. Tourist industries are of a more recent origin, and have required a novel way of acquiring capital and generating income. Businesses in either the more traditional sectors or the tourism sector could by most definitions be described as small or micro (Dahles, 1999:3-4).

From a distance the most obvious economic activity on Gili Air is coconut plantations, many dating back decades. While a thriving copra exporting industry once existed on the islands, a government regulation in the early 1970s requiring the use of an intermediary caused prices to fall, and the industry eventually collapsed. Two people on the island transport coconuts to Lombok for sale at market, but the margins are low.

Agriculture is practiced on the island, in the form of dry farming of cassava, sweet potato, corn, peanuts, soybeans, and pineapple, mostly for subsistence and local consumption, and a small amount sold in the market in Pamenang on Lombok. Many local people also raise cattle, goats, chickens, and ducks. Farmers remain the poorest people on the island, and despite the island's recent comparative affluence as a result of tourism-related activities, some still receive rice rations originating from foreign aid organizations.

Around fifty full-time fishers operate twenty-five fishing boats. These fishers sell their catch on the beach on Gili Air, if larger at the harbour on Lombok, or if particularly large at the market in Tanjung, the district capital. A further 40 dinghies and 20 boats are also used for fishing, but only for subsistence purposes. Dynamite blasting, poisoning, and anchor damage have severely eroded the reefs near Gili Air, with approximately 95% of the coral now dead. This combined with overall patterns of over-fishing have severely depleted stocks of important species, with catches well down on those of previous years.

Since 1995 locals have begun to commercially farm seaweed, which is then sold to a trader in Lombok, eventually making its way to Hong Kong. The seaweed industry was begun with the explicit purpose of creating a cash crop to relieve pressure on fish stocks. The El Niño weather phenomenon in the 1997-98 period raised sea temperatures in the area, and killed or severely weakened most of the seaweed stocks.

People on Gili Air are respected boat-builders, filling orders from Gili Air, the other two islands, Lombok, and even as far away as Europe. The industry is lucrative enough to allow these 10 people to work in the industry full-time, but they are still comparatively poor, living in simple timber, bamboo, and thatch houses.

The small government sector on Gili Air employs fifteen people on a full-time basis. These comprise five primary school teachers, the village headman, island headman, village secretary, three office staff at the village office, the paramedic, and three employees at the island's power station. Wages are low, and all but the teachers and headman have been employed only in the last five years.

Gili Air supports a sizeable transportation sector. A boat owners' cooperative operates a passenger and cargo service between Bangsal on Lombok and the three islands. Of the 52 boats in use by the cooperative, 25 are owned by people from Gili Air. About 50% of passengers are local people, and 50% tourists, with an official fixed price for all. The island supports 25 *cidomo* (two-wheeled horse carts), which carry passengers and cargo from the harbour to all points on the island

Tourism appears to have begun on Gili Air in the mid-1970s. At that time it consisted mainly of day-trippers from Mataram, the provincial capital, and those who stayed overnight in the homes of local people. The first small bungalow-style hotel was built in 1979, by a well-liked entrepreneur from Mataram, who already possessed some land on the island. The then island headman began the next hotel. Within a few years others recognized the success of both of these businesses, and slowly opened hotels of their own. In 1984 there were 4 small hotels, and by 1989 there were 12. Gili Air entered a period of rapid growth in 1990, with 3 hotels added, and in 1991 a further 7. Accommodation on Gili Air currently consists of 29 ordinary hotels, with 190 rooms in total, and 2 more up-market hotels with 45 rooms in total.

Hotels represent the largest capital inputs in the tourism industry on Gili Air. Twelve were financed primarily through savings alone, and a further twelve through a combination of savings and bank credit. Foreign spouses were the source of capital in 5 cases. Foreign business partners provided capital in two cases. Local people from Gili Air have always controlled a considerable amount of the hotel industry themselves, owning and managing 20 of the 31 hotels. Partnerships between new arrivals and foreigners account for 5 of the hotels' owners and managers. New arrivals alone own and run 3 of the hotels. Local people with foreign business partners also operate three of these businesses. Similar patterns were noted by Cohen (1996a; 1996b) in the development of the island of Koh Samui in Thailand, where local residents exerted a considerable influence over tourism by self-financing development, and retaining some control over many of the other businesses. Interestingly, Gili Air's ownership patters vary considerably from those of nearby Gili Trawangan, where resident or absentee owners from Bali and Jakarta control much of the development, and local residents are considerably marginalised (Hampton, 1998; Kamsma and Bras, 1999).

Independent restaurants began to be opened on Gili Air in 1987. There are currently six independent restaurants and two bars on the island, serving food and beverages. Six of these eight establishments are owned by local people, and all were financed via savings. One new arrival and one foreigner own the two other businesses, and financed the businesses through their own savings. This roughly parallels the ownership patterns observed by Cohen (1996a; 1996b) on both Koh Samui and Phuket in Thailand.

Scuba diving centres opened on Gili Air only in 1992, although dive schools operating from Senggigi Beach on Lombok had been bringing divers to sites near the islands for a couple of years before that. The first dive centre was a joint venture between a foreigner and a local, the following two have been entirely foreign-owned, and the most recent has been opened by a local man. All of these businesses have been financed from savings.

With only a few exceptions, tourism businesses on Gili Air are nearly exclusively very small or micro businesses, with simple organizational structures to match. Before the crisis began, there were 39 tourism businesses on the island, with 200 people directly employed in their operation. This figure works out to an average of just 5.1 people per business, but with a median of just 3. This lower figure is explicable as three businesses employed 11, 19, and 20 people respectively, one other just one person, and most just 2 or 3 people. Of these 200 people, 93 were local islanders, and 107 were from off the island. While locals can move between the economic sectors on the island if one of those sectors is performing poorly, outsiders are more or less restricted to tourism alone. The 93 local people were involved in these businesses by virtue of owning them, or being relatives of the owners. The 107 others came to the island from the Indonesian islands of Lombok, Sumbawa, Bali, and Java, and in the case of foreign or mixed foreign ownership, as far away as Australia, England, Scotland and Germany. Of the 43 businesses examined here, only one hotel and the four dive centres were staffed by people with formal qualifications. This hotel requires all staff with direct contact with guests to have diplomas from a tourism training institute. The four dive centres employed qualified dive instructors to take customers scuba diving. All of the others were run by people with no formal business or tourism industry qualifications. In 37 of the 43 businesses, owners and employees had only primary or lower secondary school qualifications. In one case the owners of a hotel were illiterate, and required their employees to read important documents to them. These businesses are small in nature, pay low wages and profits, and their owners and employees have limited education and training. For this reason no owners or employees had any formal knowledge of, or skills in, crisis management. In the crisis period on Gili Air from 1997 until 2002, the conventional advice of experts and consultants to undertake tasks such as crisis analysis, planning, or training has not occurred on the island.

CRISIS MANAGEMENT ON GILI AIR

No businesses on the island employed formal crisis management planning or contingency planning. However, several techniques were employed to cope with the double problem of low tourist arrivals and profits, and rising costs. These techniques fall under several categories. The first is essentially one of maintaining the status quo, with all staff retained, but lowered wages, full facilities and services maintained, but lowered prices, in an attempt to make their business attractive to potential tourists. The second involves lowering costs through reducing facilities and services offered. Staff were not laid off, but their wages were either cut or were commission-based. The third technique involves closing the business, so that overheads are reduced to a minimum. The next involves leasing or selling the business to an outside party, either foreigner or Indonesian. The final technique is somewhat paradoxical, and involves expanding their business in an attempt to capture a larger segment of the small market.

Tourism business owners and managers on Gili Air used these six techniques of crisis management over the five-year period are described graphically in Figure 1. In the first stage of the crisis during the normally busy mid-year period of 1997, 25 of the then 39 businesses continued to operate normally, with their full level of staff, and lowered prices. Staying open with full staff and operating as if there was no crisis became more expensive and less feasible. By January 1998, 19 of the 43 businesses on the island chose this option. By just after the presidential resignation in July 1998 this figure fell to 12. As the instability continued

FIGURE 1. Crisis Management Techniques

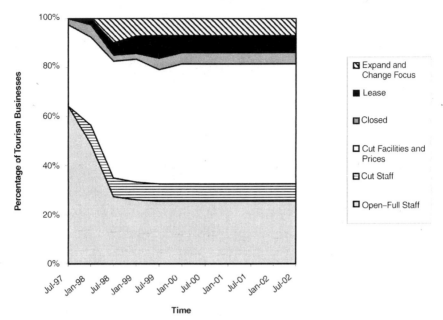

into the beginning of 1999 the number of businesses with full staff fell to 11. This was a trend which continued until the present.

At the beginning of the crisis no tourism businesses on the island employed staff shedding. With very few tourists for more than six months caused incomes to fall for many businesses, and by January 1998 three businesses decided to reduce their numbers of staff, but still provide a full range of services. This placed the remaining staff in a difficult situation, as some tasks require the same effort regardless of the presence or absence of guests. Three businesses have continued this strategy into the present.

At the outset of the crisis in July 1997 thirteen of the 43 tourism businesses coped by reducing their staff, prices and facilities. Their businesses were reduced to operating as "skeletons" of their normal selves. By the beginning of 1998 the figure rose to 14, by July 1998 there were 19, January 1999 it was 21, July 1999 was 20, and is since then has been steady at 21 of the 43 businesses. While many businesses initially chose to only reduce prices, as the crisis lengthened, they were faced with stable or rising costs, and little income.

At the outset of the crisis one tourism business on the island closed for business. In the next two periods of time this figure doubled. In July 1998 and January 1999 only one business remained closed. Since July 1999 two businesses have remained closed. This figure is surprising, as the crisis has continued for more than three years, and many more businesses could have been expected to have closed for business, and their owners turned to other sources of income.

While at the outset of the crisis no tourism businesses were leased to outsiders, in the second and third periods one owner decided to lease his business to an outsider. By July 1998 two had chosen this option. By January 1999 three had done so, and by July 1999 there were four. In the next two periods one business reverted to local ownership and management, but the other three have since remained leased to outsiders. This figure belies somewhat the desire by many other owners of tourism businesses on Gili Air to lease their businesses to outsiders, and some to sell their businesses if the opportunity presented itself. The generally unstable situation in the country which has kept many visitors away has also kept many potential outside parties from leasing locally-owned tourism businesses also.

Contrary to the prevailing political uncertainty and economic recession within the country, some businesses expanded or shifted their primary business focus. In the worst part of the crisis, in July 1998 this figure expanded to 4, with three of them engaging in expansion of the number and quality of bungalows in their hotels. Since January 1999 three businesses have been engaged in an extended period of expansion and enhancement of their facilities. The owners of these businesses have taken a more long-term perspective of the tourism industry on their island.

As I have demonstrated, the crisis management techniques utilized by tourism business owners and managers on Gili Air are comparatively limited. Operating normally, shedding staff, reducing prices and services offered, closing, and leasing to others are comparatively simple techniques, and ones which small business people in Indonesia generally have become somewhat familiar with. Their inability to analyze potential threats to their businesses, assemble crisis teams to deal with crisis management, to both produce crisis plans and deal with the crisis when things do go wrong. This is as a direct result of the small, or even micro, nature of the businesses, their low staff numbers, and their generally low levels of education and training. It is also simply as a result of their poverty and their lack of access to advice and credit.

The crisis caused by falling tourist arrivals has led many of the 43 owners and managers of tourism-oriented businesses on the island to look for additional sources of income to meet their own daily requirements, and to pay the financial overheads of their respective businesses (see Figure 2). Sixteen of

FIGURE 2. Additional Sources of Income

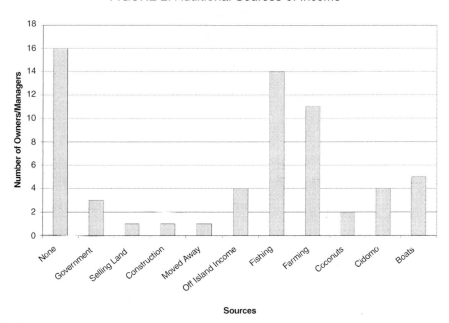

Sources

these people had no alternative source of income to call upon, and had to live off savings, or sell assets to survive. Of these sixteen, four were local people, and twelve outsiders to the island, domestic or foreign. They had no land to farm, other business opportunities, or skills, equipment, or authority to fish in the waters off the island. Because of the generally poor state of the economy generally, those from off the island were unable to call upon family and friends for income support, as many of those people were in the same, if not worse, situation. Three local people who already worked for the government relied on those positions for income during this period. However, as government wages are low, and prices continued to rise, these wages were less and less able to provide for their necessities. One local person, who was especially well-connected and respected, made the most of the opportunities to act as an agent to sell land to outsiders. It is important to note that while tourist arrivals were well down all throughout the three year period, the island is entering a stage in its tourism development when the numbers of foreigners in particular looking for land and homes on the island is increasing (Butler, 1980). Another local man decided to focus his attentions on boat building, earning a steady income during the period. One person moved away from the island and obtained work on Bali, where the crisis was not as severe. Four outsiders who owned tourism businesses on the island received money from other business interests off the island. Fourteen local people earned some income and food from fishing. Eleven local people also made some income from farming on the island. Two local people made some income from the sale of coconuts from their plantations. Four locals supplemented their income through renting their cidomo to others for a daily rental fee. Finally, five local islanders earned income from their boats which are used in the cooperative.

The four individuals who received money from outside the island, the man who acted as a real estate agent for outsiders, and the man who moved from the island have managed to secure incomes more than sufficient for their needs. These men were the best placed of all small business owners and managers on Gili Air, as five of them had obtained their original business capital from their own savings, and one man obtained it from his business partner.

Twenty-one owners or managers of tourism businesses on Gili Air received what could be termed subsistence incomes from non-tourism activities. Some of these activities, most notably fishing, provided food and little else. Other activities provided money, but only in very limited amounts. In 12 of these 21 cases the owners or managers of these businesses had self-financed, and therefore their overheads were relatively low. In 9 of the 21 cases they had borrowed at least part of their capital from banks. At a time when interest rates have been in the zone of 15-70%, repayments represent a considerable operating overhead, and one which many of the people in this category would have found difficult to cover.

An additional sixteen owners or managers had no income at all, and were forced to live off savings, or sell assets. Of these 16 people 7 financed their businesses from savings. An additional 6 people had acquired their capital from spouses or foreign business partners. These 13 people were a position to keep their businesses open, and avoid bankruptcy for some time. Three other people had no income whatsoever, but had borrowed money from banks to finance their business. Of all of the small business people on the island they were in the worst position. Within the following months these three could be expected to have to sell their assets or become bankrupt, and for those who have already done so, to go out of business.

CONCLUSION

The crisis situation in Indonesia was particularly difficult for small or micro tourism businesses on Gili Air for a number of reasons. Firstly, it was an economic, political, and social crisis, and perhaps more importantly, it was a crisis of confidence. Few people are confident of the government's ability to find a solution to the problems. The timing of the crisis was also problematic. Although the initial crisis was very sudden and severe, it has continued for three years, and the indications are that it has not yet ended. These conditions would make crisis management difficult for any business, even large corporations in developed countries.

Tourism businesses on Gili Air did not follow the three basic rules of conventional crisis management. Owners and managers did not assess the potential social, cultural, economic, or political threats to their businesses. Most of them put all of their profits back into their businesses, in an attempt to build them. This is perhaps more crucial in the tourism industry, where the types of facilities demanded by potential visitors changes over time (Butler 1980). Tourism business owners and managers also did not assemble crisis management teams. The numbers of staff in these businesses was very low, with a mean of only three people. Over time, some staff were shed, and many others, especially those whose majority of income came from commissions or tips, lived a subsistence only existence. Finally, none of the 43 tourism businesses on the island had a crisis management plan. In the 20-year history of the industry on the island, no one had experienced crisis or recession.

By Littlejohn's (1983:11) definition of crisis management as providing a systematic and orderly response to a crisis situation, tourism businesses on Gili Air did not exercise crisis management. But perhaps this has more to do with the bias in the literature on crisis management toward large or medium sized corporations. The responses of tourism businesses on Gili Air were not very systematic, nor were they orderly. Their responses have been ad hoc and unsystematic. On the whole they have no access to funds or credit facilities, and have had to deal with the crisis in this piecemeal fashion. With the exception of one business, they have been able to avoid bankruptcy or closure, have been able to repay or re-schedule bank loans to some extent, and in most cases have been able to continue operating as tourism businesses.

If the crisis management methods have been designed and marketed toward medium to large corporations, especially in developing countries, or transnational corporations, these methods are especially relevant to them. They are not as relevant to small or micro businesses, especially in the developing world. To enable the owners and managers of these small businesses to manage their businesses in crisis situations, techniques must be designed specifically for their situations. The techniques of staff shedding, reduced prices, leasing at least temporarily to outsiders, and taking advantage of low labour costs and static or falling land prices to expand, could form the basis of such crisis management for other micro or small tourism businesses.

REFERENCES

Andriole, S. J. (1985). Software Tools for High Order Corporate Crisis Management. In S. J. Andriole (Ed.), *Corporate Crisis Management* (pp. 259-278). Princeton: Petrocelli Books.

Bank of England (Quarterly Bulletin) (1999) The Asian crisis: Lessons for crisis management and prevention. Vol. 39.

Booth, S. A. (1993). *Crisis Management Strategy: Competition and change in modern enterprises.* London and New York: Routledge.

Business: The lunchbox tourists. (1998). *Economist,* 349(80): 67-68.

Butler, R.W. (1980). The Concept of a Tourist Area Cycle of Evolution: Implications For Management of Resources. *Canadian Geographer,* 24(1): 5-12.

Cohen, E. (1996a). Marginal Paradises: Bungalow Tourism on the Islands of Southern Thailand. In Cohen, E. *Thai Tourism: Hill Tribes, Islands and Open-Ended Prostitution* (pp. 179-213). Bangkok: White Lotus.

Cohen, E. (1996b). Insiders and Outsiders: The Dynamics of Development of Bungalow Tourism on the Islands of Southern Thailand. In Cohen, E. *Thai Tourism: Hill Tribes, Islands and Open-Ended Prostitution* (pp. 215-224). Bangkok: White Lotus.

Dahles, H. (1999). Tourism and Small Entrepreneurs in Developing Countries: A Theoretical Perspective. In H. Dahles and K. Bras (Eds.). *Tourism & Small Entrepreneurs: Development, National Policy, and Entrepreneurial Culture: Indonesian Cases* (pp. 1-19). New York: Cognizant Communication Corporation.

Eklof, A. K. (1998). Sun, Sand and Smoke. *Inside Indonesia,* 53: 22-23.

Fink, S. (1986). *Crisis Management: Planning for the Inevitable.* New York: AMACOM.

Hampton, M. (1998). Backpacker Tourism and Economic Development. *Annals of Tourism Research,* 25: 639-660.

Henderson, J. C. (1999). Managing the Asian financial crisis: Tourist Attractions in Singapore. *Journal of Travel Research,* 38(2): 177-181.

Kamsma, T. and K. Bras (1999). Gili Trawangan: Local Entrepreneurship in Tourism Under Pressure. In H. Dahles and K. Bras (Eds.). *Tourism & Small Entrepreneurs: Development, National Policy, and Entrepreneurial Culture: Indonesian Cases* (pp. 67-78). New York: Cognizant Communication Corporation.

Klara, R. (1998). Hawaii K-O. *Restaurant Business,* 97(10): 26.

Littlejohn, R. F. (1983). *Crisis Management: A Team Approach.* New York; American Management Associations.

Lyon, J. and A. Wheeler. (1997). *Bali and Lombok: a travel survival kit.* 6th Edition. Hawthorn: Lonely Planet Publications.

Warm climate and white sand equal gold. (1999). *Business Korea,* Vol. 16(12): 93.

Index